Historical Viewpoints

Notable Articles from *American Heritage*

SIXTH EDITION

VOLUME ONE TO 1877

Editor

John A. Garraty

Gouverneur Morris Professor of History

Columbia University

 HarperCollins*Publishers*

Sponsoring Editor: Bruce Borland
Project Editor: Eric Leonidas
Art Direction: Lucy Krikorian
Text Design: North 7 Atelier Ltd.
Cover Design: Delgado Design
Cover Photo: Fitz Hugh Lane, *View of Norwich Connecticut,* 1847. Courtesy of Mr. and
  Mrs. Thomas M. Evans.
Photo Research: Lynn Mooney
Production: Willie Lane/Sunaina Sehwani
Compositor: ComCom Division of Haddon Craftsmen, Inc.
Printer and Binder: R.R. Donnelley & Sons Company
Cover Printer: Phoenix Color Corp.

HISTORICAL VIEWPOINTS: Notable Articles from *American Heritage,* Sixth
Edition, Volume One to 1877

Library of Congress Cataloging-in-Publication Data

Historical viewpoints: notable articles from American heritage/
  editor, John A. Garraty. —6th ed.
    p. cm.
  Contents: —v.1 Since 1877.
  ISBN 0-06-042280-7
  1. United States—History. I. Garraty, John Arthur, 1920-
II. American heritage.
E178.6.H67 1991
973—dc20   90-4956
                                                   CIP

95   9 8

CONTENTS

INTRODUCTION

This sixth edition has been inspired by the encouraging reception afforded the five earlier editions of *Historical Viewpoints* and by the fact that interesting new articles continue to appear in *American Heritage.* This edition contains eight new essays. I have included these new selections because they seem ideally suited to current historical interests and because they present fresh points of view.

There are almost as many kinds of history as there are historians. In addition to the differences between political history and the social, economic, and cultural varieties, the discipline lends itself to such classifications as analytical, narrative, statistical, impressionistic, local, comparative, philosophical, and synthetic. Often the distinctions between one and another kind of history are overemphasized. No one can write good political history without some consideration of social, economic, and cultural questions; narrative history requires analysis to be meaningful; impressionistic treatments of past events are, in a way, statistical histories based on very tiny samples. Nevertheless, the different approaches exist and serve different purposes. Each focuses on part of the total human experience and sees it from a particular perspective; each, when well done, adds its own contribution to the total record.

Each perspective has its value for the introductory student. Some are perhaps more generally useful (that is, more interesting to a wider segment of the population) or more suggestive at a particular time and place than others, but the distinctions are like those between a miniature and a mural, a sonnet and an epic poem. No one would suggest that "The Moonlight Sonata" was a waste of Beethoven's time because he was capable of producing the *Choral* symphony, or that Mozart should not have written "Eine Kleine Nachtmusik" because he had within him *Don Giovanni.* In the same way a monograph or an article of twenty pages can be as well worth doing and as satisfying to read as Edward Gibbon's *Decline and Fall of the Roman Empire.*

The terms "scholarly" and "popular" history came into existence during the latter half of the nineteenth century. Before that time, all history was popular in the sense that those who wrote it, viewing themselves as possessors of special information acquired through scholarship or through having observed firsthand the events they described, aimed to transmit that knowledge to anyone interested in the subject. But when history became "scientific" and professionalized, historians began to write primarily for other historians. They assumed that nonspecialists had no interest in their work or were incapable of understanding it, and even argued that to write history for the general reader was to prostitute one's talents. Therefore, although with many notable exceptions, the best-trained and most intelligent historians tended to forswear the task of transmitting their scholarly findings to ordinary readers.

Of course popular history continued to be written and read, but most of it was produced by amateurs. Its quality varied greatly. The scholarly prejudice against "popularizers" had a solid basis in fact. Too often popular history was—and still is—shallow, error ridden, out of date before publication, a mere rehash of already written books, an exasperating mixture, as one critic has said, of "something we all knew before" and "something which is not so." Much of it was written by journalists and novelists who often lacked the patience, the professional skills, and the knowledge of sources that are as necessary for the writing of good history as narrative power, imagination, and lucidity of style.

It was chiefly with the hope of encouraging professional historians to broaden their perspectives that, beginning in the 1930s, a group of historians led by Professor Allan Nevins of Columbia University began to think of founding a general circulation magazine of American history. Their aim was a magazine in which solidly researched and significant articles would be presented in a way that would interest and educate readers who were not professional students of the past. Nevins himself, one of the great historians of the twentieth century, epitomized the combination they sought to produce. He was a prodigious scholar, author of dozens of learned volumes, and trainer of literally hundreds of graduate students, but he was also a fluent and graceful writer whose work was widely read and appreciated. Nevins's books won Pulitzer Prizes as well as academic renown.

The example provided by Nevins and a few other outstanding historians of his generation, such as Samuel Eliot Morison, undoubtedly influenced the gradual revival of concern for popular history that has occurred in recent times on the part of professional academic scholars. So did the increasing sophistication of the general reading public, which made it less difficult for these experts to write this type of history without sacrificing their intellectual standards. In any case, in 1954 the Nevins group—the Society of American Historians—joined the American Association for State and Local History in sponsoring the magazine they had envisioned: *American Heritage.*

The success of *American Heritage* was rapid and substantial. It achieved a wide circulation, and the best professional historians began to publish in its pages. Its articles, at their best, have been authoritative, interesting, significant, and a pleasure to read. They have ranged over the whole course of American history from the precolonial era to the present, and have dealt with every aspect of American development from politics to painting and from economics to architecture.

The present selection from among the hundreds of outstanding essays and book excerpts that have appeared in *American Heritage* since 1954 seeks to provide a balanced assortment of articles to supplement and enrich general college courses in American history. Keeping in mind the structure of these courses and the topics they tend to emphasize, I have reprinted here articles that, in my opinion, will add depth and breadth to the student's understanding. The articles new to this edition are William Cronon and Richard White, *The Clash of Cultures: Indians, Europeans, and the Environment;* Alfred W. Crosby, *American Indians and European Diseases;* Eric Foner, *The South's Inner Civil War;* Jack Larkin, *Everyday Life*

Before the Civil War; Robert N. Linscott, *Daily Life in Colonial Massachusetts,* Roger T. Pray, *Prison "Reform" in America;* Robert V. Remini, *Andrew Jackson and the Annexation of Texas;* and Garry Wills, *America, France, and Their Revolutions.*

This is—by definition—popular history, but it is also history written by experts. The articles differ in purpose and approach. Some present new findings, some reexamine old questions from a fresh point of view, others magisterially distill and synthesize masses of facts and ideas. From the total, readers may extract, along with the specifics of the individual essays, a sense of the variety and richness of historical literature. They will observe how different historians (not all of them academic scholars) have faced the task of presenting knowledge not to other historians alone but to an audience of intelligent and interested general readers.

Since most of the students enrolled in college history courses are not specialists—even those who intend to become professional historians stand at the very beginning of their training—this approach seems to me ideally adapted to their needs. Many, though by no means all, of the subjects treated in these essays have also been covered in articles in professional historical periodicals, often written by the same historians. But as here presented, without sacrifice of intellectual standards, the material is not so much easier to grasp as it is more meaningful. Details are clearly related to larger issues; historical characters are delineated in the round, not presented as stick figures or automatons; too much previous knowledge is not assumed. I once read the draft of an essay on the history of the Arabs that contained the sentence "The life and philosophy of Mohammed are well known" and then went on to other less universally understood topics. Such essays no doubt have their place, but that place is not in collections designed for beginners, whatever the subject.

Finally, at least some of the essays I have included here illustrate the truth that history is, at its best, an art as well as a science. After all, the ancients gave history its own Muse, Clio. I hope and expect that students, from reading the following pages, will come to realize that history is a form of literature, that it can be *enjoyed,* not merely assimilated. Even those who see college history courses exclusively as training grounds for future professionals surely will not object if their students enjoy these readings while they learn.

Needless to say, I hope the book will serve even better than its predecessors the needs and interests of students of American history.

John A. Garraty

PART ONE

A New
World

Perils of the Sea of Darkness, by sixteenth-century Flemish engraver Theodore de Bry, combines truth and fantasy to symbolize the Old World's fascination with the new.

Myths That Hide the American Indian

Oliver La Farge

As Oliver La Farge explains in this essay, the true character of the civilization of the American Indian has, from the time of Columbus, been shrouded in myth. Europeans have seen the Indians as they wished to see them, not as they really were. Naturally, there are good reasons for this as well as bad: The tribes left no written records; they were scattered and isolated over a vast continent; and they differed one from another greatly in culture and social structure.

Years of patient research by archaeologists, anthropologists, and other students have gone into the work of reconstructing their way of life. As La Farge's essay shows, that task, if not completed, has been substantially advanced. Its importance, of course, is enormous, and not merely because of our interest in the first settlers of America. Only by understanding the Indians can the early history of the Europeans in the New World be fully grasped.

An anthropologist by training, La Farge was an admirable exemplar of the role of the specialist in writing history for the general public. Besides his many scientific works and a Pulitzer Prize–winning novel, Laughing Boy, *in articles like this one he brought to thousands of readers objective and yet moving portraits of Indian life.*

Ever since the white men first fell upon them the Indians of what is now the United States have been hidden from white men's view by a number of conflicting myths. The oldest of these is the myth of the Noble Red Man or the Child of Nature, who is credited either with a habit of flowery oratory of implacable dullness or else with an imbecilic inability to converse in anything more than grunts and monosyllables.

That first myth was inconvenient. White men soon found their purposes better served by the myth of ruthless, faithless savages, and later, when the "savages" had been broken, of drunken, lazy good-for-nothings. All three myths coexist today, sometimes curiously blended in a schizophrenic confusion such as one often sees in the moving pictures. Through the centuries the mythical figure has been variously equipped; today he wears a feather headdress, is clothed in beaded buckskin, dwells in a tepee, and all but lives on horseback.

It was in the earliest period of the Noble Red Man concept that the Indians probably exerted their most important influence upon Western civilization. The theory has been best formulated by the late Felix S. Cohen, who, as a profound student of law concerning Indians, delved into early white-Indian relations, Indian political economy, and the white men's view of it. According to this theory, with which the present writer agrees, the French and English of the early seventeenth century encountered, along the East Coast of North America from Virginia southward, fairly advanced tribes whose semi-hereditary rulers depended upon the acquiescence of their people for the continuance of their rule. The explorers and first settlers interpreted these rulers as kings, their people as subjects. They found that even the commonest subjects were endowed with many rights and freedoms, that the nobility was fluid, and that commoners existed in a state of remarkable equality.

Constitutional monarchy was coming into being in England, but the divine right of kings remained firm doctrine. All European society was stratified in many classes. A somewhat romanticized observation of Indian society and government, coupled with the idea of the Child of Nature, led to the formulation, especially by French philosophers, of the theories of inherent rights in all men, and of the people as the source of the sovereign's authority. The latter was stated in the phrase, "consent of the governed." Both were carried over by Jefferson into our Declaration of Independence in the statement that "all men are created equal, that they are endowed by their Creator with certain unalienable Rights" and that governments derive "their just powers from the consent of the governed. . . ."

Thus, early observations of the rather simple, democratic organization of the more advanced coastal tribes, filtered through and enlarged by the minds of European philosophers whose thinking was ripe for just such material, at least influenced the formulation of a doctrine, or pair of doctrines, that furnished the intellectual base for two great revolutions and profoundly affected the history of mankind.

In the last paragraph I speak of "the more advanced" tribes. Part of the myth about the first Americans is that all of them, or most of them, had one culture and were at the same stage of advancement. The tribes and nations that occupied North America varied enormously, and their condition was anything but static. The advent of the white men put a sudden end to a phase of increasingly rapid cultural evolution, much as if a race of people, vastly superior in numbers, in civilization, and above all in weapons, had overrun and conquered all of Europe in Minoan times. Had that happened, also, the conquerors would undoubtedly have concluded, as so many white men like to conclude about Indians, that that peculiar race of light-skinned people was obviously inferior to their own.

Human beings had been in the New World for at least 15,000 years. During much of that time, as was the case in the beginning everywhere, they advanced but little from a Palaeolithic hunting culture. Somewhere around 2,500 B.C. farming began with the domestication of corn either in Peru or in Meso-America* in the vicinity of western Guatemala. Farming brought about the sedentary life and the increased food supply necessary for cultural progress. By the time of the birth of Christ, the influence of the high cultures, soon to become true civiliza-

---

*Meso-America denotes the area in which the highest civilizations north of Peru developed, extending from a little north of Mexico City into Honduras.

tions, in Meso-America was beginning to reach into the present United States. Within the next 1,500 years the Indians of parts of North America progressed dramatically. When the white men first landed, there were three major centers of high culture: the Southeast-Mississippi Valley, the Southwest, and the Northwest Coast. None of the peoples of these regions, incidentally, knew about war bonnets or lived in tepees.

The Southeast-Mississippi Valley peoples (for brevity, I shall refer to the area hereafter simply as "Southeast") seem to have had the strongest influences from Meso-America, probably in part by land along the coast of Texas, in part by sea across the Gulf of Mexico, whether direct from Mexico or secondhand through the peoples of the West Indies. There is a striking resemblance between some of their great earthen mounds, shaped like flat-topped pyramids, with their wood-and-thatch temples on top, and the stone-and-mortar, temple-topped pyramids of Meso-America. Some of their carvings and engravings strongly suggest that the artists had actually seen Meso-American sculptures. The list of similarities is convincingly long.

There grew up along the Mississippi Valley, reaching far to the north, and reaching also eastwards in the far south, the high culture generally called "Mound Builder." It produced a really impressive art, especially in carving and modeling, by far the finest that ever existed in North America. The history of advancing civilization in the New World is like that of the Old—a people develops a high culture, then barbarians come smashing in, set the clock part way back, absorb much of the older culture, and carry it on to new heights. A series of invasions of this sort seems to have struck the Mound Builders in late prehistoric times, when they were overrun by tribes mainly of Muskhogean and Iroquoian linguistic stock. Chief among these were the ancestors of the well-known Five Civilized Tribes—the Seminoles, Creeks, Choctaws, Chickasaws, and Cherokees. When white men first met them, their culture was somewhat lower than that of the earlier period in the land they occupied. Nonetheless, they maintained, in Florida, Alabama, Mississippi, Louisiana, and Georgia, the highest level east of the Rockies. A late movement of Iroquoian tribes, close relatives of the Cherokees, among them the Iroquois themselves, carried a simpler form of the same culture into Pennsylvania, New York, Ohio, and into the edge of Canada.

All of these people farmed heavily, their fields stretching for miles. They were few in a vast land—the whole population of the present United States was probably not over a million. Hunting and fishing, therefore, were excellent, and no reasonable people would drop an easy source of abundant meat. The development of their farming was held in check quantitatively by the supply of fish and game. They farmed the choice land, and if the fields began to be exhausted, they could move. They moved their habitations somewhat more freely than do we, but they were anything but nomadic. The southern tribesmen lived neither in wigwams nor tepees, but in houses with thatched roofs, which in the extreme south often had no walls. They had an elaborate social structure with class distinctions. Because of their size, the white men called their settlements "towns." The state of their high chiefs was kingly. They were a people well on the road toward civilization.

The Natchez of Mississippi had a true king, and a curious, elaborate social system. The king had absolute power and was known as the Sun. No ordinary man could speak to him except from a distance, shouting and making obeisances. When he went out, he was carried on a litter, as the royal and sacred foot could not be allowed to touch the ground. The Natchez nation was divided into two groups, or moieties: the aristocracy and the common people. The higher group was subdivided into Suns (the royal family), Nobles, and Honored Ones. The common people were known simply as Stinkers. A Stinker could marry anyone he pleased, but all the aristocrats had to marry out of their moiety, that is, marry Stinkers. When a female aristocrat married a Stinker man, her children belonged to her class; thus, when a Sun woman married a Stinker, her children were Suns. The children of the men, however, were lowered one class, so that the children of a Sun man, even of the Sun himself, became Nobles, while the children of an Honored One became lowly Stinkers.

This system in time, if nothing intervened, would lead to an overwhelming preponderance of aristocrats. The Natchez, however, for all their near-civilization, their temples, their fine crafts and arts, were chronically warlike. Those captives they did not torture to death they adopted, thus constantly replenishing the supply of Stinkers (a foreigner could become nothing else, but his grandchildren, if his son struck a royal fancy, might be Suns).

The Indians of the Southeast knew the Mexican–West Indian art of feather weaving, by means of which they made brilliant, soft cloaks. The Sun also wore

Two of the myths attached to the American Indian are on view in these nineteenth-century engravings: the wind, bloodthirsty savage (right) and the drunken wastrel (left).

a crown of an elaborate arrangement of feathers, quite unlike a war bonnet. In cloak and crown, carried shoulder-high on a litter, surrounded by his retainers, his majesty looked far more like something out of the Orient than anything we think of ordinarily when we hear the word "Indian."

The Natchez were warlike. All of the southeasterners were warlike. War was a man's proper occupation. Their fighting was deadly, ferocious, stealthy if possible, for the purpose of killing—men, women, or children, so long as one killed— and taking captives, especially strong males whom one could enjoy torturing to death. It is among these tribes and their simpler relatives, the Iroquois, that we find the bloodthirsty savage of fiction, but the trouble is that he is not a savage. He is a man well on the road toward civilization.

With the Iroquois, they shared a curious pattern of cruelty. A warrior expected to be tortured if captured, although he could, instead, be adopted, before torture or at any time before he had been crippled. He entered into it as if it were a contest, which he would win if his captors failed to wring a sign of pain from him and if he kept taunting them so long as he was conscious. Some of the accounts of such torture among the Iroquois, when the victim was a member of a tribe speaking the same language and holding to the same customs, are filled with a quality of mutual affection. In at least one case, when a noted enemy proved to have been too badly wounded before his capture to be eligible for adoption, the chief, who had hoped that the man would replace his own son, killed in battle, wept as he assigned him to his fate. At intervals between torments so sickening that one can hardly make one's self read through the tale of them, prisoner and captors exchanged news of friends and expressions of mutual esteem. Naturally, when tribes who did not hold to these customs, including white men, were subjected to this treatment it was not well received.

This pattern may have come into North America from a yet more advanced, truly civilized source. The Mexicans—the Aztecs and their neighbors—expected to be sacrificed if they were captured, and on occasion might insist upon it if their captors were inclined to spare them. They were not tortured, properly speaking, as a general rule, but some of the methods of putting them to death were not quick. What we find in North America may have been a debasement of the Mexican practices developed into an almost psychopathic pleasure among people otherwise just as capable of love, of kindness, of nobility, and of lofty thought as any anywhere—or what the conquistadores found in Mexico may have been a civilized softening of earlier, yet more fearful ways. The Aztecs tore fantastic numbers of hearts from living victims, and like the people of the Southeast, when not at war said "We are idle." They were artists, singers, dancers, poets, and great lovers of flowers and birds.

The Iroquois and Muskhogeans had a real mental sophistication. We observe it chiefly in their social order and what we know of their religions. The Iroquois did not have the royalty and marked divisions of classes that we find farther south, but their well-organized, firmly knit tribes were what enabled them, although few in numbers, to dominate the Algonkians who surrounded them. The Iroquois came nearer to having the matriarchy that popular fable looks for among primitive people than any other American tribe. Actual office was held by the men, but

the women's power was great, and strongly influenced the selection of the officers.

Five of the Iroquois tribes achieved something unique in North America, rare
anywhere, when in the sixteenth century they formed the League of the Five
Nations—Senecas, Onondagas, Mohawks, Cayugas, and Oneidas—to which,
later, the Tuscaroras were added. The league remained united and powerful until
after the American Revolution, and exists in shadowy form to this day. It struck
a neat balance between sovereignty retained by each tribe and sovereignty sacrificed to the league, and as so durable and effective a union was studied by the
authors of our Constitution.

The league was founded by the great leader Hiawatha. Any resemblance
between the fictional hero of Longfellow's poem and this real, dead person is
purely coincidental. Longfellow got hold of the name and applied it to some
Chippewa legends, which he rewrote thoroughly to produce some of the purest
rot and the most heavy-footed verse ever to be inflicted upon a school child.

The Iroquois lived in "long houses," which looked like extended Quonset
huts sheathed in bark. Smaller versions of these, and similarly covered, domed
or conical structures, are "wigwams," the typical housing of the Northeast. Many
people use the word "wigwam" as synonymous with "tepee," which is incorrect.
A tepee, the typical dwelling of the Plains Indians of a later period, is a functional
tent, usually covered with hides or, in recent years, canvas, and one of its essential
features is that it is the shelter of constantly mobile people. A tepee, incidentally,
is about the most comfortable tent ever invented, winter or summer—provided
you have two or three strong, competent women to attend to setting it up and
striking it.

The great tribes we have been discussing showed their sophistication in a new
way in their response to contact with Europeans. Their tribal organizations became tighter and firmer. From south to north they held the balance of power. The
British success in establishing good relations with many of them was the key to
driving the French out of the Mississippi area; to win the Revolution, the Americans had to defeat the Iroquois, whose favor up to then had determined who
should dominate the Northeast. The southern tribes radically changed their
costume, and quickly took over cattle, slaves, and many arts. By the time Andrew
Jackson was ready to force their removal, the Cherokees had a stable government
under a written constitution, with a bicameral parliament, an alphabet for writing
their language, printing presses, a newspaper, schools, and churches.

Had it not been for the white men's insatiable greed and utter lawlessness,
this remarkable nation would have ended with a unique demonstration of how,
without being conquered, a "primitive" people could adapt itself to a new civilization on its own initiative. They would have become a very rare example of how
aborigines could receive solid profit from the coming of the white men.

After the Five Civilized Tribes were driven to Oklahoma, they formed a union
and once again set up their governments and their public schools. Of course we
could not let them have what we had promised them; it turned out that we
ourselves wanted that part of Oklahoma after all, so once again we tore up the
treaties and destroyed their system. Nonetheless, to this day they are a political

power in the state, and when one of their principal chiefs speaks up, the congressmen do well to listen.

The tribes discussed until now and their predecessors in the same general area formed a means of transmission of higher culture to others, east and west. Their influence reached hardly at all to the northwards, as north of the Iroquois farming with native plants was difficult or impossible. On the Atlantic Coast of the United States the tribes were all more or less affected. Farming was of great importance. Even in New England, the status of chiefs was definite and fairly high. Confederacies and hegemonies, such as that of the Narragansetts over many of the Massachusetts tribes, occurred, of which more primitive people are incapable. Farther south, the state of such a chief as Powhatan was royal enough for Europeans to regard him as a king and his daughter as a true princess.

To the westward, the pattern of farming and sedentary villages extended roughly to the line that runs irregularly through Nebraska and Kansas, west of which the mean annual rainfall is below twenty inches. In wet cycles, there were prehistoric attempts to farm farther west, and in historic times the Apaches raised fair crops in the eastern foothills of the southern tip of the Rockies, but only the white men combined the mechanical equipment and the stupidity to break the turf and exhaust the soil of the dry, high plains.

An essay as short as this on so large a subject is inevitably filled with almost indefensible generalizations. I am stressing similarities, as in the case of the Iroquois-Southeast tribes, ignoring great unlikenesses. Generalizing again, we may say that the western farmers, whose cultures in fact differed enormously, also lived in fairly fixed villages. In the southern part, they built large houses covered with grass thatch. At the northwestern tip of the farming zone we find the Mandans, Hidatsa, and Crows, who lived in semi-subterranean lodges of heavy poles covered with earth, so big that later, when horses came to them, they kept their choice mounts inside. These three related, Siouan-speaking tribes living on the edge of the Plains are the first we have come to whose native costume, when white men first observed them, included the war bonnet. That was in the early nineteenth century; what they wore in 1600, no one knows.

The western farmers had their permanent lodges; they also had tepees. Immediately at hand was the country of the bison, awkward game for men on foot to hunt with lance and bow, but too fine a source of meat to ignore. On their hunting expeditions they took the conical tents. The size of the tepees was limited, for the heavy covers and the long poles had to be dragged either by the women or by dogs. Tepee life at that time was desirable only for a short time, when one roughed it.

The second area of Meso-American influence was the Southwest as anthropologists define it—the present states of New Mexico and Arizona, a little of the adjacent part of Mexico, and various extensions at different times to the north, west, and east. We do not find here the striking resemblances to Meso-America in numbers of culture traits we find in the Southeast; the influence must have been much more indirect, ideas and objects passing in the course of trade from tribe to tribe over the thousand miles or so of desert northern Mexico.

In the last few thousand years the Southwest has been pretty dry, although not as dry as it is today. A dry climate and a sandy soil make an archaeologist's paradise. We can trace to some extent the actual transition from hunting and gathering to hunting plus farming, the appearance of the first permanent dwellings, the beginning of pottery-making, at least the latter part of the transition from twining and basketry to true weaving. Anthropologists argue over the very use of the term "Southwest" to denote a single area, because of the enormous variety of the cultures found within it. There is a certain unity, nonetheless, centering around beans, corn, squashes, tobacco, cotton, democracy, and a preference for peace. Admitting the diversity, the vast differences between, say, the Hopi and Pima farmers, we can still think of it as a single area, and for purposes of this essay concentrate on the best-studied of its cultures, the Pueblos.

The name "Pueblo" is the Spanish for "village," and was given to that people because they lived—and live—in compact, defensible settlements of houses with walls of stone laid up with adobe mortar or entirely of adobe. Since the Spanish taught them how to make rectangular bricks, pure adobe construction has become the commoner type. They already had worked out the same roofing as was usual in Asia Minor and around the Mediterranean in ancient times. A modern Pueblo house corresponds almost exactly to the construction of buildings dating back at least as far as 600 B.C. in Asia Minor.

The Pueblos, and their neighbors, the Navahos, have become well enough known in recent years to create some exception to the popular stereotype of Indians. It is generally recognized that they do not wear feathers and that they possess many arts, and that the Pueblos are sedentary farmers.

Farming has long been large in their pattern of living, and hunting perhaps less important than with any people outside the Southwest. Their society is genuinely classless, in contrast to that of the Southeast. Before the Spanish conquest, they were governed by a theocracy. Each tribe was tightly organized, every individual placed in his niche. The power of the theocracy was, and in some Pueblos still is, tyrannical in appearance. Physical punishment was used to suppress the rebellious; now more often a dissident member is subjected to a form of being sent to Coventry. If he be a member of the tribal council, anything he says at meetings is pointedly ignored. If he has some ceremonial function, he performs it, but otherwise he is left in isolation. I have seen a once self-assertive man, who for a time had been a strong leader in his tribe, subjected to this treatment for several years. By my estimation, he lost some thirty pounds, and he became a quiet conformist.

The power of the theocracy was great, but it rested on the consent of the governed. No man could overstep his authority, no one man had final authority. It went hard with the individual dissident, but the will of the people controlled all.

The Pueblos had many arts, most of which still continue. They wove cotton, made handsome pottery, did fine work in shell. Their ceremonies were spectacular and beautiful. They had no system of torture and no cult of warfare. A good warrior was respected, but what they wanted was peace.

The tight organization of the Pueblo tribes and the absolute authority over individuals continues now among only a few of them. The loosening is in part the result of contact with whites, in part for the reason that more and more they are building their houses outside of the old, solid blocks of the villages, simply because they are no longer under constant, urgent need for defense.

It is irony that the peace-loving southwestern farmers were surrounded by the worst raiders of all the wild tribes of North America. Around A.D. 1100 or 1200 there began filtering in among them bands of primitives, possessors of a very simple culture, who spoke languages of the Athabascan stock. These people had drifted down from western Canada. In the course of time they became the Navahos and the Apaches. For all their poverty, they possessed a sinew-backed bow of Asiatic type that was superior to any missile weapon known to the Southwest. They traded with the Pueblos, learned from them, stole from them, raided them. As they grew stronger, they became pests. The Navahos and the northeastern branch of the Apaches, called Jicarilla Apaches, learned farming. The Navahos in time became artists, above all the finest of weavers, but they did not give up their raiding habits.

These Athabascans did not glorify war. They made a business of it. Killing enemies was incidental; in fact, a man who killed an enemy had to be purified afterwards. They fought for profit, and they were about the only North Americans whose attitude toward war resembled professional soldiers'. This did not make them any less troublesome.

The last high culture area occupied a narrow strip along the Pacific Coast, from northern California across British Columbia to southern Alaska, the Northwest Coast culture. There was no Meso-American influence here, nor was there any farming. The hunting and fishing were so rich, the supply of edible wild plants so adequate, that there was no need for farming—for which in any case the climate was unfavorable. The prerequisite for cultural progress is a food supply so lavish that either all men have spare time, or some men can specialize in non-food-producing activities while others feed them. This condition obtained on the Northwest Coast, where men caught the water creatures from whales to salmon, and hunted deer, mountain sheep, and other game animals.

The area was heavily forested with the most desirable kinds of lumber. Hence wood and bark entered largely into the culture. Bark was shredded and woven into clothing, twined into nets, used for padding. Houses, chests, dishes, spoons, canoes, and boats were made of wood. The people became carvers and wood-workers, then carried their carving over onto bone and horn. They painted their houses, boats, chests, and their elaborate wooden masks. They made wooden armor, including visored helmets, and deadly wooden clubs. In a wet climate, they made raincloaks of bark and wore basketry hats, on the top of which could be placed one or more cylinders, according to the wearer's rank. The chiefs placed carvings in front of their houses that related their lineage, tracing back ultimately to some sacred being such as Raven or Bear—the famous, so-called totem poles.

I have said that the finest prehistoric art of North America was that of the Mound Builders; in fact, no Indian work since has quite equaled it—but that is, of course, a matter of taste. The greatest historic Indian art was that of the Northwest Coast. Their carvings, like the Mound Builder sculptures, demand comparison with our own work. Their art was highly stylized, but vigorous and fresh. As for all Indians, the coming of the white men meant ruin in the end, but at first it meant metal tools, the possession of which resulted in a great artistic outburst.

Socially they were divided into chiefs, commoners, and slaves. Slaves were obtained by capture, and slave-raiding was one of the principal causes of war. Generosity was the pattern with most Indians, although in the dry Southwest we find some who made a virtue of thrift. In the main, a man was respected because he gave, not because he possessed. The Northwest Coast chiefs patterned generosity into an ugliness. A chief would invite a rival to a great feast, the famous potlatch. At the feast he would shower his rival and other guests with gifts, especially copper disks and blankets woven of mountain sheep wool, which were the highest units of value. He might further show his lavishness by burning some possessions, even partially destroy a copper disk, and, as like as not, kill a few slaves.

If within a reasonable time the other chief did not reply with an even larger feast, at which he gave away or destroyed double what his rival had got rid of, he was finished as a chief—but if he did respond in proper form, he might be beggared, and also finished. That was the purpose of the show. Potlatches were given for other purposes, such as to authenticate the accession of the heir to a former chief, or to buy a higher status, but ruinous rivalry was constant. They seem to have been a rather disagreeable, invidious, touchy people. The cruelty of the southeasterners is revolting, but there is something especially unpleasant about proving one's generosity and carelessness of possessions by killing a slave—with a club made for that special purpose and known as a "slave-killer."

The Meso-American culture could spread, changing beyond recognition as it did so, because it carried its food supply with it. The Northwest Coast culture could not, because its food supply was restricted to its place of origin.

North and east of the Northwest Coast area stretched the sub-Arctic and the plains of Canada, areas incapable of primitive farming. To the south and east were mountains and the region between the Rockies and the Coastal ranges called the Great Basin. Within it are large stretches of true desert; most of it is arid. Early on, Pueblo influences reached into the southern part, in Utah and Nevada, but as the climate grew drier, they died away. It was a land to be occupied by little bands of simple hunters and gatherers of seeds and roots, not strong enough to force their way into anywhere richer.

In only one other area was there a natural food supply to compare with the Northwest Coast's, and that was in the bison range of the Great Plains. But, as already noted, for men without horses or rifles, hunting bison was a tricky and hazardous business. Take the year 1600, when the Spanish were already established in New Mexico and the English and French almost ready to make settlements on the East Coast, and look for the famous Plains tribes. They are not there. Some are in the mountains, some in the woodlands to the northeast, some farming to the eastward, within the zone of ample rainfall. Instead we find scattered bands of Athabascans occupying an area no one else wanted.

Then the white men turned everything upside down. Three elements were most important in the early influence: the dislodgment of eastern tribes, the introduction of the horse, and metal tools and firearms. Let us look first at the impact on the centers of high culture.

White men came late to the Northwest Coast, and at first only as traders. As already noted, early contact with them enriched the life of the Indians and brought about a cultural spurt. Then came settlers. The most advanced, best organized tribes stood up fairly well against them for a time, and they are by no means extinct, but of their old culture there are now only remnants, with the strongest survivals being in the arts. Today, those Indians who are in the "Indian business," making money from tourists, dress in fringed buckskin and war bonnets, because otherwise the tourists will not accept them as genuine.

The tribes of the Atlantic Coast were quickly dislodged or wiped out. The more advanced groups farther inland held out all through colonial times and on into the 1830's, making fairly successful adjustments to the changed situation, retaining their sovereignty, and enriching their culture with wholesale taking over of European elements, including, in the South, the ownership of Negro slaves. Finally, as already noted, they were forcibly removed to Oklahoma, and in the end their sovereignty was destroyed. They remain numerous, and although some are extremely poor and backward, others, still holding to their tribal affiliations, have merged successfully into the general life of the state, holding positions as high as chief justice of the state supreme court. The Iroquois still hold out in New York and in Canada on remnants of their original reservations. Many of them have had remarkable success in adapting themselves to white American life while retaining considerable elements of their old culture. Adherents to the old religion are many, and the rituals continue vigorously.

The British invaders of the New World, and to a lesser degree the French, came to colonize. They came in thousands, to occupy the land. They were, therefore, in direct competition with the Indians and acted accordingly, despite their verbal adherence to fine principles of justice and fair dealing. The Spanish came quite frankly to conquer, to Christianize, and to exploit, all by force of arms. They did not shilly-shally about Indian title to the land or Indian sovereignty, they simply took over, then granted the Indians titles deriving from the Spanish crown. They came in small numbers—only around 3,000 settled in the Southwest—and the Indian labor force was essential to their aims. Therefore they did not dislodge or exterminate the Indians, and they had notable success in modifying Indian culture for survival within their regime and contribution to it.

In the Southwest the few Spaniards, cut off from the main body in Mexico by many miles of difficult, wild country, could not have survived alone against the wild tribes that shortly began to harry them. They needed the Pueblo Indians and the Pueblos needed them. The Christian Pueblos were made secure in their lands and in their local self-government. They approached social and political equality. During the period when New Mexico was under the Mexican Republic, for two years a Taos Indian, braids, blanket, and all, was governor of the territory. Eighteen pueblos survive to this day, with a population now approaching 19,000, in addition to nearly 4,000 Hopis, whose culture is Pueblo, in Arizona. They are conservative progressives, prosperous on the whole, with an excellent chance of surviving as a distinctive group for many generations to come. It was in the house of a Pueblo priest, a man deeply versed in the old religion as well as a devout Catholic, that I first saw color television.

The Spanish, then, did not set populations in motion. That was done chiefly from the east. The great Spanish contribution was loosing the horses. They did not intend to; in fact, they made every possible effort to prevent Indians from acquiring horses or learning to ride. But the animals multiplied and ran wild; they spread north from California into Oregon; they spread into the wonderful grazing land of the high Plains, a country beautifully suited to horses.

From the east, the tribes were pressing against the tribes farther west. Everything was in unhappy motion, and the tribes nearest to the white men had firearms. So the Chippewas, carrying muskets, pushed westward into Minnesota, driving the reluctant Dakotas, the Sioux tribes, out of the wooded country into the Plains as the horses spread north. At first the Dakotas hunted and ate the strange animals, then they learned to ride them, and they were off.

The Sioux were mounted. So were the Blackfeet. The semi-civilized Cheyennes swung into the saddle and moved out of the farming country onto the bison range. The Kiowas moved from near the Yellowstone to the Panhandle; the Comanches came down out of the Rocky Mountains; the Arapahos, the Crows, abandoning their cornfields, and the Piegans, the great fighting names, all followed the bison. They built their life around the great animals. They ate meat lavishly all year round; their tepees, carried or dragged now by horses, became commodious. A new culture, a horse-and-bison culture, sprang up overnight. The participants in it had a wonderful time. They feasted, they roved, they hunted,

Alfred Jacob Miller's painting of a Plains warrior—the myth still endures.

they played. Over a serious issue, such as the invasion of one tribe's territory by another, they could fight deadly battles, but otherwise even war was a game in which shooting an enemy was an act earning but little esteem, but touching one with one's bare hand or with a stick was the height of military achievement.

This influx of powerful tribes drove the last of the Athabascans into the Southwest. There the Apaches and the Navahos were also mounted and on the go, developing their special, deadly pattern of war as a business. In the Panhandle country, the Kiowas and Comanches looked westward to the Spanish and Pueblo settlements, where totally alien peoples offered rich plunder. The Pueblos, as we have seen, desired to live at peace. The original Spanish came to conquer; their descendants, becoming Spanish-Americans, were content to hold what they had, farm their fields, and graze their flocks. To the north of the two groups were Apaches and Utes; to the east, Kiowas and Comanches; to the south, what seemed like unlimited Apaches; and to the west the Navahos, of whom there were several thousands by the middle of the seventeenth century.

The tribes named above, other than the Kiowas and Comanches, did not share in the Plains efflorescence. The Navahos staged a different cultural spurt of their own, combining extensive farming with constant horseback plundering, which in turn enabled them to become herdsmen, and from the captured wool develop their remarkable weaving industry. The sheep, of course, which became important in their economy, also derived from the white men. Their prosperity and their arts were superimposed on a simple camp life. With this prosperity, they also developed elaborate rituals and an astoundingly rich, poetic mythology.

The Dakotas first saw horses in 1722, which makes a convenient peg date for the beginning of the great Plains culture. A little over a hundred years later, when Catlin visited the Mandans, it was going full blast. The memory of a time before horses had grown dim. By 1860 the Plains tribes were hard-pressed to stand the white men off; by 1880 the whole pattern was broken and the bison were gone. At its height, Plains Indian culture was brittle. Materially, it depended absolutely on a single source of food and skins; in other aspects, it required the absolute independence of the various tribes. When these two factors were eliminated, the content was destroyed. Some Indians may still live in tepees, wear at times their traditional clothing, maintain here and there their arts and some of their rituals, but these are little more than fringe survivals.

While the Plains culture died, the myth of it spread and grew to become embedded in our folklore. Not only the Northwest Coast Indians but many others as unlikely wear imitations of Plains Indian costume and put on "war dances," to satisfy the believers in the myth. As it exists today in the public mind, it still contains the mutually incongruous elements of the Noble Red Man and the Bloodthirsty Savage that first came into being three centuries and a half ago, before any white man had ever seen a war bonnet or a tepee, or any Indian had ridden a horse.

The Great Debate over Indian Policy

Lewis Hanke

 One of the most difficult problems that historians face, especially when dealing with distant events and cultures foreign to their own, is assimilating the point of view of the actors whose behavior they seek to describe and explain. Those who write about the European settlement of the New World confront this problem in one of its most knotty aspects, because from the perspective of our own times the actions of the Europeans appear so inhumane as to defy explanation, let alone justification. How can their "settlement" of the Americas be described as anything but naked, unprovoked aggression, their treatment of the native inhabitants in less blunt terms than cruel and callously overbearing? Yet we know that these Europeans were human beings, most of them—we may safely assume—no better or worse than ourselves. The historian's task is to show why they behaved as they did, and this involves understanding their values and assumptions as well as their motives. The good historian does not suspend judgment but attempts to judge the subjects under investigation only after internalizing as much as possible of the mental and emotional baggage that they carried through life.

The following essay by Lewis Hanke of the University of Massachusetts, an expert on the history of Spanish colonization and recently president of the American Historical Association, goes far toward making the behavior of the Europeans in America less incredible in modern eyes. His hero, Bartolomé de Las Casas, about whom he has written extensively, was throughout most of his long life a defender of the rights of the Indians and an admirer of their culture and their artistic achievements. But many of Las Casas's ideas and assumptions seem as narrow-minded as those of his contemporaries who considered the Indians subhuman, fit only for slavery or extinction. The essay deals on one level with the struggle waged among the Spaniards over Indian policy, but at a deeper and more important level it throws light on the whole history of the New World and on human nature itself.

W hen Hernando Cortés and his little band of Spaniards fought their way in 1519 from the tropical shores of Mexico up to the high plateau and first saw stretched below them the Aztec capital Tenochtitlán, gleaming on its lake under the morning sun, they experienced one of the truly dramatic moments in the history of America. Fortunately we have the words of a reporter worthy of the scene, the foot soldier Bernal Díaz del Castillo, whose *True History of the Conquest of New Spain* is one of the classics of the Western world. He wrote:

"Gazing on such wonderful sights we did not know what to say or whether what appeared before us was real; for on the one hand there were great cities and in the lake ever so many more, and the lake itself was crowded with canoes, and in the causeway were many bridges at intervals, and in front of us stood the great City of Mexico, and we—we did not number even four hundred soldiers!''

That was a soldier's memory, and even today the Spanish conquest of the New World is widely believed, especially by English-speaking peoples, to have been a purely military exploit of a peculiarly ruthless nature. That the period of discovery and conquest was full of violence is certain.

But what deserves more notice is quite another aspect of this turbulent period: the great struggle among the Spaniards themselves to determine how to apply Christian precepts to relations with the natives they encountered as they crossed the rivers, plains, swamps, and mountains of the New World. The going forth together of the Spanish standard and the Roman Catholic cross is well known. But too often the cross is dismissed as merely a symbol of a national church as much bent on "conquest" as the standard-bearers. The real effort to convert the natives, which moved many Spaniards and greatly concerned the Crown of Spain, and the powerful role religious conscience played throughout the conquest have been largely overlooked. Other nations sent out bold explorers and established empires. But no other European nation plunged into the struggle for Christian justice, as she understood it, that Spain engaged in shortly after Christopher Columbus first reached the New World.

So the story deserves to be told of Bartolomé de Las Casas, perhaps the most loved and hated and certainly the most influential of many Spaniards who believed the Spanish mandate in America to be primarily an obligation to convert the Indians peacefully to the Christian faith. He gave fifty strenuous years of his life to protect the natives from the treatment his fellow countrymen accorded them.

But, to be understood, he must be seen against the background of the Spanish colonial effort as a whole. Like many others who opposed a purely military conquest, Las Casas represented the church that the Spanish Crown sent to the New World in double harness with the conquistadors. For this conquest was unique. The Spaniards, with the approval of the Pope and carrying out the commands of their King, were to claim the new lands and the tribute of their inhabitants for the Spanish Crown (a worldly purpose) and bring these inhabitants into the knowledge of Christ (a spiritual purpose). The dual motivation behind the enterprise made conflict inevitable—conflict not only between the Spanish and the natives they were dealing with, but also among the Spaniards themselves, for although practically all Spaniards accepted both purposes as good, they could never agree for long on how best to achieve them.

From our vantage point, four hundred years later, we can see the tragedy of the Spanish conquest: the Crown and the nation were attempting the impossible. On the one hand, they sought imperial dominion, prestige, and revenue; on the other, the voluntary commitment of many peoples culturally different from themselves to the new religion they offered or imposed. The tragedy of the Indians was that in order to accomplish either objective the Spaniards were bound to overthrow established Indian values and to disrupt or destroy Indian cultures and civilizations, as they did in spectacular fashion in Mexico and Peru.

But from Spanish documents alone—the voices of the conquered can be heard only through Spanish materials—we may reconstruct the extraordinary story of how Christian conscience worked as a leaven during the onrushing conquest, insisting on judging men's deeds and the nation's policies. The struggle centered upon the aborigines. Influenced by the wealth of medieval legends that for centuries had circulated in Europe, the Spaniards expected to meet in America giants, pygmies, griffins, wild men, human beings adorned with tails, and other fabulous folk. When Cortés embarked from Cuba upon the conquest of Mexico, Governor Diego Velázquez instructed him to look in Aztec lands for strange beings with great flat ears and doglike faces. Francisco de Orellana was so sure that he had met warrior women on his famous voyage of 1540–41 that the mightiest river in South America was named the Amazon.

The plumed and painted peoples actually encountered soon perplexed the Spanish nation, from King to common citizen. Who were they and where did they come from? What was their nature, especially their capacity for European civilization and Christianity, and how should they be dealt with? Few significant figures of the conquest failed to deliver opinions, and the Council of the Indies held long formal inquiries on the subject. The voices of dogmatic and troubled individuals—ecclesiastics, soldiers, colonists, and royal officials in America as well as men of action and thought in Spain—rose continually in a dissident chorus of advice to Crown and Council.

Against this background of national excitement Bartolomé de Las Casas arose to devote his life to the Indians. His contemporaries saw him variously as a saintly leader, a dangerous fanatic, or a sincere fool; and, because his reputation is bound up with judgments on the conquest as a whole, his memory is kept green even today by support and attack. Of Las Casas the man, despite his powerful role, we know little. Neither friend nor enemy described his appearance, and no painter recorded it during his life. He wrote no autobiography; we must depend largely upon his historical and polemical writings for knowledge of his life and ideas.

We do know that he was born in Seville in 1474 and was there when Columbus, returning from his first voyage in 1493, triumphantly exhibited through the streets natives and parrots from the New World. His father accompanied Columbus on the second voyage and is supposed to have given the boy an Indian slave to serve as a page during his student days. Bartolomé went to America, probably with Nicolás de Ovando in 1502, and, even though he had already received minor orders, he was little better than the rest of the gentlemen-adventurers who rushed to the New World, bent on speedily acquiring fortunes. He obtained Indian slaves, worked them in mines, and attended to the cultivation of his estates. While he did not mistreat his Indians, their lowly lot seems not to have disturbed him. In 1512 he participated in the conquest of Cuba and was rewarded with both land and the service of some Indians.

It was against such men as Las Casas that a young Dominican friar named Antonio de Montesinos delivered two indignant sermons in Hispaniola in 1511. This first public cry on behalf of human liberty in the New World, whose texts were "I am a voice crying in the wilderness" and "Suffer me a little and I will show thee that I have yet to speak on God's behalf," stunned and then enraged the colonists, for Montesinos declared they were in mortal sin by reason of their cruelty to the Indians. Of Montesinos, whom the King shortly commanded to be silent, we know little except this brave moment of protest, which has been called one of the great events in the spiritual history of mankind. Las Casas shared the resistance of the other colonists to the cry. Like them, he took no steps to change his way of life, and for more than two years after the sermons he continued as a gentleman-ecclesiastic, although on one occasion a priest refused him the sacraments because he held slaves. The ensuing dispute disturbed without convincing him.

But the seed of a great decision was growing within this obstinate man, as yet unaware that he was destined to become the greatest Indian champion of them all. One day in the spring of 1514, while he was preparing a sermon for Whitsunday at the newly established Cuban settlement of Sancti Espiritus, his eye fell upon this verse in Ecclesiasticus: "He that sacrificeth of a thing wrongfully gotten, his offering is ridiculous, and the gifts of unjust men are not accepted."

Pondering on this text and on the doctrines preached by the Dominicans, he became increasingly convinced "that everything done to the Indians thus far was unjust and tyrannical." The scales fell from his eyes. He saw at last what was to be forever after the truth for him, and experienced as complete a change of life as did Saul of Tarsus on the road to Damascus.

Characteristically, he entered upon the new life immediately. He freed his Indians and preached a sermon at Sancti Espiritus against his fellow Spaniards. It shocked them as much as Montesinos had shocked his congregation. The path thus chosen in his fortieth year Las Casas was to follow for the more than fifty years that remained to him; the energy and skill hitherto employed for his own comfort and enrichment led him to far places, and many times across the Ocean Sea, to attack and astonish generations of his countrymen.

As one of the dominating personalities of Spain's most glorious age, he wrote more copiously, spoke more vigorously, and lived longer than any other prominent figure of the conquest. He was no ivory-tower scholar but a tenacious fighter always eager to put into practice the doctrines he preached. And, though he insisted that all dealing with Indians should be peaceful, those of his fellow Spaniards who opposed his views found him an aggressive and unrelenting opponent.

One of his first projects, undertaken in 1521, was an attempt to colonize the northern coast of Venezuela with Spanish farmers who were to till the soil, treat the Indians kindly, and thus lay the basis for an ideal Christian community. The colony was a complete failure, largely because the Spaniards involved sought to enrich themselves rather than to put into effect the aspirations of Las Casas. Deeply discouraged, he entered the Dominican Order and for ten years, meditating and studying, remained apart from the affairs of the world. Then he took up the battle again. Until his death in 1566 at the age of ninety-two, he fought the good fight in divers ways and places; in Nicaragua he sought to block wars he considered unjust; in Mexico he engaged in bitter debates with other ecclesiastics over justice for the Indians; in Guatemala he promoted a plan for the peaceful conquest and Christianization of the Indians; before the royal court in Spain he agitated successfully on behalf of many laws to protect the American natives. He even served as bishop for awhile, at Chiapa in southern Mexico. During his last two decades, after his final return to Spain in 1547 at the age of seventy-three, he became a sort of attorney-at-large for the Indians.

It was during this last period also that he produced and published some of his most important works. Of those writings published in his own lifetime, the tract that most immediately inflamed Spaniards was the *Very Brief Account of the Destruction of the Indies.* This thundering denunciation of Spanish cruelty and oppression, full of harsh accusations and horrifying statistics on the number of Indians killed, was printed in 1552 in Seville. Even though Las Casas believed treatment of the Indians was "less bad" in Mexico, the work is a thoroughgoing indictment of Spanish action in all parts of the "Indies."

Translations of the *Very Brief Account* brought out in English, Dutch, French, German, Italian, and Latin powerfully influenced the world to believe that Spaniards were inherently cruel. The De Bry drawings that illustrated many of the texts, depicting Spaniards hunting Indians with mastiffs and butchering even women and children, graphically underlined the charges. Thus the political use the enemies of Spain made of the writings of Las Casas helped usher in the modern age of propaganda. For, ironically enough, his zeal to touch the consciences of his own king and countrymen by stressing the cruelties of the conquistadors was largely responsible for that dark picture of Spain's work in America which has for hundreds of years borne the name, "The Black Legend"—*La leyenda negra*—which is still widely believed, at least in English-speaking lands.

Although Las Casas' principal aim was to shame the Spanish conscience, he was also a historian, and his *Historia de las Indias* remains one of the basic documents of the discovery and early conquest of America. He has also been recognized as an important political theorist, and as one of the first anthropologists of America. Although sixteenth-century Spain was a land of eminent scholars and bold thinkers, few of his contemporaries matched the wide range of Las Casas' learning or the independence of his judgments.

Two of his major convictions show how he challenged the Christian conscience of his time to confront the great issues presented by the Spanish conquest. The first was that Christianity must be preached to the Indians by peaceful means alone. The second was that the Indians were human beings to be educated and Christianized, not half-men to be enslaved and kept down in what one sixteenth-century Englishman described as "ethnique darkness."

To prove his first point Las Casas wrote an enormous treatise, *The Only Method of Attracting All People to the True Religion;* though only a portion has been preserved, that remnant is a large volume. The doctrine he enunciated in this first of his many polemical writings was simple enough. He quoted, as did Pope Paul III in the bull "Sublimis Deus," the words of Christ, "Go ye and teach all nations," and agreed that "nations" included the American Indians. As the Pope declared in Rome in that momentous pronouncement on June 9, 1537, at about the time that Las Casas was preaching the same doctrine in Guatemala:

The sublime God so loved the human race that he not only created man in such wise that he might participate in the good that other creatures enjoy, but also

D. FR. BARTHOLOME DE LAS CASAS
Del Orden de Predicadores, Obispo de Chiapa,
Varon apostolico, y el mas zeloso de la felicidad
de los Indios.
Nació en Sevilla el año de 1474, y murió en Madrid
el de 1566.

The Spanish inscription under this late eighteenth-century portrait of
Bartolomé de Las Casas reads: "Order of Preachers, Bishop of Chiapas.
Most zealous apostle and defender of the welfare of the Indians."

endowed him with capacity to attain to the inaccessible and invisible Supreme Good and behold it face to face . . . all are capable of receiving the doctrines of the faith. . . . We . . . consider that the Indians are truly men and that they are not only capable of undertaking the Catholic faith, but according to our information, they desire exceedingly to receive it. . . . The said Indians and all other people who may later be discovered by Christians are by no means to be deprived of their liberty or the possession of their property, even though they be outside the faith of Jesus Christ; and they may and should, freely and legitimately, enjoy their liberty and the possession of their property; nor should they be in any way enslaved; should the contrary happen it shall be null and of no effect. . . . By virtue of our apostolic authority, we declare . . . that the said Indians and other peoples should be converted to the faith of Jesus Christ by preaching the word of God and by the example of good and holy living.

Las Casas applied this doctrine even more specifically than the Pope. He declared that wars against the Indians were unjust and tyrannical; hence the gold, silver, pearls, jewels, and lands wrested from them were wrongfully gotten and must be restored. To subdue and convert the natives by force was not only unlawful, it was also unnecessary. For once the Indians accepted Christianity, their next and inevitable step would be to acknowledge the King of Spain as their sovereign.

Again and again Las Casas returned to his central theme. The proper method for conversion was "bland, suave, sweet, pleasing, tranquil, modest, patiently slow, and above all peaceful and reasonable." Moreover, following Saint Augustine, he insisted that faith depended upon belief, which presupposed understanding. This brought him into conflict with those who favored wholesale baptism of Indians without too many questions asked or catechisms learned. The friars who bore the brunt of the frontier missionary campaigns went about their work with uplifted hearts and a firm conviction that the souls of the Indians constituted the true silver to be mined in America. Indeed, the conquest presented them with a wonderful opportunity, for, though Luther was challenging the Church in Europe, they were determined to build it anew and make it unassailable in the New World. They recorded impressive baptismal statistics. The Franciscans, who believed in mass baptism and sprinkled holy water over Indian heads until their hands could no longer hold the hyssop, calculated that in Mexico alone, between 1524 and 1536, they had saved four million souls. Urged on by flaming zeal, they were exasperated by Las Casas, who wanted each Indian properly instructed in the faith before baptism.

Influenced by Las Casas' doctrine of peaceful persuasion, his Dominican brothers actually tried to put it into effect beginning in 1537, in the spirit of one of Las Casas' favorite authorities, St. John Chrysostom, who had declared: "Men do not consider what we say but what we do—we may philosophize interminably, but if when the occasion arises we do not demonstrate with our actions the truth of what we have been saying, our words will have done more harm than good." For this demonstration of Las Casas' ideas they chose the only land left unconquered in that region, the province of Tuzutlán in present-day Guatemala. It was a mountainous, rainy tropical country filled with fierce beasts, snakes, and large monkeys. Worst of all, it lacked salt. The ferocious natives there were impossible to subjugate, or so believed the conquistadors, who had invaded the region three times and had as often returned "holding their heads." *Tierra de guerra,* they named it—"Land of War."

To this province and people Las Casas offered to go, to induce them voluntarily to become vassals of the King of Spain and pay him tribute according to their ability, to teach them and to preach the Christian faith. All this he proposed to do without arms or soldiers, his only weapon being the word of God and the "reasons of the Holy Gospel." Governor Alonso Maldonado speedily granted his two modest requests: that Indians won over by peaceful methods should not be parceled out to serve Spaniards but should be declared direct dependents of the King, with only moderate tribute to pay; and that for five years no Spaniards except Las Casas and his brother Dominicans should enter the province, so that secular Spaniards might not disturb the Indians or "provoke scandal."

It would be gratifying to report that the experiment in Guatemala went smoothly, but the facts are otherwise. For ten years the colonists in the nearby capital and the ecclesiastics fought stubbornly over the peaceful preaching of the faith. During this time the municipal council of Santiago informed the King that Las Casas was an unlettered friar, an envious, turbulent, most unsaintly fellow, who kept the land in an uproar and would, unless checked, destroy Spanish rule in the New World; furthermore, that the so-called "peaceful" Indians revolted every day and killed many Spaniards. But royal orders continued to flow from Spain supporting the Dominicans and—amid the sardonic laughter of the colonists—the Land of War was officially christened "the Land of True Peace."

In 1544 Las Casas was appointed Bishop of Chiapa, a region which included Tuzutlán. His battle with the colonists grew so hot that a royal investigator was sent to that area in 1547 to look into alleged mistreatment of the Dominicans by the Spanish colonists and reported that much supporting evidence could be found. For a time the Bishop himself fled to Nicaragua to escape his irate flock, many of whom, including the judges of the royal *audiencia,* he had excommunicated.

The end of the experiment is chronicled in a sad letter the friars sent to the Council of the Indies in May, 1556. Writing so that the King might clearly understand what had happened, they described the strenuous work they had done for years, despite the great heat and difficulty of the land. But always "the devil was vigilant" and finally he had stirred up the pagan priests, who called in some neighboring infidel Indians to help provoke a revolt in which the friars and their followers were burned out of their homes and some thirty were killed by arrows, one being sacrificed before a pagan idol. Among those who died was a zealous missionary able to preach in seven Indian languages. The Spaniards in Santiago, citing the royal order forbidding them to enter the territory, had unctuously declined the friars' request for help. The story ended when the King ordered the punishment of the rebellious Indians; the Land of True Peace became even poorer, and the peaceful conversion of Indians there ceased.

Despite this failure, Las Casas, remaining true to his idea, returned to Spain in 1547 to urge his point of view before King and Council. Now seventy-three, after nearly half a century of experience in Indian affairs, he arrived just in time to direct the campaign for his second great conviction: that the aborigines were human beings with the same essential rights as Spaniards. It was a dangerous moment for the Indians, for the ancient theory of Aristotle—that some men are by nature slaves—had been invoked, had been gratefully received by colonists and officials, and had been found conveniently applicable to Indians from the coasts of Florida to the mountains of far-distant Chile. The proposal that some-one else should do the physical work of the world appealed strongly to sixteenth-century Spaniards, whose taste for martial glory and religious conquest and distaste for labor came from their forefathers, who had struggled for centuries to eject the Moslems from Spain. And when to this doctrine was linked the concept that the inferior beings were actually benefited by the labor they performed, the proposition became invincibly attractive.

The Aristotelian doctrine had first been applied to the American Indians in 1519, when Las Casas at the age of forty-five clashed with Juan Quevedo, Bishop of Darién, at Barcelona before the young Emperor Charles V. Las Casas had denounced the bishop for invoking such a non-Christian idea and had dismissed Aristotle as a "gentile burning in Hell, whose doctrine we need not follow except in so far as it conforms to Christian truth." At the same time Las Casas enunciated the basic concept which would guide his action on behalf of the Indians all the rest of his agitated life: "Our Christian religion is suitable for and may be adapted to all the nations of the world, and all alike may receive it; and no one may be deprived of his liberty, nor may he be enslaved on the excuse that he is a natural slave, as it would appear that the reverend bishop of Darién advocates." But no decision had emerged from the debate; the episode was merely a prelude to the important drama that unfolded thirty years later when Las Casas confronted the scholar Juan Ginés de Sepúlveda in Valladolid, the somber Spanish capital on the desolate plain of Castile.

This great dispute originated when the Council of the Indies declared to the King on July 3, 1549, that the dangers both to the Indians and to the King's conscience which the conquests incurred were so great that no future military expedition should be licensed without his express permission and that of the Council. The Council declared:

> The greed of those who undertake conquests and the timidity and humility of the Indians is such that we are not certain whether any instruction will be obeyed. It would be fitting for Your Majesty to order a meeting of learned men, theologians, and jurists . . . to . . . consider the manner in which these conquests should be carried on . . . justly and with security of conscience.

Accordingly, in April of 1550 the King, Charles I of Spain and Charles V of the Holy Roman Empire, ordered that all New World conquests be suspended until a special group of theologians and counselors—to be convened that very year—should decide upon a just method of conducting them.

In 1550 Charles' influence was felt in every country of Europe. His posses-sions stretched to the Netherlands in the north and Milan in the south; in the New

World his bold captains had raced over a vast territory from northern Mexico some seven thousand miles south to Buenos Aires, and his ships had even reached Manila far across the Pacific. In the fifty-eight years since Columbus' landfall Spaniards had discovered one thousand times more new land than had been explored in the previous one thousand years of medieval Europe. In the New World great Indian empires—the Inca and the Aztec being the most notable—had toppled before Spanish soldiers, while in the Old, Charles sturdily fought back both Protestants and Turks. Probably never before had such a mighty sovereign ordered his conquests to cease until it should be decided if they were just.

We do not know where in Valladolid the sessions of the "Council of Fourteen"—which began in mid-August—were held. Perhaps the Council sat in the halls of the ancient university or in the Dominican monastery of San Gregorio, whose imposing buildings still stand. Among the judges were outstanding theologians and veteran members of the councils of Castile and of the Indies; this was the last significant dispute on the nature of the Indians and the justice of Spain's dominion over America.

Las Casas was bold indeed to engage Sepúlveda in learned combat, for this humanist scholar, who had given comfort to Spanish officials and conquistadors by composing a treatise defending the Spanish conquest, had one of the best trained minds of his time. During years of study in Italy he had become one of the principal scholars in the recovery of the "true" Aristotle, and he enjoyed great prestige at court. In 1548, not long before joining battle with Las Casas, he had published in Paris his Latin translation of Aristole's *Politics,* which he considered his principal contribution to knowledge.

The disputants had been summoned to Valladolid to answer the question, Is it lawful for the King of Spain to wage war on the Indians before preaching the faith to them in order to subject them to his rule, so that afterward they may be more easily instructed in the faith? Sepúlveda had come to prove that this was "both lawful and expedient." Las Casas was there to declare it "iniquitous, and contrary to our Christian religion."

On the first day of the dispute Sepúlveda spoke for three hours, giving a résumé of his work "Demócrates." On the second day Las Casas appeared, armed with a monumental treatise, still unpublished, which he proceeded to read word for word. This scholastic onslaught continued for five days, until the reading was completed or—as Sepúlveda suggested—until the members of the Council could bear no more. The two principals did not appear together, but the judges discussed the issues with them separately and also carried on discussions among themselves.

Sepúlveda's fundamental idea was simple. It was lawful and necessary to wage war against the natives for four reasons: (1) For the gravity of the sins which the Indians had committed, especially their idolatries and their "sins against nature"—cruelty to their fellows, cannibalism, and use of human sacrifice in religious ceremonies; (2) On account of the rudeness of their natures, which obliged them to serve persons, like the Spaniards, having a more refined nature; (3) In order to spread the faith, which would be more easily accomplished by the prior subjugation of the natives; (4) To protect the weak among the natives themselves.

The arguments of Las Casas require little detailed analysis: he simply called for justice for the Indians. But the judges at Valladolid, like the later Scottish philosopher who declared, "Blessed are they that hunger and thirst after justice, but it is easier to hunger and thirst after it than to define it," inquired of Las Casas exactly how the conquest ought to proceed. He replied that, when no danger threatened, preachers alone should be sent. In particularly dangerous parts of the Indies, fortresses should be built on the borders, and little by little the people would be won over to Christianity by peace, love, and good example. It is clear that Las Casas, despite the failure at Tuzutlán, never abandoned his hopes for peaceful colonization and persuasion.

The focal point of the argument was Sepúlveda's second justification for the Spaniards' rule: the "natural rudeness and inferiority" of the Indians, which, he declared, accorded with the doctrine of philosophers that some men are born to be natural slaves. Indians in America were without exception rude persons born with a limited understanding, he claimed, and therefore they were to be classed as *servi a natura,* bound to serve their superiors and natural lords, the Spaniards. These inferior people "require, by their own nature and in their own interests, to be placed under the authority of civilized and virtuous princes or nations, so that they may learn, from the might, wisdom, and law of their conquerors, to practice better morals, worthier customs and a more civilized way of life." The Indians are as inferior "as children are to adults, as women are to men, as different from Spaniards as cruel people are from mild people."

> Compare then those blessings enjoyed by Spaniards of prudence, genius, magnanimity, temperance, humanity, and religion with those of the *homunculi* [little men] in whom you will scarcely find even vestiges of humanity, who not only possess no science but who also lack letters and preserve no monument of their history except certain vague and obscure reminiscences of some things in certain paintings. Neither do they have written laws, but barbaric institutions and customs. They do not even have private property.

The fatuity of Sepúlveda's utterances is the more striking when one considers how much information on Indian culture and intellectual capacity was then available. It had been thirty years since the German artist Albrecht Dürer had seen the artistic booty that Cortés had dispatched from Montezuma's Mexico to Charles V and had written in his diary: " I saw among them amazing artistic objects, and I marvelled over the subtle ingenuity of the men in these distant lands, indeed I cannot say enough about the things that were brought before me." Few were equipped to judge as expertly as Dürer the artistic accomplishments of the New World, but by 1550 much of the Aztec, Maya, and Inca culture had come to the notice of Spaniards, and a mass of material rested in the archives of the Council of the Indies. The mathematical achievements of the Mayas and the art and engineering feats of the Incas were not fully appreciated then, but much information was available. Even Cortés, whom Sepúlveda so admired, had been much impressed by some of the Indian laws and achievements, which surprised him since he considered them "barbarians lacking in reason, and in knowledge of God, and in communication with other nations."

But Spaniards who had not been to America had no basis for understanding

*The title page of the earliest printed Spanish-Mexican
Indian dictionary, published in 1555 by the
scholar-friar Alonso de Molina.*

Indians or assessing their cultural power and potentiality, and many were ready
to agree with Sepúlveda when he asked: "How can we doubt that these people, so uncivilized, so barbaric, so contaminated with many sins and obscen-
ities . . . have been justly conquered by such an excellent, pious, and most just
king as was Ferdinand the Catholic and as is now Emperor Charles, and by such
a humane nation which is excellent in every kind of virtue?"

In reply to Sepúlveda's wholesale denigration of the Indians, Las Casas presented to the judges his 550-page Latin manuscript "Apologia," sixty-three chap-
ters of close reasoning and copious citations dedicated to demolishing the arguments of his opponent. He also seems to have presented a summary, perhaps for
those judges who might falter in plowing through his detailed treatise.

Bringing into court his long experience in the Indies, he stressed heavily that

"God had deprived Sepúlveda of any personal knowledge of the New World."
Painting a glowing picture of Indian ability and achievement, he drew heavily
upon his earlier *Apologetic History,* a tremendous accumulation of 870 folio pages
on Indian culture that he had begun in 1527 and completed some twenty years
later, to refute the charge that the Indians were semi-animals whose property and
services could be commandeered by Spaniards and against whom war could justly
be waged. Here he advanced the astonishing idea that the American Indians
compared favorably with the Egyptians, Greeks, and Romans—were indeed superior to them in some ways—and in fact fulfilled every one of Aristotle's requirements for the good life. In several aspects, he insisted, they even surpassed the
Spaniards themselves! His closing argument pulled no punches:

> Doctor Sepúlveda founds these rights upon our superiority . . . and upon our
> having more bodily strength than the Indians. . . . This is simply to place our
> kings in the position of tyrants. The right of those kings rests upon their
> extension of the gospel in the New World, and their good government of the
> Indian nations. These duties they would be bound to fulfill even at their own
> expense; much more so considering the treasures they have received from the
> Indies. To deny this doctrine is to flatter and deceive our monarchs, and to
> put their salvation in peril. The doctor perverts the natural order of things,
> making the means the end, and what is accessory, the principal. . . . He who
> is ignorant of this, small is his knowledge, and he who denies it is no more of
> a Christian than Mahomet was.

The judges at Valladolid, probably exhausted and confused by this mighty
conflict, fell into argument with one another and reached no collective decision.
Both disputants claimed victory, but the facts now available do not conclusively
support either one. The judges went home after the final meeting, and for years
afterward the Council of the Indies struggled to get them to write out their
opinions. In vain. We can sympathize with the judges, for they had been besieged
by two formidable men committed to two conflicting visions of Indian reality, and
each had insisted that the whole structure of Spain's action in America must
conform to his single vision.

After the last meeting, Las Casas and his companion, Rodrigo de Andrada,
made final arrangements with the San Gregorio monastery in Valladolid to spend
the rest of their lives there. According to the contract drawn up on July 21, 1551,
they were to be accorded three new cells—one of them presumably for the large
collection of books and manuscripts Las Casas had amassed—a servant, first place
in the choir, freedom to come and go as they pleased, and burial in the San
Gregorio sacristy.

Las Casas did not, however, settle down to a life of quiet contemplation. The
failure of the Valladolid disputation to produce a resounding public triumph for
his ideas may have convinced him that his efforts on behalf of the Indians needed
a more permanent record. He was now seventy-eight years old, weary from half
a century of involvement in Indian affairs, and he probably hoped to use the
printing press to place his propositions and projects before Spaniards whom he

could not otherwise reach. At any rate, he left San Gregorio and sallied forth the next year, 1552, to Seville, where he spent many months recruiting friars for America and preparing a series of nine remarkable treatises, printed there in 1552 and early 1553, which served as textbooks and guides to friars scattered over the vast stretches of America.

But his opponents made use of them too. His summaries of the debates with Sepúlveda—printed in Seville and later translated in England—of course included Sepúlveda's arguments. These, ironically, so impressed the town council of Mexico, the richest and most important city in all the Indies, that it voted in February of 1554 to buy Sepúlveda "jewels and clothing from this land to the value of two hundred pesos" in recognition of his soundness and "to encourage him in the future." Sepúlveda himself fired a new salvo by issuing a reply to Las Casas under the somewhat pejorative title, "Rash, Scandalous and Heretical Propositions which Dr. Sepúlveda Noted in the Book on the Conquest of the Indies which Friar Bartolomé de Las Casas Printed Without a License."

Las Casas never wavered in his convictions, and in his will, dated March 17, 1564, prophesied darkly: "Surely God will wreak his fury and anger against Spain some day for the unjust wars waged against the Indians." In the last few months of his life he made a final appeal to Rome for support, but his long and passionate crusade ended when death overtook him in July, 1566.

The struggle itself did not end. In fact, the Crown pursued a steady course during the years after Valladolid in the direction of the doctrine set forth by Las Casas: friendly persuasion and not general warfare to attract the Indians to the faith. And though Sepúlveda's views had been widely circulated in manuscript form and presented in detail at the Valladolid meeting, his treatise "Demó-crates," which had set off the controversy, was never approved for publication. The generous terms of the standard law on new discoveries—promulgated in July of 1573 by Charles' successor, Philip II, and designed to regulate all future discoveries and conquests—were probably attributable to the battle Las Casas fought at Valladolid.

The law decreed particularly that, instead of "conquest" the term "pacifica-tion" should henceforth be used. The vices of the Indians were to be dealt with very gently at first "so as not to scandalize them or prejudice them against Christianity." If, after all the explanations, natives still opposed a Spanish settle-ment and the preaching of Christianity, the Spaniards might use force but were to do "as little harm as possible," a measure that Las Casas would never have approved. No license was given to enslave the captives. In theory this general order governed conquests as long as Spain ruled her American colonies, although some Spaniards could always be found who thought that the Indians should be subjugated by arms because they were not Christians.

What if Spain had followed the precepts of Las Casas to the letter? Would every friar eventually have been enslaved or killed, and Spanish America overrun by other, less squeamish Europeans? We shall never know, for the history of the expansion of Europe includes no examples of the wholly peaceful penetration of new lands. We do know, however, that for generations the Dominican attempt to preach the faith peacefully in Guatemala influenced Spaniards throughout

Spain's vast American empire to use persuasion rather than a "fire and sword" policy in bringing Catholicism to the Indians.

In the end, no simplification of the Valladolid controversy is satisfactory. For in this struggle between learned, bitterly divided men of the same nation, other considerations besides theories on the nature of the Indians—economic striving, personality clashes, and the Crown's interest—all played a part. But it was significant that the Crown permitted fundamental disputes in those tumultuous years in which its policies were evolving. To Spain's everlasting credit she allowed men to insist that all her actions in America be just, and at times she listened to those voices.

The attempt in 1573 to regulate all future conquests and the many other laws on behalf of the Indians would never have been promulgated if Sepúlveda's ideas on just war against the Indians had triumphed. Nor would this passage have appeared in the fundamental code, the Laws of the Indies, printed in 1681: "War cannot and shall not be made on the Indians of any province to the end that they may receive the Holy Catholic Faith or yield obedience to us, or for any other reason."

But the Valladolid dispute lives on principally because of the ideas on the nature of man which Las Casas enunciated there. One fine passage shows the great eloquence of which he was sometimes capable:

> Thus mankind is one, and all men are alike in that which concerns their creation and all natural things, and no one is born enlightened. . . . All of us must be guided and aided at first by those who were born before us. And the savage peoples of the earth may be compared to uncultivated soil that readily brings forth weeds and useless thorns, but has within itself such natural virtue that by labor and cultivation it may be made to yield sound and beneficial fruits.

No single individual completely typifies the nation which established Spanish power in the New World. Rather, the sixteenth-century Spanish character may be likened to a medal stamped on each of its sides with a resolute face. One is that of an imperialistic conquistador; the other, that of a friar devoted to God. Both were imprisoned within the thinking of their own kind and their own time. Neither, when he was most himself, could wholly understand or forgive the other. Yet they were sent yoked together into a new world and together were responsible for the action and the achievement of Spain in America. Even to begin to understand the extremely complex movement of men and ideas which is called the Spanish conquest, we must see that both these bold faces were truly Spanish.

The struggle which Montesinos started in Cuba and Las Casas and many others carried forward throughout the Spanish empire in America is not yet over. The dust on centuries-old manuscripts that recount the Spanish struggle for Christian justice cannot obscure the vitality of the issues, which still disturb the world today. The cry of Montesinos denouncing the enslavement of Indians and the loud voice of Las Casas proclaiming that all the peoples of the world are men are valid today and will still be valid tomorrow, for they are timeless. And in the perspective of centuries the decision of the Spaniards not to stigmatize the Indians as natural slaves may be seen as a milestone on the long road, still under construction, which winds slowly toward civilizations based on the dignity of all men.

The Clash of Cultures: Indians, Europeans, and the Environment

William Cronon and Richard White

One of the most interesting and productive recent developments in the study of American history has been work dealing with the interrelations between people and their environment. In part, this work is a result of our current concern with pollution and the exhaustion of valuable natural resources, but it has also proved to be a valuable way of learning more about how people of past generations and different cultures dealt with nature and with one another. The following discussion of two leading American "environmental" historians makes clear how much light this approach throws on the culture of the American Indians and their relations with European colonists.

William Cronon of Yale University is the author of Changes in the Land: Indians, Colonists and the Ecology of New England. *This book, which won the 1984 Parkman Prize, is a study of how Indians and European settlers shaped and were in turn influenced by the New England landscape. Richard White, a professor of history at the University of Utah, has published* Land Use, Environment, and Social Change *and* The Roots of Dependency, *an environmental history of three Indian tribes.*

WILLIAM CRONON: If historians thought about the environment at all up until a few years ago, they thought of it in terms of an older school of American historians who are often called "environmental determinists." People like Frederick Jackson Turner argued that Europeans came to North America, settled on the frontier, and began to be changed by the environment.

RICHARD WHITE: In a delayed reaction to Turner, historians in the late 1960s and early 1970s reversed this. They began to emphasize a series of horror stories when they wrote about the environment. The standard metaphor of the time was "the rape of the earth," but what they were really describing was the way Americans moving west cut down the forests, ploughed the land, destroyed the grasslands, harnessed the rivers—how they in effect transformed the whole appearance of the North American landscape.

WILLIAM CRONON: Since then, I think, we've realized that both positions are true, but incomplete. The real problem is that human beings reshape the earth as they live upon it, but as they reshape it, the new form of the earth has an influence on the way those people can live. The two reshape each other. This is as true of Indians as it is of European settlers.

RICHARD WHITE: My first connections with Indians in the environment was very immediate. I became interested because of fishing-rights controversies in the Northwest, in which the Indians' leading opponents included several major environmental organizations. They argued that Indians were destroying the fisheries. What made this odd was that these same groups also held up Indians as sort of primal ecologists. I remember reading a Sierra Club book which claimed that Indians had moved over the face of the land and when they left you couldn't tell they'd ever been there. Actually, this idea demeans Indians. It makes them seem simply like an animal species, and thus deprives them of culture. It also demeans the environment by so simplifying it that all changes come to seem negative—as if somehow the ideal is never to have been here at all. It's a crude view of the environment, and it's a crude view of Indians.

WILLIAM CRONON: Fundamentally, it's an ahistorical view. It says not only that the land never changed—"wilderness" was always in this condition—but that the people who lived upon it had no history, and existed outside of time. They were "natural."

RICHARD WHITE: That word *natural* is the key. Many of these concepts of Indians are quite old, and they all picture Indians as people without culture. Depending on your view of human nature, there are two versions. If human beings are inherently evil in a Calvinistic sense, then you see Indians as inherently violent and cruel. They're identified with nature, but it's the nature of the howling wilderness, which is full of Indians. But if you believe in a beneficent nature, and a basically good human nature, then you see Indians as noble savages, people at one with their environment.

WILLIAM CRONON: To understand how Indians really did view and use their environment, we have to move beyond these notions of "noble savages" and "Indians as the original ecologists." We have to look instead at how they actually lived.

RICHARD WHITE: Well, take the case of fire. Fire transformed environments all over the continent. It was a basic tool used by Indians to reshape landscape,

A mountain lion, a wold, and a scalp lock are some of the elements in the design of this Pueblo buffalo-hide shield. It was obtained about 1890.

enabling them to clear forests to create grasslands for hunting and fields for planting. Hoe agriculture—as opposed to the plow agriculture of the Europeans—is another.

WILLIAM CRONON: There's also the Indians' use of "wild" animals—animals that were not domesticated, not owned in ways Europeans recognized. Virtually all North American Indians were intimately linked to the animals around them, but they had no cattle or pigs or horses.

RICHARD WHITE: What's hardest for us to understand, I think, is the Indians' different way of making sense of species and the natural world in general. I'm currently writing about the Indians of the Great Lakes region. Most of them thought of animals as a species of *persons.* Until you grasp that fact, you can't really understand the way they treated animals. This is easy to romanticize—it's easy to turn it into a "my brother the buffalo" sort of thing. But it wasn't. The Indians *killed* animals. They often overhunted animals. But when they overhunted, they did so within the context of a moral universe that both they and the animals inhabited. They conceived of animals as having, not rights—that's the wrong word—but *powers.* To kill an animal was to be involved in a social relationship with the animal. One thing that has impressed me about Indians I've known is their realization that this is a harsh planet, that they survive by the deaths of other creatures. There's no attempt to gloss over that or romanticize it.

WILLIAM CRONON: There's a kind of debt implied by killing animals.

RICHARD WHITE: Yes. You incur an obligation. And even more than the obligation is your sense that those animals have somehow surrendered themselves to you.

WILLIAM CRONON: There's a gift relationship implied. . . .

RICHARD WHITE: . . . which is also a *social* relationship. This is where it becomes almost impossible to compare Indian environmentalism and modern white environmentalism. You cannot take an American forester or an American wildlife manager and expect him to think that he has a special social relationship with the species he's working on.

WILLIAM CRONON: Or that he owes the forest some kind of gift in return for the gift of wood he's taking from it.

RICHARD WHITE: Exactly. And it seems to me hopeless to try to impose that attitude onto Western culture. We distort Indian reality when we say Indians were conservationists—that's not what conservation means. We don't give them full credit for their view, and so we falsify history.

Another thing that made Indians different from modern Euro-Americans was their commitment to producing for *security* rather than for maximum yield. Indians didn't try to maximize the production of any single commodity. Most tried to attain security by diversifying their diet, by following the seasonal cycles: they ate what was most abundant. What always confused Europeans was why Indians didn't simply concentrate on the most productive part of the cycle: agriculture, say. They could have grown more crops and neglected something else. But once you've done that, you lose a certain amount of security.

WILLIAM CRONON: I like to think of Indian communities having a whole series of ecological nets under them. When one net failed, there was always another underneath it. If the corn died, they could always hunt deer or gather wild roots. In hard times—during an extended drought, for instance—those nets became crucial.

All of this was linked to seasonal cycles. For me, one of the best ways of understanding the great diversity of environmental practices among Indian peoples is to think about the different ways they moved across the seasons of the year. Because the seasons of North America differ markedly between, say, the Eastern forests and the Great Plains and the Southwestern deserts, Indian groups devised quite different ways of life to match different natural cycles.

New England is the region I know best. For Indians there, spring started with hunting groups drawing together to plant their crops after having been relatively dispersed for the winter. While women planted beans, squash, and corn, men hunted the migrating fish and birds. They dispersed for summer hunting and gathering while the crops matured, and then reassembled in the fall. The corn was harvested and great celebrations took place. Then, once the harvest was done and the corn stored in the ground, people broke up their villages and fanned out in small bands for the fall hunt, when deer and other animals were at their fattest. The hunt went on until winter faded and the season of agriculture began again. What they had was agriculture during one part of the year, gathering going on continuously, and hunting concentrated in special seasons. That was typical not just of the Indians of New England but of eastern Indians in general.

RICHARD WHITE: For me the most dramatic example of seasonal changes among Indian peoples would be the horticulturists of the eastern Great Plains. The Pawnees are the example I know best. Depending on when you saw the Pawnees, you might not recognize them as the same people. If you came upon them in the spring or early fall, when they were planting or harvesting crops, you would have found a people living in large, semisubterranean earth lodges and surrounded by scattered fields of corn and beans and squash. They looked like horticultural people. If you encountered the Pawnees in early summer or late fall, you would have thought you were seeing Plains nomads—because then they followed the buffalo, and their whole economy revolved around the buffalo. They lived in tepees and were very similar, at least in outward appearance, to the Plains nomads who surrounded them.

For the Pawnees, these cycles of hunting and farming were intimately connected. One of my favorite examples is a conversation in the 1870s between the Pawnee Petalesharo and a Quaker Indian agent who was trying to explain to him why he should no longer hunt buffalo. Suddenly a cultural chasm opens between them, because Petalesharo is trying to explain that the corn will not grow without the buffalo hunt. Without buffalo to sacrifice at the ceremonies, corn will not come up and the Pawnee world will cease. You see them talking, but there's no communication.

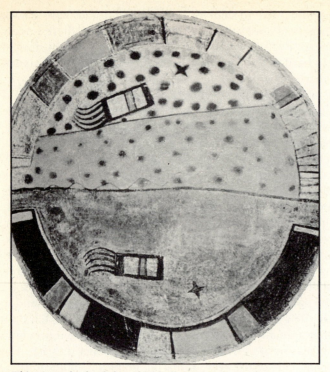

*This Arapaho buckskin shield shows two bear paws set
among stars and land and rimmed with a rainbow.
Collected about 1875.*

WILLIAM CRONON: It's difficult for a modern American hearing this to see Petalesharo's point of view as anything other than alien and wrong. This notion
of sacrificing buffalo so corn will grow is fundamental to his view of nature,
even though it's utterly different from what *we* mean when we call him a
conservationist.

RICHARD WHITE: And yet, if you want to understand people's actions historically,
you have to take Petalesharo seriously.

WILLIAM CRONON: Environmental historians have not only been reconstructing
the ways Indians used and thought about the land, they've also been analyz-
ing how those things changed when the Europeans invaded. A key discovery
of the last couple of decades had been our radically changed sense of how
important European disease was in changing Indian lives.

RICHARD WHITE: It was appalling. Two worlds that had been largely isolated
suddenly came into contact. The Europeans brought with them diseases the
Indians had never experienced. The resulting death rates are almost impossible to imagine: 90 to 95 percent in some places.

WILLIAM CRONON: The ancestors of the Indians came to North America from ten
to forty thousand years ago. They traveled through an Arctic environment
in which many of the diseases common to temperate and tropical climates

simply couldn't survive. They came in groups that were biologically too small to sustain those diseases. And they came without the domesticated animals with which we share several of our important illnesses. Those three circumstances meant that Indians shed many of the most common diseases of Europe and Asia. Measles, chicken pox, smallpox, and many of the venereal diseases vanished during migration. For over twenty thousand years, Indians lived without encountering these illnesses, and so lost the antibodies that would ordinarily have protected them.

RICHARD WHITE: Most historians would now agree that when the Europeans arrived, the Indian population of North America was between ten and twelve million (the old estimate was about one million). By the early twentieth century it had fallen to less than five hundred thousand. At the same time, Indian populations were also under stress from warfare. Their seasonal cycles were being broken up, and they were inadequately nourished as a result. All these things contributed to the tremendous mortality they suffered.

WILLIAM CRONON: Part of the problem was biological; part of it was cultural. If a disease arrived in mid-summer, it had quite different effects from one that arrived in the middle of the winter, when people's nutrition levels were low and they were more susceptible to disease. A disease that arrived in spring, when crops had to be planted, could disrupt the food supply for the entire year. Nutrition levels would be down for the whole subsequent year, and new diseases would find readier victims as a result.

RICHARD WHITE: The effects extended well beyond the original epidemic—a whole series of changes occurred. If Indian peoples in fact shaped the North American landscape, this enormous drop in their population changed the way the land looked. For example, as the Indians of the Southeast died in what had once been a densely populated region with a lot of farmland, cleared areas reverted to grassy woodland. Deer and other animal populations increased in response. When whites arrived, they saw the abundance of animals as somehow natural, but it was nothing of the sort.

Disease also dramatically altered relationships among Indian peoples. In the 1780s and 1790s the most powerful and prosperous peoples of the Great Plains margins were the Mandans, the Arikaras, the Hidatsas, the Pawnees, all of whom raised corn as part of their subsistence cycles. Nomadic, nonagricultural groups like the Sioux were small and poor. Smallpox changed all that. Those peoples living in large, populous farming villages were precisely those who suffered the greatest death rates. So the group that had once controlled the region went into decline, while another fairly marginal group rose to historical prominence.

WILLIAM CRONON: That's a perfect example of biological and cultural interaction, of how complex it is. A dense population is more susceptible to disease than a less dense one: that's a biological observation true of any animal species. But which Indian communities are dense and which are not, which ones are living in clustered settlements and which ones are scattered thinly on the ground—these aren't biological phenomena but *cultural* ones.

RICHARD WHITE: Perhaps the best example of this is the way different Plains Indian responded to the horse, which, along with disease, actually preceded the arrival of significant numbers of Europeans in the region. The older conception of what happened is that when the horse arrived, it transformed the world. That may have been true for the Sioux, but not for the Pawnees. The Sioux became horse nomads; the Pawnees didn't. They were not willing to give up the security of raising crops. For them, the horse provided an ability to hunt buffalo more efficiently, but they were not about to rely solely on buffalo. If the buffalo hunt failed, and they had neglected their crops, they would be in great trouble. As far as I know, there is no agricultural group, with the exception of the Crows and perhaps the Cheyennes, that *willingly* gave up agriculture to rely solely on the buffalo. The people like the Sioux who became Plains nomads had always been hunters and gatherers, and for them horses represented a *more* secure subsistence, not a less secure one.

WILLIAM CRONON: It's the ecological safety net again. People who practiced agriculture were reluctant to abandon it, because it was one of their strongest nets.

RICHARD WHITE: And they didn't. When given a choice, even under harsh circumstances, people tried to integrate the horse into their existing economy, not transform themselves.

The horse came to the Sioux at a time when they were in trouble. Their subsistence base had grown precarious: the buffalo and beavers they'd hunted farther east were declining, and the decline of the farming villages from disease meant the Sioux could no longer raid or trade with them for food. The horse was a godsend: buffalo hunting became more efficient, and the buffalo began to replace other food sources. Having adopted the horse, the Sioux moved farther out onto the Plains. By the time they had their famous conflicts with the United States in the 1860s and 1870s, they were the dominant people of the Great Plains. Their way of life was unimaginable without the horse and buffalo.

WILLIAM CRONON: The result was that the Sioux reduced the number of ecological nets that sustained their economy and way of life. And although the bison were present in enormous numbers when the Sioux began to adopt the horse, by the 1860s the bison were disappearing from the Plains; by the early eighties they were virtually gone. That meant the Sioux's main ecological net was gone, and there wasn't much left to replace it.

RICHARD WHITE: To destroy the buffalo was to destroy the Sioux. Of course, given time, they might have been able to replace the buffalo with cattle and become a pastoral people. That seems well within the realm of historical possibility. But they were never allowed that option.

WILLIAM CRONON: Disease and the horse are obviously important factors in Indian history. But there's a deeper theme underlying these things. All North American Indian peoples eventually found themselves in a relationship of dependency with the dominant Euro-American culture. At some point, in various ways, they ceased to be entirely autonomous peoples, controlling their own resources and their own political and cultural life. Is environmental history fundamental to explaining how this happened?

RICHARD WHITE: I think it's absolutely crucial. Compare the history of European settlement in North America with what happened in Asia and Africa. Colonialism in Asia and Africa was very important, but it was a passing phase. It has left a strong legacy, but Africa is nonetheless a continent inhabited by Africans, Asia a continent inhabited by Asians. American Indian peoples, on the other hand, are a small minority in North America. Part of what happened was simply the decline in population, but as we've said, that decline was not simple at all. To understand it, we have to understand environmental history.

Many Indians were never militarily conquered. They nonetheless became dependent on whites, partly because their subsistence economy was systematically undercut. Virtually every American Indian community eventually had to face the fact that it could no longer feed or shelter itself without outside aid. A key aspect of this was the arrival of a market economy in which certain resources came to be overexploited. The fur trade is the clearest example of this.

WILLIAM CRONON: No question. The traditional picture of the fur trade is that Europeans arrive, wave a few guns and kettles and blankets in the air, and Indians come rushing forward to trade. What do they have to trade? They have beaver pelts, deerskins, bison robes. As soon as the incentive is present, as soon as those European goods are there to be had, the Indians sweep across the continent, wipe out the furbearing animals, and destroy their own subsistence. That's the classic myth of the fur trade.

RICHARD WHITE: It simply didn't happen that way. European goods often penetrated Indian communities slowly; Indian technologies held on for a long time. Indians wanted European goods, but for reasons that could be very different from why *we* think they wanted them.

WILLIAM CRONON: One of my favorite examples is the kettle trade. Indians wanted kettles partly because you can put them on a fire and boil water and they won't break. That's nice. But many of those kettles didn't stay kettles for long. They got cut up and turned into arrowheads that were then used in the hunt. Or they got turned into high-status jewelry. Indians valued kettles because they were such an extraordinarily flexible resource.

RICHARD WHITE: The numbers of kettles that have turned up in Indian graves proves that their value was not simply utilitarian.

WILLIAM CRONON: The basic facts of the fur trade are uncontestable. Europeans sought to acquire Indian furs, food, and land; Indians sought to acquire European textiles, alcohol, guns, and other metal goods. Indians began to hunt greater numbers of furbearing animals, until finally several species, especially the beaver, were eliminated. Those are the two end points of the fur-trade story. But understanding how to get from one to the other is very complicated. Why did Indians engage in the fur trade in the first place? That's the question.

RICHARD WHITE: We tend to assume that exchange is straightforward, that it's simply giving one thing in return for another. That is not how it appeared to Indian peoples.

WILLIAM CRONON: Think of the different ways goods are exchanged. One is how we usually perceive exchange today: we go into the local supermarket, lay down a dollar, and get a candy bar in return. Many Europeans in the fur trade thought that was what they were doing—giving a gun, or a blanket, or a kettle and receiving a number of furs in return. But for the Indians the exchange looked very different.

RICHARD WHITE: To see how Indians perceived this, consider two things we all know, but which we don't ordinarily label as "trade." One is gifts. There's no need to romanticize the giving of gifts. Contemporary Americans exchange gifts at Christmas or at weddings, and when those gifts are exchanged, as anybody who has received one knows, you incur an obligation. You often have relatives who never let you forget the gift they've given you, and what you owe in return. There's no *price* set on the exchange, it's a *gift,* but the obligation is very real. That's one way Indians saw exchange. To exchange goods that way, the two parties at least had to pretend to be friends.

At the other extreme, if friendship hadn't been established, goods could still change hands, but here the basis of exchange was often simple theft. If you had enemies, you could rob them. So if traders failed to establish some friendship, kinship, or alliance, Indians felt perfectly justified in attacking them and taking their goods. In the fur trade there was a fine line between people who sometimes traded with each other and sometimes stole from each other.

WILLIAM CRONON: To make that more concrete, when the Indian handed a beaver skin to the trader, who gave a gun in return, it wasn't simply two goods that were moving back and forth. There were *symbols* passing between them as well. The trader might not have been aware of all those symbols, but for the Indian the exchange represented a statement about their friendship. The Indian might expect to rely on the trader for military support, and to support him in return. Even promises about marriage, about linking two communities together, might be expressed as goods passed from hand to hand. It was almost as if a language was being spoken when goods were exchanged. It took a long time for the two sides to realize they weren't speaking the same language.

RICHARD WHITE: Right. But for Indians the basic meanings of exchange were clear. You gave generously to friends; you stole from enemies. Indians also recognized that not everybody could be classified simply as a friend or an enemy, and this middle ground is where trade took place.

But even in that middle ground, trade always began with an exchange of gifts. And to fail to be generous in your gifts, to push too hard on the price—Indians read that as hostility. When Europeans tried to explain the concept of a "market" to Indians, it bewildered them. The notion that demand for furs in London could affect how many blankets they would receive for a beaver skin in Canada was quite alien to them. How on earth could events taking place an ocean away have anything to do with the relationship between two people standing right here who were supposed to act as friends and brothers toward each other?

WILLIAM CRONON: So one thing Indian peoples had trouble comprehending at certain stages in this dialogue was the concept of *price:* the price of a good fluctuating because of its abundance in the market. Indian notions were much closer to the medieval "just price." This much gunpowder is always worth this many beaver skins. If somebody tells me they want twice as many skins for the same gunpowder I bought last year at half the price, suddenly they're being treacherous. They're beginning to act as an enemy.

RICHARD WHITE: Or in the words Algonquians often used, "This must mean my father doesn't love me any more." To Europeans that kind of language seems ludicrous. What in the world does love have to do with giving a beaver skin for gunpowder? But for Indians it's absolutely critical.

Of course, exchange became more commercial with time. Early in the fur trade, Indians had received European goods as gifts, because they were allies against other Indians or other Europeans. But increasingly they found that the only way to receive those goods was through direct economic exchange. Gift giving became less important, and trading goods for set prices became more important. As part of these commercial dealings, trad-

Feathers decorate this Sioux buckskin dance shield; its mysterious design includes birds and lizards.

ers often advanced loans to Indians before they actually had furs to trade. By that mechanism, gifts were transformed into debts. Debts could in turn be used to coerce greater and greater hunting from Indians.

WILLIAM CRONON: As exchange became more commercial, the Indians' relationship to animals became more commercial as well. Hunting increased with the rise in trade, and animal populations declined in response. First the beaver, then the deer, then the bison disappeared from large stretches of North America. As that happened, Indians found themselves in the peculiar position of relying more and more on European goods but no longer having the furs they needed to acquire them. Worse, they could no longer even *make* those same goods as they once had, in the form of skin garments, wild meat, and so on. That's the trap they fell into.

RICHARD WHITE: And that becomes dependency. That's what Thomas Jefferson correctly and cynically realized when he argued that the best way for the United States to acquire Indian lands was to encourage trade and have government storehouses assume Indian debts. Indians would have no choice but to cede their lands to pay their debts, and they couldn't even renounce those debts because they now needed the resources the United States offered them in order to survive. Not all tribes became involved in this, but most who relied on the fur trade eventually did.

Of course, the effects go both ways. As whites eliminated Indians and Indian control, they were also, without realizing it, eliminating the forces that had shaped the landscape itself. The things they took as natural—why there were trees, why there weren't trees, the species of plants that grew there—were really the results of Indian practices. As whites changed the practices, those things vanished. Trees began to reinvade the grassland, and forests that had once been open became closed.

WILLIAM CRONON: Once the wild animals that had been part of the Indians' spiritual and ecological universe began to disappear, Europeans acquired the land and began to transform it to match their assumptions about what a "civilized" landscape should look like. With native animals disappearing, other animals could be brought in to use the same food supply that the deer, the moose, and the bison had previously used. And so the cow, the horse, the pig—the animals so central to European notions of what an animal universe looks like—began to move across the continent like a kind of animal frontier. In many instances the Indians turned to these domesticated European species to replace their own decreasing food supply and so adopted a more pastoral way of life. As they lost their lands, they were then stuck with the problem of feeding their animals as well as themselves.

RICHARD WHITE: The Navajos are a good example of this. We tend to forget that Indians don't simply vanish when we enter the twentieth century. The Navajos are perhaps the group who maintained control over their own lands for the longest time, but their control was increasingly subject to outside pressures. They very early adopted European sheep, which became more and more important to their economy, both because wild foods were eliminated and because the government strongly encouraged the Navajos to raise more

Pueblo designs are easier to decipher than those of the Plains Indians. This shield shows a moon, rainbow, and falling rain.

sheep. They built up prosperous herds but were gradually forced to confine them to the reservation instead of the wider regions they had grazed before.

The result was a crisis on the Navajo reservation. The land began to erode. By the 1920s and 1930s the Navajos had far more sheep than could be sustained during dry years. And here's where one of the more interesting confrontations between Indians and conservationists took place. The government sought to reduce Navajo stock, but its own motives were mixed. There was a genuine fear for the Navajos, but the main concern had to do with Boulder Dam. Conservationists feared Lake Mead was going to silt up, and that the economic development of the Southwest would be badly inhibited.

What they didn't understand were the causes of erosion. They blamed it all on Navajo sheep, but it now appears that there was a natural gullying cycle going on in the Southwest. Anybody familiar with the Southwest knows that its terrain is shaped by more than sheep and horses, no matter how badly it is overgrazed. So the result of government conservation policy for the Navajos was deeply ironic. Having adjusted to the European presence, having prospered with their sheep, they found their herds being undercut by the government for the good of the larger economy. It's a classic case

of Indians—as the poorest and least powerful people in a region—forced to
bear the brunt of economic-development costs. So the Navajo economy was
again transformed. As the Navajos became poorer and poorer, they grew
more willing to lease out oil and allow strip mining on the reservation. They
found themselves in the familiar situation of being forced to agree to practices that were harmful, even in their view, to the land. They had to do it
in order to survive, but they were then attacked by white conservationists
for abandoning their own values.

WILLIAM CRONON: A real no-win situation.

RICHARD WHITE: There are lessons in all this. We can't copy Indian ways of
understanding nature, we're too different. But studying them throws our
own assumptions into starker relief and suggests shortcomings in our relationships with nature that could cost us dearly in the long run.

WILLIAM CRONON: I think environmental history may be capable of transforming
our perspective, not just on Indian history, but on all human history. The
great arrogance of Western civilization in the industrial and postindustrial
eras has been to imagine human beings existing somehow apart from the
earth. Often the history of the industrial era has been written as if technology has liberated human beings so that the earth has become increasingly
irrelevant to modern civilization—when in fact all history is a long-standing
dialogue between human beings and the earth. It's as if people are constantly speaking to the earth, and the earth is speaking to them. That's a way
of putting it that Indians would be far more capable of understanding than
most modern Americans. But this dialogue, this conversation between earth
and the inhabitants of earth, is fundamental to environmental history. With
it we can try to draw together all these pieces—human population changes,
cultural changes, economic changes, environmental changes—into a complicated but unified history of humanity upon the earth. That, in rather
ambitious terms, is what environmental historians are seeking to do.

PART TWO

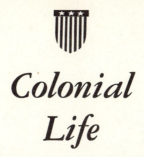

Colonial Life

Fox hunting was a passion that colonial gentry gladly indulged. This rendering of a hunting party is a detail from an overmantel painting of the late seventeenth century.

American Indians and European Diseases

Alfred W. Crosby

In "The Clash of Cultures," William Cronon and Richard White explained why European diseases had such devastating effects on American Indians. In this essay, Professor Alfred W. Crosby of the University of Texas shows how European diseases affected the Indians of New England both physically and psychologically. That the Europeans were as ignorant of what was actually happening as the "primitive" native inhabitants and, indeed, that they attributed the Indians' diseases to the same supernatural cause that the Indians did is an added illustration of how environment and culture interact.

Professor Crosby, a pioneer in the field of environmental history, is the author of The Columbian Exchange, *a book that deals with the ways Indian and European cultures influenced each other in America.*

I n December of 1620, a group of English dissenters who "knew they were pilgrimes," in the words of William Bradford, stepped ashore on the southern coast of Massachusetts at the site of the Wampanoag Indian village of Pawtuxet. The village was empty, abandoned long enough for the grasses and weeds to have taken over the cornfields, but not long enough for the trees to have returned. The Pilgrims occupied the lonely place and called it Plymouth.

It was pestilence that had cleared the way for this tiny foothold in New England, and the shadow of death would be a major factor in giving the settlement form and substance in the months ahead.

New England Indians and European fishermen and traders had been in intermittent contact for a century, and it was inevitable that more than otter skins, beaver pelts, knives, and kettles would be exchanged. Disease was among the commodities, and in this trade the Indians would come off second best. Europe, with ancient contact by land and new ones by sea with the chief disease communities of the world, and with her relatively dense populations of often hungry and always filthy people, had all the advantages of her disadvantages: an arsenal of diseases.

Europe was in the midst of a golden age for infectious disease organisms, an era ushered in by the Black Death in the fourteenth century. To such old regulars as smallpox and consumption were added such new, or newly recognized, diseases as plague, typhus, and syphilis. Bubonic plague, the greatest killer of them all, smoldered continually and broke out periodically in consuming epidemics. Early in 1617 southeast gales drove whales ashore in the Netherlands. The fearful thought them a portent of plague, and sure enough, by August the plague was general throughout the land. London had full-scale epidemics of that killer in 1603 and again in 1625, and the plague—or something very like it—soon made its presence felt among the Indians of the Northeast coast of America. Innocent of immunity or experience, the Indians were helpless. . . .

When did this pestilence first appear in New England? Probably no earlier than 1616 and no later than 1617, and it lasted until at least 1619. What vessel brought it? It is improbable that we will ever know. What was the disease? Another difficult question. We know it lasted through winters, which suggests that it wasn't a mosquito-borne disease, like yellow fever. We know that the few Europeans who actually saw its victims did not identify it as smallpox, measles, mumps, chicken pox, or any of Europe's common diseases, which they certainly would have recognized. We know it spread along the coast no farther southwest than Narragansett Bay, nor farther northeast than the Kennebec River or possibly Penobscot Bay, nor did it penetrate inland more than twenty or thirty miles. The narrow geographical limitations of the epidemic suggest that the disease was not one of the breath-borne maladies, like smallpox or measles, which normally surge across vast areas. A flea- or louse-borne disease like typhus or plague seems more likely.

We know that the disease produced spots on its victims' skins; and we know by hearsay that some Englishmen in New England at the peak of the epidemic slept in huts with dead and dying Indians, but that not one of these whites fell ill or even so much as "felt their heads to ache while they stayed there." Spots certainly suggest typhus. The Europeans' freedom from infection suggests some disease so common in Europe that they all had acquired immunity to it at home, or that they didn't stay around long enough to get a proper dose of the disease— or that the account is in part or whole false.

Most of the seventeenth-century chroniclers called the disease the plague. "Plague" was and is a word often used to mean any pestilence, but these chroniclers often called it *the* plague." Captain Thomas Dermer, one of the few Europeans actually to see Indians who were freshly recovering from the experience, called their infection in 1619 "the Plague, for wee might perceive the sores of some that had escaped, who described the spots of such as usually died."

Plague is certainly capable of doing what this pestilence did, and Europeans certainly knew it well enough to recognize it by sight or description. And it is true that plague was well established in Western Europe in the early years of the seventeenth century. Like some kinds of typhus, it is a disease carried by rats and their attendant vermin, rats which swarmed in the holds of the sailing vessels of that era. The disease travels readily by ship, as the European colonists in America knew. Many Britons fell ill and died on the vessels of the Third Supply sailing to Virginia in 1609, and the rumor was that one of the vessels had plague on board. In the 1660's, during London's last great siege of plague, Virginians fled from their ports for fear of the disease coming across on the ships from England.

Fear was justified because ship rats were coming across and establishing beachheads in America. Captain John Smith tells us that they already numbered in the thousands in Jamestown in 1609, when the rats almost starved out the colony by eating its stores of food. They were present and prospering in New England by at least the 1660's, and probably a great deal earlier. It is likely that they found living in the layered bark walls of the Indian wigwams warm and comfortable, and the Indian food-storage practices and eating habits conducive to good diet. Once the rats were established, the transfer of their plague-ridden fleas to the Indians would have been almost automatic and perhaps not even noticed by the new hosts. Body lice were even more common among New England Indians than among white settlers, and the natives commonly passed the time by picking lice and killing them between their teeth.

It is disturbing, though, to those who diagnose the pestilence as plague, that Dermer described its chief signs as sores and spots, rather than the terrible buboes or boils of the groin and armpits that are impossible to overlook in typical victims of the plague. And it is even more odd that the plague-infected fleas did not establish themselves and their bacilli permanently among the wild rodents of New England, as they did in those of the western United States at the end of the nineteenth century. A diagnosis of typhus is tempting, but the historian is reluctant to contradict firsthand witnesses.

Whether plague or typhus, the disease went through the Indians like fire. Almost all the seventeenth-century writers say it killed nine of ten and even nineteen of twenty of the Indians it touched—an incredible mortality rate. But if it was, indeed, plague, it could well have killed that proportion. In the fourteenth century, plague killed one-third of all the people in Europe and a much higher percentage than that in many towns and districts. Further, the Indians knew nothing of the principle of contagion and had an ancient custom of visiting the sick, jamming into extremely hot little huts with them, assuring maximum dispersal of the illness. Their methods of treating illness, which usually featured a stay in a sweatbox, followed by immersion in the nearest cold pond or river, would have been a dreadful trauma for a person with a high fever, and a fine way to encourage pneumonic complications. Consider, too, that the epidemic could not have failed to disrupt food-procurement patterns, as women lay too ill to tend the corn and the men too weak to hunt. Starvation often gleans what epidemic disease has missed. Consider, finally, that after the Indians realized the full extent of the disease, some of them, at least, ran away and left the sick and convalescent to die of neglect. In short, one does not necessarily have to accept a 90 per cent death rate for a given village or area in order to accept a 90 per cent depopulation rate.

It is undeniable that the pestilence largely emptied the Indian villages of coastal New England by 1619. That year, Thomas Dermer found "ancient plantations, not long since populous, now utterly void; in other places a remnant remains, but not free of sickness."

In 1621 a party of Pilgrims went to visit Massasoit, the most powerful Wampanoag sachem, at his summer quarters on a river about fifteen miles from Plymouth. They saw the remnants of many villages and former Indian cornfields along both sides of the river grown up in weeds higher than a man's head: "Thousands of men have lived there, which died in a great plague not long since:

and pity it was and is to see so many goodly fields, and so well seated, without men to dress and manure the same."

Near Boston Bay, Thomas Morton saw even more vivid indications of the plague: "For in a place where many inhabited, there hath been but one left alive, to tell what became of the rest, the livinge being (as it seemed) not able to bury the dead, they were left for Crowes, kites and vermin to prey upon. And the bones and skulls upon the severall places of their habitations, made such a spectacle after my coming into those partes, that as I travailed in that Forrest, nere the Massachusets, it seemed to mee a new found Golgotha."

What destroyed Indian bodies also undermined Indian religion—the Indian's entire view of the universe and of himself. Disease was always considered a manifestation of spiritual influences, and the power of the powwows (medicine men) to direct and cure disease was central to the Indian religion. Later in the century we hear of powwows being hounded, punished, and even killed for failing to produce promised cures. What was the impact when hundreds, even thousands, died under the hands of leaders whose chief distinction was their ability to cure? Many of the powwows themselves, in constant contact with the sick they sought to cure, must have died. What was the impact of this final and irrevocable defeat of these priestly physicians?

What seemed cosmically appalling to the Indians was interpreted as clear proof of God's love by the Pilgrims—a divine intercession that revealed itself from the beginning. They had planned to settle in the Hudson River area or thereabouts, but the master of the *Mayflower* deposited them on the coast of New England. His inability or refusal to take them where they wanted to go proved a bit of luck—"God outshoots Satan oftentimes in his own bow"—for the lands about the Hudson's mouth, though more attractive because more fertile than Plymouth's, were "then abounding with a multitude of pernicious savages. . . ." God had directed the Pilgrims to a coast His plague had cleared of such savages: "whereby he made way for the carrying of his good purpose in promulgating his gospel. . . ." There were no Indians at Plymouth and none for eight or ten miles, and yet it had recently been a village of Wampanoags who had, over the years, cut away the tough climax growth of forest to plant corn. When the weak and hungry Colonists went out to plant in the following spring, all they had to do was to clear out the weeds. Death, it seemed obvious, was God's handyman and the Pilgrim's friend.

The wind of pestilence did more than merely clear a safe place for the Pilgrim to settle; in the long run, it enabled that settlement not only to survive, but to take root and, in the end, to prosper with a minimum of native resistance. The natives of coastal Massachusetts were fewer in number than in a very long time, possibly than in several thousand years, but there were still quite enough of them to wipe out the few Europeans from the *Mayflower,* and they had reason to hate whites. In addition to kidnapings, Europeans—English, the Indians told Dermer—recently had lured a number of Wampanoags on board their ship and had then "made great slaughter of them with their murderers [small ship's cannon]. . . ." When a party of Pilgrims visited the next tribe to the south, the Nausets, in 1621, they met an old woman who broke "forth into great passion, weeping and crying excessively." She had lost three of her sons to kidnapers, and now was without comfort in her old age. A Wampanoag said that the Nausets had killed three English interlopers in the summer of 1620.

Half the English at Plymouth died of malnutrition, exhaustion, and exposure that first winter. Indian anger and Indian power could have made Plymouth one of the lost colonies, like the one Columbus left behind on La Española in 1493 or Sir Walter Raleigh's Roanoke colony of the 1580's.

At some time during this low ebb of Pilgrim history the powwows gathered in the fastnesses of a swamp, where, for three days, they "did curse and execrate" the newcomers to destroy them or drive them away. It almost worked: at times the number of English healthy enough to offer any real help to the sick and, if necessary, any real resistance to attackers was as low as six or seven. But in the end the Indian's gods failed, and the English survived, "having borne this affliction with much patience, being upheld by the Lord."

What held the Indians back from physical attack? They had the strength and motive, and bloody precedent had been set by both whites and Indians. The answer must be fear. The coastal Indians may have been second only to the Pilgrims in New England as believers in the power of the white man's god. A visitor to Plymouth in 1621 wrote that the plague had sapped Wampanoag courage, as well as the tribe's numbers: "their countenance is dejected, and they seem as a people affrighted." They were coming to the English settlement in great numbers every day, "and might in one hour have made a dispatch of us, yet such a fear was upon them, as that they never offered us the least injury in word or deed."

Direct relations between the Wampanoags and the Pilgrims began in March of 1621, approximately three months after the English arrival. An Indian walked out of the woods and through the fields and into Plymouth. He was Samoset, who spoke some English, having learned it from English fishermen on the coast of Maine. He asked for beer, and received "strong water," biscuit, butter, cheese, pudding, and a piece of duck. It was he who told the Pilgrims the old Indian name for their village and explained what had happened to its original inhabitants. A few days later he returned with the individual whom the Pilgrims would soon rank as "a special instrument sent of God for their good beyond their expectation." The man was Squanto, a Pawtuxet who had been kidnaped, had escaped in Spain, and had lived in Cornhill, London, before making his way back to America.

An hour later the sachem, Massasoit, walked in with a train of sixty men. If he had come to fight, he could have swept Plymouth out of existence, but he came in peace, and what amounts to a nonaggression and mutual defense pact was soon agreed upon—the Treaty of Plymouth. Massasoit, wrote Edward Winslow in his first-person account of that day in March, "hath a potent adversary, the Narrohigansets [Narragansets], that are at war with him, against whom he thinks we may be some strength to him, for our peeces are terrible unto them."

In the eyes of the native people of New England, the whites possessed a greater potency, a greater mana, than any Indian people. Nothing could be more immediately impressive than firearms, which made clouds of smoke and a sound like the nearest of thunderclaps and killed at a distance of many paces. And what could seem more logical but to see a similarity between the muskets and cannon, which reached out invisibly and tore bodies, and the plague, which reached out invisibly and corrupted bodies? In the 1580's, Indians in the vicinity of Roanoke had blamed the epidemic then raging on "invisible bullets" that the whites could shoot any distance desired; and it is quite like that Massasoit and his followers had a similar interpretation of their experience with epidemic disease. No wonder the mighty sachem literally trembled as he sat beside the governor of Plymouth that day in March of 1621.

The following year, the Pilgrims learned that Squanto, taking advantage of his position as go-between for the Indians and English, had been telling the former that he had such control over the latter that he could persuade them to unleash the plague again, if he wished. He tried to use this claim of immense power to persuade the Wampanoags to shift their allegiance from Massasoit to himself. It was a game which nearly cost the schemer his life, and he had to spend the rest of his days living with the Pilgrims.

He told the Indians that the plague was buried under the storehouse in Plymouth, where, interestingly enough, the Pilgrims did have something buried: their reserve kegs of gunpowder. He told the Wampanoags that the English could send the plague forth to destroy whomever they wished, while not stirring a foot from home. When, in May of 1622, the Pilgrims dug up some of the gunpowder kegs, another Wampanoag, understandably disturbed, asked the English if they did, indeed, have the plague at their beck and call. The answer he got was as honest a one as could be expected from a seventeenth-century Christian: "No; but the God of the English has it in store, and could send it at his pleasure, to the destruction of his or our enemies." Not long after, Massasoit asked Governor William Bradford if "he would let out the plague to destroy the Sachem, and his men, who were his enemies, promising that he himself, and all his posterity, would be their everlasting friends, so great an opinion he had of the English."

Those enemies were the Narragansets, whose presence was the greatest immediate threat to Plymouth, and whose fear of the Englishmen's power was Plymouth's (and the Wampanoags') best shield. In the late fall of 1621 Canonicus, the Narragansets' greatest sachem, sent a bundle of arrows wrapped in a snakeskin to Squanto at Plymouth. Squanto was not present when they arrived, for which the messenger who brought the bundle was visibly thankful, and he departed "with all expedition." When Squanto returned and examined Canonicus' package, he explained that it signified a threat and a challenge to the new colony. The governor, who as a European of the Reformation era knew as much of threat and challenge as any Indian, stuffed the skin with gunpowder and shot, and sent it back to Canonicus. The great and terrible sachem refused to accept it, would not touch the powder and shot, nor suffer the bundle to remain in Narraganset country. The sinister package, "having been posted from place to place a long time, at length came whole back again." The plague perhaps had taught the Indian the principle of contagion.

Disease, real and imagined, remained a crucial element in English-Indian relations for at least the next two years, and seemingly always to the advantage of the English. In 1622 and 1623 the Pilgrims were still so incompetent at living in America that only the abundance of shellfish and corn obtained from the

Indians kept them from starvation: a dangerous situation, because by then the Indians' fear of and respect for the whites were declining. As one Pilgrim chronicler put it, the Indians "began again to cast forth many insulting speeches, glorying in our weakness, and giving out how easy it would be ere long to cut us off. Now also Massassowat [Massasoit] seemed to frown on us, and neither came or sent to us as formerly." A letter arrived from Jamestown far to the south in Virginia telling of how the Indians had risen there, killing hundreds of the colonists. In the summer of 1622 a band of ne'er-do-well English settled at Wessagusset (Weymouth), not far from Plymouth, and after begging food from the impoverished Pilgrims, set about stealing it from the Indians. That fall Squanto, the almost indispensable man in the Pilgrims' dealings with the Indians, fell ill on a trip to collect corn from the natives. After fever and nosebleeds he died, asking the governor to pray for him "that he might go to the Englishman's God in heaven. . . ."

The Indians, apparently with the Massachusets tribe in the lead, began to plot to exterminate the Wessagusset settlement. They were less intolerant of the Plymouth than the Wessagusset people, but their plan was to destroy the Pilgrims, as well, for fear that the latter would take revenge for the murder of any English. The scheme never got beyond the talking stage. Why weren't the Indians able to organize themselves and take the action they planned? Pilgrims collecting corn from the Massachusets in the latter part of 1622 learned of a "great sickness" among them "not unlike the plague, if not the same." Soon after, Wampanoag women bringing corn to Plymouth were struck with a "great sickness," and the English were obliged to carry much of the corn home on their own backs.

Disease or, at least, bodily malfunction most dramatically affected New England history in 1623 when Massasoit developed a massive case of constipation. In March the news arrived in Plymouth that Massasoit was close to death and that a Dutch vessel had grounded on the sands right in front of his current home. The English knew of the Indian custom that any and all friends must visit the ill, especially the very ill, and they also wanted to meet with the stranded Dutch; so a small party set out from Plymouth for the sachem's sickbed. The Pilgrims found the Dutch afloat and gone, and Massasoit's dwelling jammed to bursting with well-wishers and powwows "making such a hellish noise, as it distempered us that were well, and therefore unlike to ease him that was sick."

Edward Winslow undertook the sachem's case and managed to get between his teeth "a confection of many comfortable conserves, on the point of my knife. . . ." He then washed out his patient's mouth, put him on a light diet, and soon his bowels were functioning again. The Englishman had, with the simplest of Hippocratic remedies, apparently saved the life of the most powerful man in the immediate environs of Plymouth. For the next day or so Winslow was kept busy going from one to another of the sachem's sick or allegedly sick followers, doling out smidgens of his confection and receiving "many joyful thanks." In an era which was, for the Indians, one of almost incomprehensible mortality, Winslow had succeeded where all the powwows had failed in thwarting the influences drawing Massasoit toward death. The English could not only persuade a profoundly malevolent god to kill, but also *not* to kill.

The most important immediate product of Massasoit's recovery was his gratitude. He revealed the details of the Indian plot against Wessagusset and Plymouth, a plot involving most of the larger tribes within two or three days travel of Plymouth, and even the Indians of Capawack (Martha's Vineyard). He said he had been asked to join when he was sick, but had refused for himself and his people. The Pilgrims probably had already heard rumors of the plot, and the sachem's story was confirmed by Phineas Pratt, one of the ne'er-do-wells from Wessagusset, who made his way by fleetness of foot and luck through hostile Indians to Plymouth.

Captain Miles Standish sailed to Boston Bay with a small group of armed men, tiny in number but gigantic in the power the Indians thought they possessed. They killed five or so of the alleged leaders of the plot and returned home with the head of one of them. The remnants of the Wessagusset colony were swept together and brought to Plymouth, where in time most of them made the decision to go back to Europe as hands on the vessels fishing along the Maine coast. The Indian head was set up at Plymouth fort as a visual aid to Indian education.

The Indian plan to wipe out the white colonies fell to pieces. Members of the several tribes within striking distance of Plymouth "forsook their houses, running to and fro like men distracted, living in swamps and other desert places, and so brought manifold diseases amongst themselves, whereof very many are dead. . . ." Ianough, sachem of the Massachusetts, said "the God of the English was offended with them, and would destroy them in his anger. . . ." The Pilgrims noted smugly that the mortality rate among their opponents was, indeed, high, and "neither is there any likelihood it will easily cease; because through fear they set little or no corn, which is the staff of life, and without which they cannot long preserve health and strength."

By 1622 or so the very last cases of the plague had occurred in New England—if indeed these were examples of plague and not of misdiagnosis—and the only remains of the great pestilence were disarticulating bones lost in fallen walls of rotting bark that had once been homes. But it had done its work. In 1625 the Pilgrims, for the first time, raised enough corn to fill their own stomachs *and* trade with the Indians. The Pilgrims had survived and were getting stronger, thanks more to biology than religion, despite Pilgrim preconceptions, but Thomas Morton nevertheless was reminded of a line from Exodus: "By little and little (saith God of old to his people) will I drive them out from before thee; till thou be increased, and inherit the land."

Daily Life in Colonial Massachusetts

Robert N. Linscott

This article by the late Robert N. Linscott was written after his retirement as an editor at a leading New York publishing house. It is a most unusual piece, a labor of love about a labor of love. Back in the early nineteenth century a self-trained historian named Sylvester Judd became fascinated by the history of the Connecticut River valley of his native Massachusetts. By interviewing elderly inhabitants of the region and burrowing deeply into old records, he collected a vast amount of information, the kind of detail about everyday life that is so often lost to history. In the 1960s Linscott located Judd's diary and much of the material he had brought together in manuscript form. He used the Judd manuscripts to write this account.

When Hadley, Massachusetts, was settled in 1659, there were only about eight hundred Indians within that area of the Connecticut Valley that now lies in Massachusetts. During the first forty years, the attitude of the whites to the Indians was friendly but wary. Squaws and braves, in scanty attire, were common sights in the village streets, and the greeting *Netop* ("my friend") was often heard.

In this region the popular belief that the Indians surrendered their lands unwillingly to the whites and were cheated to boot had no basis in fact. On the contrary the Indians sold their lands gladly, and the price they received seemed to them clear profit. Except for their village sites and the scanty cornfields their squaws cultivated, which totaled only seventy acres in the entire valley, land was regarded by the Indians merely as a place to hunt and fish. These rights, in most cases, they reserved. And in return for half the crops, the whites not only let the squaws have their cornfields but even ploughed them, thus more than doubling the yield.

How fairly the Indians were treated is shown by this deed of sale for the land now occupied by the town of Hadley: "Be it known to all men by these presents that Chickwollop alias Wahillowa, Umpanchala alias Womscom, and Quomquont alias Wompshaw, the sachems on Nolwotogg, the sole and proper owners of all the land on the east side of the Quonicticot River . . . do give, grant, bargain and sell unto John Pynchon, of Springfield . . . his assigns and successors forever, all the grounds, woods, ponds, waters, meadows, trees, stones, etc., lying on the east side of Quonictocot River within the compass aforesaid . . . for and in consideration of two hundred fathoms [of wampum]. . . ."

The deed was signed by the marks (Indian signatures to such deeds as these were in the form of pictorial marks: a beaver, a snake, a snowshoe, a bow, a hand) of the three sachems, by John Pynchon, and by five witnesses. It was subscribed below: "The Indians desired that they might set their wigwams at some time within the tract of ground they sold without offense, and that the English would be kind and neighborly to them in not prohibiting them firewood out of the woods, etc., which was promised them." The deed was then assigned by John Pynchon to the "present inhabitants of Hadley," he having acted as their agent for the purchase.

The currency of the Indians was wampum, and the 228 fathoms for which this land was sold was then the equivalent of somewhere in the neighborhood of sixty English pounds sterling. Wampum was made from shells and was of two kinds: white, made from the shells of the whelk, and black (actually darkish blue), made from the shells of the quahog clam, and having twice the value of the white. These shells were collected by the Indians along the shores of Long Island Sound, cut into tiny beads, polished to a glassy smoothness, bored, and strung on thin strips of deer sinew. If used for decoration, the strings of wampum were worn about the neck and wrists, or the beads were embroidered on deerskin to make a belt that was a prestige symbol, with the width of the belt and the number of beads, sometimes as many as three thousand, indicating the power and wealth of the wearer.

If used as currency, the wampum was usually strung in units of a fathom, or six feet, containing from 240 to 360 beads and worth from five to ten shillings if white, ten to twenty if black.

By enactment of the Great and General Court (the Massachusetts legislature) in 1641, wampum became legal currency in the Bay Colony for sums of ten pounds or less at the rate of six pieces of white wampum for a penny, and half as many black. However, wampum currency was soon debased by the influx of ill-made shells. In 1648 it was ordered that "it shall be entire without deforming spots" and strung in different lengths worth from one to twelve pence in white and from two pence to ten shillings in black, thus making it conveniently passable in lieu of small coins, which were very scarce.

In the early years of the colony, wampum was a sound currency, since it could always be exchanged with the Indians for beaver skins, which were readily salable in England at a good profit. However, as beaver grew scarce, debasement continued, and when silver from the West Indian trade grew more abundant, the value of wampum continued to slip. In 1661 the law making it legal tender was repealed. In 1675 a penny would buy twenty-four wampums, and by the end of the century it was no longer used except in remote villages, and then only for small change.

Meanwhile, the desire of the Indians for wampum and of the English for furs was gratified by a shrewd English gentleman. William Pynchon, a fur trader and one of the original proprietors of the Bay Colony, transferred his operations in 1636 to what is now Springfield, Massachusetts. He built a warehouse and trading post on the banks of the Connecticut River and quickly monopolized the fur trade of the great river and its tributaries. Prudently, and from sources unknown, he acquired bushels of loose wampum shells, and these he hired the women and children of his settlement to string for him to the extent of twenty thousand fathoms, paying them at the rate of three half-pence a fathom. By turning shells into currency, he accumulated capital worth somewhere between five and ten thousand pounds with which to pay the Indians for their furs.

How well the scheme worked is shown by the Pynchon account books now in the Connecticut Valley Historical Museum in Springfield. In six years William, and his son, John, secured from the Indians over nine thousand beaver skins, weighing about fourteen thousand pounds, which he paid for in wampum and in bartered goods. They also bought thousands of skins of otter, muskrat, mink, fox, raccoon, wildcat, and moose. These skins were packed in hogsheads and carted down the river to his warehouse just below the rapids, in what is now Windsor Locks, where they were transferred to coastal vessels for shipment to Boston and thence by packet to London. There they were sold, partly for cash and partly in exchange for bright-colored cloth and coats, knives, awls, axes, and trinkets for their trading posts.

For years William Pynchon paid over half the taxes of Springfield and ruled his growing settlement with the aid of a "cabinet" consisting of his son and two sons-in-law. Eventually he had the temerity to write a theological treatise that was denounced by the clergy and publicly burned in Boston, whereupon he returned in 1652 to England, leaving his wilderness empire to his son, twenty-six-year-old John.

John Pynchon continued and extended the fur monopoly, establishing additional posts in the Connecticut and Housatonic valleys and building up extensive interests in the West Indies, where he traded with his own fleet of ships. In addition to his trading enterprises, he was an early and successful real estate operator. As settlers pushed into the fertile valley, he would buy tracts of land from the Indian sachems who were supplying him with furs, giving them credit at his trading posts to the extent of the price agreed upon, and sell the land to the colonists at the same price, having made his profit on the goods which the Indians took in payment. . . .

John Pynchon's account books were kept in fathoms and hands of wampum. (Fathoms he wrote *fadams*.) He computed ten hands of wampum as equal to a fathom of six feet, making his hands a little over seven inches instead of the usual four. The white wampum he valued at five shillings (in 1660) a fathom. At his death in 1702 he was worth about five thousand pounds, a vast estate for that place and time.

Amicable though the relations were between Indians and whites in the Connecticut Valley during the first quarter-century, the abyss that separated the two civilizations was too wide to be permanently bridged. In 1675 years of peace were shattered by King Philip's War when Indian treacheries and torturings led to reprisals. Perhaps the most chilling example is a terse note scribbled on the margin of a letter in which the captain of a troop of soldiers in Springfield forwarded to the governor in Boston information that had been extorted from a captured squaw. The note reads, "This aforesaid Indian was ordered to be tourne to peeces by dogs, and she was so dealt with."

From the beginning the Great and General Court set bounties on wolves, wildcats, and other predators. During the long terror of the French and Indian

Wars in the first half of the eighteenth century, the largest bounty of all was set on Indians. Ten pounds was paid for each Indian scalp taken by a soldier or one hundred pounds if taken by a volunteer; later the amount was raised to forty pounds to soldiers and three hundred to volunteers for Indian braves and twenty pounds for squaws or children under twelve. Men of the Connecticut Valley ventured into the wilderness on scalping parties, and [Sylvester] Judd reports that the accounts of the treasurer for Hampshire County during 1757 and 1758 show that he paid bounties of fifteen hundred pounds for five scalps.

In order that money might not be wasted on nonessentials, the General Court passed a law in 1651 forbidding persons whose estate did not exceed two hundred pounds, and those dependent on them, to wear gold or silver lace, gold or silver buttons, bone lace above two shillings a yard, or silk scarves or hoods, under penalty of ten shillings for each offense. The first attempt to enforce this law in Hampshire County (Massachusetts) was made in 1673 when twenty-five wives and five maids were haled into court as "persons of small estate who used to wear silk contrary to law." Of the thirty only three were fined.

In 1676 there was a roundup of the younger set with thirty-eight wives and maids and thirty young men brought into court—the men, "some for wearing silk, and that in a flaunting manner, and others for long hair and other extravagancies." Only two of the sixty-eight were fined, which seems to have had a discouraging effect upon the officers of the law, as six years later, in a curious reversal, the officials of five towns were brought to court for *not* arresting such inhabitants of their towns as wore unsuitable and excessive apparel. The battle was over and the younger set had won, but for many years their elders continued to wag their heads over the degeneracy of the age.

Flaunters were bad enough, but witches were even more troublesome. The first was Mary Parsons of Springfield, who was indicted in 1651 for having been seduced by the Devil; for having used "divers" hellish practices on the persons of two children of the Springfield minister; and for having murdered her own child. At her trial in Boston (local courts could not try capital offenses) she pleaded not guilty to witchcraft and was acquitted but she was found guilty of murder and was condemned to death. Her husband, Hugh, was also indicted for witchcraft, largely on the word of his wife, who testified that "sometymes he hath puld of the Bed Clothes and left me naked abed. . . . Sometimes he hath thrown pease about the Howse and made me pick them up. . . . Oftentymes in his sleep he makes a gablings Noyse." Hugh was found guilty by the jury, but the verdict was overruled by the magistrates.

In 1674 another Mary Parsons, this one of Northampton, was accused of familiarity with the Devil and of having caused the death of Mary Bartlett. The accused was a respectable woman and the wife of one of Northampton's richest citizens, but according to Judd, she was proud and high-spirited to a point that had excited the ill will of her neighbors. At the preliminary hearing she vehemently asserted her innocence, whereupon the magistrate appointed a "jury of soberized, chaste women to make a diligent search upon the body of Mary Parsons, whether any marks of witchcraft might appear." Suspicious marks were discovered, and she was sent to Boston for trial but there found innocent and discharged. . . .

When the white men came to the valley, it was not, as supposed, covered with dense forests. The Indian custom of burning over the land each year to destroy the undergrowth and facilitate hunting had made it like a park where a deer could be seen at forty rods. Pine gradually took the place of oak for building, but all pine trees of two feet or more in diameter were reserved for the king's navy, a law that produced more discontent than logs. In Northampton, Massachusetts, for example, of 363 logs marked for the king, all but 37 were poached for private use.

During the seventeenth century wheat was the staple crop. Corn, peas, and oats, rye for bread, barley for malt, and flax for cloth were also raised. Horses, cattle, and sheep were pastured in the forest, and hogs and young stock ran wild. To help in sorting them out, each town was required by law to have its own brand mark. Cattle and horses were driven to pasture before the sun was an hour high by the town herdsmen and brought back "seasonably" at night. Sheep were watched by the town shepherd and "folded" at night in hurdles, or movable pens. Geese often wore a shingle with a hole bored in it about their necks to keep them from straying. They splashed and honked in the puddles of the common and slept at night before their owners' houses, being much esteemed as watchdogs. Four times a year the women of the village plucked them for feather beds, first pulling stockings over the heads of the geese to keep them from biting. Many families kept skeps (hives) of bees, and the only way they knew to get the honey was to kill the bees with brimstone.

In the seventeenth century horses were cheaply raised, little tended, and sold for as low as thirty shillings in barter or twenty in money. Fourteen hands was set by law as the proper height for a horse. They were used only under the saddle and could be hired for a penny and a half a mile or twopence if the horse carried double.

By 1655 cattle were being driven to Boston for market and sold for a penny a pound. When a farmer slaughtered, he "lent" his neighbors what meat he could not use before it spoiled and expected an equal return when they slaughtered. By 1700 milch cows were plentiful, and the tinkling of their bells as they browsed along the roads made a pleasant background to the sounds of the village.

For nearly a century all travel was on foot, by boat, or on horseback with goods and chattels fastened to the saddle and probably a batch of journeycake (later corrupted to *johnnycake*) in the saddlebag. Roads were merely paths through the woods. Indian paths were hardly more than a foot wide, and the first paths of the whites were scarcely wider. Not until the eighteenth century was there a cart road from Hadley to Boston. Before then produce was carried by canoe down the river to a point below the rapids and there transshipped to coastal vessels. Oxen were the beasts of burden, and oxcarts were used in farm work. The gradual increase in the use of horse carts and carriages, sleds and sleighs, and the subsequent opening up of highways, revolutionized travel and the conveyance of goods. . . .

By colony law of 1647, every town of fifty families was required to provide a school where children could learn to read and write, and towns of a hundred families had also to provide a grammar school with a master able to fit young men for college. The schools were supported in part by the town and in part by the parents of the pupils. Teachers were paid about thirty pounds a year, and to guard against truancy, parents were compelled to contribute their share whether or not their children attended school. Free schools were long a bone of contention, as the less well-to-do favored them, while the more well-to-do looked askance at the increased taxes this would entail. The former won but not until well into the eighteenth century.

Girls were commonly taught at home, as it was deemed improper for the sexes to mingle at school. As a result there were many private schools kept by "dames" in their own homes where girls were taught at minimum cost to read and sew. Writing was thought unnecessary for females in the seventeenth century, and not one in ten could sign her name.

By the standards of the times, ministers were well paid. The first minister of Hadley received an allotment of land and eighty pounds a year in produce, as well as free wood for his fireplace. (Since ministers sat at home to write sermons instead of working outdoors, they used prodigious amounts of firewood. The average Hadley family burned thirty cords a year but some ministers used up to seventy cords. A cord is a stack of wood four feet wide, four feet high, and eight feet long.) One shrewd minister of the eighteenth century stipulated a cost-of-living clause in his contract—that is, his salary should rise or fall as the prices of eight commodities of the period rose and fell.

In the old meetinghouses the allotting of places was done by a committee on the basis of the age, estate, and honors of each parishioner. Since prestige was involved, a man's standing in the community being publicly proclaimed by the seat given him, quarrels were common. Sermons in the unheated churches never diminished in length, even in zero weather, though they were sometimes hard to hear above the stamping of numbed feet. . . .

The standard dish of early New England was made of cornmeal and water and called hasty pudding or mush. On Saturday a huge batch was cooked to be eaten for breakfast and often for supper throughout the week. Pumpkins, another early favorite, were adopted from the Indians. They were pared and cut into circular slices through which poles were passed and on which they were then suspended from the kitchen ceiling to dry.

Salt pork was the principal meat dish. . . . Some pork was kept in brine, but most was salted in large pieces and hung in the great kitchen chimney to smoke. These smoked sides were called flitches of bacon.

Contrary to popular belief, baked beans were not eaten till the eighteenth century. Potatoes were first raised in the valley about 1750; tomatoes and rhubarb were unknown until well into the nineteenth century.

Candlewood (pine knots or silvers of pine) was commonly used for light in the seventeenth century as it was much easier to come by than candles, which country people made by spinning wicks of tow and dipping them in melted tallow.

The favorite drinks of the early settlers were beer and cider. Beer was the most popular, and almost every household made its own. Brew day was once a week, and into the kettle went not only malt and hops but also dried pumpkins, dried apple parings, and sometimes rye bran and birch twigs. After brewing, the beer was strained through a sieve, and from the emptyings (the settlings in the barrel) yeast was made. Of cider, the average country family drank four or five barrels a year, and innumerable apple trees were planted to supply this demand. At first the apples were pounded by hand in a trough, but cider mills came in around 1700. In winter, when milk was scarce, children were given cider sweetened with molasses and warmed in a pan.

Because the word *alehouse* had fallen into bad repute, inns or drinking places were called *ordinaries* and were strictly regulated. Indeed, governmental regulations today would have seemed puny to the Puritans, who believed that well-being could be assured by legislative enactment. The first ordinaries, for example, were not allowed to serve strong drinks, nor even cakes and buns except at weddings and funerals, nor to force meals costing twelve pennies or above on poor people.

This first law was soon repealed, but the strength of liquor continued to be regulated; four bushels of malt, for example, had to be used in making a sixty-three-gallon hogshead of beer under penalty of a stiff fine. Moreover, liquor could be sold only to "governors of families of sober carriage," as complaints were being made even then of drinking by wild youths. . . .

Clocks and watches were rare before the Revolution. A few country people had hourglasses or sundials, but for the most part, time was told by the sun or by a "noon mark," which many houses had on the bottom casing of a south window. The month of March, when most town meetings are still held, once marked the beginning of the new year. Some towns figured it as beginning March 1, but most towns began it on March 25 and called the days from January 1 to March 24, inclusive, mongrel time, to be written down thus: March 3, 167¾, the upper figure in the fraction denoting the year commencing March 25, the lower the year commencing January 1. This confusion continued until the calendar was reformed in 1752.

Country folk seldom used titles in the early days except for military officers. A few leading members of the community, including the minister, would be called Mister, but it would have been thought quite shocking to use it for a farmer or mechanic. Goodman and Goodwife (or Goody) were the titles for a yeoman (a farmer who owned or occupied land) and his wife. Until about 1720 both the wife and daughter of a Mister were called Mistress (abbreviated to Mrs.) and, for some time after that, Miss and Mrs. were used indiscriminately for married and unmarried females. Middle names came in during the eighteenth century; before then only one given name was used.

During its first half-century Hadley sometimes aided the aged and worthy poor by boarding them out around town; two weeks with one family, then moved on to the next. (A stay so brief might indicate that a fortnight was as long as any one family could tolerate them.) By the next century, when the number of paupers had increased, they were annually put up at vendue and knocked down to the lowest bidder; that is, each pauper was put on the block and auctioned off to the person who would keep him a year for the smallest sum.

The first minister of Hadley had three Negro slaves; a man, woman, and child, valued at sixty pounds. The peak year for slaves was 1754, when the number reached eighteen—a surprisingly large number for a New England village of about five hundred inhabitants. . . .

William Byrd II of Virginia

Marshall Fishwick

Whether William Byrd II was actually as unique a person as he seems can never be known, for it is only because of his marvelously candid diary that we know him as well as we do. Perhaps if others among the privileged but hard-working tobacco planters of eighteenth-century Virginia had left similar records, we would have had to conclude that Byrd was merely typical. In any case, Byrd the historical figure is important not because of his personal qualities, fascinating as these were, but because of what the story of his life tells us about the society of colonial Virginia.

If Byrd was, as Professor Marshall Fishwick, director of the American Studies Institute, Lincoln University, notes in the following essay, a "Renaissance man," he was one no doubt in part because the world he inhabited demanded versatility and rewarded achievement. His career helps explain the extraordinary self-confidence, imagination, and energy of several generations of Americans, not only his own but even more those that immediately followed and, in the single case of his native Virginia, that produced Washington, Jefferson, Madison, Patrick Henry, and a host of others—the great Virginia leaders of the American Revolution.

He could never resist an old book, a young girl, or a fresh idea. He lived splendidly, planned extensively, and was perpetually in debt. Believing perhaps, like Leonardo, that future generations would be more willing to know him than was his own, he wrote his delicious, detailed diaries in code. Only now that they have been translated, and time has put his era in perspective, do we see what William Byrd of Westover was: one of the half-dozen leading wits and stylists of colonial America.

In the popular imagination, to be an American hero means to rise from rags to riches. William Byrd reversed the pattern, as he did so many other things: born to wealth, he never seemed able to hold on to it. His father, William Byrd I (1653–1704), was one of the most powerful and venerated men of his generation. Not only had he inherited valuable land on both sides of the James River, he had also won the hand of Mary Horsmanden, and a very dainty and wealthy hand it was, too. Some of the bold and red knight-errant blood of the Elizabethans flowed through the veins of William Byrd I. He had the same knack as did Captain John Smith (in whom that blood fairly bubbled) for getting in and out of scrapes. For example, William Byrd I joined Nathaniel Bacon in subduing the Indians, but stopped short of joining the rebellion against Governor William Berkeley, withdrawing in time to save his reputation and his neck. Later on he became receiver-general and auditor of Virginia, a member of the Council of State, and the colony's leading authority on Indians. The important 1685 treaty with the Iroquois bore his signature. Death cut short his brilliant career soon after his fiftieth birthday, and suddenly thrust his son and namesake into the center of the colonial stage. The boy, who had spent much of his time in England getting an education and, later, as an agent for Virginia, must now return to America and assume the duties of a man.

No one can read the story of young Will Byrd's early years, and his transformation, without thinking of Will Shakespeare's Prince Hal. If ever a young Virginian behaved scandalously in London, it was Will Byrd. "Never did the sun shine upon a Swain who had more combustible matter in his constitution," Byrd wrote of himself. Love broke out upon him "before my beard." Louis Wright, to whose editing of Byrd's diaries we are indebted for much of our knowledge of the man, says that he was notoriously promiscuous, frequenting the boudoirs of highborn and lowborn alike. Indeed, as his diary shows, he was not above taking to the grass with a *fille de joie* whom he might encounter on a London street.

Once, when he arrived for a rendezvous with a certain Mrs. A-l-n, the lady wasn't home, so he seduced the chambermaid. Just as he was coming down the steps Mrs. A-l-n came in the front door. Then Will Byrd and Mrs. A-l-n went back up the stairs together. Several hours later, he went home and ate a plum cake.

On his favorites he lavished neoclassic pseudonyms and some of the era's most sparkling prose. One such lady (called "Facetia" and believed to have been Lady Elizabeth Cromwell) was his preoccupation during 1703. When she left him to visit friends in Ireland, Will Byrd let her know she would be missed:

> The instant your coach drove away, madam, my heart felt as if it had been torn up by the very roots, and the rest of my body as if severed limb from limb. . . . Could I at that time have considered that the only pleasure I had in the world was leaving me, I had hung upon your coach and had been torn in pieces sooner than have suffered myself to be taken from you.

Having said all the proper things, he moved on to relate, in a later letter, some of the juicier bits of London gossip. Mrs. Brownlow had finally agreed to marry Lord Guilford—"and the gods alone can tell what will be produced by the conjunction of such fat and good humour!" The image is Falstaffian, as were many of Byrd's friends. But with news of his father's death he must, like Prince Hal, scorn his dissolute friends and assume new duties. With both Hal and Will the metamorphosis was difficult and partial, but nonetheless memorable.

The Virginia to which in 1705 William Byrd II returned—the oldest permanent English settlement in the New World and the first link in the chain that would one day be known as the British Empire—was a combination of elegance and crudity, enlightenment and superstition. While some of his Virginia neighbors discussed the most advanced political theories of Europe, others argued about how to dispose of a witch who was said to have crossed over to Currituck Sound in an eggshell. In 1706, the same year that Byrd was settling down in Virginia after his long stay in England, a Virginia court was instructing "as many Ansient and

Knowing women as possible . . . to search her Carefully For teats spotts and marks about her body." When certain mysterious marks were indeed found, the obvious conclusion was drawn, and the poor woman languished in ye common gaol. Finally released, she lived to be eighty and died a natural death.

Other Virginia ladies faced problems (including, on occasions, Will Byrd) that were far older than the colony or the witch scare. A good example was Martha Burwell, a Williamsburg belle, who rejected the suit of Sir Francis Nicholson, the governor, so she might marry a man more to her liking. If she did so, swore the enraged Nicholson, he would cut the throat of the bridegroom, the clergyman, and the issuing justice. Unaware that females are members of the weaker sex, Martha refused to give in—even when Nicholson threw in half a dozen more throats, including those of her father and brothers. She married her true love. No throats were cut—but visitors to the Governor's palace in Williamsburg observed that His Excellency made "a Roaring Noise."

In those days Tidewater Virginia was governed by benevolent paternalists. The aristocrats intermarried, and the essential jobs—sheriff, vestryman, justice of the peace, colonel of militia—stayed in the family. The support of the gentry was the prerequisite to social and political advancement. Wealth, status, and privilege were the Tidewater trinity, and it was a case of three in one: wealth guaranteed status; status conveyed privilege; and privilege insured wealth.

Will Byrd both understood and mastered the world to which he had returned. He retained the seat in the House of Burgesses which he had won before going to England, and turned his attention to finding a suitable wife. Like many of his contemporaries, he confined "romantic love" to extracurricular affairs, and called on common sense to help him in matrimony. Both Washington and Jefferson married rich widows. Ambitious young men found they could love a rich girl more than a poor one, and the colonial newspapers reported their marriages with an honesty that bordered on impropriety. One reads, for example, that twenty-three-year-old William Carter married Madam Sarah Ellson, widow of eighty-five, "a sprightly old Tit, with three thousand pounds fortune."

Will Byrd's choice was the eligible but fiery Lucy Parke, daughter of the gallant rake Daniel Parke, who had fought with Marlborough on the Continent and brought the news of Blenheim to Queen Anne. Many a subsequent battle was fought between Lucy Parke and William Byrd after their marriage in 1706, though neither side was entirely vanquished. Byrd was quick to record his victories, such as the one noted in his diary for February 5, 1711: "My wife and I quarrelled about her pulling her brows. She threatened she would not go to Williamsburg if she might not pull them; I refused, however, and got the better of her and maintained my authority."

That Mrs. Byrd had as many good excuses for her fits of temper and violence as any other lady in Virginia seems plain—not only from her accusations, but from her husband's admissions. From his diary entry of November 2, 1709, for example, we get this graphic picture of life among the planters:

In the evening I went to Dr. [Barrett's], where my wife came this afternoon. Here I found Mrs. Chiswell, my sister Custis, and other ladies. We sat and talked till about 11 o'clock and then retired to our chambers. I played at [r-m] with Mrs. Chiswell and kissed her on the bed till she was angry and my wife also was uneasy about it, and cried as soon as the company was gone. I neglected to say my prayers which I should not have done, because I ought to beg pardon for the lust I had for another man's wife. However I had good health, good thoughts, and good humor, thanks be to God Almighty.

As we read on, we begin to realize that we are confronting a Renaissance man in colonial America—a writer with the frankness of Montaigne and the zest of Rabelais. Philosopher, linguist, doctor, scientist, stylist, planter, churchman, William Byrd II saw and reported as much as any American who died before our Revolution.

Here was a man who, burdened for most of his life with the responsibility of thousands of acres and hundreds of slaves, never became narrow or provincial. Neither his mind, nor his tongue, nor his pen—the last possibly because he wrote the diaries in code—was restrained by his circumstances, and no one at home or abroad was immune from the barbs of his wit. When we read Byrd, we know just what Dean Swift meant when he said: "We call a spade a spade."

One of Byrd's most remarkable achievements, and one not nearly well enough known and appreciated, is his sketch of himself, attached to a letter dated February 21, 1722. For honesty and perception, and for the balance that the eighteenth century enthroned, it has few American counterparts.

Poor Inamorato [as Byrd calls himself] had too much mercury to fix to one thing. His Brain was too hot to jogg on eternally in the same dull road. He liv'd more by the lively moment of his Passions, than by the cold and unromantick dictates of Reason. . . . He pay'd his Court more to obscure merit, than to corrupt Greatness. He never cou'd flatter any body, no not himself, which were two invincible bars to all preferment. . . . His religion is more in substance than in form, and he is more forward to practice vertue than profess it. . . . He knows the World perfectly well, and thinks himself a citizen of it without the . . . distinctions of kindred sect or Country.

He goes on to explain why, for most of his life, he began his day by reading ancient classics, and frowned upon morning interruptions:

A constant hurry of visits & conversations gives a man a habit of inadvertency, which betrays him into faults without measure & without end. For this reason, he commonly reserv'd the morning to himself, and bestow'd the rest upon his business and his friends.

The reason for his own candor is clearly stated:

He Lov'd to undress wickedness of all its paint, and disguise, that he might loath its deformity.

The extent of his philosophizing and his admitted heresy is made clear by this remarkable passage:

This portrait of William Byrd was painted in London by Sir Godfrey Kneller between 1715 and 1720 when the aristocratic Virginian was in his prime.

He wishes every body so perfect, that he overlooks the impossibility of reaching it in this World. He wou'd have men Angells before their time, and wou'd bring down that perfection upon Earth which is the peculiar priviledge of Heaven.

Byrd left us a scattered and largely unavailable body of litera—ture—*vers de société,* historical essays, character sketches, epitaphs, letters, poems, translations, and humorous satires. Of this work Maude Woodfin, one of the few scholars to delve adequately into Byrd's work, wrote:

"There is a distinctly American quality in these writings of the latter half of Byrd's life, in direct contrast to the exclusively English quality in the writings of his earlier years. Further study and time will doubtless argue that his literary work in the Virginia period from 1726 on, with its colonial scene and theme, has greater literary merit than his work in the London period."

Byrd has a place in our architectural history as well. His manor house, Westover, is in many ways the finest Georgian mansion in the nation. Triumphant architectural solutions never came quickly or easily: only first-rate minds can conjure up first-rate houses. In the spring of 1709, we know from Byrd's diary, he had workmen constructing brick. Five years later, stonecutters from Williamsburg were erecting the library chimney. There were interruptions, delays, faulty shipments, workmen to be trained. But gradually a masterpiece—noble in symmetry, proportion, and balance—emerged.

Built on a little rise a hundred yards from the James River, Westover has not changed much over the generations. The north and south façades are as solid and rhythmical as a well-wrought fugue, and the beautiful doorways would have pleased Palladio himself. Although the manor is derived from English standards (especially William Salmon's *Palladio Londinensis*), Westover makes such superb use of the local materials and landscape that some European critics have adjudged it esthetically more satisfying than most of the contemporary homes in England.

Like other buildings of the period, Westover was planned from the outside in. The main hallway, eighteen feet wide and off center, goes the full length of the house. The stairway has three runs and a balustrade of richly turned mahogany. The handsomely paneled walls of the downstairs rooms support gilded ceilings. Underneath the house is a complete series of rooms, converging at the subterranean passage leading to the river. Two underground chambers, which could be used as hiding places, are reached through a dry well. Since he liked nothing less than the idea of being dry, William Byrd kept both chambers stocked with claret and Madeira.

Westover takes its place in the succession of remarkable Virginia manors that remain one of the glories of the American past. It was completed probably by 1736, after Stratford Hall, with its masculine vigor, and Rosewell, with its mahogany balustrade from San Domingo. Westover would be followed by Brandon, with chaste cornices and fine simplicity; Gunston Hall, with cut-stone quoins and coziness; Sabine Hall, so reminiscent of Horace's villa at Tivoli; and Pacatone, with its wonderful entrance and its legendary ghosts.

These places were more than houses. They were little worlds in themselves,

The front elevation of Westover as it appears today.

part of a universe that existed within the boundaries of Virginia. The planters lavished their energy and their lives on such worlds. They were proud of their crops, their horses, their libraries, their gardens. Byrd, for example, tells us about the iris, crocus, thyme, marjoram, phlox, larkspur, and jasmine in his formal two-acre garden.

At Westover one might find the Carters from Shirley, the Lees from Stratford, the Harrisons from Randolph, or the Spotswoods from Germanna. So might one encounter Byrd's brother-in-law, that ardent woman-hater, John Custis, from Arlington. Surely the ghost of William Byrd would not want any tale of Westover to omit a short tribute to Custis' irascible memory.

While other founding fathers left immortal lines about life and liberty to stir our blood, Custis left words to warm henpecked hearts. With his highhanded lady he got on monstrous poor.

After one argument Custis turned and drove his carriage into the Chesapeake Bay. When his wife asked where he was going, he shouted, "To Hell, Madam." "Drive on," she said imperiously. "Any place is better than Arlington!" So that he might have the last word, Custis composed his own epitaph, and made his son execute it on pain of being disinherited:

UNDER THIS MARBLE TOMB LIES THE BODY
OF THE HON. JOHN CUSTIS, ESQ.,

* * *

AGE 71 YEARS, AND YET LIVED BUT SEVEN YEARS,
WHICH WAS THE SPACE OF TIME HE KEPT
A BACHELOR'S HOME AT ARLINGTON
ON THE EASTERN SHORE OF VIRGINIA.

Still Custis came to Westover, like all others who could, to enjoy the fairs, balls, parlor games, barbecues—but above all, the conversation.

One should not conclude that entertaining friends was the main occupation of William Byrd. As soon as he awoke he read Latin, Greek, or Hebrew before breakfast. His favorite room was not the parlor but the library, in which were collected over 3,600 volumes dealing with philosophy, theology, drama, history, law, and science. Byrd's own writings prove his intimate knowledge of the great thinkers and writers of the past.

Of those works, none except his diary is as interesting as his *History of the Dividing Line.* On his fifty-third birthday, in 1727, Byrd was appointed one of the Virginia commissioners to survey the disputed Virginia-North Carolina boundary; the next spring saw the group ready to embark on their task. Byrd's *History,* which proves he was one of the day's ablest masters of English prose, is a thing of delight. For days comedy and tragedy alternated for supremacy. Indians stole their food. Bad weather and poor luck caused Byrd to swear like a trooper in His Majesty's Guards. To mend matters, Byrd's companions arranged a party around a cheerful bowl, and invited a country bumpkin to attend. She must have remembered the party for a long time:". . . they examined all her hidden Charms and play'd a great many gay Pranks," noted Byrd, who seems to have disapproved of the whole affair. "The poor Damsel was disabled from making any resistance by the Lameness of her Hand."

Whenever matters got too bad, the party's chaplain "rubbed up" his aristocratic swamp-evaders with a seasonable sermon; and we must adjudge all the hardships a small price to pay for the *History.* This was followed by *A Journey to Eden,* which tells of Byrd's trip to survey twenty thousand acres of bottom land. On September 19, 1733, Byrd decided to stake out two large cities: "one at Shacco's, to be called Richmond, and the other at the point of the Appomattuck River, to be called Petersburg."

It is a generally accepted belief that only in politics did eighteenth-century America reach real distinction. But as we look more closely at our colonial literature and architecture, and apply our own criteria rather than those imposed upon us by the English, we find that this may not be so. How, for example, could we have underestimated William Byrd's importance all these years? There are several answers. He never pretended to be a serious writer (no gentleman of his time and place would), any more than Jefferson would have set himself up as a professional architect. But at least we have Jefferson's magnificent buildings to refute the notion that he was a mere dabbler, and for years we had little of Byrd's prose. Because he did "call a spade a spade," many of his contemporaries, and even more of their descendants, have not wanted his work and allusions made public.

The Latin motto of William Byrd's coat of arms reads, appropriately enough, "No guilt to make one pale."

Byrd had been dead almost a century when Edmund Ruffin published fragments of his writings in the *Virginia Farmers' Register.* Only in our own generation have the diaries been deciphered: not until 1941 did a major publisher undertake to set part of them into print; not until 1958 did we have *The London Diary* (1717–21); not even now can we read all that Byrd left for us.

No amount of reappraisal can turn Byrd into a figure of the highest magnitude. What it might do is to reveal a man who for candor, self-analysis, and wit is unsurpassed—this in an age that produced Washington, Adams, Franklin, Henry, and Jefferson. Could any other colonial American, for example, have written such a delightful and ribald satire on women as "The Female Creed," which has an eighteenth-century lady profess: "I believe in astrologers, coffee-casters, and Fortune-tellers of every denomination, whether they profess to read the Ladys destiny in their faces, in their palms or like those of China in their fair posteriors."

Nor will one often encounter in a colonial writer the desire to exhume his father's corpse, and then to report: "He was so wasted there was not one thing to be distinguished. I ate fish for dinner."

When William Byrd II died in the summer of 1744, the pre-Revolutionary ethos and attitudes were dying too. They have not attracted historians and novelists as have the earlier adventurous days of settlement or the later days that tried men's souls. The period from 1700 to 1750 remains the forgotten one in American history and literature, despite much excellent but rather specialized work in it since 1930.

When we know more of that important and colorful half century, William Byrd's reputation will rise. In him we shall find the most complete expression of a man who lived with us but belongs to the world. In his work we shall see, more clearly than in that of his contemporaries, the emerging differences between England and the American colonies destined to grow into their own nationhood. Beside him, the so-called Connecticut Wits of the late eighteenth century seem to be lacking half their title. Compared to his prose, the tedious sermonizing of the Puritan and Anglican ministers seems like copybook work in an understaffed grammar school. Not that William Byrd was a saint, or a model husband—as he would have been the first to point out. But as with the saints, we admire him all the more because he tells us about his faults and lets us tabulate the virtues for ourselves. All told, we can say of him what Abraham Lincoln supposedly said when he saw Walt Whitman far down the corridors of a building: "There goes a man." William Byrd of Westover would have settled for this.

Witchcraft in Colonial New England

John Demos

The notorious Salem witchcraft trials of 1692 were one of the most shocking incidents in colonial history, but as Professor John Demos of Yale University explains in the following essay, they were by no means unique. Demos is not content, however, to describe other New England cases where persons were accused of being witches. Nor does he write off the phenomenon as an example of mass hysteria, ignorant prejudice, and the miscarriage of justice. If everyone believed that witches existed, he argues, some people surely believed (or feared) that they were themselves witches, and of these, some no doubt deliberately tried to practice witchcraft. Demos's tale is fascinating, and it also shows how important it is for historians to immerse themselves in the times they study. To do their job properly, they must see that world as those who actually lived in it saw it and at the same time maintain the perspective of their own time.

Professor Demos is the author of A Little Commonwealth: Family Life in Plymouth Colony *and* Entertaining Satan: Witchcraft and the Culture of Early New England.

The place is the fledgling community of Windsor, Connecticut: the time, an autumn day in the year 1651. A group of local militiamen has assembled for training exercises. They drill in their usual manner through the morning, then pause for rest and refreshment. Several of the younger recruits begin a moment's horseplay; one of these—a certain Thomas Allen—cocks his musket and inadvertently knocks it against a tree. The weapon fires, and a few yards away a bystander falls heavily to the ground. The unfortunate victim is an older man, also a trainee, Henry Stiles by name. Quickly, the group converges on Stiles, and bears him to the house of the local physician. But the bullet has fatally pierced his heart.

One month later the "particular court" of the Connecticut colony meets in regular session. On its agenda is an indictment of Thomas Allen: "that . . . [thou] didst suddenly, negligently, carelessly cock thy piece, and carry the piece . . . which piece being charged and going off in thine hand, slew thy neighbor, to the great dishonor of God, breach of the peace, and loss of a member of this commonwealth." Allen confesses the fact, and is found guilty of "homicide by misadventure." For his "sinful neglect and careless carriages" the court orders him to pay a fine of twenty pounds sterling. In addition he is bound to good behavior for the ensuing year, with the special proviso "that he shall not bear arms for the same term."

But this is not the end of the matter. Stiles's death remains a topic of local conversation, and three years later it yields a more drastic result. In November, 1654, the court meets in special session to try a case of witchcraft—against a woman, Lydia Gilbert, also of Windsor: "Lydia Gilbert, thou art here indicted . . . that not having the fear of God before thine eyes, thou hast of late years or still dost give entertainment to Satan, the great enemy of God and mankind, and by his help hast killed the body of Henry Stiles, besides other witchcrafts, for which according to the law of God and the established law of this commonwealth thou deservest to die." The court, in effect, is considering a complicated question: did Lydia Gilbert's witchcraft *cause* Thomas Allen's gun to go off, so as to kill Henry Stiles? Evidence is taken on various points deemed relevant. Henry Stiles was a boarder in the Gilbert household for some while before his death. The arrangement was not a happy one; neighbors could recall the sounds of frequent quarreling. From time to time Stiles loaned money and property to his landlord, but this served only to heighten the tension. Goodwife Gilbert, in particular, violated her Christian obligation of charitable and peaceable behavior. A naturally assertive sort, she did not conceal her sense of grievance against Goodman Stiles. In fact, her local reputation has long encompassed some unfavorable elements: disapproval of her quick temper, envy of her success in besting personal antagonists, suspicion that she is not above invoking the "Devil's means." The jury weighs the evidence and reaches its verdict—guilty as charged. The magistrates hand down the prescribed sentence of death by hanging. A few days thereafter the sentence is carried out.

On the next succeeding Sabbath day, and with solemn forewarning, the pastor of the Windsor church climbs to the pulpit to deliver his sermon. Directly he faces the questions that are weighing heavily in the minds of his parishioners. Why has this terrible scourge of witchcraft been visited on their little community? What has created the opportunity which the Devil and his legions have so untimely seized? For what reason has God Almightly condoned such a tragic intrusion on the life of Windsor? The pastor's answer to these questions is neither surprising nor pleasant for his audience to hear, but it carries a purgative force. The Windsor townsfolk are themselves at least partially to blame. For too long they have strayed from the paths of virtue: overvaluing secular interests while neglecting religious ones, tippling in alehouses, "nightwalking," and—worst of all—engaging one another in repeated strife. In such circumstances the Devil always finds an opening; to such communities God brings retribution. Thus the recent witchcraft episode is a lesson to the people of Windsor, and a warning to mend their ways.

Lydia Gilbert was not the first witch to have lived at Windsor, nor would she be the last. For so-called Puritans, the happenstance of everyday life was part of a struggle of cosmic dimensions, a struggle in which witchcraft played a logical part. The ultimate triumph of Almighty God was assured. But in particular times and places Satan might achieve some temporary success—and claim important victims. Indeed he was continually adding earthly recruits to his nefarious cause. Tempted by bribes and blandishments, or frightened by threats of torture, weak-willed persons signed the "Devil's Book" and enrolled as witches. Thereafter they were armed with his power and obliged to do his bidding. God, meanwhile, opposed this onslaught of evil—and yet He also permitted it. For errant men and women there was no more effective means of "chastening."

In a sense, therefore, witchcraft was part of God's own intention. And the element of intention was absolutely central, in the minds of the human actors. When a man lay dead from a violent accident on a training field, his fellow townspeople would carefully investigate how events had proceeded to such an end. But they sought, in addition, to understand the *why* of it all—the motives, whether human or supernatural (or both), which lay behind the events. The same was true for other forms of everyday mischance. When cows took strangely ill, when a boat capsized in a sudden storm, when bread failed to rise in the oven or beer went bad in the barrel, there was cause for careful reflection. Witchcraft would not necessarily provide the best explanation, but it was always a possibility—and sometimes a most convenient one. To discover an unseen hand at work in one's life was to dispel mystery, to explain misfortune, to excuse incompetence. Belief in witchcraft was rooted in the practical experience no less than the theology of the time.

A single shocking episode—the Salem "hysteria" of 1692—has dominated the lore of this subject ever since. Yet the Salem trials were distinctive only in a quantitative sense—that is, in the sheer numbers of the accused. Between the late 1630's and 1700 dozens of New England towns supported proceedings against witchcraft; some did so on repeated occasions. The total of cases was over a hundred (and this includes only actual trials from which some record survives today). At least forty of the defendants were put to death; the rest were acquitted or convicted of a lesser charge. Numerous additional cases went unrecorded because they did not reach a court of law; nonetheless they generated much excitement—and distress. "Witches" were suspected, accused informally, and condemned in unofficial ways. Gossip and rumor about such people constituted a staple part of the local culture.

The typical witch was a woman of middle age. Like Lydia Gilbert, she was married, had children, and lived as a settled member of her community. (However, widows and childless women were also suspected, perhaps to an extent disproportionate to their numbers in the population at large.) Some of the accused were quite poor and a few were given to begging; but taken altogether they spanned the entire social spectrum. (One was the wife of a leading magistrate in the Massachusetts Bay Colony.) Most seemed conspicuous in their personal behavior: they were cantankerous, feisty, quick to take offense, and free in their expression of anger. As such they matched the prevalent stereotype of a witch, with its emphasis on strife and malice and vengeance. It was no accident, in a culture which valued "peaceableness" above all things, that suspected witches were persons much given to conflict. Like deviant figures everywhere, they served to mark the accepted boundaries between Good and Evil.

Their alleged victims, and actual accusers, are much harder to categorize. Children were sometimes centrally involved—notoriously so at Salem—but witchcraft evidence came from people of both sexes and all ages. The young had their "fits"; older witnesses had other things of which to complain. Illness, injury, and the loss of property loomed largest in such testimony; but there were reports, too, of strange sights and sounds, of portents and omens, of mutterings and cures—all attributable in some way to the supposed witch. The chances for conviction were greatest when the range of this evidence was wide and the sources numerous. In some cases whole neighborhoods joined the ranks of the accusers.

Usually a trial involved only a single witch, or perhaps two; the events at issue were purely local. A finding of guilt would remove the defendant forever from her community. An acquittal would send her back, but with a clear warning to watch her step. Either way tension was lowered.

Occasionally the situation became more complicated. In Connecticut, during the years from 1662 to 1665, the courts heard a long sequence of witchcraft cases—perhaps as many as a dozen. Some of the accused were eventually executed; others fled for their lives to neighboring colonies. Almost none of the legal evidence has survived; it is known, however, that Connecticut was then experiencing severe problems of religious factionalism. The witch trials may well have been a direct result.

The context for the other wide-scale outbreak is much clearer. Salem, in the closing decades of the seventeenth century, was a town notorious for internal contention. An old guard of village farmers was arrayed against newly prosperous merchants and townsmen. For years, indeed decades, local governance was disrupted: town meetings broke up with important issues unresolved, ministers came and left (out of favor with one side or the other), lawsuits filled the court dockets. Thus when the first sparks of witchcraft were fanned, in a small group of troubled girls, they acted like tinder on a dried-out woodpile. Suspicion led immediately to new suspicion, and accusation to accusation—with results that every schoolchild knows. Soon the conflagration burst the boundaries of Salem itself; eventually it claimed victims throughout eastern Massachusetts. By the time cooler heads prevailed—especially that of the new governor, Sir William Phips—twenty witches had been executed and dozens more were languishing in local jails.

But the Salem trials—to repeat—were highly unusual in their sheer scope: witch-hunting gone wild. In the more typical case, events moved slowly, even carefully, within a limited and intensely personal framework. This dimension of the witchcraft story also deserves close attention.

October, 1688. A cart stops by the roadside in the south part of Boston. A tall man alights and hurries along a pathway toward a small house. A door opens to admit him and quickly closes again. The visitor is Rev. Cotton Mather, a young but already eminent clergyman of the town. The house is occupied by the family of a mason named John Goodwin.

Immediately upon entering, Mather becomes witness to an extraordinary scene. On the parlor floor in front of him two small human forms are thrashing about. A girl of thirteen (named Martha) and a boy of eleven (John, Jr.) are caught in the throes of agonizing fits. Their bodies contort into strange, distended shapes. Their eyes bulge. Their mouths snap open and shut. They shriek uncontrollably. From time to time they affect the postures of animals, and crawl about the room, barking like dogs or bellowing like frightened cows. Their father and

These scenes of the work of witches, devils, and other supernatural beings appeared in a treatise entitled "Saducismus Triumphatus, or a Full and Plain Evidence concerning Witches and Apparitions," published in London in 1726. They reflect common beliefs about what such creatures might do.

several neighbors look on in horror, and try by turns to prevent serious damage to persons or property.

Mather waits for a moment's lull; then he opens a Bible, kneels, and begins to pray. Immediately the children stop their ears and resume their shrieking. "*They* say we must not listen," cries the girl, while hurling herself toward the fireplace. Her father manages to block the way; briefly he catches her in an awkward embrace. But she reels off and falls heavily on her brother.

Soon it is time for supper. The children quiet temporarily, and come to the table with their elders. However, when food is offered them, their teeth are set as if to lock their mouths shut. Later there are new troubles. The children need assistance in preparing for bed, and they tear their nightclothes fearfully. At last they quiet and pass into a deep sleep.

Mather sits by the fireside and reviews the history of their affliction with the distraught parents. The family is a religious one, and until the preceding summer the children were unfailingly pious and well behaved. Martha's fits had begun first, John's soon thereafter; indeed, two still younger children in the family have also been affected from time to time. A physician had been summoned, but he could discover no "natural maladies" at work.

The parents recall an episode that had directly preceded the onset of Martha's fits. The girl was sent to retrieve some family linen from a laundress who lived nearby. Several items had disappeared, and Martha complained—intimating theft. The laundress angrily denied the charges, and was joined in this by her own mother, an Irishwoman named Glover. Goodwife Glover was already a feared presence in the neighborhood; her late husband, on his deathbed, had accused her of practicing witchcraft. Now she poured out her retaliative anger on young Martha Goodwin. The girl has not been the same since.

Late in the evening, having listened with care to the entire story, Mather prepares to leave. John Goodwin explains that several neighbors have been urging the use of "tricks"—countermagic—to end his children's difficulties. But Goodwin prefers a strategy based on orthodox Christian principles.

In this Cotton Mather is eager to cooperate. He returns to the Goodwin house each day for a week, and on one particular afternoon he is joined by his fellow clergymen from all parts of Boston. Eventually he invites Martha Goodwin into his own home for a period of intensive pastoral care. (Martha's younger brother is taken, at the same time, into the home of the minister at Watertown.) Their afflictions continue, though with lessened severity.

Meanwhile the courts intervene and Goodwife Glover is put on trial for her alleged crimes. She has difficulty answering the prosecutor's questions; she can speak only in her native tongue (Gaelic), so the proceedings must involve interpreters. Her house is searched, and "poppets" are discovered—small images, made of rags, believed to be instrumental in the perpetration of witchcraft. Eventually she confesses guilt and raves wildly in court about her dealings with the Devil. The judges appoint six physicians to assess her sanity; they find her *compos mentis*. The court orders her execution.

On her way to the gallows Goodwife Glover declares bitterly that the children will not be cured after her death, for "others had a hand in it as well." And in fact, the fits suffered by Martha and young John increase immediately thereafter. Winter begins, and suspicion shifts to another woman of the neighborhood. However, the new suspect dies suddenly, and under strange circumstances, before she can be brought to trial. At last the children show marked improvement, and by spring they are virtually their former selves. Meanwhile a relieved, and triumphant, Cotton Mather is spending long days in his study, completing a new book that will soon be published under the title *Memorable Providences, Relating to Witchcrafts and Possessions.* A central chapter deals at length with selected "examples," and includes the events in which Mather himself has so recently participated. The Goodwin children will be leading characters in a local best seller.

Goodwife Glover was relatively rare, among those accused of witchcraft in early New England, in confessing guilt. Only at Salem did any considerable number choose to convict themselves—and there, it seemed, confession was the strategy of choice if one wished to avoid the gallows. Were Goody Glover's admissions, in effect, forced out of her? Was she perhaps seriously deranged (the opinion of the court-appointed physicians notwithstanding)? Did she truly believe herself guilty? Had she, in fact, sought to invoke the power of the Devil, by stroking poppets with her spittle—or whatever?

We have no way now to answer such questions; the evidence comes to us entirely through persons who believed—and prosecuted—the case against her. It does seem likely, in a community where virtually everyone accepted the reality of witchcraft, that at least a few would have tried to practice it. In a sense, however, it no longer matters whether specific individuals were guilty as charged. What does matter is that many of them were believed guilty—and that this belief was itself efficacious. As anthropologists have observed in cultures around the world, people who regard themselves as objects of witchcraft are vulnerable to all manner of mischance. They blunder into "accidents," they lose their effectiveness in work and social relations, they occasionally sicken and die.

No less was true in early New England. The victims of witchcraft—whatever the variety of their particular afflictions—had this in common: they believed *beforehand* that they had been marked as targets for attack. Their fearful expectation became, at some point, incapacitating—and yielded its own directly feared result. Thus the idea of witchcraft served both as the *ad hoc* cause of the victim's troubles and as the *post hoc* explanation. The process was neatly circular, for each explanation created a further cause—which, in turn, required additional explanation. In the language of modern medicine, these episodes were "symptoms," and their basis was "psychogenic."

The seizures of the afflicted children were but the extreme end of the symptomatic continuum. When Martha Goodwin had been drawn into a bitter exchange with a suspected witch, she was left deeply unsettled. She feared retaliation; she wished to retaliate herself; she felt acutely uncomfortable with the anger she had already expressed. Henceforth an anguished "victim" of witchcraft, she was, in effect, punished for her own vengeful impulse. Yet, too, she *had* her revenge, for her accusations led straight to the trial and conviction of her antagonist. The same inner processes, and a similar blend of wish and fear, served to energize fits in victims of witchcraft all across New England.

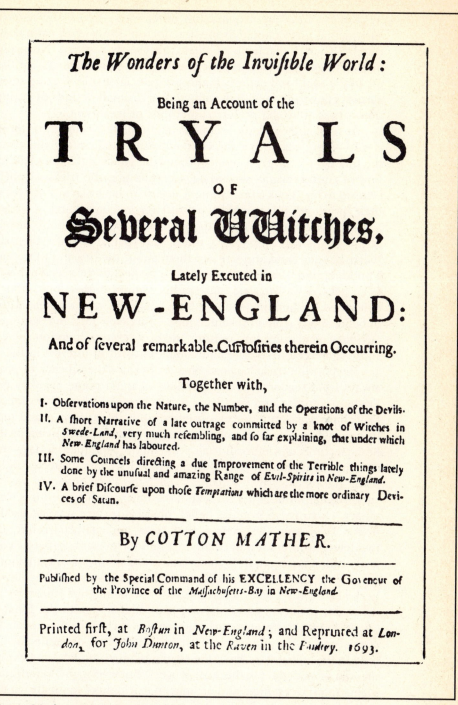

The Wonders of the Invisible World:

Being an Account of the

TRYALS

OF

Several Witches,

Lately Excuted in

NEW-ENGLAND:

And of several remarkable Curiosities therein Occurring.

Together with,

I. Observations upon the Nature, the Number, and the Operations of the Devils.

II. A short Narrative of a late outrage committed by a knot of Witches in *Swede-Land*, very much resembling, and so far explaining, that under which *New-England* has laboured.

III. Some Councels directing a due Improvement of the Terrible things lately done by the unusual and amazing Range of *Evil-Spirits* in *New-England*.

IV. A brief Discourse upon those *Temptations* which are the more ordinary Devices of Satan.

By COTTON MATHER.

Published by the Special Command of his EXCELLENCY the Governeur of the Province of the *Massachusetts-Bay* in *New-England*.

Printed first, at *Boston* in *New-England*; and Reprinted at *London*, for *John Dunton*, at the *Raven* in the *Poultry*. 1693.

Cotton Mather wrote several pamphlets on the Salem trials; this is the title page of one of them, as reprinted in London from an earlier Boston edition.

But fits could be explained in other ways—hence the requirement that all such victims be examined by medical doctors. Only when natural causes had been ruled out was a diagnosis of witchcraft clearly justified. Normally, beyond this point, clergymen would assume control of the proceedings, for they were "healers of the soul" and experts in the struggle against Evil. Long sessions of prayer, earnest conversation with the afflicted, occasional periods of fasting and humiliation—these were the preferred methods of treatment.

At least they were the *Christian* methods. For—much to the chagrin of the clergy—there were other ways of combating witchcraft. From obscure sources in the folk culture of pre-Christian times the New Englanders had inherited a rich lore of countermagic—including, for example, the tricks which John Goodwin refused to try. Thus a family might decide to lay branches of "sweet bays" under their threshold. ("It would keep a witch from coming in.") Or a woman tending a sick child would perform elaborate rituals of protection. ("She smote the back of her hands together sundry times, and spat in the fire; then she . . . rubbed [herbs] in her hand and strewed them about the hearth.") Or a man would hurl a pudding into a fire in order to draw a suspect to the scene of his alleged crimes. ("To get hay was no true cause of his coming thither, but rather the spirit that bewitched the pudding brought him.") All this was of a piece with other strands of belief and custom in seventeenth-century New England: fortunetelling, astrology, healing charms, love potions and powders—to mention a few. Witchcraft, in short, belonged to a large and complex world of interest in the supernatural.

Beyond the tricks against witches, besides the efficacy of prayer, there was always legal recourse. Witchcraft was a capital crime in every one of the New England colonies, and thus was a particularly solemn responsibility of the courts. Procedure was scrupulously observed: indictment by a grand jury, depositions from qualified witnesses, verdict by a jury of trials, sentencing by the magistrates. Some features of witchcraft trials seem highly repugnant today—for example, the elaborate and intimate body searches of defendants suspected of having "witch's teats" (nipplelike growths through which the witch or wizard was believed to give suck to Satan). But in the context of the times, such procedures were not extraordinary. Contrary to popular belief, physical torture was *not* used to obtain evidence. Testimony was taken on both sides, and character references favorable to the defendant were not uncommon. Guilt was never a foregone conclusion; most trials ended in acquittal. Perhaps *because* the crime was a capital one, many juries seemed reluctant to convict. Some returned verdicts like the following: "[We find her] not legally guilty according to indictment, but [there is] just ground of vehement suspicion of her having had familiarity with the Devil."

At Salem, to be sure, such caution was thrown to the winds. The creation of special courts, the admission of "spectral evidence" (supplied by "shapes" visible only to the afflicted victims), the strong momentum favoring conviction—all this marked a decided tilt in the legal process. But it brought, in time, its own reaction. Magistrates, clergymen, and ordinary participants eventually would see the enormity of what they had done at Salem in the name of law and religion. And they would not make the same mistakes again.

Thus the eighteenth century, in New England, was essentially free of *legal* action against witchcraft. However, the belief which had sustained such action did not evaporate so quickly.

Hampton, New Hampshire: March 26, 1769. The finest house in the town, a mansion by any standard, is destroyed in a spectacular fire. The owner is General Jonathan Moulton—scion of an old family, frequent town officer, commander of the local forces in various Indian wars, businessman of extraordinary skill and energy. Yet despite these marks of eminence, Moulton is no favorite of his fellow townsmen. To them he seems ruthless, crafty, altogether a "sharp dealer." Indeed, the local gossips have long suggested that Moulton is in league with the Devil. There is no easier way to explain, among other things, his truly prodigious wealth.

The ashes of Moulton's house are barely cold when a new story circulates in the town: the fire was set by the Devil, because the General had cheated him in a bargain. The details are told as follows. Moulton had pledged his soul to the Devil, in exchange for regular payments of gold and silver coins. The payments were delivered down his chimney and into his boot, which was hung there precisely for this purpose. The arrangement went smoothly for awhile, but then came

A mezzotint portrait of Cotton Mather, done many years after the Salem trials.

a time when the boot took far more coins than usual. The Devil was perplexed, and decided to go down the chimney to see what was wrong. He found that the General had cut off the foot of the boot; the room was so full of money that there was scarcely air to breathe.

The fire—and this account of it—notwithstanding, Moulton quickly recoups. He builds a new mansion even more grand than the first one. His business enterprises yield ever greater profit. He serves with distinction in the Revolutionary War and also in the convention which draws up the constitution of the state of New Hampshire. Yet his local reputation shows little change with the passage of years. When he dies, in 1788, the news is carried to the haymakers on the Hampton marsh: "General Moulton is dead!" they call to one another in tones of evident satisfaction. And there is one final peculiarity about his passing. His body, prepared for burial, is suddenly missing from the coffin. The people of Hampton are not surprised. "The Devil," they whisper knowingly to one another, "has got his own at last."

Similar stories are preserved in the lore of many New England towns. Through them we can trace an enduring interest in the idea of witchcraft—and also an unmistakable change. The figure of the witch gradually lost its power to inspire fear. In many towns, for many generations, there were one or two persons suspected of practicing the black arts, but the effects of such practice were discounted. Witches were associated more and more with simple mischief—and less with death and destruction. There was even, as the Moulton story shows, an element of humor in the later lore of witchcraft.

In our own time the wheel has turned full circle. There are many new witches among us—self-proclaimed, and proud of the fact. They haunt our television talk-shows and write syndicated columns for our newspapers. Their witchcraft is entirely constructive—so they assure us—and we are all invited to join in their celebration of things occult. Meanwhile some of the old witches have been rehabilitated.

Hampton, New Hampshire: March 8, 1938. A town meeting considers the case of a certain Eunice Cole, whose witchcraft was locally notorious three centuries before. The following motion is made: "*Resolved,* that we, the citizens . . . of Hampton . . . do hereby declare that we believe that Eunice (Goody) Cole was unjustly accused of witchcraft and familiarity with the Devil in the seventeenth century, and we do hereby restore to the said Eunice (Goody) Cole her rightful place as a citizen of the town of Hampton." The resolution is passed unanimously. In fact, the legend of Goody Cole has become a cherished part of the local culture. A bronze urn in the town hall holds material purported to be her earthly remains. A stone memorial on the village green affirms her twentieth-century rehabilitation. There are exhibits on her life at the local historical society. There are even some *new* tales in which she plays a ghostly, though harmless part: an aged figure, in tattered shawl, seen walking late at night along a deserted road, or stopping in the early dawn to peer at gravestones by the edge of the green.

And now an author's postscript:

Hampton, New Hampshire: October, 1972. The living room in a comfortable house abutting the main street. A stranger has come there, to examine a venerable manuscript held in this family through many generations. Laboriously his eyes move across the page, straining to unravel the cramped and irregular script of a bygone era. Two girls, aged nine or ten, arrive home from school; after a brief greeting they move off into an alcove and begin to play. Awash in the sounds of their game, the stranger looks up from his work and listens. "I'll be Goody Cole!" cries one of the girls. "Yes," responds the other, "and I'll be the one who gives you a whipping—you mean old witch!"

It is a long way from their time to ours, but at least a few of the early New England witches have made the whole journey.

The Middle Passage

Daniel P. Mannix and Malcolm Cowley

To Europeans like William Byrd, America offered an environment of unparalleled freedom and stimulation; for those of lesser fortune, as the historical record shows, it supplied only somewhat less opportunity for self-expression and improvement. But for Africans—roughly ten percent of all the colonists by the middle of the eighteenth century—America meant the crushing degradation of slavery. Until recently, without excusing or justifying slavery, most historians have tended not so much to ignore as to compartmentalize (one is almost tempted to say "segregate") the history of Afro-Americans from the general stream of American development. When generalizing about American "free institutions," "opportunity," and "equality," the phrase "except for blacks" needs always to be added if the truth is to be told.

Historical arguments have developed about the condition of slaves in America, about the differences between the British-American and Latin-American slave systems, and about other aspects of the history of blacks in the New World. But there has been only unanimity among historians about the horrors associated with the capture of blacks in Africa and with the dread "middle passage" over which the slaves were shipped to the Americans. In this essay the literary critic Malcolm Cowley and the historian Daniel P. Mannix combine their talents to describe what it meant to be wrenched from one's home and native soil, herded in chains into the foul hold of a slave ship, and dispatched across the torrid mid-Atlantic into the hell of slavery.

Long before Europeans appeared on the African coast, the merchants of Timbuktu were exporting slaves to the Moorish kingdoms north of the Sahara. Even the transatlantic slave trade had a long history. There were Negroes in Santo Domingo as early as 1503, and the first twenty slaves were sold in Jamestown, Virginia, about the last week of August, 1619, only twelve years after the colony was founded. But the flush days of the trade were in the eighteenth century, when vast supplies of labor were needed for the sugar plantations in the West Indies and the tobacco and rice plantations on the mainland. From 1700 to 1807, when the trade was legally abolished by Great Britain and the United States, more than seventy thousand Negroes were carried across the Atlantic in any normal year. The trade was interrupted by wars, notably by the American Revolution, but the total New World importation for the century may have amounted to five million enslaved persons.

Most of the slaves were carried on shipboard at some point along the four thousand miles of West African coastline that extend in a dog's leg from the

Sahara on the north to the southern desert. Known as the Guinea Coast, it was feared by eighteenth-century mariners, who died there by hundreds and thousands every year.

Contrary to popular opinion, very few of the slaves—possibly one or two out of a hundred—were free Africans kidnapped by Europeans. The slaving captains had, as a rule, no moral prejudice against manstealing, but they usually refrained from it on the ground of its being a dangerous business practice. A vessel suspected of man-stealing might be "cut off" by the natives, its crew killed, and its cargo of slaves offered for sale to other vessels.

The vast majority of the Negroes brought to America had been enslaved and sold to the whites by other Africans. There were coastal tribes and states, like the Efik kingdom of Calabar, that based their whole economy on the slave trade. The slaves might be prisoners of war, they might have been kidnapped by gangs of black marauders, or they might have been sold with their whole families for such high crimes as adultery, impiety, or, as in one instance, stealing a tobacco pipe. Intertribal wars, the principal source of slaves, were in many cases no more than large-scale kidnapping expeditions. Often they were fomented by Europeans, who supplied both sides with muskets and gunpowder—so many muskets or so much powder for each slave that they promised to deliver on shipboard.

The ships were English, French, Dutch, Danish, Portuguese, or American. London, Bristol, and finally Liverpool were the great English slaving ports. By 1790 Liverpool had engrossed five eighths of the English trade and three sevenths of the slave trade of all Europe. Its French rival, Nantes, would soon be ruined by the Napoleonic wars. During the last years of legal slaving, Liverpool's only serious competitors were the Yankee captains of Newport and Bristol, Rhode Island.

Profits from a slaving voyage, which averaged nine or ten months, were reckoned at thirty per cent, after deducting sales commissions, insurance premiums, and all other expenses. The Liverpool merchants became so rich from the slave trade that they invested heavily in mills, factories, mines, canals, and railways. That process was repeated in New England, and the slave trade provided much of the capital that was needed for the industrial revolution.

A slaving voyage was triangular. English textiles, notions, cutlery, and firearms were carried to the Guinea Coast, where they were exchanged for slaves. These were sold in America or the West Indies, and part of the proceeds was invested in colonial products, notably sugar and rice, which were carried back to England on the third leg of the voyage. If the vessel sailed from a New England port, its usual cargo was casks of rum from a Massachusetts distillery. The rum was exchanged in Africa for slaves—often at the rate of two hundred gallons per man—and the slaves were exchanged in the West Indies for molasses, which was carried back to New England to be distilled into rum. A slave ship or Guineaman was expected to show a profit for each leg of its triangular course. But the base of the triangle, the so-called Middle Passage from Africa to the New World with a black cargo, was the most profitable part of the voyage, at the highest cost in human suffering. Let us see what happened in the passage during the flush days of the slave trade.

As soon as an assortment of naked slaves was carried aboard a Guineaman, the men were shackled two by two, the right wrist and ankle of one to the left wrist and ankle of another; then they were sent below. The women—usually regarded as fair prey for the sailors—were allowed to wander by day almost anywhere on the vessel, though they spent the night between decks, in a space partitioned off from that of the men. All the slaves were forced to sleep without covering on bare wooden floors, which were often constructed of unplaned boards. In a stormy passage the skin over their elbows might be worn away to the bare bones.

William Bosman says, writing in 1701, "You would really wonder to see how these slaves live on board; for though their number sometimes amounts to six or seven hundred, yet by the careful management of our masters of ships"—the Dutch masters, in this case—"they are so regulated that it seems incredible: And in this particular our nation exceeds all other Europeans; for as the French, Portuguese and English slave-ships are always foul and stinking; on the contrary ours are for the most part clean and neat."

Slavers of every nation insisted that their own vessels were the best in the trade. Thus, James Barbot, Jr., who sailed on an English ship to the Congo in 1700, was highly critical of the Portuguese. He admits that they made a great point of baptizing the slaves before taking them on board, but then, "It is pitiful," he says, "to see how they crowd those poor wretches, six hundred and fifty or seven hundred in a ship, the men standing in the hold ty'd to stakes, the women between decks and those that are with child in the great cabin and the children in the steeridge which in that hot climate occasions an intolerable stench." Barbot adds, however, that the Portuguese provided the slaves with coarse thick mats, which were "softer for the poor wretches to lie upon than the bare decks . . . and it would be prudent to imitate the Portuguese in this point." The English, however, did not display that sort of prudence.

There were two schools of thought among the English slaving captains, the "loose-packers" and the "tight-packers." The former argued that by giving the slaves a little more room, better food, and a certain amount of liberty, they reduced the death rate and received a better price for each slave in the West Indies. The tight-packers answered that although the loss of life might be greater on each of their voyages, so too were the net receipts from a larger cargo. If many of the survivors were weak and emaciated, as was often the case, they could be fattened up in a West Indian slave yard before being offered for sale.

The argument between the two schools continued as long as the trade itself, but for many years after 1750 the tight-packers were in the ascendant. So great was the profit on each slave landed alive that hardly a captain refrained from loading his vessel to its utmost capacity. Says the Reverend John Newton, who was a slaving captain before he became a clergyman:

The cargo of a vessel of a hundred tons or a little more is calculated to purchase from 220 to 250 slaves. Their lodging rooms below the deck which are three (for the men, the boys, and the women) besides a place for the sick, are sometimes more than five feet high and sometimes less; and this height is divided toward the middle for the slaves to lie in two rows, one above the other, on each side of the ship, close to each other like books upon a shelf. I have known them so close that the shelf would not easily contain one more.

The poor creatures, thus cramped, are likewise in irons for the most part which makes it difficult for them to turn or move or attempt to rise or to lie down without hurting themselves or each other. Every morning, perhaps, more instances than one are found of the living and the dead fastened together.

Newton was writing in 1788, shortly before a famous parliamentary investigation of the slave trade that lasted four years. One among hundreds of witnesses was Dr. Alexander Falconbridge, who had made four slaving voyages as a surgeon. Falconbridge testified that "he made the most of the room," in stowing the slaves, "and wedged them in. They had not so much room as a man in his coffin either in length or breadth. When he had to enter the slave deck, he took off his shoes to avoid crushing the slaves as he was forced to crawl over them." Falconbridge "had the marks on his feet where the slaves bit and pinched him."

Captain Parrey of the Royal Navy was sent to measure the slave ships at Liverpool and make a report to the House of Commons. That was also in 1788. Parrey discovered that the captains of many slavers possessed a chart showing the dimensions of the half deck, lower deck, hold, platforms, gunroom, orlop, and great cabin, in fact of every crevice into which slaves might be wedged. Miniature black figures were drawn on some of the charts to illustrate the most effective method of packing in the cargo.

On the *Brookes,* which Parrey considered to be typical, every man was allowed a space six feet long by sixteen inches wide (and usually about two feet seven inches high); every woman, a space five feet ten inches long by sixteen inches wide; every boy, five feet by fourteen inches; every girl, four feet six inches by twelve inches. The *Brookes* was a vessel of 320 tons. By a new law passed in 1788 it was permitted to carry 454 slaves, and the chart, which later became famous, showed where 451 of them could be stowed away. Parrey failed to see how the captain could find room for three more. Nevertheless, Parliament was told by reliable witnesses, including Dr. Thomas Trotter, formerly surgeon of the *Brookes,* that before the new law she had carried 600 slaves on one voyage and 609 on another.

Taking on slaves was a process that might be completed in a month or two

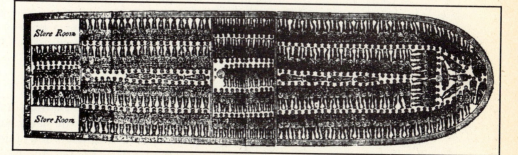

This diagram is a typical example of the "tight packing" techniques of many slavers.

by vessels trading in Lower Guinea, east and south of the Niger delta. In Upper Guinea, west and north of the delta, the process was longer. It might last from six months to a year or more on the Gold Coast, which supplied the slaves most in demand by the English colonies. Meanwhile the captain was buying Negroes, sometimes one or two a day, sometimes a hundred or more in a single lot, while haggling over each purchase.

Those months when a slaver lay at anchor off the malarial coastline were the most dangerous part of her voyage. Not only was her crew exposed to African fevers and the revenge of angry natives; not only was there the chance of her being taken by pirates or by a hostile man-of-war; but there was also the constant threat of a slave mutiny. Captain Thomas Phillips says, in his account of a voyage made in 1693–94:

> When our slaves are aboard we shackle the men two and two, while we lie in port, and in sight of their own country, for 'tis then they attempt to make their escape, and mutiny; to prevent which we always keep centinels upon the hatchways, and have a chest full of small arms, ready loaden and prim'd, constantly lying at hand upon the quarter-deck, together with some granada shells; and two of our quarter-deck guns, pointing on the deck thence, and two more out of the steerage, the door of which is always kept shut, and well barr'd; they are fed twice a day, at 10 in the morning, and 4 in the evening, which is the time they are aptest to mutiny, being all upon the deck; therefore all that time, what of our men are not employ'd in distributing their victuals to them, and settling them, stand to their arms; and some with lighted matches at the great guns that yaun upon them, loaden with partridge, till they have done and gone down to their kennels between decks.

In spite of such precautions, mutinies were frequent on the Coast, and some of them were successful. Even a mutiny that failed might lead to heavy losses among the slaves and the sailors. Thus, we read in the Newport, Rhode Island, *Mercury* of November 18, 1765:

> By letters from Capt. Hopkins in a Brig belonging to Providence arrived here from Antigua from the Coast of Africa we learn That soon after he left the Coast, the number of his Men being reduced by Sickness, he was obliged to permit some of the Slaves to come upon Deck to assist the People: These Slaves contrived to release the others, and the whole rose upon the People, and endeavoured to get Possession of the Vessel; but was happily prevented by the Captain and his Men, who killed, wounded and forced overboard, Eighty of them, which obliged the rest to submit.

There are scores of similar items in the colonial newspapers.

William Richardson, a young sailor who shipped on an English Guineaman in 1790, tells of going to the help of a French vessel on which the slaves had risen while it was at anchor. The English seamen jumped into the boats and pulled hard for the Frenchman, but by the time they reached it there were "a hundred slaves in possession of the deck and others tumbling up from below." The slaves put up a desperate resistance. "I could not but admire," Richardson says, "the courage of a fine young black who, though his partner in irons lay dead at his feet, would not surrender but fought with his billet of wood until a ball finished his existence. The others fought as well as they could but what could they do against fire-arms?"

There are fairly detailed accounts of fifty-five mutinies on slavers from 1699 to 1845, not to mention passing references to more than a hundred others. The list of ships "cut off" by the natives—often in revenge for the kidnapping of free Africans—is almost as long. On the record it does not seem that Africans submitted tamely to being carried across the Atlantic like chained beasts. Edward Long, the Jamaica planter and historian, justified the cruel punishments inflicted on slaves by saying, "The many acts of violence they have committed by murdering whole crews and destroying ships when they had it in their power to do so have made these rigors wholly chargeable on their own bloody and malicious disposition which calls for the same confinement as if they were wolves or wild boars." For "wolves or wild boars" a modern reader might substitute "men who would rather die than be enslaved."

With the loading of the slaves, the captain, for his part, had finished what he regarded as the most difficult part of his voyage. Now he had to face only the ordinary perils of the sea, most of which were covered by his owners' insurance against fire, shipwreck, pirates and rovers, letters of mart and counter-mart, barratry, jettison, and foreign men-of-war. Among the risks not covered by insurance, the greatest was that of the cargo's being swept away by disease. The underwriters refused to issue such policies, arguing that they would expose the captain to an unholy temptation. If insured against disease among his slaves, he

In 1839 some 53 captives revolted aboard the slaver Amistad. *They were recaptured but later freed in a case that reached the Supreme Court.*

might take no precautions against it and might try to make his profit out of the insurance.

The more days at sea, the more deaths among his cargo, and so the captain tried to cut short the next leg of his voyage. If he had shipped his slaves at Bonny, Old Calabar, or any port to the southward, he might call at one of the Portuguese islands in the Gulf of Guinea for an additional supply of food and fresh water, usually enough, with what he had already, to last for three months. If he had traded to the northward, he made straight for the West Indies. Usually he had from four to five thousand nautical miles to sail—or even more, if the passage was from Angola to Virginia. The shortest passage—that from the Gambia River to Barbados—might be made in as little as three weeks, with favoring winds. If the course was much longer, and if the ship was becalmed in the doldrums or driven back by storms, the voyage might take more than three months, and slaves and sailors would be put on short rations long before the end of the Middle Passage.

On a canvas of heroic size, Thomas Stothard, Esquire, of the Royal Academy, depicted *The Voyage of the Sable Venus from Angola to the West Indies.* His painting is handsomely reproduced in the second volume of Bryan Edwards' *History of the British Colonies in the West Indies* (1793), where it appears beside a poem on the same allegorical subject by an unnamed Jamaican author, perhaps Edwards himself.

The joint message of the poem and the painting is simple to the point of coarseness: that slave women are preferable to English girls at night, being passionate and accessible; but the message is embellished with classical details, to show the painter's learning.

Meanwhile the Sable Venus, if she was a living woman carried from Angola to the West Indies, was roaming the deck of a ship that stank of excrement; as was said of any slaver, "You could smell it five miles down wind." She had been torn from her husband and her children, she had been branded on the left buttock, and she had been carried to the ship bound hand and foot, lying in the bilge at the bottom of a dugout canoe. Now she was the prey of the ship's officers.

Here is how she and her shipmates spent the day.

If the weather was clear, they were brought on deck at eight o'clock in the morning. The men were attached by their leg irons to the great chain that ran along the bulwarks on both sides of the ship; the women and half-grown boys were allowed to wander at will. About nine o'clock the slaves were served their first meal of the day. If they were from the Windward Coast—roughly, the shore-line of present-day Liberia and Sierra Leone—the fare was boiled rice, millet, or corn meal, sometimes cooked with a few lumps of salt beef abstracted from the sailors' rations. If they were from the Bight of Biafra, at the east end of the Gulf of Guinea, they were fed stewed yams, but the Congos and the Angolas preferred manioc or plantains. With the food they were all given half a pint of water, served out in a pannikin.

After the morning meal came a joyless ceremony called "dancing the slaves." "Those who were in irons," says Dr. Thomas Trotter, surgeon of the *Brookes* in 1783, "were ordered to stand up and make what motions they could, leaving a passage for such as were out of irons to dance around the deck." Dancing was prescribed as a therapeutic measure, a specific against suicidal melancholy, and also against scurvy—although in the latter case it was a useless torture for men with swollen limbs. While sailors paraded the deck, each with a cat-o'-nine-tails in his right hand, the men slaves "jumped in their irons" until their ankles were bleeding flesh. Music was provided by a slave thumping on a broken drum or an upturned kettle, or by an African banjo, if there was one aboard, or perhaps by a sailor with a bagpipe or a fiddle. Slaving captains sometimes advertised for "A person that can play on the Bagpipes, for a Guinea ship." The slaves were also told to sing. Said Dr. Claxton after his voyage in the *Young Hero,* "They sing, but not for their amusement. The captain ordered them to sing, and they sang songs of sorrow. Their sickness, fear of being beaten, their hunger, and the memory of their country, etc., are the usual subjects."

While some of the sailors were dancing the slaves, others were sent below to scrape and swab out the sleeping rooms. It was a sickening task, and it was not well performed unless the captain imposed an iron discipline. James Barbot, Sr., was proud of the discipline maintained on the *Albion-Frigate.* "We were very nice," he says, "in keeping the places where the slaves lay clean and neat, appointing some of the ship's crew to do that office constantly and thrice a week we perfumed betwixt decks with a quantity of good vinegar in pails, and red-hot iron bullets in them, to expel the bad air, after the place had been well washed and scrubbed with brooms." Captain Hugh Crow, the last legal English slaver, was famous for his housekeeping. "I always took great pains," he says, "to promote the health and comfort of all on board, by proper diet, regularity, exercise, and cleanliness, for I considered that on keeping the ship clean and orderly, which was always my hobby, the success of our voyage mainly depended." Certainly he lost fewer slaves in the Middle Passage than the other captains, some of whom had the filth in the hold cleaned out only once a week.

At three or four in the afternoon the slaves were fed their second meal, often a repetition of the first. Sometimes, instead of African food, they were given horse beans, the cheapest provender from Europe. The beans were boiled to a pulp, then covered with a mixture of palm oil, flour, water, and red pepper, which the sailors called "slabber sauce." Most of the slaves detested horse beans, especially if they were used to eating yams or manioc. Instead of eating the pulp, they would, unless carefully watched, pick it up by handfuls and throw it in each other's faces.

That second meal was the end of their day. As soon as it was finished they were sent below, under the guard of sailors charged with stowing them away on their bare floors and platforms. The tallest men were placed amidships, where the vessel was widest; the shorter ones were tumbled into the stern. Usually there was only room for them to sleep on their sides, "spoon fashion." Captain William Littleton told Parliament that slaves in the ships on which he sailed might lie on their backs if they wished—"though perhaps," he conceded, "it might be difficult all at the same time."

After stowing their cargo, the sailors climbed out of the hatchway, each clutching his cat-o'-nine-tails; then the hatchway gratings were closed and barred. Sometimes in the night, as the sailors lay on deck and tried to sleep, they heard from below "an howling melancholy noise, expressive of extreme anguish."

When Dr. Trotter told his interpreter, a slave woman, to inquire about the cause of the noise, "she discovered it to be owing to their having dreamt they were in their own country, and finding themselves when awake, in the hold of a slave ship."

More often the noise heard by the sailors was that of quarreling among the slaves. The usual occasion for quarrels was their problem of reaching the latrines. These were inadequate in size and number, and hard to find in the darkness of the crowded hold, especially by men who were ironed together in pairs.

In squalls or rainy weather, the slaves were never brought on deck. They were served their two meals in the hold, where the air became too thick and poisonous to breathe. Dr. Falconbridge writes:

> For the purpose of admitting fresh air, most of the ships in the slave-trade are provided, between the decks, with five or six airports on each side of the ship, of about six inches in length and four in breadth; in addition to which, some few ships, but not one in twenty, have what they denominate wind-sails [funnels made of canvas and so placed as to direct a current of air into the hold]. But whenever the sea is rough and the rain heavy, it becomes necessary to shut these and every other conveyance by which the air is admitted. . . . The negroes' rooms very soon become intolerably hot. The confined air, rendered noxious by the effluvia exhaled from their bodies and by being repeatedly breathed, soon produces fevers and fluxes which generally carry off great numbers of them.

Dr. Trotter says that when tarpaulins were thrown over the gratings, the slaves would cry, "Kickeraboo, kickeraboo, we are dying, we are dying." Falconbridge gives one instance of their sufferings:

> Some wet and blowing weather having occasioned the portholes to be shut and the grating to be covered, fluxes and fevers among the negroes ensued. While they were in this situation, I frequently went down among them till at length their rooms became so extremely hot as to be only bearable for a very short time. But the excessive heat was not the only thing that rendered their situation intolerable. The deck, that is, the floor of their rooms, was so covered with the blood and mucus which had proceeded from them in consequence of the flux, that it resembled a slaughter-house.

While the slaves were on deck they had to be watched at all times to keep them from committing suicide. Says Captain Phillips of the *Hannibal,* "We had about 12 negroes did wilfully drown themselves, and others starv'd themselves to death; for," he explained, " 'tis their belief that when they die they return home to their own country and friends again."

This belief was reported from various regions, at various periods of the trade, but it seems to have been especially strong among the Ibos of eastern Nigeria. In 1788, nearly a hundred years after the *Hannibal's* voyage, Dr. Ecroide Claxton was the surgeon who attended a shipload of Ibos. Some, he testified, wished to die on an idea that they should then get back to their own country. The captain in order to obviate this idea, thought of an expedient viz. to cut off the heads of those who died intimating to them that if determined to go, they must return without heads. The slaves were accordingly brought up to witness the operation. One of them by a violent exertion got loose and flying to the place where the nettings had been unloosed in order to empty the tubs, he darted overboard. The ship brought to, a man was placed in the main chains to catch him which he perceiving, made signs which words cannot express expressive of his happiness in escaping. He then went down and was seen no more.

Dr. Isaac Wilson, a surgeon in the Royal Navy, made a Guinea voyage on the *Elizabeth,* the captain of which John Smith, . . . was said to be very humane. Nevertheless, Wilson was assigned the duty of flogging the slaves. "Even in the act of chastisement," Wilson says, "I have seen them look up at me with a smile, and, in their own language, say 'presently we shall be no more.' " One woman on the *Elizabeth* found some rope yarn, which she tied to the armorer's vise; she fastened the other end round her neck and was found dead in the morning.

On the *Brookes* when Thomas Trotter was her surgeon, there was a man who, after being accused of witchcraft, had been sold into slavery with all his family. During the first night on shipboard he tried to cut his throat. Dr. Trotter sewed up the wound, but on the following night the man not only tore out the stitches but tried to cut his throat on the other side. From the ragged edges of the wound and the blood on his fingers, he seemed to have used his nails as the only available instrument. His hands were then tied together, but he refused all food, and he died of hunger in eight or ten days.

Besides the propensity for suicide, another deadly scourge of the Guinea cargoes was a phenomenon called "fixed melancholy." Even slaves who were well fed, treated with kindness, and kept under relatively sanitary conditions would often die, one after another, for no apparent reason; they had simply lost the will to live. Dr. Wilson believed that fixed melancholy was responsible for the loss of two thirds of the slaves who died on the *Elizabeth*. "No one who had it was ever cured," he says, "whereas those who had it not and yet were ill, recovered. The symptoms are a lowness of spirits and despondency. Hence they refuse food. This only increases the symptoms. The stomach afterwards got weak. Hence the belly ached, fluxes ensued, and they were carried off." But in spite of the real losses from despair, the high death rate on Guineamen was due to somatic more than to psychic afflictions.

Along with their human cargoes, crowded, filthy, undernourished, and terrified out of the wish to live, the ships also carried an invisible cargo of microbes, bacilli, spirochetes, viruses, and intestinal worms from one continent to another; the Middle Passage was a crossroad and market place of diseases. From Europe came smallpox, measles (somewhat less deadly to Africans than to American Indians), gonorrhea, and syphilis (which last Columbus' sailors had carried from America to Europe). The African diseases were yellow fever (to which the natives were resistant), dengue, blackwater fever, and malaria (which was not specifically

African, but which most of the slaves carried in their blood streams). If anopheles mosquitoes were present, malaria spread from the slaves through any new territories to which they were carried. Other African diseases were amoebic and bacillary dysentery (known as "the bloody flux"), Guinea worms, hookworm (possibly African in origin, but soon endemic in the warmer parts of the New World), yaws, elephantiasis, and leprosy.

The particular affliction of the white sailors after escaping from the fevers of the Guinea Coast was scurvy, a deficiency disease to which they were exposed by their monotonous rations of salt beef and sea biscuits. The daily tot of lime juice (originally lemon juice) that prevented scurvy was almost never served on merchantmen during the days of the legal slave trade, and in fact was not prescribed in the Royal Navy until 1795. Although the slaves were also subject to scurvy, they fared better in this respect than the sailors, partly because they made only one leg of the triangular voyage and partly because their rough diet was sometimes richer in vitamins. But sailors and slaves alike were swept away by smallpox and "the bloody flux," and sometimes whole shiploads went blind from what seems to have been trachoma.

Smallpox was feared more than other diseases, since the surgeons had no way of curing it. One man with smallpox infected a whole vessel, unless—as sometimes happened—he was tossed overboard when the first scabs appeared. Captain Wilson of the *Briton* lost more than half his cargo of 375 slaves by not listening to his surgeon. It was the last slave on board who had the disease, says Henry Ellison, who made the voyage. "The doctor told Mr. Wilson it was the small-pox," Ellison continues. "He would not believe it, but said he would keep him, as he was a fine man. It soon broke out amongst the slaves. I have seen the platform one continued scab. We hauled up eight or ten slaves dead of a morning. The flesh and skin peeled off their wrists when taken hold of, being entirely mortified."

But dysentery, though not so much feared, probably caused more deaths in the aggregate. Ellison testified that he made two voyages on the *Nightingale*. On the first voyage the slaves were so crowded that thirty boys "messed and slept in the long boat all through the Middle Passage, there being no room below"; and still the vessel lost only five or six slaves in all, out of a cargo of 270. On the second voyage, however, the *Nightingale* buried "about 150, chiefly of fevers and flux. We had 250 when we left the coast."

The average mortality in the Middle Passage is impossible to state accurately from the surviving records. Some famous voyages were made without the loss of a single slave. On one group of nine voyages between 1766 and 1780, selected at random, the vessels carried 2,362 slaves and there were no epidemics of disease. The total loss of slaves was 154, or about six and one-half per cent. That figure is to be compared with the losses on a list of twenty voyages compiled by Thomas Clarkson, the abolitionist, in which the vessels carried 7,904 slaves with a mortality of 2,053, or twenty-six per cent. Balancing high and low figures together, the English Privy Council in 1789 arrived at an estimate of twelve and one-half per cent for the average mortality among slaves in the Middle Passage. To this figure it added four and one-half per cent for the deaths of slaves in harbors before they were sold, and thirty-three per cent for deaths in the so-called "seasoning" or acclimatizing process, making a total of fifty per cent. If these figures are correct, only one slave was added to the New World labor force for every two purchased on the Guinea Coast.

To keep the figures in perspective, it might be said that the mortality among slaves in the Middle Passage was possibly no greater than that of white indentured servants or even of free Irish, Scottish, and German immigrants in the North Atlantic crossing. On the better-commanded Guineamen it was probably less, and for a simple economic reason. There was no profit on a slaving voyage until the Negroes were landed alive and sold; therefore the better captains took care of their cargoes. It was different on the North Atlantic crossing, where even the hold and steerage passengers paid their fares before coming aboard, and where the captain cared little whether they lived or died.

After leaving the Portuguese island of São Tomé—if he had watered there—a slaving captain bore westward along the equator for a thousand miles, and then northwestward toward the Cape Verde Islands. This was the tedious part of the Middle Passage. "On leaving the Gulf of Guinea," says the author of a *Universal Geography* published in the early nineteenth century, ". . . that part of the ocean must be traversed, so fatal to navigators, where long calms detain the ships under a sky charged with electric clouds, pouring down by torrents of rain and of fire. This *sea of thunder,* being a focus of mortal diseases, is avoided as much as possible, both in approaching the coasts of Africa and those of America." It was not until reaching the latitude of the Cape Verde Islands that the vessel fell in with the northeast trades and was able to make a swift passage to the West Indies.

Dr. Claxton's ship, the *Young Hero,* was one of those delayed for weeks before reaching the trade winds. "We were so streightened for provisions," he testified, "that if we had been ten more days at sea, we must either have eaten the slaves that died, or have made the living slaves *walk the plank,*" a term, he explained, that was widely used by Guinea captains. There are no authenticated records of cannibalism in the Middle Passage, but there are many accounts of slaves killed for various reasons. English captains believed that French vessels carried poison in their medicine chests, "with which they can destroy their negroes in a calm, contagious sickness, or short provisions." They told the story of a Frenchman from Brest who had a long passage and had to poison his slaves; only twenty of them reached Haiti out of five hundred. Even the cruelest English captains regarded this practice as Latin, depraved, and uncovered by their insurance policies. In an emergency they simply jettisoned part of their cargo.

Often a slave ship came to grief in the last few days of the Middle Passage. It might be taken by a French privateer out of Martinique, or it might disappear in a tropical hurricane, or it might be wrecked on a shoal almost in sight of its harbor. On a few ships there was an epidemic of suicide at the last moment.

These, however, were exceptional disasters, recounted as horror stories in the newspapers of the time. Usually the last two or three days of the passage were a comparatively happy period. All the slaves, or all but a few, might be released from their irons. When there was a remaining stock of provisions, the slaves were given bigger meals—to fatten them for market—and as much water as they could

In April of 1860 these despondent and emaciated slaves reached Key West in the bark Wildfire. *From an etching published in* Harper's Weekly.

drink. Sometimes on the last day—if the ship was commanded by an easy-going captain—there was a sort of costume party on deck, with the women slaves dancing in the sailors' castoff clothing. Then the captain was rowed ashore, to arrange for the disposition of his cargo.

This was a problem solved in various fashions. In Virginia, if the vessel was small, it might sail up and down the tidal rivers, bartering slaves for tobacco at private wharves. There were also public auctions of newly imported slaves, usually at Hampton, Yorktown, or Bermuda Hundred. In South Carolina, which was the great mainland slave market, the cargo was usually consigned to a commission merchant, who disposed of the slaves at auction, then had the vessel loaded with rice or indigo for its voyage back to England.

In the smaller West Indian islands, the captain sometimes took charge of selling his own slaves. In this case he ferried them ashore, had them drawn up in a ragged line of march, and paraded them through town with bagpipes playing, before exposing them to buyers in the public square. In the larger islands, commission merchants took charge of the cargo, and the usual method of selling the slaves at retail was a combination of the "scramble"—to be described in a moment—with the vendue or public auction "by inch of candle."

First the captain, with the commission merchant at his side, went over the cargo and picked out the slaves who were maimed or diseased. These were carried

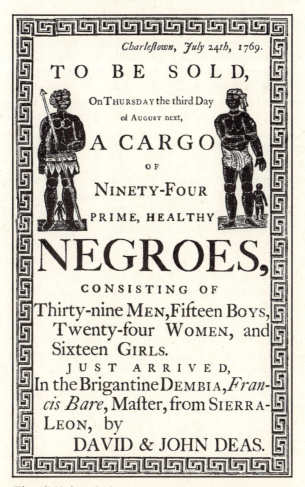

The 1769 broadside is typical of those posted in southern ports to advertise the arrival of slave ships from Africa's west coast.

to a tavern and auctioned off, with a lighted candle before the auctioneer; bids were received until an inch of candle had burned. The price of so-called "refuse" slaves sold at auction was usually less than half of that paid for a healthy Negro. "I was informed by a mulatto woman," Dr. Falconbridge says, "that she purchased a sick slave at Grenada, upon speculation, for the small sum of one dollar, as the poor wretch was apparently dying of the flux." There were some slaves so diseased and emaciated that they could not be sold for even a dollar, and these might be left to die on the wharves.

The healthy slaves remaining after the auction were sold by "scramble," that is, at standard prices for each man, each woman, each boy, and each girl in the cargo. The prices were agreed upon with the purchasers, who then scrambled for their pick of the slaves. During his four voyages Falconbridge was present at a number of scrambles. "In the *Emilia*," he says,

> at Jamaica, the ship was darkened with sails, and covered round. The men slaves were placed on the main deck, and the women on the quarter deck. The purchasers on shore were informed a gun would be fired when they were ready to open the sale. A great number of people came on board with tallies or cards in their hands, with their own names upon them, and rushed through the barricado door with the ferocity of brutes. Some had three or four handkerchiefs tied together, to encircle as many as they thought fit for their purposes.

For the slaves, many of whom believed that they were about to be eaten, it was the terrifying climax of a terrifying voyage.

The parliamentary investigations of 1788–1791 presented a complete picture of the Middle Passage, with testimony from everyone concerned except the slaves, and it horrified the English public. Powerful interests in Parliament, especially those representing the Liverpool merchants and the West Indian planters, prevented the passage of restrictive legislation at that time. But the Middle Passage was not forgotten, and in 1807 Parliament passed a law forbidding any slaver to sail from a British port after May 1 of that year. At about the same time, Congress prohibited the importation of slaves into American territory from and after January 1, 1808. All the countries of Europe followed the British and American example, if with some delay. During the next half century, however, reformers would learn that the trade was difficult to abolish in fact as well as in law, and that illegal slaving would continue as long as slavery itself was allowed to flourish.

The Scotch-Irish in America

James G. Leyburn

That we are a nation of immigrants and that each national and ethnic strain in our society has "contributed" to the shaping of American civilization are commonplace observances. We tend, however, to assume that before the arrival of the great waves of Irish and German immigrants in the 1840s the country was populated almost entirely by people of English descent. This was far from the case. There were, aside from small groups of Dutch, Portuguese, Swedish, and French settlers, the "Pennsylvania Dutch" (actually Germans), who flocked into Pennsylvania in the late seventeenth century, and far more important—because the Pennsylvania Dutch formed a relatively isolated enclave—the thousands of Scotch-Irish settlers, whose origins and influence are discussed in this essay by James G. Leyburn.

The Scotch-Irish were English in the political sense, but as Leyburn shows, they possessed a distinct culture and had a distinctive and long-lasting impact on American civilization. Leyburn, emeritus professor of sociology at Washington and Lee University, is the author of, among other books, The Scotch-Irish: A Social History.

Millions of Americans have Scotch-Irish ancestors, for when this country gained its independence perhaps one out of every ten persons was Scotch-Irish. Few descendants among these millions, however, know much about their ancestors—about what the hyphenated name implies, where the original Scotch-Irishmen came from and why, or what part this vigorous folk played in early American history.

Because the thirteen original American colonies were English, with government in English hands and the population predominantly from England, the tendency of our history books has been to make us see colonial history as the product of transplanted Englishmen. Every American child learns about Jamestown, Pilgrims and Puritans, Tidewater planters, landed proprietors and gentry—all English; but few schoolbooks make a child aware of the non-English "first Americans." In quite recent years our attention has been insistently called to the blacks who made up one sixth of our first census in 1790; and the very names of German, Dutch, Portuguese, Jewish, and French Huguenot elements tell us who these early Americans were. But who were the Scotch-Irish?

Next to the English they were the most numerous of all colonists, with settlements from Maine to Georgia. Some historians suggest that they were "archetypal" Americans, in the sense that their ideals and attitudes, limitations and prepossesions, virtues and vices, proved to be common national characteristics of nineteenth-century Americans. If such a claim has any validity, the people themselves deserve to be more than a vague name.

To English colonists who were their neighbors from 1717 to 1775 any idea that immigrants from northern Ireland might presage future American character would have been startling if not dismaying. Few of the settled colonists had kind words for the newcomers in those days. Pennsylvania received the largest numbers of them, and James Logan, secretary to the Penn family and an Irishman himself, lamented that "the settlement of five families of [Scotch-Irishmen] gives me more trouble than fifty of any other people." When they continued to pour into the colony, Logan, fearing that the recent Quaker element might be submerged, fumed: "It is strange that they thus crowd where they are not wanted." Cotton Mather in Massachusetts was more forthright; he fulminated against their presence as one of "the formidable attempts of Satan and his Sons to Unsettle us." On the eve of the Revolution a loyal English colonist declared the Scotch-Irish to be, with few exceptions, "the most God-provoking democrats on this side of Hell."

Such initial hostility toward a wave of foreigners was to become commonplace during the next century, when America received some thirty million immigrants from Europe. By comparison with these late-comers, however, the Scotch-Irish were fortunate, since they experienced active hostility for only a brief time. Practically all of them pushed as quickly as possible to the cheap lands of the back country, where, out of sight, they no longer offended the sensibilities of English colonists by their "oddities."

In many ways the Scotch-Irish pioneers were indeed an augury of Americans-to-be. They were probably the first settlers to identify themselves as Americans—not as Pennsylvanians or Virginians or citizens of some other colony, nor as Englishmen or Germans or any European nationality. Their daily experience of living on the outer fringe of settlement, of making small farms in the forests, of facing the danger of Indian attack and fighting back, called for qualities of self-reliance, ingenuity, and improvisation that Americans have ranked high as virtues. They were inaugurators of the heroic myth of the winning of the West that was to dominate our nineteenth-century history. Their Presbyterian Church, with its tradition of formality in worship and its insistence upon an educated ministry, was the first denomination to make tentative, if reluctant, adjustments to the realities of frontier life. Social mixing and intermarriage with their neighbors, irrespective of national background, made any such qualifier as Scotch-Irish (or northern Irish or Ulsterman) disappear within a generation.

When the Revolutionary War came, Scotch-Irishmen were the most whole-hearted supporters of the American cause in each of the thirteen colonies. If before 1775 they were still regarded as aliens and immigrants, their zeal as patriots and soldiers changed all that. At home and abroad they were credited with playing a vital part in the struggle for independence. A Hessian captain wrote in 1778, "Call this war by whatever name you may, only call it not an American rebellion; it is nothing more or less than a Scotch Irish Presbyterian rebellion." King George was reported to have characterized the Revolution as "a Presbyterian war," and Horace Walpole told Parliament that "there is no use crying about it. Cousin America has run off with a Presbyterian parson, and that it is the end of it." A representative of Lord Dartmouth wrote from New York in 1776 that "Presbyterianism is really at the Bottom of this whole Conspiracy, has supplied it with Vigour, and will never rest, till something is decided upon it." Such testimony to enthusiasm for the American cause was not given to any other group of immigrants.

Upon the conclusion of the war, when the great Ohio and Mississippi valleys were opened up and the rush westward began, sons and daughters of the original Scotch-Irishmen led the way across the mountains to the new frontiers. Theodore Roosevelt is not the only historian who suggests that the institutions, attitudes, and characteristics of these trans-Allegheny pioneers constituted the practical middle ground into which the diversities of easterners and southerners might merge into something new—American culture.

The hyphenated term "Scotch-Irish" is an Americanism, generally unknown in Scotland and Ireland and rarely used by British historians. In American usage it refers to people of Scottish descent who, having lived for a time in the north of Ireland, migrated in considerable numbers to the American colonies during the half century before the Revolutionary War. Perhaps 250,000 of them actually crossed the sea to America, and they bred rapidly; their sons, like later arrivals from Ulster, constantly extended settlements westward to the Appalachians. The mountains then sent the flow of newcomers north and especially south from Pennsylvania until they constituted a dominant element in many colonies.

Only occasionally were these people then called Scotch-Irish; the usual designation was simply "Irish." "Scotch-Irish" is accurate, yet many Irish-American critics assert that it is an appellation born of snobbish pride and prejudice. . . .

Yet for all the implicit snobbishness in the double name, it directs attention to geographical, historical, and cultural facts in the background of the Scotch-Irish people. The persistence of ancestral traits of character can be exaggerated and even given a mystical quality; but there is no doubt that tradition, ancient "sets" of mind, religious convictions, limitations of outlook, and abiding prejudices gave the Scotch-Irish qualities of personality and character that affected their life in America.

The people who began to come to America in 1717 were not Scots, and certainly they were not Irish: already they were Scotch-Irish, even though this name was rarely given them. The hyphen bespeaks two centuries of historical events, many of them tragic ("dark and drublie" was the Scottish phrase), some of them heroic. The ancestors of these people had come, in the century after 1610, from the Lowlands of Scotland across the twenty-mile channel to the northern province of Ireland (Ulster) as a result of a political experiment undertaken by England. It was called the Plantation of Ulster, and it was simply one of England's many attempts to solve "the Irish problem."

For five centuries, ever since the time of Henry II (1133–89), England had tried to rule Ireland, but the Irish refused to become docile subjects. Their resistance was intensified into bitterness when England became Protestant and tried to extirpate the Roman Catholic religion in Ireland. Finally, in Queen

This pioneer settlement in colonial New Hampshire is reasonably typical of the rough and primitive cabins and stockades built by the earliest Scotch-Irish in America.

Elizabeth's closing years, Irish earls in the north, after a desperate struggle, were defeated and exiled, and the Crown confiscated all their lands. James I, who followed Elizabeth in 1603, proposed (at the suggestion of Edmund Spenser and others of his counsellors) to settle this region with loyal English and Scottish Protestants who, in return for cheap land, would keep the Irish under control. Since the king had been James VI of Scotland before succeeding to the English crown, he was successful in persuading thousands of his Scottish subjects to cross to Ulster and start a new life there under advantageous economic circumstances.

Only a vivid modern imagination can conceive the squalor, indeed the near savagery, of the northern Irish counties around 1600. Queen Elizabeth called the inhabitants "the wild Irish." She and her advisors looked upon them as Victorians did African natives and other "lesser breeds without the law." These Irishmen had no cities, no education, no refinements; they lived from hand to mouth at a primitive level (maintained, of course, by centuries of guerrilla fighting against the English). Their Catholic religion, a patriotic rallying point and a blessed solace, had acquired many elements of magic and superstition. Almost utter demoralization had ensued upon the defeat and exile of their leaders in the 1590's.

The Scots who were invited (along with English Protestants) by King James to settle Ulster and subdue its natives were thus the first Scotch-Irishmen. They came from the Lowlands, that region nearest the English border and longest in contact with English ways, language, and ideas. They were not the romantic Highland figures of Scott's novels. They were not clansmen who wore kilts and who marched, complete with dirk, sporran, brooch, and bonnet, to the skirling of bagpipes in the glens. On the contrary, they were farmers who eked out a bare living on thin soil as tenants of a laird. Three words best characterize them: they were poor, Presbyterian, and pertinacious.

Their farming methods were primitive. Crops were not rotated, and the yield was meager; starvation was always imminent in the long winters, for both man and beast. King James's offer of a new start in Ireland on larger farms whose land had lain fallow was, therefore, very appealing, all the more because lairds in the Lowlands had recently demanded higher rents and contracts that made farmers feel a loss of traditional rights and dignity.

The first Scotsmen to pioneer in Ulster succeeded well enough to allure other thousands of Lowlanders, and when, in mid-century, troubles arose with the English king and his church, the exodus increased. The new Ulstermen ran the gamut of character, as pioneers do. Their motives for migration—desire for a better living, escape from problems and debts—indicate ambition and initiative. Some of the adventurers proved to be shiftless; others had qualities needing only opportunity to bring them to full flower. Most of the "planters" took their families with them, thus proclaiming their intention to stay and establish themselves. Socially, they were generally humble folk (aristocrats rarely migrate), but with tenacious qualities indispensable for pioneers.

They were Presbyterians to a man, and Scottish Presbyterianism was unique in its intensity, even in those religious days. The Reformation in Scotland, led by John Knox, had achieved immediate and almost universal success among Lowlanders. Their Calvinist "kirk" became the Church of Scotland, a nationalist symbol for the people, who supported it all the more loyally because of the initial struggle against "popery" and the subsequent resistance against royal efforts to make it Anglican. A notable aspect of the Reformation in Scotland was the enthusiastic commitment of the people to education, not only for ministers but also for laymen. It was as if a dormant ideal had suddenly and permanently come to flower. The highest aspiration of a Lowland family was that a son might attend a university and become a minister or dominie. The passion for education carried over to northern Ireland and to America, with far-reaching results in the colonies.

It is likely that the quality of the Lowlanders that made the king most hopeful of their success in the Ulster Plantation was their well-known stubbornness and dourness ("dour" and "durable" are linguistically related). He counted on these traits to hold them in Ulster even when things went badly, and to make them keep the "wild Irish" in tow, and his confidence proved justified. Had not an elder of the kirk besought the Lord that he might always be right, "for Thou knowest, Lord, that I am unco' hard to turn"?

In the century between 1610 and 1717 perhaps as many as one hundred thousand Lowlanders came across from Scotland, and by the latter date there were some five Scots to every three Irishmen and one Englishman in Ulster. The English planters represented the Establishment: high civil officials, Anglican churchmen, businessmen, and the Army; but the preponderant Scots set the tone of the new culture of northern Ireland. It is a culture that, as the recent troubles there have painfully shown, is still self-consciously different from that of the rest of the island.

The Ulster experience was a fitting preparation for pioneering in America. The farmers had constantly to be on guard against native Irish uprisings. Agricultural methods decidedly improved under English example. Feudalism, which still existed in Scotland, simply disappeared in Ulster, for farmers were no longer subject to an overlord or attached to one locality. The Presbyterian Church, with its members "straitly" watched over and disciplined by the session of each parish kirk, stiffened the moral fiber of the people, and with its own presbyteries, not subject to the Scottish Kirk, gave the members experience in self-government.

In one respect, however, the Scotch-Irish seemed to be deficient. The Renaissance did not reach Scotland until the eighteenth century, many years after the Lowlanders had left. From the moment of their arrival in northern Ireland comment was made by Englishmen on the apparently complete lack of aesthetic sensibility on the part of these Scots. As one observer remarked, if a Scotsman in Ulster "builds a cottage, it is a prison in miniature; if he has a lawn, it is only grass; the fence of his grounds is a stone wall, seldom a hedge. He has a sluggish imagination: it may be awakened by the gloomy or terrific, but seldom revels in the beautiful." The same limitations apparently characterized the Scotch-Irish in America.

In the very decades when at last the Ulster Plantation seemed to be achieving its purpose, with the Irish subdued, Protestantism dominant, English rule secured, and prosperity imminent, the great migration to America got under way. As usually happens when thousands of people undertake so hazardous an enterprise as crossing an ocean to find a new home, there was both a push from the old country and a pull from the new.

Paradoxically, Ulster's growing prosperity was one cause of the first wave of migration. A lucrative woolen and linen industry, developing since the 1690's, alarmed the English Parliament and led to the passage of a series of crippling protective acts whose results were resentment on the part of Ulstermen, economic depression, and recurrent unemployment. A second cause touched men personally and turned many thoughts to migration: this was the hated practice of rack-renting. The term referred to a landlord's raising rent when a long lease on his land expired—and in the decade after 1710 hundreds of leases came up for renewal. To us, such a practice seems normal; but Ulster farmers felt it to be a violation of tradition, a moral injury, because a tenant was treated impersonally. If the farmer could not or would not pay the higher rent, he had only two practical alternatives: a return to the poverty of Scotland, or migration to the New World.

Still other causes stimulated emigration. Six years in succession after 1714 brought dire drought, with depression in the flax industry and soaring costs of food. In 1716 sheep were afflicted with a destructive disease; severe frosts throughout the decade discouraged farmers; a smallpox epidemic scourged Ulster. In addition there was a goad from the Anglican religious establishment. Deserting the tolerant policy of William III, the High-Church party, ascendant during the reign of Queen Anne (1702–14), secured the passage of a Test Act, requiring all officeholders in Ireland to take the sacrament according to prescriptions of the Church of England. Although aimed at Irish Catholics, the weight of this requirement fell heavily upon substantial Presbyterians who held magistracies and other civil posts. By extension, Presbyterian ministers could no longer perform legal marriages or even bury the dead, nor could "dissenters" teach school. This unwise law, though not everywhere rigidly enforced, caused resentment among the stubborn Scots, intensified by the fact that they had been loyal to the Crown and had proved a bulwark of defense against the rampageous Irish.

For all these reasons some five thousand Ulster Scots went to America in 1717 and 1718. After that initial migration, the pull of America began to exert more effect than the push from northern Ireland. Reports coming from the colonies were highly favorable, especially from Pennsylvania. Land was cheap and plentiful, authorities were well disposed, the soil was fertile beyond all imagination, and opportunities were boundless. Only two drawbacks loomed: the perils of an ocean crossing, and the expense of the passage. The former was very real in those days; but optimism persuaded young people that the nightmare of several weeks on a tiny, overcrowded ship, with much illness, was rarely fatal and that grim memories would soon fade. As for passage money, the practice of indenture had long been a familiar device. Few who had made up their minds to go would be deterred by having to work for a master in America for a period of years to pay off their passage fee, for then came freedom and a new life in a country which, according to some, resembled paradise.

Five great waves brought a quarter million Ulster Scots to America, turned them into Scotch-Irish Americans, depressed the economy of Ulster, and depopulated parts of that province. The tides ebbed and flowed partly with conditions in Ulster, partly with upsurges of what was called migration fever. The chief waves were those of 1717–18, 1725–29, 1740–41, 1754–55, and 1771–75; and each benefited particular colonies. The first two helped fill up the back country of Pennsylvania and soon began spilling over into the Shenandoah Valley of Virginia. The third further peopled the Shenandoah Valley and spread into the piedmont and upcountry of North Carolina. That colony and South Carolina

The port of Londonderry in northern Ireland in the 1700s was one of the major embarkation points for the Scotch-Irish emigrating to the New World.

drew most of the people in the fourth wave, while the final group, coming just before the Revolutionary War, spread out widely from New York to Georgia.

In each wave, other colonies drew settlers. Because the Delaware River early proved the favorite entryway, the colonies of New Jersey, Delaware, and Maryland soon had many Ulstermen. Massachusetts reluctantly admitted a few but so disliked their uncongenial ways that later arrivals in Boston went on to New Hampshire or Maine.

Two facts about the migration are significant for American history. First, there was almost no further influx from northern Ireland after the Revolutionary War; thus, there was no addition to the Scotch-Irish element from abroad nor any inducement to maintain sentimental ties or a "national" identity with a country ruled by England. Second, the concentration of Scotch-Irishmen in the geographically central colonies of Pennsylvania and Virginia made a kind of reservoir from which the people spread north and south through all other colonies; moreover, their farms just east of the Alleghenies were nearest the Great West when that vast territory opened up after 1783. Scotch-Irishmen were thus the vanguard of the trans-Allegheny pioneers. . . .

Scotch-Irishmen struck a real blow for religious liberty in this country. In 1738 the royal governor of Virginia and the Tidewater planters actively sought to persuade newcomers to the Pennsylvania frontier to leave that crowded region and settle in the Shenandoah Valley. An ancestor of John C. Calhoun presented to Governor William Gooch a memorial drawn up by the Presbyterian Synod of Philadelphia requiring religious toleration as a prerequisite for settlement. Gooch acceded to the demand, to the benefit of Virginia and of later American freedom. . . .

In education and religion it may be asserted that many American ideals and standards derive from the happy agreement of two self-assured colonial groups, the Scotch-Irish and the New England Yankees. Alone, neither people might have been weighty enough or (in the case of the Yankees) unprovincial enough to have prevailed; but their common Calvinism and earnestness gave America its first commitment to general education as well as its tendency to identify religion with upright moral character.

For both people, schools followed churches as the first institutions to be formed. The word of God must be expounded by educated ministers, and colonists could not send their sons abroad for training. The connection between church and school, going back to the Reformation, was to remain close for descendants of both Presbyterians and Puritans until the present century. Ministers were schoolmasters as well as preachers. Curricula in Scotch-Irish log schools on the frontier resembled those of the town schools in earlier New England, with training in the three R's, the Bible, and the catechisms, while higher education was directed toward training for the ministry. The Puritans founded Harvard and Yale well before the Presbyterians established Princeton and Hampden-Sydney and Dickinson; but from these first colleges came a host of others, whose students were not wholly ministerial. Until the Civil War the great majority of colleges in the country were founded by religious denominations and still remained under their control. (The state's responsibility for higher education had not yet been widely claimed.) Of the 207 permanent colleges founded before 1861, well over half were established by Presbyterians and New Englanders; and many of them were notable as "mothers" of still other colleges.

The distinctive religious influence of the Scotch-Irish and New Englanders was not in their common Calvinism, though certainly Calvinist theology has had its effect upon America: it was rather in persuading millions of Americans that religion and character are synonyms. In most other parts of the world religion is likely to mean ritual observance, adherence to a creed, customary pious acts, or some combination of these; but when an American says that a person is deeply religious he is likely to mean first of all that he is upright and highly moral. Both Puritans and Scotch-Irish insisted upon rectitude of life and behavior, stubborn adherence to principle, scorn of compromise, and a stern severity that could be as hard upon others as upon self. Neither people could accept the idea that a man's religious duty consisted only of acts performed on Sunday or of doctrinal orthodoxy. Since America quickly became pluralistic in religion, there could never have been agreement upon ritual, creed, or observances to unify us religiously; but all Americans could agree on admirable character and high moral rectitude. What the Puritans and Scotch-Irish made of religion was immensely reinforced when the Baptist and Methodist movements, rising to ascendancy in the nineteenth century, taught the same ideas.

In certain ways the Presbyterian Church of the Scotch-Irish was the first important denomination to become "Americanized" and broadly "American." In log churches on a frontier, with a congregation of pioneer farmers, many formal traditions of the dignified Presbyterian Church quietly vanished—the Geneva gown and stock, the separate pulpit, the attendance of the minister by a beadle, the set prayers. Many of the colonial Presbyterian ministers experimented with unconventional, direct methods of evangelism, in order to speak clearly to a people losing interest in dignity for the sake of tradition. (The approval of the presbyteries for this informality was not won, however; and because the dynamic Methodist and Baptists felt free to adopt resourceful methods of evangelism, they drew thousands of adherents among descendants of the Scotch-Irish.)

The Church of England was the established religion in six colonies and the Congregational faith in three others; both, then, were identified with the upper-class English Establishment; but the Presbyterian Church was nowhere official, elite, or English. Moreover, these other two dominant churches were regional, strong only in the Tidewater and in New England; but the Presbyterian Church, like the Scotch-Irish people, was present in every colony. Its ministers were supported not by legally exacted tithes but by free contributions of members; these ministers in their work moved freely from one region to another. The organization of the church was controlled by presbyteries that ranged from New York to the South. The "federal" structure of the church of the Scotch-Irish seemed congenial to American conditions and exerted a unifying influence in our early history.

If we of the twentieth century wish to admire the Scotch-Irish as representative prototypes of later Americans, we must ruefully note that their Ulster forefathers' neglect of things aesthetic was carried over to the new country. European visitors and critics in the nineteenth century, indeed, considered all Americans deficient in such matters; but we now know how wrong they were, for our museums are full of beautiful early American art and artifacts from New England, from the Tidewater, from German farmlands, and from many other regions and districts—but not from Scotch-Irish settlements. Nothing in the background of these people in either Scotland or northern Ireland had attracted them to painting, sculpture, architecture, music, and literature, and nothing in their way of life in the colonies apparently changed their attitude. They liked what was practical and seemed indifferent to whether it was beautiful. The lists of distinguished scions of the Scotch-Irish in nineteenth-century America include no names of artists and poets.

By 1800 the young United States was growing strong and self-confident, with a continent to win. Already the authority of the thirteen original states was losing its hold over the rising generation. If a farsighted historian of the time had been inclined to identify representative types of inhabitants who would probably become the most characteristic Americans of the new century, he might well have named the restless frontiersman and the rising middle-class townsman. The former was rapidly winning the West, clearing the wilderness, exploiting America's fabulous wealth, adding romance to the American myth; the latter was establishing law and order, building industry, adding comfort to utility, and treasuring respectability and responsibility. If the same historian had sought to find the embodiment of each of his representative types, he could have pointed immediately to the descendants of the vigorous Scotch-Irish, now thoroughly American, with no further accretions from abroad. Most of them had even forgotten the adjective formerly applied to them. The daily life of being an American was too absorbing to permit adulation of one's ancestors, even though these had been the admirable Scotch-Irish.

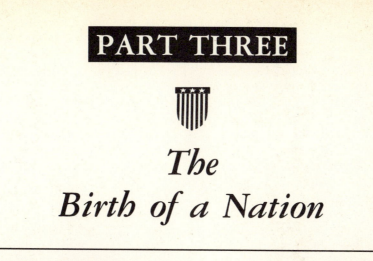

PART THREE

The
Birth of a Nation

In Daniel Berger's 1784 engraving, defiant Bostonians burn newspapers and documents carrying the stamp demanded by the act of 1765.

George III, Our Last King

J. H. Plumb

One of the most difficult tasks of the historian is to deal fairly with failure, with incompetence—even with evil. He must try to honor Othello's plea and speak of men (and institutions) as they actuallywere—"nothing extenuate, nor set down aught in malice." In this essay one of England's premier historians, Professor J. H. Plumb of Cambridge University, succeeds brilliantly in achieving this objective.

Professor Plumb's analysis of America's last king, the unfortunate and much-maligned George III, lays bare the monarch's inadequacies but describes him with sympathy and understanding. As a result, we learn a great deal not only about George III but also about eighteenth-century British politics and thus about the causes of the American Revolution. George III is easy to caricature or to portray as the devil incarnate, and as Plumb points out, historians have done both these things repeatedly. Their accounts have often been entertaining, but they have explained very little about the man and his times. By treating him as he has, however, Plumb makes George III and the tragic events of the early years of his long reign plausible and thus meaningful.

Professor Plumb has written, among many books, The First Four Georges, England in the Eighteenth Century: 1714–1815 *and two volumes of a definitive biography of Sir Robert Walpole.*

Poor George III still gets a bad press. In a famous television talk in London, the Prime Minister of Great Britain suggested to the President of the United States that the kind of colonial policy associated with the name of George III still distorted the American view of the nature and function of the British Empire, and Mr. Eisenhower smilingly agreed. It is not surprising. Since Jefferson's great philippic in the Declaration of Independence, few historians, English or American, have had many good words to say for him. True, he has been excused direct responsibility for many items of the catalogue of enormities that Jefferson went on to lay at his door, but to the ordinary man he remains one of England's disastrous kings, like John or the two Jameses.

Actually, . . . toward the end of his life and immediately after it his reputation improved, and even the writers of American school textbooks did not at first hold him personally responsible for the disasters that led to independence. They held his ministers responsible. It was after the publication of Horace Walpole's *Memoirs* in 1845 that George III began to be blamed. Walpole's gossip appeared to give substance to Burke's allegations that the King deliberately attempted to subvert the British constitution by packing ministries and Parliament with his personal party—the King's friends—a collection of corrupt politicians bought with place and with pension.

Later historians held that these Tory incompetents, bent on personal government for their master, pursued a ruinous policy that ended only with the breakup of the first British Empire and a return of the Whigs to power. Historians reminded themselves not only of the disasters in America, but the failure of parliamentary reform in England, of the oppressions of the Irish, the Catholics, the Dissenters; they remembered the treatment of radicals at the time of the French Revolution; they recalled the merciless suppression of trade unions; the violent opposition to the abolition of slavery. It all added up to a huge indictment of George III and a magnificent justification for Whig doctrine. Here and there a scholar urged caution, but was little heeded. What the great historians formulated, the textbook writers cribbed. When English historians found so much to condemn, why should Americans lag behind? In 1954, two American historians—Leon Canfield and Howard Wilder—could write:

In 1760, George III mounted the throne. A young man of twenty-two, he was unwilling to accept the idea that the King's power should be limited. His mother had always said to him: "George, be King!" When he became ruler this obstinate young man put his mother's advice into swift action. He set out to get his way not by ignoring Parliament but by building up a personal following. He made free use of bribes and appointments, and presently the King's friends were strong in Parliament.

The increase in royal power drove the wedge of misunderstanding deeper between England and the colonies.

The young George III was portrayed in his coronation robes by court painter Allan Ramsay.

In 1959, an English historian, Jack Lindsay, was still writing in much the same vein. These views, however, are no longer fashionable. The greatest living English historian of the eighteenth century, Sir Lewis Namier, has hammered at them for thirty years. His friend, Romney Sedgwick, with a more caustic pen and no less scholarship, has subjected them to ridicule in review after review, sinking his verbal darts into reputations as skillfully as a savage at his blowpipe. Professor Herbert Butterfield has not only traced the origins of the myths of George III's tyranny but has also shown how the now-fashionable view of George III was held by historians and textbook writers long, long ago in the early nineteenth century. So the wheel has come full circle. Will it turn again? Or will blame and justification give way simply to understanding? Shall we at last have a balanced portrait of America's last king?

On one thing historians are agreed. To understand the part played by George III in the great tragedy of his reign, one must begin with the King's own personality and with the environment in which he was reared. David and Absalom provided the pattern of family relationship of European monarchs and their sons and heirs in the eighteenth century, except that most of the monarchs were less controlled than David. Peter the Great of Russia had his son Alexis executed—slowly and painfully. The Elector of Prussia, Frederick William, insisted that his son, whom he had kept in close confinement, watch the death of his dearest friend for what only a madman could call treason. So it is not surprising to learn that George III's grandmother wished that her son, Frederick, father of George III, were in the bottommost pit of hell or that she became almost hysterical on her deathbed when she thought he might inherit some of her personal possessions. The Lord Chancellor had to be sent for to lull her fears.

George II's opinion of his own lackluster son matched his wife's. He quite simply hated him as he had hated his own father, who, at one time, had put him under house arrest and removed his children. (It had required all the persuasive powers of the Cabinet to get him released.) This fantastic antagonism between father and son that went on from generation to generation found a situation in English politics that fitted it like a glove. The House of Commons always harbored a number of disappointed politicians who were so hated by the ministers in power that they had few prospects of immediate advancement. But as Sir Robert Walpole bluntly phrased it: "Everybody who could get no ready money had rather have a bad promissory note than nothing." So they made their court to the heir, who found them jobs in his household, and plotted the political changes that they would make when Father died. So throughout the century a Prince of Wales as soon as he was grown up became the leader of the Opposition. At times the Opposition made such a nuisance of itself that the monarch and his ministry decided to buy it off by giving jobs to the leaders, and the astonished heir apparent found his friends deserting him with alacrity. This happened both to George III and to his father. The politics of hatred and the politics of betrayal, therefore, became a part of the environment of the adolescence and early manhood of the Hanoverian kings.

It was in an atmosphere of faction that George III was born; an environment that might have taxed the most gifted of men. Unfortunately George III was as unlucky in his heredity as in his environment. Neither George II nor his Queen, Caroline, was devoid of character or without some gifts above the commonplace. Her intelligence and his memory were unusual in monarchs, and their hatred of their son was tinged with genuine disappointment. Frederick, George III's father, was known to posterity as "Poor Fred," and the epithet was not unjust. He possessed a small talent for music, a mild interest in games, particularly cricket, and little else. The unsympathetic Lord Shelburne described his life as a "tissue of childishness and falsehood"; and his friends as well as his enemies despised him. George II married his son to Princess Augusta of Saxe-Gotha simply because there was no one else. The other Protestant princesses of sufficiently high birth had madness in their families, and George II rejected them, for as he said, "I did not think ingrafting my half-witted coxcomb upon a madwoman would mend the breed." As it turned out, it could not have made matters much worse, for an astonishing number of Princess Augusta's children and grandchildren turned out to be congenital idiots, or subject to fits of insanity, or mentally unbalanced, or blind; the rest were odd or wicked or both.

In some ways George III can be described as the best of the bunch. He was very stupid, really stupid. Had he been born in different circumstances it is unlikely that he could have earned a living except as an unskilled manual laborer. He was eleven before he could read, and he never mastered grammar or spelling or punctuation. He was lethargic, apathetic, childish, a clod of a boy whom no one could teach. His major response to life was a doting love for his brother, Edward. In late adolescence he began to wake up, largely because of a passionately romantic attachment to Lord Bute, the close friend and confidant of his mother.* Somehow Bute made the young prince conscious not only of his destiny but also of his shortcomings. The Prince promised time and time again to throw off his lethargy so that he could accomplish great things for Bute's sake. Naturally the greatest of things was to get rid of his grandfather's evil ministers and to install Bute in a position of power. The ill-spelt, ungrammatical, childish, heart-felt notes that he sent to Bute make pathetic reading. They are charged with a sense of inadequacy, a feeling of hopelessness before the immensity of the burden which destiny had laid on his shoulders, and with an anxious need for help that is almost neurotic in its intensity.

Every year his reverence for the concept of kingship grew stronger; nothing illustrates his regard more than his behavior over Lady Sarah Lennox. This charming girl of fifteen swept him off his feet just before he succeeded to the throne. He longed to marry her. Bute said no, and George III wrote that "he [*i.e.,* Bute] has thoroughly convinced me of the impropriety of marrying a country woman; the interest of my country ever shall be my first care, my own inclinations shall ever submit to it." And submit he did and married a dull, plain, German Protestant princess who bore him the huge family that was to plague his days.

A sexually timid, if nonetheless passionate man, George may have found it

---

*The public thought she was his mistress. Almost certainly she was not. The slander deeply distressed George III and made his attachment to Bute firmer.

James Gillray did this caricature of the penny-wise and pound-foolish monarch in 1791.

easier to take Bute's advice than many have thought. Lady Sarah attracted lovers as a candle moths, and George, conscious of his faults and of his inadequacies, must have realized that he cut a poor figure amidst *her* brilliant courtiers. His Queen, Charlotte, attracted no one. And yet sacrifice there was, and George paid for it. Shortly after his marriage he experienced his first bout of insanity. Later in life these periods of madness grew longer. It was only during these attacks that his thoughts escaped from his strict concept of marriage, and rioted in adultery. Then, and then only, was it unsafe for a lady of his court to be alone with him.

During these years of delayed adolescence George III learned, too, that kings had to make other sacrifices. Men powerfully backed in the Lords and Commons, and with an experience of a lifetime's politics behind them, could not easily be dismissed. The great Whig families had ruled since the Hanoverian accession in 1714. They had filled the court of the Georges, monopolized the great offices of state, controlled the Cabinet, dominated the House of Lords, managed the Commons, and run the war with France which had lasted more or less for twenty years. The Duke of Newcastle, George II's Secretary of State, had held an important position in government since he had reached his majority. The Dukes of Devonshire took their high offices as if they belonged to them by hereditary right. Even the Whig career politicians, such as the Lord Chancellor Hardwicke, had been in power for so long that they had come to regard themselves as practically irreplaceable.

These men were not to be easily swept away and replaced by Bute; they possessed too much cunning, too much political experience, too many followers whom they had gratified with places. They doubted Bute's capacity to survive. And still time was on George III's side. The great Whig leaders were old men; indeed their party was known as the Old Corps. And in their long lives they had made plenty of enemies. They had disappointed some members of Parliament, made others impatient, and many disapproved of their policy. Chatham, that hawk-eyed man of destiny who had been responsible more than any other man for the sweeping English victories in the Seven Years' War, deplored their caution, ignored their advice, and treated them, as one of his colleagues grumbled, "as inferior animals." And behind Chatham was the restless brood of Grenvilles, his relations by marriage—difficult, disloyal, able and ambitious men. There was yet another powerful group, led by the immensely rich Duke of Bedford, who thought it high time for the old Whigs to retire, and let them enjoy the rich pastures of court patronage.

The King's intentions, of course, were known to all these groups in 1760. His aversion to Newcastle and to Chatham, whom he labeled "the blackest of hearts," was common court gossip. And after all, he was a young king with old ministers; many time-serving politicians thought that it might be wise to trim their sails and wait for the new breeze, from whatever quarter it might blow. Of course the old Whigs, and even Chatham, realized they had to accept Bute and somehow or other please the King, if they were to survive. They soon had the measure of Bute. He lacked a personal following, felt unequal to the supreme task of ruling the country and running the war. His dependable allies in the House of Commons were few. He faltered; he hesitated; he failed to force a showdown and kick out the old Whigs. True, Chatham resigned in a huff because, knowing the King's pacific sentiments, the Cabinet refused to go along with him and declare war on Spain and seize her trade. Instead, as Chatham forecast, Spain declared war on England.

But Chatham gone did little to strengthen Bute. By the end of January, 1763, the consummate skill of those hoary old politicians Newcastle and Hardwicke had so undermined Bute's confidence that he was little better than a nervous wreck. He told George III that even the Angel Gabriel would find it difficult to govern England; that his own life was rendered intolerable by infamous scenes and blackened by ingratitude and that he felt himself on the brink of a precipice. George III was too young, too inept, too unpracticed in the arts of politics to help Bute, and so Bute resigned. George III tried to keep him as a private and secret adviser; the politicians would not let him. They grumbled, they nagged, they bullied. The King had to face his future on his own.

He was most reluctant to do so. Although peace had been achieved in 1763— he had ardently desired this—he soon found himself in the thick of problems which he felt too vast for his poor comprehension. Yet he knew that the fate of his people and his Empire was *his* responsibility to God. He felt so young, so hopeless, so desperately in need of help for someone who thought as he did on men and affairs yet was strong enough to force his will on the warring political factions. Although the old Whig empire had broken up under the strain of Chatham's resignation and the Treaty of Paris, yet the King found no stability. The King's necessity drove him back to Chatham. Chatham prided himself on being above party. The King's need, the nation's need, required men of ability, not politicians; sentiments that thrilled George III. But unfortunately Chatham's

*George III's closet adviser, Frederick Lord North,
from a mezzotint published in 1775.*

mental health was far from good, and no sooner had he become Prime Minister
than the strain of office sent him off his head. He shut himself up, would speak
to no one, and had his meals served through a trap door. The King waited and
waited for him to recover for two long years, during which a leaderless ministry
drove his country nearer to ruin. Chatham recovered only to resign and became
a passionate supporter of the American cause and so, once more, the object of
George III's hate. The ministries that followed earned neither the country's
confidence nor the King's.

Thus the first ten years of George III's reign passed in political chaos; slowly,
however, he learned the devious ways of politics, the price of men, and above all
the necessity for a man who could manage the Commons in *his* interest. In 1770
he discovered Lord North, the eldest son of the Earl of Guilford; North, whose
association with the King was to prove so disastrous for England and so fortunate
for America, was an odd character. An excellent administrator, a witty and practiced debater, full of good humor and charm, he always pleased and soothed the
members of the Commons; nevertheless his soft, fat, rounded body and full,
piglike face bespoke an indolence that bordered on disease, a physical incapacity
that made his laborious days an intolerable burden on his spirit. Time and time
again he begged the King to release him from office. The King would not, for
North reverenced as he did the mystical power of monarchy and thought as he
did on the two grave political problems which vexed his country—Wilkes and
America.

Without North, he could see only ruin for himself and his people. The
constantly changing ministries and the bitter factional strife of George III's first
ten years had bedeviled both problems. John Wilkes, wit, libertine, master tacti-
cian, raised fundamental issues concerning the liberty of the British subject. None

of the cases in which he was involved was clear-cut; in each the ministerial cause was handled with massive ineptitude. Wilkes divided the Whig groups in Parliament as effectively as he united the discontented in London. George hated "that devil Wilkes," and let this hatred be known to all and sundry. Thus Wilkes's supporters could talk of royal despotism and get others to believe them. In America Wilkes's name became a byword for liberty and for resistance to royal tyranny from Boston down the seaboard to Charleston.

America proved a graver problem than Wilkes; and the effect of ministerial changes far worse. After the great war with France which, through the Treaty of Paris, deprived her of Canada, the majority of Englishmen, and, indeed, many colonists, felt that some of the expenses of the conflict should be borne by the Americans. Each ministry from 1760–70 differed in its views as to how this should be done, and each had a separate solution for assuaging the bitterness aroused in the Americans by the inept attempts to get revenue. Acts passed by one ministry were repealed by its successor, and party maneuver became more important than the fate of America. Nor was it the question of revenue alone that infuriated the colonists—the British constantly betrayed their ignorance of American needs and American aspirations. They tried to restrict settlement beyond the Allegheny Mountains, took Indian affairs into their own hands, attempted to suppress paper currency, renovated oppressive customs laws, and restricted trade with the West Indies. No Englishman realized that the American colonies were moving toward a rapid expansion in trade, wealth, and power, just as no American could conceive of the huge expense of war that arose from Britain's vast imperial connections.

By the late 1760's, hope for compromise was probably a delusive dream of men of good will such as Chatham and Franklin. But whether it had a chance or not, there can be no doubt that the known attitude of the King made matters worse. George III revered, naturally enough, the concept of kingship. Kings were God's immediate servants. Their duties were clear—to pass on all the rights, obligations, powers, territories, undiminished, to their heirs. The constitution was sacrosanct and unchangeable. And so absolutely did George III identify himself with the English Crown that any criticism of monarchical powers, any suggestion of reform or change, he regarded as a personal affront.

The King was so stupid that he could not distinguish between himself as a person and his constitutional position as ruler. Although he accepted the American policies—either of compromise or coercion—with which his ministers presented him, placing his signature first on the Stamp Act and then on its repeal, his heart was always with the physical-force party, and he moved with uttermost reluctance to the idea of compromise, which, he thought, would infuriate as well as ruin Britain.* Those politicians, therefore, who were prepared to bring the

---

*As may be seen from his letter to North of January 31, 1776: "You will remember that before the recess, I strongly advised you not to bind yourself to bring forward a proposition for restoring tranquillity to North America, not from any absurd ideas of unconditional submission my mind never harboured; but from foreseeing that whatever can be proposed, will be liable, not to bring America back to a sense of attachment to the Mother Country, yet to dissatisfy this Country, which has in the

"American rebels," as the King called them, to their senses were the recipients of his warmhearted loyalty and devotion. In the small world of English political society, the King's views did not go for nothing. He was the fountain of patronage, the ultimate executive authority, the man who could make and break ministers and ministries. In consequence, the King's attitude began to polarize new attitudes in politics. He became the symbol of conservatism and reaction; his opponents, the men who thought that the liberties for which Wilkes and the Americans fought were essential, too, for all Englishmen, began to take a more radical attitude not only to the Crown but also to the very structure of English society. Naturally, the first effect of this was to disrupt the old political alignments; Whiggery began to break up into two groups, a right and a left wing; the Tories, who had been in opposition since 1714, now felt that they could support George III body and soul. It took many years for these new forces to push their way through into public consciousness, redefined, but George III's own personality—his meddling interference and his blind, obstinate conservatism—sharpened many men's intention to reduce the powers of the Crown even further.

The first twenty years of George III's reign were a public and a personal failure. He had done his duty conscientiously. He had tried, according to his lights, to put the government in the hands of tried and able men. The ills which assailed his country, he sincerely believed, were not of his making. Scarcely a man pitied him; the majority thought he had only himself to blame when disaster came. Yorktown ended his hopes that the tide might turn, and finished North.

During the long years of British defeat, the Old Corps of Whigs, now led by the Marquis of Rockingham, had developed a new view of the role of kingship; and their great publicist and philosopher, Edmund Burke, had persuasively pleaded for a new attitude to party and to politics. When, at last, the failures in America led the independent members of the Commons to desert North, and thereby compelled the King to send for Rockingham to take over the reins of government, George found Rockingham's terms hard to accept: freedom for America, peace with France, and hardest of all, no say in the appointment of his ministers, which he regarded as the darling prerogative of the Crown.

The King, despite himself, now had to accept what the Whigs offered him—a revolutionary action that cut at the root of royal power. He had been broken by forces that his poor brain could not understand. And, perhaps not without justice, he was held to blame for England's defeat in America by contemporaries in both countries, and by generations of historians, though justice would also demand that the shortsighted, quarrelsome, ignorant, power-seeking politicians who had made policy toward America as changeable as the British climate should be held equally responsible. We, at least, can feel pity for him—ignorant, stupid, conscientious, prejudiced, a victim of his own inadequate temperament. . . .

His motives were honorable; he gave all of his pitifully small abilities to the defense of what he thought to be the vital interests and essential rights of the

---

most handsome manner cheerfully carried on the contest, and therefore has a right to have the struggle continued, until convinced that it is in vain."

The second Marquis of Rockingham, leader of the Whigs, the party that forced George III to accept peace with the rebellious colonies.

British nation. Had he been as wise as Solomon, Britain and America would have gone their separate ways. The forces that crushed him would have crushed greater men. As it is, he remained a pathetic figure of tragicomedy; and, as the years passed, he acquired even a certain grandeur. There had been many worse kings to exercise rule over America and Britain. If he is to be blamed, it must be not for what he did but for what he was—an unbalanced man of low intelligence. And if he is to be praised, it is because he attempted to discharge honorably tasks that were beyond his powers.

The Ordeal of Thomas Hutchinson

Bernard Bailyn

The furor that erupted in the colonies in 1765 when Great Britain attempted to collect new stamp taxes on legal documents, periodicals, and all sorts of printed matter has long interested historians because the Stamp Act was a major milestone along the road that led to the American Revolution. The sacking of the house of Lieutenant Governor Thomas Hutchinson of Massachusetts by a Boston mob was one of the most shocking examples of the violence that occurred at this time. It has often been said that Hutchinson was singled out because he was a vigorous supporter of the Stamp Act. Actually, as Bernard Bailyn of Harvard University points out in the following pages, Hutchinson considered the Stamp Act a mistake and had sought to prevent its passage by Parliament. Why, in spite of this, he was so cordially disliked by the people of Boston is the subject of this essay. Professor Bailyn is the author of a biography of Hutchinson and, among other books, The Origins of American Politics *and* Pamphlets of the American Revolution.

On the night of August 26, 1765, a mob, more violent than any yet seen in America, more violent indeed than any that would be seen in the entire course of the Revolution, attacked the Boston mansion of Thomas Hutchinson, chief justice and lieutenant governor of Massachusetts. Hardly giving Hutchinson and his family time to flee from the supper table into the streets, the rioters smashed in the doors with axes, swarmed through the rooms, ripped off wainscoting and hangings, splintered the furniture, beat down the inner walls, tore up the garden, and carried off into the night, besides £900 sterling in cash, all the plate, decorations, and clothes that had survived, and destroyed or scattered in the mud all of Hutchinson's books and papers, including the manuscript of Volume I of his *History of the Colony and Province of Massachusetts-Bay* and the collection of historical papers that he had been gathering for years as the basis for a public archive. The determination of the mob was as remarkable as its savagery: "they worked for three hours at the cupola before they could get it down," Governor Francis Bernard reported; only the heavy brickwork construction of the walls prevented their razing the building completely, "though they worked at it till daylight. The next day the streets were found scattered with money, plate, gold rings, etc. which had been dropped in carrying off." Hutchinson was convinced that he himself would have been killed if he had not given in to his daughter's frantic pleading and fled. He estimated the loss of property at £2,218 sterling.

People of all political persuasions, everywhere in the colonies, were shocked at such "savageness unknown in a civilized country." Hutchinson appeared in court the next day without his robes, and as the young lawyer Josiah Quincy, Jr., who would later pursue him like a fury, reported, the chief justice, "with tears starting from his eyes and a countenance which strongly told the inward anguish of his soul," addressed the court. He apologized for his appearance: he had no other clothes but what he wore, he said, and some of that was borrowed. His family was equally destitute, and their distress was "infinitely more insupportable than what I feel for myself."

> Sensible that I am innocent, that all the charges against me are false, I cannot help feeling—and though I am not obliged to give an answer to all the questions that may be put me by every lawless person, yet I call GOD to witness (and I would not for a thousand worlds call my *Maker* to witness to a falsehood)—I say, I call my *Maker* to witness that I never, in New England or Old, in Great Britain or America, neither directly nor indirectly, was aiding, assisting, or supporting, or in the least promoting or encouraging what is commonly called the STAMP ACT, but on the contrary, did all in my power, and strove as much as in me lay, to prevent it. This is not declared through timidity, for I have nothing to fear. They can only take away my life, which is of but little value when deprived of all its comforts, all that is dear to me, and nothing surrounding me but the most piercing distress. . . .

What had caused the riot? Resistance to the Stamp Act had generally been violent; and individuals, especially the would-be stamp distributors, had commonly been attacked. But no one in America had been as deliberately and savagely assaulted as Hutchinson, though he had not been appointed a stamp master

The imposing town mansion of Thomas Hutchinson before the mob attacked.

and though, as he said, he had opposed the Stamp Act. What was the meaning and what would be the ultimate effect of the attack?

On July fourth, 1776, almost eleven stormy years after the sack of his mansion, Thomas Hutchinson, by now the exiled Loyalist governor of Massachusetts, was awarded an honorary doctorate of civil laws by Oxford University. "Probably no distinction which Hutchinson ever attained was more valued by him," his nineteenth-century biographer wrote; certainly none so fittingly symbolizes the tragedy of his life. For he was honored as an American—the most distinguished as well as the most loyal colonial-born official of his time. Provincial assemblyman, speaker of the Massachusetts House of Representatives, councillor, lieutenant governor, chief justice, governor, he had gone through the entire course of public offices and of official honors, and he was in addition America's most accomplished historian. But to the people who on the day of Hutchinson's award proclaimed their nation's independence, he was one of the most hated men on earth—more hated than Lord North, more hated than George III (both of whom, it was believed, he had secretly influenced). . . .

. . . The feeling was widespread among well-informed Americans that Thomas Hutchinson had betrayed his country; that for sordid, selfish reasons he had accepted and abetted—even stimulated—oppressive measures against the colonies; that he had supported them even in the face of a threat of armed resistance; and that in this sense his personal actions lay at the heart of the Revolution. So it was said, again and again. Was it true?

It is hard to imagine a man less disposed by background or heritage to betray his countrymen than Thomas Hutchinson. His family had helped to found New England, and they had prospered with its growth. Until Thomas only one of the family had been famous: the notorious seventeenth-century Anne, who had refused to adjust her singular convictions to the will of the community, for which she had been banished, to die in exile. But the family's main interest had never been hers. The Hutchinsons had been tradesmen in London before the Puritan migration; in New England they became merchants and remained merchants, with remarkable consistency, generation after generation. In the course of a century and a half they produced, in the stem line of the family, not a single physician, not a single lawyer, and not a single teacher or minister. The entire clan devoted itself to developing its property and the network of trade, based on kinship lines at every point, that Anne's brothers and nephews had created in the mid-seventeenth century. They prospered solidly but not greatly. Their enterprises were careful, not grand. They were accumulators, down-to-earth, unromantic middle-men, whose solid, petit-bourgeois characteristics became steadily more concentrated in the passage of years until in Thomas, in the fifth generation, they reached an apparently absolute and perfect form.

He was born in Boston in 1711. His father, Colonel Thomas Hutchinson, had risen somewhat, though not greatly, beyond the level of his two prosperous merchant-shipowner relatives, Elisha and Eliakim. The colonel served on the provincial Council for over twenty years, donated the building for a Latin grammar school (which his son would attend), and improved into provincial magnificence the imposing town house bequeathed to him by a widowed aunt. The

colonel's marriage fitted perfectly the pattern of his classically bourgeois existence. His wife, Sarah Foster, ten years his senior, was the daughter of John
Foster, the Boston merchant to whom he had been apprenticed in trade, of status
identical to the Hutchinson family's, who engaged in the same kinds of trade as
they did and to whom, by force of the remarkable endogamy that characterizes
the family history, Colonel Thomas became triply related by other marriages
between the two families.

Colonel Thomas set the pattern for young Thomas' life. He was industrious,
charitable, unaffected, unworldly, and clannish. A strait-laced, pious provincial,
he read the Scriptures to his family mornings and evenings and devoted himself
to trade and to the welfare of his kin and community. For over thirty years, his
son later recorded, Colonel Thomas "kept a table on Saturdays with a salt fish
or bacalao [codfish] dinner." To this unpretentious feast he regularly invited only
four close friends, all of them merchants, two of them relatives; only "now and
then," his son recalled, was a clergyman added to the group.

For young Thomas, the future governor, there was no break in the continuity
of family and community life. He entered Harvard at the age of twelve, where he
developed not so much the intellectual interests that later became important to
him as his ability and resources in trade. At the time he entered college, he
recalled a half century later, his father undertook his proper education by presenting him with "two or three quintals of fish." From this humble capital he managed
to build, by "adventuring to sea" through his college years, a fund of £4–500
sterling, which, combined with an inheritance from his father, became a fortune,
by provincial standards, by the time of the Revolution: in cash fifteen times his
original capital, and in real estate eight houses, including the Boston mansion he
had inherited, two wharves and a variety of lots and shop properties in Boston,
and in suburban Milton a country house universally admired for its simple beauty
and splendid setting and a hundred acres of choice land.

. . . At the age of twenty-six, Hutchinson entered politics. He was never
thereafter out of it, and he maintained an altogether consistent policy in defense
of what, until the great issues of the 1760's intervened, were widely considered
to be the basic interests of the colony. As representative of Boston to the Massachusetts House from 1737 to 1749 (with the exception of a single year) and a
councillor for the succeeding seventeen years, he distinguished himself by his
effective defense of a hard-money policy and by his equally determined defense
of the territorial integrity of Massachusetts and of its chartered rights. So convinced was the community of Hutchinson's "disinterestedness and integrity,"
Pownall reported in 1757, that even those who most sharply disagreed with him
continued to respect him, even to revere him. In the end Hutchinson's views on
the money question prevailed, in part because of the shrewd use that Massachusetts, led by Hutchinson, was able to make of the specie it received from the
English government as repayment for its contribution to the war against France;
and in part because when in 1741 the issue developed into a crisis that threatened
violence, Governor Jonathan Belcher had seized the initiative and stamped out
the incipient rebellion by force. There was no limit, Belcher wrote Hutchinson
in a portentous letter of 1741, to what political fanatics would do; they would even
defy Parliament, for the common people were told by their leaders that they were

out of the reach of the government of England, and the Assembly was made to think they were as big as the Parliament of Great Britain. "They are grown so brassy and hardy as to be now combining in a body to raise a rebellion. . . . I have this day sent the sheriff and his officers to apprehend some of the heads of the conspirators, so you see we are becoming ripe for a smarter sort of government."

In 1740 Hutchinson was sent by the colony to England to plead the case of certain Massachusetts landowners whose property had fallen to New Hampshire in a Crown ruling on the colony's boundary, and he negotiated repeatedly, almost annually, with the border Indians in the interest of his native colony, managed the province's lottery, supervised the financing of the Louisbourg expedition of 1745, dealt with other colonies on joint military efforts, and adjudicated boundary disputes with Connecticut and Rhode Island.

It is hard to see what more he could have done to serve his countrymen or how, as a leader of the establishment in trade and politics, he could have been more enlightened.

Yet in the end his services were forgotten and he was cursed as a traitor in the land of his birth—cursed not merely by the wild men, the alarmists, the political paranoids, and the professional agitators, but by some of the most stable, sensible people of the time, many of whom knew him personally. There was, they said, some deep flaw in his character, some perversion of personality, some profound "malignancy of heart," that had turned his patriotism into treason andled him to sacrifice the general good for the most sordid, selfish gain. . . .

Until 1757 Hutchinson had been one of those establishment figures who knew how to find their way successfully through the paths of factional intrigue. As a young man he had had Governor Belcher's favor, and in 1740 Hutchinson had gravitated to Belcher's successor, the ambitious and well-connected English lawyer William Shirley. For almost two decades thereafter Hutchinson had remained a leader of Governor Shirley's unusually stable political coalition.

Governor Thomas Pownall, who succeeded Shirley as governor in 1757, elevated Hutchinson to the lieutenant governorship, but he was a man with whom Hutchinson would struggle, directly or indirectly, for the rest of his life.

Pownall's administration was a brief interlude between the long, late-colonial era of William Shirley, which had nourished the young Thomas Hutchinson's success in trade and politics, and the disastrous decade of Sir Francis Bernard, in which Hutchinson's failure began; but though brief it was a critical interlude. For in these years Hutchinson's devotion to the welfare of the empire and his identification of America's well-being with the strength of Great Britain had become an intense commitment. At the same time his differences with the momentarily triumphant opposition forces, with which Pownall had allied himself, had become charged with more than ordinary political meaning. They were of course his rivals in quite traditional factional contests for the control of public offices. But beyond that he had been shocked by their pursuit of private gain at the expense of the general welfare, which he took to mean the welfare of the pan-Atlantic polity that had protected the infant colonies for a century and a half, and he distrusted the glib libertarianism by which they justified their resistance to appeals for wartime sacrifices.

The new governor, Francis Bernard, was the ideal type of the patronage

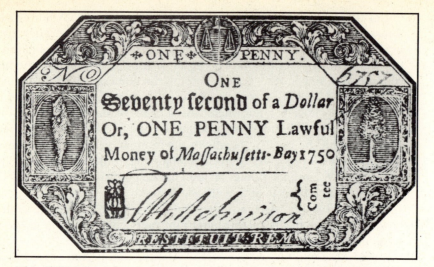

This 1750 Massachusetts paper penny bears the signature of Hutchinson,
who was a member of a committee in charge of issuing letters of credit.

appointee in the first British Empire. A well-educated barrister whose only administrative or political office in England had been the recordership of the town of
Boston in Lincolnshire, he had practiced law until the financial needs of his ten
children drove him to seek more lucrative employment in the colonies. Through
the patronage of his wife's influential uncle, Viscount Barrington, he was appointed to the governorship of New Jersey in 1758 and then, feeling socially and
culturally isolated there and seeking a better-paying position, managed to have
himself transferred, at the age of fifty, to Massachusetts. He was a decent man who
had simple, uncomplicated desires: peace and quiet, the respect of those he ruled,
some comradeship in literary matters, appointments for his six sons, and a substantial income—from salary, from fees, and from lucrative investments. As far
as he knew, the prospects in Massachusetts were excellent. "I am assured," he
wrote shortly before he arrived in Boston, "that I may depend upon a quiet and
easy administration." True, he had heard from Pownall the discouraging news
(along with accounts of investment opportunities in northern New England land)
that the total income of the Massachusetts governor, from salary and "all advantages and contingencies," was only £1,200 sterling; but he thought he could live
more cheaply in Boston than in many other places, and in addition he would have
far better opportunities for educating and providing jobs for his children there
than he had had in Perth Amboy. Moreover, in Boston, "perhaps the most
polished and scientific town in America," he was sure he would find the "refined
conversation and the amusements that arise from letters, arts, and sciences
. . . many very conversable men, tolerable music, and other amusements to which
I had bid adieu not without regret." Finally, he had heard that the Massachusetts
governor had (in the fortress to which he would repeatedly flee in the years to
come) "a very pretty place to retire to, a pleasant apartment in Castle William,
which stands in an island about three miles from the town at the entrance of the
Bay."

He was thus a well-disposed and ordinary man, with ordinary desires, but he was no politician and he was innocent of the arts of governance. "Open in his behavior," Hutchinson wrote of him, "regardless of mere forms, and inattentive to the fashionable arts of engaging mankind," he was destined by his manner alone to offend the sensibilities of the proud Bostonians. But it was not simply a question of manner and sensibilities. He was determined to get every penny to which his office entitled him. It was this mainly that led him to his fatal decision to appoint Hutchinson to the vacant chief justiceship; and it was this—well before the Stamp Act raised fundamental questions of principle—that first pitched Hutchinson into open conflict with the opposition merchants and populist politicians.

Hutchinson had not sought the chief justiceship, which fell vacant when the incumbent, Stephen Sewall, died five weeks after Bernard arrived in Boston, nor had he attempted to solicit Bernard's patronage or to forge a political alliance with him. But if Hutchinson did not seek Bernard's support, Bernard had reason to seek his. Though the Assembly quickly granted the new governor a substantial salary and then went beyond that to give him the gift of Mount Desert Island, off the southeast coast of Maine, he quickly discovered the difficulty of maintaining the "quiet and easy" administration he had expected. The province, he found, was "divided into parties so nearly equal that it would have been madness for me to have put myself at the head of either of them." In this situation "management and intrigue," he wrote to Barrington, were required to preserve the force of government and at the same time convey at least "the appearance" of respect for the colonists' cherished liberties, "of which they formed high and sometimes unconstitutional ideas."

The appointment of the new chief justice was crucial to the success of this delicate balance. For it was the superior court in the end that would largely determine whether the interest of the state would be sustained in general, and in particular whether the trade regulations would be enforced and whether therefore the governor would receive his statutory third of the income from forfeited goods.

Bernard knew that Governor Shirley had promised the next court vacancy to the venerable Barnstable lawyer James Otis, Sr., then speaker of the House and, in Shirley's time, a political colleague of Hutchinson's. But word reached Bernard that Otis' appointment at this juncture would be inadvisable, perhaps because his brilliant but unstable son James, Jr., was leading the family into doubtful political alliances and was reluctant to use his office as deputy advocate-general of the vice-admiralty court to prosecute violations of the navigation laws. Hutchinson's commitment to maintaining close ties between England and America, on the other hand, was beyond question, as was his reputation with all parties for integrity, industry, judiciousness, and devotion to public service.

The day after Sewall died, "several gentlemen" (Bernard said they were "the best men in the government") told Hutchinson they were proposing him for the vacancy. He was pleasantly surprised, but he immediately expressed what he called "a diffidence of my own abilities," for he was no lawyer and he was not at all certain "that it would be advisable for me to undertake so great a trust." He repeated these same doubts "of my abilities to give the country satisfaction" when young James Otis called on him to seek his support for the elder Otis' appointment; and while he did not promise the Otises his help and said merely that the whole question was new to him and that he would have to think about it, he went out of his way to praise the elder Otis and to register his own lack of enthusiasm for the appointment. His passivity persisted even though most of the judiciary assured him of their support. When, after a month, Bernard finally broached the subject to him, explaining that "the major voices seemed to be in my favor," Hutchinson replied that while recognizing the importance of the position, he knew "the peculiar disadvantages I should be under" in following so distinguished a jurist as Sewall. And when some weeks later Bernard told him that he had definitely decided to appoint him and indicated that even if he refused he would not turn to Otis, Hutchinson "still expressed my doubts of the expedience of it. . . ."

Bernard was well aware of the problems: years later he would apologize to Lord Mansfield for having appointed a chief justice"not . . . bred to the law"; but he knew that the essential qualifications were as much political and intellectual as strictly legal, and he could count on Hutchinson's diligence in perfecting his knowledge of the law. So Hutchinson, still concerned about his lack of technical qualifications and having refused to solicit actively for the appointment but always eager for advancement, prestige, and a major public role, accepted. His appointment was announced on November 13, and on December 30, 1760, his commission was issued.

The general transformation of Hutchinson's reputation proceeded gradually in the months and years that followed his appointment to the chief justiceship, but John Adams and James Otis, Jr., who would ultimately shape opinion most powerfully, reached immediate conclusions. The 1760's were years in which the Massachusetts bar reached a high point of professionalization; its practitioners were exceptionally conscious of their craft and proud of their skills—and none more so than the twenty-five-year-old apprentice John Adams. Adams never forgot the outrage he felt at this elevation of a layman to the chief justiceship, so thwarting, insulting, and humiliating to his excruciatingly sensitive self-esteem. An appointment so unmerited, so perverse, and so unjust to those like himself who were sacrificing their lives to the law could only be the result of dangerous secret forces whose power would no doubt otherwise be felt and that would otherwise block the aspirations of powerless but honest and able new men.

Otis helped to substantiate these fears and to publicize this affront to the dignity of "old practitioners at the bar." Like Adams, Otis too registered shock that the new chief justice was "bred a merchant," but that was not the main burden of his response. Nor was it simply the rage of wounded pride at his family's humiliation . . . Hutchinson, Otis pointed out, was a dominant figure in the executive by virtue of being lieutenant governor, in the legislature as a councillor ("I have long thought it . . . a great grievance that the chief justice should have a seat in the Council and consequently so great a share of influence in making those very laws he is appointed to execute upon the lives and property of the people"), and in the judiciary as chief justice. "Mixed monarchy," Otis agreed, was, as everyone knew, the most perfect form of government, but—what everyone did not know—fundamental to it was the separation of legislative and executive powers, and without this, free government would dissolve. Montesquieu was right: "when the legislative and executive powers are united in the same person, or in the same body of magistrates (or nearly so) there can be no liberty because (just and great) apprehensions may arise lest the same monarch or senate (or junto) should enact *tyrannical* laws to execute them in a *tyrannical* manner." Within a few months of Hutchinson's appointment to the high bench Otis' attacks, cast in these terms and publicized again and again, became a blistering indictment.

The case of the writs of assistance—to support customs officers in searching for contraband—came before the superior court almost as soon as Hutchinson took his seat on the bench. The episode not only served to fuse Adams' resentment at unmerited professional advancement with Otis' fear of monopolized power, but it brought all of this into conjunction with the hostilities of a significant part of the merchant community for whom strict enforcement of trade regulations was a novel threat.

Hutchinson was especially well informed on the problems of these general search warrants, and he was as much concerned to limit their use to the strict letter of the law as anyone in the colony. It had been he, in fact, in 1757, who had prevented the governor from issuing general warrants on his own authority, and as a result the power to grant these potentially dangerous instruments had been confined to the superior court acting as a court of exchequer. He knew of the warrants' unquestioned legality in England and of their common use there, and he knew, too, that they had been issued before in Massachusetts without provoking public controversy.

But if the positive law was clear (and the doubts it raised were quickly settled by queries to England), the higher law of "natural equity" was not, and it was to this that Otis, who formally represented the merchant opposition, in the end directed his plea. It was the moral basis of the law, not the literal provisions, that primarily concerned him. "This writ," he charged, in words that John Adams, an eager attendant at the trial, recorded on the spot, "is against the fundamental principles of law. The privilege of house. A man who is quiet is as secure in his house as a prince in his castle," and no act of Parliament can contravene this privilege. "An act [of Parliament] against the constitution is void, an act against natural equity is void. . . .The executive courts must pass such acts into disuse"— precedents to the contrary notwithstanding, Adams later recalled him saying, for "ALL PRECEDENTS ARE UNDER THE CONTROL OF THE PRINCIPLES OF THE LAW."

The *principles* of law? Who was to say what they were? Yet it was Otis' extravagant transjuridical claim that entered American awareness, not Hutchinson's scrupulous regard for the law as it existed. Fifty-six years later John Adams—as romantic in old age as he had been in youth—caught the inner, quasi-mythological meaning of the event in his famous description of the scene:

> near the fire were seated five judges, with Lieutenant Governor Hutchinson
> at their head as chief justice, all in their new fresh robes of scarlet English
> cloth, in their broad bands, and immense judicial wigs [and against them James

A portrait of Hutchinson attributed to John Singleton Copley. It is considered the only authentic portrait of him in existence.

Otis,] a flame of fire! With the promptitude of classical allusions, a depth of research . . . a profusion of legal authorities, a prophetic glare of his eyes into futurity, and a rapid torrent of impetuous eloquence, he hurried away all before him. . . . Every man of an [immense] crowded audience appeared to me to go away, as I did, ready to take up arms against writs of assistance. . . . Then and there the child Independence was born.

Hutchinson had strongly disapproved of the Stamp Act from the time he first heard of it. . . . [He] had summarized his views in four forceful arguments against the projected stamp tax: first, that the Crown and Parliament had long ago conceded to the colonies the power to make their own laws and to tax themselves by their own representatives; second, that Americans were in no sense represented in Parliament and hence that the justification for parliamentary taxation based on presumptive representation was invalid; third, that the colonies owed no debt to the English government for their settlement and development—the colonies had been founded and sustained by private enterprise, at times in the face of state opposition; and finally, that economic arguments in favor of the act were fallacious, since England's natural profit from the colonies, which would be endangered by taxation, was greater than any prospective tax yield.

These were hardheaded arguments—all matters of historical fact or irrefutable logic. They contained no challenge to English authority as such and indulged in no speculative distinctions in Parliament's power. For Parliament's ultimate control, Hutchinson believed, was the price of American freedom, and that control must remain paramount, he concluded—in words that a decade later would toll through the continent, the death knell of his political ambition—even if it became necessary for that body to abridge "what are generally called natural-rights. . . . The rights of parts and individuals must be given up when the safety of the whole shall depend on it . . . it is no more than is reasonable . . . in return for the protection received against foreign enemies." It was better, he said, "to submit to some abridgment of our rights than to break off our connection."

The Massachusetts legislature undertook to prepare a petition to Parliament protesting the proposed stamp tax. The lead was taken by the "heads of the popular party" in the House, Hutchinson explained, who drafted a document that stated the colony's objections to the stamp duties in passionate and highly theoretical terms, grounded in principles of natural rights and in constitutional guarantees. The Council, over which Hutchinson as lieutenant governor presided, rejected this "informal and incautiously expressed" draft, and a joint committee of the two Houses was formed to frame an acceptable document. Hutchinson was chosen chairman of this committee, and he led it in rejecting two new versions, "both very exceptionable." "Ten days were spent in this manner," Hutchinson confided to Jackson, "which I thought time not ill spent as I had the more opportunity of showing them the imprudence of every measure which looked like opposition to the determinations of Parliament." He explained to them the folly of pressing principles merely because they seemed grand and glittering and somehow pure; he stated the need for calm and compromise; and he expounded the value of supporting existing structures because they were the basis of civil order. But the conferees resisted and in draft after draft confronted him with demands that the *theory* of the matter, the *principles* at stake, the commitments that were involved, should be clearly stated. But Hutchinson kept control, of himself and of the situations, and waited, patiently and skillfully, for precisely the right moment to resolve the controversy. He found it when his opponents were altogether "perplexed and tired" and about to resolve wearily on yet another unacceptable proposal; he then "drew a petition to the House of Commons, not just such as I would have chosen if I had been the sole judge but such as I thought the best I could hope for being accepted," and he pressed this version through. In this way the effort of the "popular party" to draw Massachusetts into "an ample and full declaration of the exclusive right of the people to tax themselves" had been defeated. The address as adopted, Hutchinson explained with some pride, assumed that American control of its own taxation was an indulgence which the colonists prayed the continuance of—"a matter of favor," he wrote in his *History*, "and not a claim of right."

Thus Hutchinson, and prudence, prevailed—but only briefly, and for the last time, and at great cost. Two developments quickly turned his victory into a dangerous defeat. Reports from the other colonies began to come in. Their petitions—especially New York's—appeared to be "so high," Hutchinson wrote, "that the heroes of liberty among us were ashamed of their own conduct," and they would have reversed their action if it had not been too late. Second, news soon arrived that the Stamp Act had in fact passed despite all the agitation against it in America and that in passing it Parliament had made no distinctions whatever among the various petitions filed against it; no purpose at all had been served by the prudence Hutchinson had imposed on the House. The reaction in Boston was immediate and severe. It was instantly concluded, he reported, "that if all the colonies hadshown . . . firmness and asserted their rights, the act would never have passed," and therefore if some one person had deliberately destroyed that unanimity, his aim could only have been secretly to promote, not defeat, the Stamp Act, protestations to the contrary notwithstanding. And so it was that Hutchinson, as he later realized, because he had been "the promoter of the [Massachusetts petition], was charged with treachery and . . . [with] betraying his country."

So the charge originated; and it stuck, as passions rose in the months between the passage of the Stamp Act and the date of its legal inception, and seemed in fact more and more persuasive. Everything served to confirm the suspicions of Hutchinson's duplicity that had first been generated by his prudent refusal to defy Parliament's power in principle. When the stamp master for Massachusetts was announced, he proved to be none other than Hutchinson's brother-in-law, fellow councillor, and protégé, the colony's secretary, Andrew Oliver: by this appointment alone Hutchinson's secret motives seemed to be revealed. Vituperative squibs began to appear in the newspapers. Rumors (lies, Hutchinson said, that shocked him) circulated that he had written secretly to England to encourage the promoters of the act and that copies of those letters had been returned confidentially from London and were available in Boston to be read. Otis swore he knew for a fact that the whole idea of a stamp act had been hatched by Hutchinson and Bernard and that he could point to the very house in Boston—indeed, the very room—in which the act itself had been conceived. Hutchinson fought back. He explained his views again and again, but the only effect this had, he confessed, was to confirm "the groundless suspicions of my having promoted the act."

By the summer of 1765 suspicious episodes throughout the entire span of Hutchinson's long career were being recalled in public prints. He still commanded the respect of informed people; he was still a natural as well as a legal leader of his native society. Yet something crucial in all of his activities had been missing—some recognition that security is not all nor prudence necessarily the wisest guide to action, some understanding that in the end law to be effective must reflect human sensibilities, and authority must deserve the respect it would command. Gradually the law he represented had begun to seem arbitrary, his honors to seem undeserved, and the government he led to become distant and insensitive to the needs of the governed.

As his prominence had grown so too had his vulnerability. In the scorching heat of the Stamp Act resistance he became a marked man, and explanations were demanded. On August 14 crowds directed by well-known opposition leaders turned to Hutchinson for the first time, surrounding his mansion and demanding that he "declare to them I had never wrote to England in favor of the Stamp Act." Since, the leaders said, they respected Hutchinson's private character, they would accept his personal assurance that he did not favor the act. He knew he had nothing to hide, but should he concede to such intimidation? Was he responsible to a mob? Surely he was "not obliged to give an answer to all the questions that may be put me by every lawless person." Fortunately an unnamed "grave, elderly tradesman" who was a noted town-meeting speaker intervened and "challenged every one of them to say I had ever done them the least wrong [and] charged them with ingratitude in insulting a gentleman who had been serving his country all his days." Somehow the speaker convinced the crowd that Hutchinson was not likely to have done anything deliberately to hurt his country and got them to move off. The day closed for Hutchinson with a fervent prayer for "a greater share of fortitude and discretion here than I have ever yet been master of." Twelve days later the "hellish fury" of August 26 descended on him, his family, and his property in "the most barbarous outrage which ever was committed in America."

Women in the American Revolution

Mary Beth Norton

The liberating effects of the War of Independence on women were far smaller and less revolutionary than were the effects of the struggle on American men. The Declaration of Independence, it will be recalled, claimed that all men were created equal but said nothing about women. This did not mean that American women as a group were less patriotic than men or that their contributions to the war effort were unimportant or entirely in the conventional "female" mold typified by Betsy Ross's sewing of the flag. Hundreds of women got close to the fighting. They traveled with the army, doing most of the cooking and laundering and otherwise assisting the soldiers in the field. The famous "Molly Pitcher" really did help fire cannon at the Battle of Monmouth, but the soldiers gave her that nickname (her actual name was Mary Ludwig Hays) because of her labor of bringing pitchers of water for the wounded from a nearby well.

In this essay Mary Beth Norton, a professor at Cornell University, describes the wartime activities of an organization of patriotic Philadelphia women. Professor Norton is the author of The British Americans *and of* Liberty's Daughters, *an account of how women were affected by the Revolution.*

When news that the British had taken Charleston, South Carolina, reached Philadelphia in May of 1780, merchants and government officials reacted to the disaster by taking steps to support the inflated Pennsylvania currency and solicit funds to pay new army recruits. And in a totally unexpected move, the women of Philadelphia emerged from their usual domestic roles to announce their intention of founding the first large-scale women's association in American history. As the *Pennsylvania Gazette* put it delicately, the ladies adopted "public spirited measures."

Up until then, American women had not engaged in any organized support of the war effort. Now that the American soldiers were suffering a serious loss of morale in the aftermath of the fall of Charleston, the women proposed a nation-wide female-conceived and -executed relief effort to aid the hard-pressed troops. The campaign began June 10, 1780, with the publication of a broadside, *The Sentiments of an American Woman.* It was composed by thirty-three-year-old Esther de Berdt Reed, who was to become president of the Ladies Association. The daughter of a prominent English supporter of America, Esther had lived in Pennsylvania only since her 1770 marriage to Joseph Reed, but she was nonetheless a staunch patriot. Her *Sentiments* asserted forcefully that American women were determined to do more than offer "barren wishes" for the success of the army: they wanted to be "really useful," like "those heroines of antiquity, who have rendered their sex illustrious."

Mrs. Reed built her case carefully. She began by reviewing the history of women's patriotic activity, referring alike to female monarchs, Roman matrons, and Old Testament women. Linking herself explicitly to such foremothers, she declared, "I glory in all which my sex has done great and commendable. I call to mind with enthusiasm and with admiration all those acts of courage, of constancy and patriotism, which history has transmitted to us." Mrs. Reed held up Joan of Arc as an especially appropriate model, for she had driven from France "the ancestors of these same British, whose odious yoke we have just shaken off, and whom it is necessary that we drive from this Continent."

Esther Reed went on to address the question of propriety. She admitted that some men might perhaps "disapprove" women's activity. But in the current dismal state of public affairs anyone who raised this objection would not be "a good citizen." Any man who truly understood the soldiers' needs could only "applaud our efforts for the relief of the armies which defend our lives, our possessions, our liberty." By thus hinting that critics of her scheme would be unpatriotic, Mrs. Reed cleverly defused possible traditionalist objections.

Finally, she outlined her plan. Female Americans should renounce "vain ornaments," donating the money they would no longer spend on elaborate clothing and hairstyles to the patriot troops as *"the offering of the Ladies."*

Her appeal drew an immediate response. Three days after the publication of the broadside, thirty-six Philadelphia women met to decide how to carry out its suggestions. The results of their deliberations were printed as an appendix to *Sentiments* when it appeared in the June 21 issue of the *Pennsylvania Gazette.* Entitled "Ideas, relative to the manner of forwarding to the American Soldiers, the Presents of the American Women," the plan proposed nothing less than the mobilization of the entire female population. Contributions would be accepted from any woman, in any amount. A "Treasuress" appointed in each county would oversee the collection of money, keeping careful records of all sums received. Overseeing the work of each state's county treasuresses would be the wife of its governor, who would serve as "Treasuress-General." Ultimately, all contributions would be sent to Martha Washington to be used for the benefit of the troops. Only one restriction was placed on the contributions' use: "It is an extraordinary bounty intended to render the condition of the soldier more pleasant, and not to hold place of the things which they ought to receive from the Congress, or from the States."

The Philadelphians set to work collecting funds even before the publication of their "Ideas." Dividing the city into ten equal districts, they assigned between two and five women to each area. Traveling in pairs, the canvassers visited every house, requesting contributions from "each woman and girl without any distinction." Among the collectors in the fifth ward, Market to Chestnut Streets, were Sarah Franklin Bache, the daughter of Benjamin Franklin, and Anne Willing (Mrs. Tench) Francis; Julia Stockton (Mrs. Benjamin) Rush worked in district six; and in the eighth ward, Spruce to Pine Streets, the canvassers included Alice Lee Shippen, a member of the prominent Virginia family and wife of a Philadelphia physician; Mrs. Robert Morris; and Sally McKean, wife of the Pennsylvania chief justice. The fact that women of such social standing undertook the very unfeminine task of soliciting contributions not only from friends and neighbors but also from strangers, poor people, and servants supports the contention of one of the Philadelphians that they "considered it as a great honour" to be invited to serve as canvassers. In a letter to a friend in Annapolis, an anonymous participant declared that "those who were in the country returned without delay to the city to fulfil their duty. Others put off their departure; those whose state of health was the most delicate, found strength in their patriotism." When a nursing mother was reluctant to leave her baby, this witness recorded, a friend volunteered to nurse the child along with her own.

Accounts of the women's reception differ. The anonymous letter-writer claimed that "as the cause of their visit was known, they were received with all the respect due to so honourable a commission." She explained that no house was omitted, not even those inhabited by the pacific Quakers, and that even there the subscription met with success, for "nothing is more easy than to reconcile a beneficent scheme with a beneficent religion." But Anna Rawle—herself a Quaker—described the canvass of Quaker homes quite differently. "Of all absurdities the Ladies going about for money exceeded everything," she told her mother Rebecca Shoemaker, whose second husband, Samuel, was a loyalist exile. Sarah Bache had come to their door, Anna reported, but had turned away, saying that "she did not chuse to face Mrs. S. or her daughters." Anna characterized the collectors as "so extremely importunate that people were obliged to give them something to get rid of them." Even "the meanest ale house" did not escape their net, and men were harassed until they contributed in the name of their wives or sweethearts. "I fancy they raised a considerable sum by this extorted contribu-

An engraved portrait of Martha Washington, based on an unfinished painting by Gilbert Stuart. The likeness was made at about the time of the Ladies Association fund-raising drive.

tion," Anna concluded, but she felt the requests were "carried to such an excess of meaness as the nobleness of no cause whatsoever could excuse."

It is impossible to know whether the letter-writer's examples of women proudly giving to the cause or Anna Rawle's account of reluctant contributors dunned into paying up is more accurate. But by the time the Philadelphia canvass was completed in early July, more than $300,000 Continental dollars had been collected from over sixteen hundred people. Because of inflation, this amount when converted to specie equaled only about $7,500, but even that represented a considerable sum. In financial terms, the city canvass was a smashing success. And it was a success in other ways as well, for the Philadelphia women sought and achieved symbolic goals that went far beyond the collection of money. As the anonymous canvasser put it, the women hoped that the "general beneficent" subscription "will produce the happy effect of destroying *intestine discords,* even to the very last seeds." That hope was particularly appropriate for Philadelphia women, some of whom had become notorious during the British occupation in 1777–78 for consorting with enemy troops. The author of the 1780 letter alluded delicately to that conduct when she explained that the canvassers wanted to "give some of our female fellow citizens an opportunity of relinquishing former errors and of avowing a change of sentiments by their contributions to the general cause of liberty and their country."

The symbolism of the fund drive was national as well as local. The participant, who had so enthusiastically described the canvassing, stressed that through their gifts American women would "greatly promote the public cause, and blast the hopes of the enemies of this country" by demonstrating the people's unanimous support of the war. Others also viewed the women's efforts in this light: as early as June 27, a laudatory essay signed "Song of Debora" appeared in the *Pennsylvania Packet.* "It must strike the enemy as with an apoplexy, to be informed, that the women of America are attentive to the wants of the Soldiery," the author declared, arguing that "it is not the quantity of the money that may be collected, but the idea of favour and affection discovered in this exertion, that will principally give life to our cause, and restore our affairs." Urging others to copy the Philadelphians, she predicted that "the women will reinspire the war; and ensure, finally, victory and peace."

In July, newspapers throughout the country reprinted *Sentiments,* usually accompanied by the detailed collection plan, and editors occasionally added exhortations of their own to the women's call for action. The symbolic importance of the subscription was conveyed to the nation by a frequently reprinted "Letter from an Officer at Camp, dated June 29, 1780." The patriotism of Philadelphia women "is a subject of conversation with the army," the officer wrote. "We do not suppose that these contributions can be any stable support to the campaign for any length of time; but, as it is a mark of respect to the army, it has given particular satisfaction, and it may be a great temporary service," for the soldiers had felt themselves "neglected" and forgotten by their fellow citizens.

Successful as this publicity was in spreading the news of the Philadelphians' plan, Esther Reed and her fellow organizers did not rely solely upon print to involve other women in their association. The anonymous participant told her

Annapolis friend that after they completed the city collections the women wrote circular letters to acquaintances in other counties and towns, "and we have it in charge to keep up this correspondence until the whole subscription shall be completed."

The women of Trenton, New Jersey, were the first to copy the Philadelphians' lead. In late June they began to organize their own subscription campaign, and on July 4 at a general meeting they outlined plans for a statewide association. When they announced their scheme in the newspapers, they published "Sentiments of a Lady in New Jersey" in deliberate imitation of the Philadelphians. "Let us animate one another to contribute from our purses in proportion to our circumstances towards the support and comfort of the brave men who are fighting and suffering for us on the field," the author urged her female compatriots. Although the final accounts of the New Jersey campaign have evidently failed to survive, in mid-July the secretary forwarded nearly $15,500 to George Washington as an initial contribution to the fund.

Maryland women also responded quickly to the Philadelphians' request. Mrs. Thomas Sim Lee, the wife of the governor, wrote to friends in each county to ask them to serve as treasuresses, and by July 14 the organization was actively soliciting money in Annapolis. In that city alone, even though many residents had left town for the summer, more than $16,000 in currency was collected, with additional sums in specie. Writing with particular reference to the Marylanders, the editor of the *Pennsylvania Packet* rhapsodized that "the women of every part of the globe are under obligations to those of America, for having shown that females are capable of the highest political virtue."

Only in one other state, Virginia, is there evidence of successful Ladies Association activity. Martha Wayles Jefferson, whose husband Thomas was then the governor, received a copy of the Philadelphians' plan directly from Martha Washington. Since she was in poor health, Mrs. Jefferson decided to encourage her friends to take part but not to assume an active role herself. Interestingly enough, the letter she wrote on August 8 to Eleanor Madison is the sole piece of her correspondence extant today. In it she asserted that "I undertake with chearfulness the duty of furnishing to my countrywomen an opportunity of proving that they also participate of those virtuous feelings" of patriotism. The following day an announcement of the campaign appeared in the *Virginia Gazette.* Only fragmentary records of the campaign have ever been located, but they indicate that county treasuresses gathered total currency contributions ranging from £1,560 (Albemarle) to $7,506 (Prince William).

The association's organizing efforts in other states seem to have failed not because of lack of will or interest but because of lack of financial resources. Hannah Lee Corbin, a Virginia widow, told her sister Alice Shippen that "the scheme of raising money for the Soldiers would be good—if we had it in our power to do it." But she was already "so heavily Laded" that she was having to sell her property just to obtain "common support." Catharine Littlefield (Mrs. Nathanael) Greene, replying to Esther Reed's circular letter, told a similar story. "The distressed exhausted State of this little Government [Rhode Island] prevents us from gratifying our warmest Inclinations," she declared, because one-fifth of its territory, including Newport, was still in British hands. "The Women of this State are animated with the liveliest Sentiments of Liberty" and wish to offer relief to "our brave and patient Soldiery," she exclaimed, "but alas! the peculiar circumstances of this State renders this impracticable."

Nevertheless, the women's association still collected substantial sums of money. Its organizers next had to decide how to disburse the funds in accordance with their original aim of presenting soldiers with "some extraordinary and unexpected relief . . . *the offering of the Ladies.*" Since Martha Washington had returned to Virginia by the time the collection was completed, the association's leaders agreed to leave the disposition of the funds to her husband. There was only one problem: George Washington had plans for the money that differed sharply from theirs. "Altho' the terms of the association seem in some measure to preclude the purchase of any article, which the public is bound to find," Washington told Joseph Reed in late June, "I would, nevertheless, recommend a provision of shirts in preference to any thing else." On July 31, Esther Reed responded to the general. Her much revised, amended, and overwritten draft, with all its tactful phrasing, suggests something of the consternation his proposal caused among the canvassers who had worked so hard and so long to collect the money.

Not only had she found it difficult to locate linen, she reported, she had also learned that Pennsylvania was planning to send two thousand shirts to its troops and that a large shipment of clothing had recently arrived from France, "These Circumstances togather with an Idea which prevails that the Soldiers might not consider it in the Light," she began, then crossed out the words following "Soldiers," and continued, "Soldiers woud not be so much gratified by bestowing an article to which they look upon themselves entitled from the public as in some other method which woud convey more fully the Idea of a reward for past Services & an incitement to future Duty." There she ended the sentence, having been so involved in her intricate prose that she failed to realize she had composed a fragment without a verb. Undaunted, she forged breathlessly ahead. "Some who are of this Opinion propose turning the whole of the Money into hard Dollars & giving each Soldier 2 at his own disposal." Having made her point, Mrs. Reed attempted to soften the fact that she was daring to dispute the judgment of the Commander-in-Chief of the American army. "This method I hint only," she added, "but would not by any means wish to adopt that or any other without your full approbation." To further lessen her apostasy, she also assured Washington that if shirts were still needed after the "fresh supplies" had been distributed, some of the money could be applied to that use.

Washington's response was, as Mrs. Reed later told her husband, "a little formal as if he was hurt by our asking his Opinion a second time & our not following his Directions after desiring him to give them." In his letter, the general suggested that "a taste of hard money may be productive of much discontent as we have none but depreciated paper for their pay." He also predicted that some soldiers' taste for drink would lead them "into irregularities and disorders" and that therefore the proposed two-dollar bounty "will be the means of bringing punishment" on them. No, he insisted; if the ladies wanted to employ their "benevolent donation" well, the money should be used for shirts—which they should make to save the cost of hiring seamstresses. Faced with Washington's adamant stance, Esther Reed retreated. "I shall now endeavour to get the Shirts made as soon as possible," she told her husband, and he agreed with her decision. "The General is so decided that you have no Choice left so that the sooner you finish the Business the better," he wrote on August 26, reminding her that "it will be necessary for you to render a publick Account of your Stewardship in this Business & tho you will receive no thanks if you do it well, you will bear much Blame should it be otherwise."

Unfortunately, however, Esther de Berdt Reed had no chance to "finish the Business" she had so ably begun; she died of dysentery the following month. The leadership of the association was assumed by Sarah Franklin Bache, with the assistance of four other women. They took control of the funds that had been in Mrs. Reed's possession, overseeing the purchase of linen and the shirtmaking process. By early December, when the Marquis de Chastellux visited Sarah Bache's home, more than two thousand shirts had been completed. He recorded that "on each shirt was the name of the married or unmarried lady who made it." Late that same month, the women gave the shirts to the Deputy Quartermaster General in Philadelphia, and Mrs. Bache told General Washington that "we wish them to be worn with as much pleasure as they were made."

In February, 1781, Washington offered profuse thanks to the members of the

Sarah Franklin Bache took over the leadership of the Association after Mrs. Reed died in 1780. This portrait by John Hoppner was painted a number of years later. Mrs. Bache was Benjamin Franklin's daughter.

committee that had succeeded Esther Reed as leaders of the association. The organization's contributions, he declared, entitled its participants "to an equal place with any who have preceded them in the walk of female patriotism. It embellishes the American character with a new trait; by proving that the love of country is blended with those softer domestic virtues, which have always been allowed to be more peculiarly *your own.*"

Washington's gratitude was genuine, and the army certainly needed the shirts, but the fact remains that the members of the association, who had embarked on a very unfeminine enterprise, were ultimately deflected into a traditional domestic role. The general's encomium made this explicit by its references to "female patriotism" and "those softer domestic virtues," which presumably included the ability to sew. Ironically and symbolically, the Philadelphia women of 1780, who had tried to chart an independent course for themselves and to establish an unprecedented nationwide female organization, ended up as what one amused historian has termed "General Washington's Sewing Circle."

The amusement has not been confined to subsequent generations, for male Revolutionary leaders too regarded the women's efforts with wry condescension. John Adams wrote to Benjamin Rush, "the Ladies having undertaken to support American Independence, settles the point." The women, on the other hand, saw nothing to smile at in the affair. Kitty Livingston, whose mother was a New Jersey canvasser, sent a copy of *The Sentiments of an American Woman* to her sister Sarah Jay, then in Spain. "I am prouder than ever of my charming countrywomen," Sarah told her husband John in forwarding the broadside to him. Abigail Adams had a similar reaction, one that stands in sharp contrast to her husband's. Mrs. Adams took the association as a sign that "virtue exists, and publick spirit lives— lives in the Bosoms of the Fair Daughters of America. . . ."

The anonymous Philadelphian who kept her Annapolis friend up-to-date on the ladies' organization was still more forthright: "Some persons have amused themselves with the importance which we have given it," she remarked, alluding to what must have been widespread condescension. "I confess we have made it a serious business, and with great reason; an object so interesting was certainly worthy an extraordinary attention." She and her fellow canvassers had "consecrated every moment we could spare from our domestic concerns, to the public good," enduring "with pleasure, the fatigues and inconveniences inseparable from such a task," because they could reflect proudly on the fact that "whilst our friends were exposed to the hardships and dangers of the fields of war for our protection, we were exerting at home our little labours to administer to their comfort and alleviate their toil."

The Most Successful Revolution

Irving Kristol

In recent years, responding to the celebration of the bicentennial of the Declaration of Independence, historians have devoted much effort to reexamining the American Revolution. They have attempted to explain why it occurred, how different social groups felt about it, and what its results and influences have been—in America and elsewhere in the world. As is usual with the study of complicated events, no general agreement has emerged from this research. Some historians of the Revolution, examining it "from the bottom up," have seen it as a radical effort of artisans and other ordinary people to reshape the society in which they lived. Other historians have viewed it as an ideological struggle led by people defending "the rights of Englishmen" against a clique of reactionary conspirators centered in London. Still others (Irving Kristol, the author of the following essay, is a prominent member of this school) have adopted a more conservative approach. They stress the limited, essentially practical objectives of the revolutionary leaders. They say, in effect, "less was more" and they attribute the enduring achievements of the revolutionary era to the restraint and conservatism of the Founding Fathers of the nation.

Kristol, a leading American conservative critic and essayist, urges us to "ignore" Tom Paine's radical interpretation of the Revolution on the grounds that Paine "never really understood America." One need not agree with all of Kristol's arguments to profit from his approach. That there was a profoundly conservative side to the Revolution, that George Washington, for example, was basically different from revolutionaries like Robespierre, Lenin, and Mao Tse-tung, are facts that must be accounted for in any well-rounded interpretation of the events of 1776. Kristol is editor of the journal The Public Interest *and author of* On the Democratic Idea in America, America's Continuing Revolution *and other works.*

For several decades now there has been a noticeable loss of popular interest in the Revolution, both as a historic event and as a political symbol. The idea and very word, "revolution," are in good repute today; the American Revolution is not. We are willing enough, on occasion, to pick up an isolated phrase from the Declaration of Independence or a fine declamation from a Founding Father—Jefferson, usually—and use these to point up the shortcomings of American society as it now exists. Which is to say, we seem to be prompt to declare that the Revolution was a success only when it permits us to assert glibly that we have subsequently failed it. But this easy exercise in self-indictment, though useful in some respects, is on the whole a callow affair. It doesn't tell us, for instance, whether there is an important connection between that successful revolution and our subsequent delinquencies. It merely uses the Revolution for rhetorical-political purposes, making no serious effort at either understanding it or understanding ourselves. One even gets the impression that many of us regard ourselves as too sophisticated to take the Revolution seriously—that we see it as one of those naive events of our distant childhood which we have since long outgrown but which we are dutifully reminded of, at certain moments of commemoration, by insistent relatives less liberated from the past than we.

I think I can make this point most emphatically by asking the simple question: what ever happened to George Washington? He used to be a Very Important Person—indeed, *the* most important person in our history. Our history books used to describe him, quite simply, as the Father of his Country, and in the popular mind he was a larger-than-life figure to whom piety and reverence were naturally due. In the past fifty years, however, this figure has been radically diminished in size and virtually emptied of substance. In part, one supposes, this is because piety is a sentiment we seem less and less capable of, and most especially piety toward fathers. We are arrogant and condescending toward all ancestors because we are so convinced we understand them better than they understood themselves—whereas piety assumes that they still understand us better than we understand ourselves. And reverence, too, is a sentiment that we, in our presumption, find somewhat unnatural. Woodrow Wilson, like most Progressives of his time, complained about the "blind worship" of the Constitution by the American people; no such complaint is likely to be heard today. We debate whether or not we should obey the laws of the land, whereas for George Washington—and Lincoln, too, who in his lifetime reasserted this point most eloquently—obedience to law was not enough: they thought that Americans, as citizens of a self-governing polity, ought to have *reverence* for their laws. Behind this belief, of course, was the premise that the collective wisdom incarnated in our laws—and especially in the fundamental law of the Constitution—understood us better than any one of us could ever hope to understand it. Having separated ourselves from our historic traditions, and no longer recognizing the power inherent in tradition itself, we find this traditional point of view close to incomprehensible.

Equally incomprehensible to us is the idea that George Washington was the central figure in a real, honest-to-God revolution—the first significant revolution of the modern era and one that can lay claim to being the only truly successful revolution, on a large scale, in the past two centuries. In his own lifetime no one doubted that he was the central figure of that revolution; subsequent generations did not dispute the fact; our textbooks, until about a quarter of a century ago, took it for granted, albeit in an ever more routine and unconvincing way. We today, in contrast, find it hard to take George Washington seriously as a successful revolutionary. He just doesn't fit our conception of what a revolutionary leader is supposed to be like. It is a conception that easily encompasses Robespierre, Lenin, Mao Tse-tung, or Fidel Castro—but can one stretch it to include a gentleman like George Washington? And so we tend to escape from that dilemma by deciding that the American Revolution was not an authentic revolution at all, but rather some kind of pseudorevolution, which is why it could be led by so unrevolutionary a character as George Washington.

Hannah Arendt, in her very profound book *On Revolution,* has written: ". . . Revolutionary political thought in the nineteenth and twentieth centuries has proceeded as though there never had occurred a revolution in the New World and as though there never had been any American notions and experiences in the realm of politics and government worth thinking about." And it is certainly indisputable that the world, when it contemplates the events of 1776 and after, is inclined to see the American Revolution as a French Revolution that never quite came off—whereas the Founding Fathers thought they had cause to regard the French Revolution as an American Revolution that had failed. Indeed, the differing estimates of these two revolutions are definitive of one's political philosophy in the modern world: there are two conflicting conceptions of politics, in relation to the human condition, which are symbolized by these two revolutions. There is no question that the French Revolution is, in some crucial sense, the more "modern" of the two. There is a question, however, as to whether it is a good or bad thing to be modern in this sense. . . .

Every revolution unleashes tides of passion, and the American Revolution was no exception. But it *was* exceptional in the degree to which it was able to subordinate these passions to serious and nuanced thinking about fundamental problems of political philosophy. The pamphlets, sermons, and newspaper essays of the Revolutionary period—only now being reprinted and carefully studied— were extraordinarily academic, in the best sense of that term. Which is to say, they were learned and thoughtful and generally sober in tone. This was a revolution infused by *mind* to a degree never approximated since and perhaps never approximated before. By mind, not by dogma. The most fascinating aspect of the American Revolution is the severe way it kept questioning itself about the meaning of what it was doing. Enthusiasm there certainly was—a revolution is impossible without enthusiasm—but this enthusiasm was tempered by doubt, introspection, anxiety, skepticism. This may strike us as a very strange state of mind in which to make a revolution; and yet it is evidently the right state of mind for making a successful revolution. That we should have any difficulty in seeing this tells us something about the immaturity of our own political imagination—an immaturity not all incompatible with what we take to be sophistication.

One of our most prominent statesmen [recently] remarked to an informal group of political scientists that he had been reading *The Federalist Papers* and he was astonished to see how candidly our Founding Fathers could talk about the frailties of human nature and the necessity for a political system to take such frailties into account. It was not possible, he went on to observe, for anyone active in American politics today to speak publicly in this way: he would be accused of an imperfect democratic faith in the common man. Well, the Founding Fathers for the most part, and most of the time, subscribed to such an "imperfect" faith. They understood that republican self-government could not exist if humanity did not possess—at some moments, and to a fair degree—the traditional "republican virtues" of self-control, self-reliance, and a disinterested concern for the public

One of the many portraits of George Washington by Gilbert Stuart.

good. They also understood that these virtues did not exist everywhere, at all times, and that there was no guarantee of their natural preponderance. As James Madison put it:

> As there is a degree of depravity in mankind which requires a certain degree of circumspection and distrust; so there are other qualities in human nature which justify a certain portion of esteem and confidence. Republican govern-

ment presupposes the existence of these qualities in a higher degree than any other form.

Despite the fact that Christian traditions are still strong in this country, it is hard to imagine any public figure casually admitting, as Madison did in his matter-of-fact way, that "there is a degree of depravity in mankind" which statesmen must take account of. We have become unaccustomed to such candid and unflattering talk about ourselves—which is, I suppose, only another way of saying that we now think democratic demagoguery to be the only proper rhetorical mode of address as between government and people in a republic. The idea, so familiar to the Puritans and still very much alive during our Revolutionary era, that a community of individual sinners could, under certain special conditions, constitute a good community—just as a congregation of individual sinners could constitute a good church—is no longer entirely comprehensible to us. We are therefore negligent about the complicated ways in which this transformation takes place and uncomprehending as to the constant, rigorous attentiveness necessary for it to take place at all. The Founders thought that self-government was a chancy and demanding enterprise and that successful government in a republic was a most difficult business. We, in contrast, believe that republican self-government is an easy affair, that it need only be instituted for it to work on its own, and that when such government falters, it must be as a consequence of personal incompetence or malfeasance by elected officials. Perhaps nothing reveals better than these different perspectives the intellectual distance we have travelled from the era of the Revolution. . . .

In what sense can the American Revolution be called a successful revolution? And if we agree that it was successful, why was it successful? . . . To begin at the beginning: the American Revolution was successful in that those who led it were able, in later years, to look back in tranquillity at what they had wrought and to say that it was good. This was a revolution that, unlike all subsequent revolutions, did not devour its children: the men who made the revolution were the men who went on to create the new political order, who then held the highest elective positions in this order, and who all died in bed. Not very romantic, perhaps; indeed positively prosaic; but it is this very prosaic quality of the American Revolution that testifies to its success. It is the pathos and poignancy of unsuccessful revolutions that excite the poetic temperament; statesmanship that successfully accomplishes its business is a subject more fit for prose. Alone among the revolutions of modernity the American Revolution did not give rise to the pathetic and poignant myth of "the revolution betrayed." It spawned no literature of disillusionment; it left behind no grand hopes frustrated, no grand expectations unsatisfied, no grand illusions shattered. Indeed, in one important respect the American Revolution was so successful as to be almost self-defeating: it turned the attention of thinking men away from politics, which now seemed utterly unproblematic, so that political theory lost its vigor, and even the political thought of the Founding Fathers was not seriously studied. The American political tradition became an inarticulate tradition: it worked so well we did not bother to inquire why it worked, and we are therefore intellectually disarmed before those moments when it suddenly seems not to be working so well after all.

The American Revolution was also successful in another important respect: it was a mild and relatively bloodless revolution. A war was fought, to be sure, and soldiers died in that war; but the rules of civilized warfare, as then established, were for the most part quite scrupulously observed by both sides—there was little of the butchery that we have come to accept as a natural concomitant of revolutionary warfare. More important, there was practically none of the off-battlefield savagery that we now assume to be inevitable in revolutions. There were no revolutionary tribunals dispensing "revolutionary justice"; there was no reign of terror; there were no bloodthirsty proclamations by the Continental Congress. Tories were dispossessed of their property, to be sure, and many were rudely hustled off into exile; but . . . not a single Tory was executed for harboring counter-revolutionary opinions. Nor, in the years after the Revolution, were Tories persecuted to any significant degree (at least by today's standards) or their children discriminated against at all. As Tocqueville later remarked, with only a little exaggeration, the Revolution "contracted no alliance with the turbulent passions of anarchy, but its course was marked, on the contrary, by a love of order and law."

A law-and-order revolution? What kind of revolution is that, we ask ourselves? To which many will reply that it could not have been much of a revolution, after all—at best a shadow of the real thing, which is always turbulent and bloody and shattering of body and soul. Well, the possibility we have to consider is that it was successful precisely because it wasn't that kind of revolution and that it is we rather than the American revolutionaries who have an erroneous conception of what a revolution is. . . .

One does not want to make the American Revolution a more prosaic affair than it was. This was a revolution—a real one—and it was infused with a spirit of excitement and innovation. After all, what the American Revolution was trying to do, once it got under way, was no small thing. It was nothing less than the establishment, for the first time since ancient Rome, of a large republican nation; and the idea of re-establishing under modern conditions the glory that had been Rome's could hardly fail to be intoxicating. This revolution did indeed have grand—even millenial—expectations as to the future role of this new nation in both the political imagination and the political history of the human race. But certain things have to be said about these large expectations if we are to see them in proper perspective.

The main thing to be said is that the millenarian tradition in America long antedates the Revolution and is not intertwined with the idea of revolution itself. It was the Pilgrim Fathers, not the Founding Fathers, who first announced that this was God's country, that the American people had a divine mission to accomplish, that this people had been "chosen" to create some kind of model community for the rest of mankind. This belief was already so firmly established by the time of the Revolution that it was part and parcel of our political orthodoxy, serving to legitimate an existing "American way of life" and most of the institutions associated with that way of life. . . .

To this traditional millenarianism the Revolution added the hope that the establishment of republican institutions would inaugurate a new and happier political era for all mankind. This hope was frequently expressed enthusiastically, in a kind of messianic rhetoric, but the men of the Revolution—most of them, most of the time—did not permit themselves to become bewitched by that rhetoric. Thus, though they certainly saw republicanism as the wave of the future, both Jefferson and Adams in the 1780's agreed that the French people were still too "depraved," as they so elegantly put it, to undertake an experiment in self-government. Self-government, as they understood it, presupposed a certain way of life, and this in turn presupposed certain qualities on the part of the citizenry—qualities then designated as republican virtues—that would make self-government possible.

Similarly, though one can find a great many publicists during the Revolution who insisted that, with the severance of ties from Britain, the colonies had reverted to a Lockean "state of nature" and were now free to make a new beginning for all mankind and to create a new political order that would mark a new stage in human history—though such assertions were popular enough, it would be a mistake to take them too seriously. The fact is that Americans had encountered their state of nature generations earlier and had made their social compact at that time. The primordial American social contract was signed and sealed on the *Mayflower*—literally signed and sealed. The subsequent presence of all those signatures appended to the Declaration of Independence, beginning with John Hancock, are but an echo of the original covenant.

To perceive the true purposes of the American Revolution it is wise to ignore some of the more grandiloquent declamations of the moment—Tom Paine, an English radical who never really understood America, is especially worth ignoring—and to look at the kinds of political activity the Revolution unleashed. This activity took the form of constitution making, above all. In the months and years immediately following the Declaration of Independence all of our states drew up constitutions. These constitutions are terribly interesting in three respects. First, they involved relatively few basic changes in existing political institutions and almost no change at all in legal, social, or economic institutions. Second, most of the changes that were instituted had the evident aim of *weakening* the power of government, especially of the executive; it was these changes—and especially the strict separation of powers—that dismayed Turgot, Condorcet, and the other French philosophes, who understood revolution as an expression of the people's will to power rather than as an attempt to circumscribe political authority. Third, in no case did any of these state constitutions tamper with the traditional system of local self-government; indeed they could not, since it was this traditional system of local self-government that created and legitimized the constitutional conventions themselves.

In short, the Revolution reshaped our political institutions in such a way as to make them more responsive to popular opinion and less capable of encroaching upon the personal liberties of the citizen—liberties that long antedated the new constitutions and that in no way could be regarded as the creation or consequence of revolution. Which is to say that the purpose of this revolution was to bring our political institutions into a more perfect correspondence with an actual American way of life that no one even dreamed of challenging. This restructuring, as we should now call it, because it put the possibility of republican self-govern-

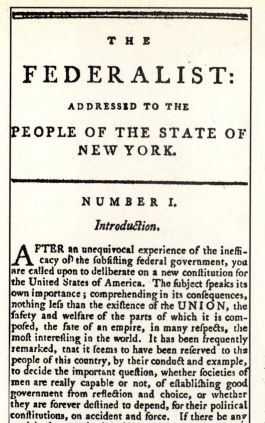

T H E

FEDERALIST:

ADDRESSED TO THE

PEOPLE OF THE STATE OF NEW YORK.

NUMBER I.

Introduction.

AFTER an unequivocal experience of the ineffi-
cacy of the fubfifting federal government, you
are called upon to deliberate on a new conftitution for
the United States of America. The fubject fpeaks its
own importance; comprehending in its confequences,
nothing lefs than the exiftence of the UNION, the
fafety and welfare of the parts of which it is com-
pofed, the fate of an empire, in many refpects, the
moft interefting in the world. It has been frequently
remarked, that it feems to have been referved to the
people of this country, by their conduct and example,
to decide the important queftion, whether focieties of
men are really capable or not, of eftablifhing good
government from reflection and choice, or whether
they are forever deftined to depend, for their political
conftitutions, on accident and force. If there be any
truth in the remark, the crifis, at which we are arrived,
may with propriety be regarded as the æra in which

A   that

A facsimile of the first page of The Federalist, *Number 1 (published in 1788)—a compilation in book form of the papers published in a New York newspaper one year earlier. These documents came to be known as* The Federalist Papers.

ment once again on the political agenda of Western civilization, was terribly exciting, to Europeans as well as Americans. But for the Americans involved in this historic task it was also terribly frightening. It is fair to say that no other revolution in modern history made such relatively modest innovations with such an acute sense of anxiety. The Founding Fathers were well aware that if republi-canism over the centuries had become such a rare form of government, there must be good reasons behind this fact. Republican government, they realized, must be an exceedingly difficult regime to maintain—it must have grave inherent problems. And so they were constantly scurrying to their libraries, ransacking classical and contemporary political authors, trying to discover why republics fail, and endeavoring to construct a new political science relevant to American condi-tions that would give this new republic a fair chance of succeeding. That new political science was eventually to be embodied in *The Federalist Papers,* the only original work of political theory ever produced by a revolution and composed by successful revolutionaries. . . .

The French Revolution promised not only a reformation of France's political

Alexander Hamilton, the driving force behind The Federalist
Papers *(and author of the reproduction shown on page 149).
This is the well-known portrait by John Trumbull.*

institutions but far more than that. It promised, for instance—as practically all
revolutions have promised since—the abolition of poverty. The American Revolution promised no such thing, in part because poverty was not such a troublesome issue in this country, but also, one is certain, because the leaders of this
revolution understood what their contemporary Adam Smith understood and
what we today have some difficulty in understanding: namely, that poverty is
abolished by economic growth, not by economic redistribution—there is never
enough to distribute—and that rebellions, by creating instability and uncertainty,
have mischievous consequences for economic growth. Similarly, the French Revolution promised a condition of "happiness" to its citizens under the new regime,
whereas the American Revolution promised merely to permit the individual to
engage in the "pursuit of happiness." . . .

   To the teeming masses of other nations the American political tradition says:
to enjoy the fruits of self-government you must first cease being "masses" and
become a "people," attached to a common way of life, sharing common values,

and existing in a condition of mutual trust and sympathy as between individuals and even social classes. It is a distinctly odd kind of revolutionary message, by twentieth-century criteria—so odd that it seems not revolutionary at all, and yet so revolutionary that it seems utterly utopian. What the twentieth century wants to hear is the grand things that a new government will do for the people who put their trust in it. What the American political tradition says is that the major function of government is to supervise the orderly arrangement of society and that a free people does not make a covenant or social contract with its government, or with the leaders of any "movement," but among themselves.

In the end what informs the American political tradition is a proposition and a premise. The proposition is that the best national government is, to use a phrase the Founding Fathers were fond of, "mild government." The premise is that you can only achieve mild government if you have a solid bedrock of local self-government, so that the responsibilities of national government are limited in scope. And a corollary of this premise is that such a bedrock of local self-government can only be achieved by a people who—through the shaping influence of religion, education, and their own daily experience—are capable of governing themselves in those small and petty matters which are the stuff of local politics. . . .

Though we have been a representative democracy for two centuries now, we have never developed an adequate theory of representation. More precisely, we have developed two contradictory theories of representation, both of which can claim legitimacy within the American political tradition and both of which were enunciated—often by the same people—during the Revolution. The one sees the public official as a "common man" who has a mandate to reflect the opinions of the majority; the other sees the public official as a somewhat uncommon man—a more-than-common man, if you will—who because of his talents and character is able to take a larger view of the public interest than the voters who elected him or the voters who failed to defeat him. One might say that the first is a democratic view of the legislator, the second a republican view. The American political tradition has always had a kind of double vision on this whole problem, which in turn makes for a bewildering moral confusion. Half the time we regard our politicians as, in the nature of things, probably corrupt and certainly untrustworthy; the other half of the time we denounce them for failing to be models of integrity and rectitude. . . . But politicians are pretty much like the rest of us and tend to become the kinds of people they are expected to be. The absence of clear and distinct expectations has meant that public morality in this country has never been, and is not, anything we can be proud of.

In a way the ambiguity in our theory of representation points to a much deeper ambiguity in that system of self-government which emerged from the Revolution and the Constitutional Convention. That system has been perceptively titled, by Professor Martin Diamond, "a democratic republic." Now, we tend to think of these terms as near-synonyms, but in fact they differ significantly in their political connotations. . . . What is the difference between a democracy and a republic? In a democracy the will of the people is supreme. In a republic it is not the will of the people but the rational consensus of the people—a rational consensus that is implicit in the term "consent"—which governs the people. That is to say, in a democracy popular passion may rule—it need not, but it may; in a republic popular passion is regarded as unfit to rule, and precautions are taken to see that it is subdued rather than sovereign. In a democracy all politicians are, to some degree, demagogues: they appeal to people's prejudices and passions, they incite their expectations by making reckless promises, they endeavor to ingratiate themselves with the electorate in every possible way. In a republic there are not supposed to be such politicians, only statesmen—sober, unglamorous, thoughtful men who are engaged in a kind of perpetual conversation with the citizenry. In a republic a fair degree of equality and prosperity are important goals, but it is liberty that is given priority as the proper end of government. In a democracy these priorities are reversed: the status of men and women as consumers of economic goods is taken to be more significant than their status as participants in the creation of political goods. A republic is what we would call moralistic in its approach to both public and private affairs; a democracy is more easygoing, more permissive, as we now say, even more cynical.

The Founding Fathers perceived that their new nation was too large, too heterogeneous, too dynamic, too mobile for it to govern itself successfully along strict republican principles, and they had no desire at all to see it governed along strict democratic principles, since they did not have that much faith in the kinds of "common men" likely to be produced by such a nation. So they created a new form of popular government, to use one of their favorite terms, that incorporated both republican and democratic principles in a complicated and ingenious way. This system has lasted for two centuries, which means it has worked very well indeed. But in the course of that time we have progressively forgotten what kind of system it is and *why* it works as well as it does. Every now and then, for instance, we furiously debate the question of whether or not the Supreme Court is meeting its obligations as a democratic institution. The question reveals a startling ignorance of our political tradition. The Supreme Court is not—and was never supposed to be—a democratic institution; it is a republican institution that counterbalances the activities of our various democratic institutions. . . .

So it would seem that two hundred years after the American Revolution we are in a sense victims of its success. The political tradition out of which it issued, and the political order it helped to create, are imperfectly comprehended by us. What is worse, we are not fully aware of this imperfect comprehension and are frequently smug in our convenient misunderstandings. . . .

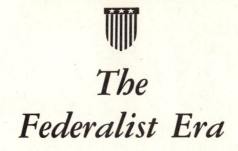

PART FOUR

The
Federalist Era

*Delegates of the first Continental Congress leaving Carpenters Hall,
Philadelphia, in 1774.*

Shays' Rebellion

Alden T. Vaughan

During the American Revolution a people rose against an oppressive government without losing their respect for government itself or for law. The American revolutionaries sought drastic change but pursued it, as Jefferson put it in the Declaration of Independence, with "a decent respect to the opinions of mankind." However, the dislocations that the Revolution produced were severe, and in the years after Yorktown the young nation had its full share of social and economic problems, some of which threatened to destroy the respect of the people for legally established authority. Whether this was truly a "critical period" has long been debated; the current opinion of historians seems to be that conditions, in the main, were not as bad as they have sometimes been pictured. But the new national government did lack many important powers, and many of the state governments displayed insufficient will and confidence and thus failed to assume responsibility for governing with the force and determination that critical times require.

In this essay Professor Alden T. Vaughan of Columbia University describes the difficulties that plagued Massachusetts in the 1780s and produced what is known as Shays' Rebellion. How the fundamental conservatism and respect for democratic values of the citizens of Massachusetts eventually resolved this conflict is the theme of his narrative, although he also weighs the influence of the affair on the Constitutional Convention at Philadelphia, which followed closely upon it.

October, 1786: "Are your people . . . mad?" thundered the usually calm George Washington to a Massachusetts correspondent. Recent events in the Bay State had convinced the General, who was living the life of a country squire at Mount Vernon, that the United States was "fast verging to anarchy and confusion!" Would the nation that had so recently humbled the British Empire now succumb to internal dissension and die in its infancy? To many Americans in the fall of 1786 it seemed quite possible, for while Washington was writing frantic notes to his friends, several thousand insurgents under the nominal leadership of a Revolutionary War veteran named Daniel Shays were closing courts with impunity, defying the state militia, and threatening to revamp the state government.

The uprising in Massachusetts was serious in itself, but more frightening was the prospect that it could spread to the other states. It had, in fact, already tainted Rhode Island, Vermont, and New Hampshire, and it showed some danger of infecting Connecticut and New York as well. By the spring of 1787, American spokesmen from Maine to Georgia were alarmed, Congress had been induced to raise troops for possible deployment against the rebels, and observers on both sides of the Atlantic voiced concern for the future of the nation. Even John Adams in London and Thomas Jefferson in Paris took time from their critical diplomatic duties to comment—the former, as might be expected, pessimistically; the latter with his usual optimism—on the causes and consequences of Shays' Rebellion. And well they might: the Massachusetts uprising of 1786–87 was to make a lasting contribution to the future of the United States by magnifying the demand for a stronger central government to replace the one created by the Articles of Confederation—a demand that reached fruition in the drafting and ratification of the Constitution in 1787–88. From the vantage point of the twentieth century, the rebellion of Daniel Shays stands—with the exception of the Civil War—as the nation's most famous and most important domestic revolt.

The root of the trouble in Massachusetts lay in the economic chaos that accompanied political independence. The successful war against Great Britain had left the thirteen former colonies free to rule themselves, but it had also left them without the commercial ties that had done so much to promote colonial prosperity. While American producers, merchants, and shippers scurried after new goods and new markets to replace the old, the ill effects of economic independence crept across the nation.

Of all the American states, perhaps none felt the postwar slump so grievously as did Massachusetts. Its $14 million debt was staggering, as was its shortage of specie. Bay Staters once again swapped wheat for shoes, and cordwood for help with the plowing. They suffered too from the ruinous inflation that afflicted the entire nation as the value of Continental currency fell in the three years after 1777 to a ridiculous low of four thousand dollars in paper money to one dollar in silver or gold. But in addition, Massachusetts caught the full brunt of England's decision—vengeful, the Americans considered it—to curtail trade between the United States and the British West Indies. To New Englanders, more than half of whom lived in Massachusetts, the new British policy threatened economic disaster. Gone was their dominance of the carrying trade, gone the booms in shipbuilding, in distilling, in food and lumber exporting, and in the slave trade. Gone too was New England's chief source of hard cash, for the West Indies had been the one place with which New England merchants enjoyed a favorable balance of trade.

Most residents of Massachusetts were probably unaware of the seriousness of their plight until it came close to home. By the early 1780's the signs were unmistakable. Men in debt—and debt was epidemic in the late seventies and eighties—saw their farms confiscated by the state and sold for as little as a third of what they considered to be the true value. Others, less fortunate, found themselves in the dark and filthy county jails, waiting helplessly for sympathetic friends or embarrassed relatives to bail them out of debtors' prison. As the economic crisis worsened, a gloomy pessimism spread among the farmers and tradesmen in the central and western parts of the state.

The economic problems of Massachusetts were difficult, but probably not insoluble. At least they could have been lessened by a wise and considerate state government. Unfortunately for the Bay Stater, good government was as scarce as good money in the early 1780's. After creating a fundamentally sound framework of government in the state constitution of 1780, the voters of Massachusetts failed to staff it with farsighted and dedicated servants of the people. "Thieves, knaves, and robbers," snorted one disgruntled citizen. With mounting grievances and apathetic legislators, the people increasingly took matters into their own hands.

As early as February, 1782, trouble broke out in Pittsfield in the Berkshires, and before the year was over, mob actions had disrupted the tranquillity of several other towns in the western part of the state. The immediate target of the Pittsfield agitators was the local court, which they temporarily closed by barring the door to members of the bench. A court that did not sit could not process foreclosures, pass judgments on debts, or confiscate property for defaulted taxes. In April, violence broke out at Northampton, where a former Connecticut clergyman named Samuel Ely—branded by one early historian as "a vehement, brazen-faced declaimer, abounding in hypocritical pretensions to piety, and an industrious sower of discord"—led the attack on the judges. Ely harangued a Northampton crowd to "go to the woodpile and get clubs enough, and knock their grey wigs off, and send them out of the world in an instant." Ely was promptly arrested and sentenced to six months in prison, but a mob soon freed him from the Springfield jail. The ex-parson found refuge in Vermont.

Instead of recognizing the validity of such protests, the Massachusetts legislature countered with a temporary suspension of habeas corpus and imposed new and higher court costs as well. And while the government did bend to the extent of authorizing certain foodstuffs and lumber to be used in lieu of money, the net effect of its measures was to rub salt into wounds already smarting. Currency remained dear, foreclosures mounted, the shadow of debtors' prison continued to cast a pall, and the state's legal system remained unduly complicated and expensive. Many citizens of western Massachusetts now began to question the benefits of independence; a few even concluded that the patriot leaders of 1776 had deluded them, and cheers for King George III were heard once again in towns that a few years before had cursed his name. And unrest continued to spread. In May, 1783, a mob tried to prevent the opening of the spring session of the Hampshire County Court at Springfield.

Perhaps the major outbreak of 1786 would have occurred a year or so sooner had it not been for a fortuitous combination of events that made the years 1784 and 1785 relatively easy to bear. In 1784 came news that a final peace had been signed with England; in 1785 Massachusetts farmers enjoyed their best harvest in several years, while the legislature, in one of its conciliatory if vagrant moods, refrained from levying a state tax. Although tempers continued to simmer, no serious outbreaks marred the period from early 1783 to midsummer 1786.

The episodes of 1782–83 and those that followed held a particular appeal for veterans of the Revolution. Even more than their civilian neighbors, the former soldiers nursed grievances that they could attribute to incompetent, if not dishonest, government. They had left their farms and shops to fight the hated redcoats, but they could not even depend on the paltry sums their services had earned for them. Inflation had made their Continental currency almost worthless, and now the government set up by the Articles of Confederation was delaying payment of overdue wages and retracting its promises of lifetime pensions to officers.

One lesson of the Revolution not lost on the Massachusetts veterans was that in times of necessity the people could reform an insensitive government by force of arms, and many of them still had in their possession the weapons they had used so effectively against the British and Hessian troops. Old habits and old weapons increasingly took on new meaning to the men of Massachusetts as the economic and political crisis of the 1780's deepened. The veterans of the Bay State knew where to find leadership, too, for among those hard-pressed by the economic problems of the decade were many who had served as officers during the War for Independence.

By 1786 several of these officers had emerged as acknowledged leaders in their own localities, although not until the final stages of the rebellion would any single commander claim the allegiance of more than a few hundred men at most.

In the eastern part of the state the most prominent leader was Captain Job Shattuck of Groton, a veteran of the French and Indian War as well as of the Revolution. Now in his fifties, Shattuck had been protesting vehemently, and sometimes violently, since 1781. His principal lieutenant in Middlesex County was Nathan Smith of Shirley, a tough veteran of both wartime and peacetime conflict—with a patch over one eye as testimony to his involvement in the latter. It was the burly Smith who on one occasion gave his hearers the unhappy choice of joining his band or being run out of town.

Farther west the rebels looked to other leaders. In Springfield and neighboring towns it was to Luke Day, said by some to be "the master spirit of the insurrection." A former brevet major in the Continental Army, Day seems to have had the inclination as well as the experience necessary to command a rebellion. In the dismal eighties he was often found grumbling his discontent in West Springfield's Old Stebbin's Tavern or drilling his followers on the town common.

But it was not upon Shattuck or Smith or Day that the final leadership devolved, with its mixed portions of glory and infamy, but on Captain Daniel Shays of Pelham. In some respects Shays was an improbable leader for a popular revolt, for he seems to have been a reluctant rebel in the first place; as late as the fall of 1786 he insisted: "I at their head! I am not." And even after he had assumed command of the bulk of the rebel army, he expressed eagerness to accept a pardon. But at the same time, Shays had attributes that made him a likely prospect for gaining the loyalty of the insurgents. Unlike the others, Shays presented a calm moderation that inspired confidence and respect. He also had a penchant for military courtesy and protocol, a quality that would have undoubtedly been repugnant to the veterans if overdone, but one that was essential if the "mobbers," as they were often called, were to acquire the discipline and organization necessary to resist the forces of government.

Daniel Shays also attracted confidence through his impressive Revolutionary War record. Joining the Continental Army at the outbreak of hostilities, he fought bravely at Bunker Hill (where his courage earned him a promotion to sergeant), served under Ethan Allen at Ticonderoga, helped thwart Gentleman Johnny Burgoyne at Saratoga, and stormed Stony Point with Mad Anthony Wayne. For recruiting a company of volunteers in Massachusetts Shays ultimately received a commission as their captain, a position he seems to have filled adequately if not outstandingly. And before leaving the service, Shays suffered at least one wound in battle.

Shays resigned from the army in 1780 and turned his hand to farming in the small town of Pelham, a few miles east of the Connecticut River. There his popularity, undoubtedly enhanced by his military reputation, won him election to various local offices. At the same time, Shays learned at first hand the problems that can beset a returned veteran. He had already sold for cash the handsome ceremonial sword that the Marquis de Lafayette had presented to him in honor of the victory at Saratoga. On long winter evenings at Conkey's Tavern, Daniel Shays listened to his neighbors' tales of distress. In 1784 he was himself sued for a debt of twelve dollars; by 1786 he was deeply involved in the insurrection. Like so many other men in western and central Massachusetts, Shays had been maneuvered by events of the postwar period into actions that he would hardly have contemplated a few years earlier.

The relative calm that followed the outbreaks of 1782–83 was abruptly shattered in 1786. To make up for the low revenue of the previous year, the legislature in the spring of 1786 imposed unusually heavy poll and property taxes, amounting to one third of the total income of the people. In 1774 taxes had been fifteen cents per capita; in 1786 they leaped to $1.75—a hefty sum for heads of families in frontier areas where a skilled laborer earned thirty to fifty cents a day. Protested one poor cobbler, "The constable keeps at us for rates, rates, rates!" Besides, the new tax schedule was notorious for its inequity, placing heavy duties on land without regard to its value—a palpable discrimination against the poorer farmers. The new schedule also worked injury on the least affluent classes by seeking almost forty per cent of its revenue through a head tax, asking equal amounts from pauper and merchant prince. As court and jail records poignantly testify, many people in the central and western parts of the state could not pay both the new taxes and their old debts. Worcester County, for example, had four thousand suits for debt in 1785–86 (double the total of the preceding two years), and the number of persons imprisoned for debt jumped from seven to seventy-two during that period. In 1786 debtors outnumbered all other criminals in Worcester County prisons 3 to 1.

The new taxes would probably have caused considerable anger by themselves, but when added to old grievances they were sure to bring trouble. During the summer of 1786, conventions met in several western counties—in Worcester, in Hampshire, in Berkshire—and even as far east as Middlesex, only a few miles from Boston. From these quasi-legal meetings came resolutions to the Massachusetts legislature calling for a variety of reforms: reduction of court and lawyers' fees, reduction of salaries for state officials, issuance of paper money, removal of the state capital from Boston (where it was deemed too susceptible to the influence of eastern commercial interests), reduction of taxes, redistribution of the tax load, and many similar changes. A few protests called for still more drastic reforms, such as abolition of the state senate and curtailment of the governor's appointive power, while some petitioners insisted on a state-wide convention to amend the constitution of 1780, now barely six years old. But on the whole the petitions demanded evolution, not revolution. This was a tempered and healthy challenge to an administration that had shown itself insensitive and incompetent.

In the protests about the government, two categories of citizens were singled out for criticism by the petitioners. First were the merchants and professional men, who enjoyed an unfair advantage within the tax system. Second were the lawyers, who seemed to be conspiring with judges and creditors to force the debtor still further into obligation. Perhaps not all lawyers were so harshly judged, but the condemnation was certainly meant to apply to those whom John Adams called "the dirty dabblers in the law," men who often created more litigation than they resolved. In contrast to the turbulent days before the Revolution, the new era in Massachusetts did not find lawyers in the vanguard of the movement for reform.

But in one respect, at least, the 1780's bore resemblance to the years before Lexington: peaceful protest soon gave way to more forceful action. In late August, following a Hampshire County convention at Hatfield, a mob of 1,500 men "armed with guns, swords, and other deadly weapons, and with drums beating and fifes playing" took command of the county courthouse at Northampton and forced the judges of the Court of Common Pleas and General Sessions of the Peace to adjourn sine die. During the next few months, similar conventions with similar results took place in Middlesex, Bristol, and Worcester counties. By early fall, mobs armed with muskets or hickory clubs and often sporting sprigs of hemlock in their hats as a sign of allegiance to the rebel cause moved at will through the interior counties.

The rebels did not go unopposed. In each county there were some citizens who looked askance at the growing anarchy and did their best to thwart it. In Worcester, seat of Worcester County, Judge Artemas Ward showed the mettle of those who would not succumb to mob rule. When on the fifth of September two hundred armed men blocked his path to the courthouse, the aging but still impressive ex-general defied the bayonets that pierced his judicial robes and for two hours lectured the crowd on the dangers of anarchy and the meaning of treason. A heavy downpour finally silenced the judge, though not until he had intoned a timely plea that "the sun never shine on rebellion in Massachusetts." But neither rain nor words had got the judge and his colleagues into the courthouse.

Elsewhere the story was much the same: a few citizens tried to stem the tide of rebellion but in the end were swept aside. At Great Barrington, in Berkshire County, a mob of 800 stopped the court, broke open the jail and released its prisoners, and abused the judges who protested. At Springfield, Daniel Shays and Luke Day made sure that the courthouse doors remained shut, while at Concord, less than twenty miles from Boston, Job Shattuck, aided by Nathan Smith and his brother Sylvanus, prevented the sitting of the Middlesex County court. Only at Taunton, in Bristol County, did a sizable mob meet its match. There Chief Justice (and former general) David Cobb was ready with a field piece, thirty volunteers, and a determination to "sit as a judge or die as a general." The Bristol court met as scheduled.

*Farmers threatened with foreclosure seize a
Massachusetts court, depicted in 1884 by the noted
illustrator, Howard Pyle.*

Governor James Bowdoin and the legislature responded to the latest outbreaks with a confusing mixture of sternness, concession, and indecision. In early
September, the Governor issued his first proclamation, condemning the mobbers' flirtation with "riot, anarchy and confusion." In October the legislature
suspended habeas corpus, but it also authorized some categories of goods as legal
tender for specified kinds of public and private debts, and it offered full pardon
to all rebels who would take an oath of allegiance before the end of the year. Yet
the government failed to find solutions to the major complaints. No significant
reforms were made in court procedures, the tax load was not reduced, officials'
salaries were not lowered, the capital was not moved, and no curbs were placed
on lawyers' machinations.

As mob violence continued through the fall of 1786, spokesmen in the Bay

State and elsewhere voiced a growing fear that the anarchy of Massachusetts might infect the entire nation. Several months earlier John Jay had predicted a crisis—"something I cannot foresee or conjecture. I am uneasy and apprehensive; more so than during the war." Now Secretary of War Henry Knox, Massachusetts statesman Rufus King, and others began to have similar apprehensions. They wrote frantic letters to one another, asking for news and predicting disaster. Abigail Adams, then in London, bristled at the "ignorant and wrestless desperadoes," while reports of the uprising helped prod her husband John into writing his ponderous *Defence of the Constitutions.* Even General Washington lost his equanimity. "[For] God's sake, tell me," he wrote to his former aide-de-camp, David Humphreys, in October, "what is the cause of all these commotions? Do they proceed from licentiousness, British influence disseminated by the tories, or real grievances which admit of redress? If the latter, why were they delayed 'till the public mind had been so much agitated? If the former, why are not the powers of Government tried at once?"

Fearful that the powers of state government would not be sufficient to thwart the rebellion, Governor Bowdoin and Secretary of War Knox hatched a scheme for employing federal troops should the need arise. Knox discussed the matter with Congress: the outcome was a call for 1,340 volunteers for the federal army (which then numbered only 700), most of them to be raised in Massachusetts and Connecticut. The additional troops were ostensibly to be used against the Indians of the Northwest, but in secret session Congress acknowledged the possibility that they might be sent instead against the self-styled "regulators" in New England, and that they might be needed to protect the federal arsenal in Springfield—a likely target for the rebellious veterans. Meanwhile the Massachusetts Council authorized a state army of 4,400 men and four regiments of artillery, to be drawn largely from the militia of the eastern counties.

Command of the state forces fell to Major General Benjamin Lincoln, a battle-tested veteran of the Revolution, and a man of tact and humanity as well as martial vigor. But before taking the field, Lincoln served a brief stint as fundraiser for his own army, for the cost of a thirty-day campaign had been calculated at about £5,000, or about $20,000, and the impoverished state treasury could offer nothing but promises of eventual reimbursement to any who would lend cash to the government. In less than twenty-four hours General Lincoln collected contributions from 130 of Boston's wealthy citizens, including £250 from Governor Bowdoin.

By the time Lincoln's army was equipped for action, the rebellion was over in eastern Massachusetts. It had never been strong there, but in November of 1786 a mob tried to halt the Middlesex County court. This time the militia was alert. After a brief skirmish in which Job Shattuck received a crippling wound, the Groton leader and two of his lieutenants were captured. While Shattuck languished in the Boston jail, his followers drifted west to join other rebel groups.

The situation now grew alarming in Worcester, where the Supreme Court was scheduled to meet on December 5; by late November, mobs of armed men drifting into town had closed the Court of Common Pleas and made it obvious that no court could meet without an army to back it up. Local officials looked on helplessly. Even bold Sheriff Greenleaf, who offered to help alleviate the high court costs by hanging every rebel free of charge, was powerless in the face of such numbers, and he became a laughingstock to boot when he strode away from the courthouse one day unaware that someone had adorned his hat with the symbolic hemlock tuft.

At first the rebels at Worcester suffered from lack of a universally recognized leader. Then in early December Daniel Shays rode in from Pelham, mounted on a white horse and followed by 350 men. He had not come to do battle if he could avoid it; to a friend he confided: "For God's sake, have matters settled peaceably: it was against my inclinations I undertook this business; importunity was used which I could not withstand, but I heartily wish it was well over." Still, as a showdown with the judges approached, Shays increasingly assumed the role of spokesman for the disparate forces. And it was just as well; with milling crowds of disgruntled veterans and a frightened and divided populace, violence might well have erupted. Instead, choosing wisdom as the better part of valor, the rebels put their energies into drafting a petition to the legislature for a redress of grievances and into several wordy defenses of their own actions. Violence was scrupulously avoided. And their immediate point, after all, had been won; the Worcester court gathered meekly in the Sun Tavern and adjourned until January 23. The insurgents then gave way before the more impressive force of winter blizzards and dispersed to the west. Friends of the rebels were not greatly heartened, however, for the basic grievances remained. Friends of the government rejoiced at the retreat of the rebels, and chanted:

Says sober Bill, "Well Shays has fled,
And peace returns to bless our days!"
"Indeed," cries Ned, "I always said
He'd prove at last a fall-back Shays,
    And those turned over and undone
Call him a worthless Shays, to run!"

But Shays was only running to a new scene of action. The Hampshire County court, scheduled to meet in Springfield in late January, should be stopped. Besides, the federal arsenal in that town had the only cache of arms the rebels could hope to capture, and without weapons the rebellion must collapse.

General Lincoln was preparing to defend the January session of the Worcester court when news reached him of the crisis in Springfield. The arsenal there boasted a garrison of some 1,100 militia under General William Shepard, but surrounding the troops were three rebel forces: Daniel Shays commanded 1,200 men at Wilbraham, eight miles to the east; Eli Parson had 400 at Chicopee, three miles to the north; Luke Day led another 400 at West Springfield, just across the Connecticut River to the west. There was every reason to believe they could overwhelm Shepard's garrison if they were willing to risk some bloodshed. General Lincoln headed for Springfield on the double.

Had Shays and his cohorts carried out their original plan they would in all likelihood have had possession of the arsenal before Lincoln arrived with rein-

After Shays' followers were repulsed at the Springfield armory, as shown here, the rebellion quickly fell apart.

forcements. The attack had been set for January 25: Shays was to have led a frontal assault from the southeast while Day directed a flanking movement from the west. But at the last minute Day decided to wait until the twenty-sixth, and his note informing Shays of the change was intercepted by Shepard's men. When Shays moved forward on the afternoon of the twenty-fifth, Shepard confidently grouped his full strength against the lone attack. But not much strength was needed. Shepard fired only three cannon shots. When two warning volleys failed to turn back the rebels, Shepard aimed the third into their midst. Three insurgents fell dead in the snow, a fourth lay mortally wounded. The remainder fled in confusion. It was a shattered band that Shays succeeded in regrouping a few miles from the scene of conflict.

At this point General Lincoln arrived and took position between Day and Shays. Both rebel armies at once broke camp and headed for safer territory—

Day's men so hastily that they left pork and beans baking in their ovens and discarded knapsacks strewn along their route. The main force, under Shays, beat a rapid retreat to the northeast, passing through Ludlow, South Hadley, Amherst, and Pelham. Lincoln followed in close pursuit, moving overland after Shays, while General Shepard marched up the frozen Connecticut River to prevent a reunion of the rebel army's eastern and western wings.

At Hadley, General Lincoln halted his pursuit long enough to discuss surrender proposals with Shays. The rebel leader was willing to negotiate, but his insistence on an unconditional pardon for himself and his men was more than General Lincoln was authorized to grant. With no agreement likely, Shays suddenly shifted his men to the relative security of Petersham, a center of regulator sentiment which lay in terrain easier to defend. It was midwinter—an unusually cold and stormy winter—and deep snow blanketed the Connecticut Valley. Perhaps the militia would not bother to follow.

But Shays reckoned without General Lincoln. Ever since 1780, when he had surrendered Charleston, South Carolina, and its garrison of 5,400 men to the British in the most costly American defeat of the Revolution, Benjamin Lincoln had had to endure charges of cowardice and indecision. Although he had been officially exonerated, a few critics persisted; in a vigorous suppression of the Shaysites General Lincoln could perhaps fully restore himself in the public's esteem. With superb stamina and determination, Lincoln marched his men the thirty miles from Hadley to Petersham through a blinding snowstorm on the night of Saturday, February 3, arriving at Petersham early the next morning. Taken completely by surprise, the insurgents were routed: some 150 were captured; the rest, including Shays, escaped to the north. Lincoln then moved across the Connecticut River to disperse rebel nests in the Berkshires. By the end of February only scattered resistance remained. What the legislature had recently condemned as a "horrid and unnatural Rebellion and War . . . traiterously raised and levied against this Commonwealth" had come to an inglorious end.

While the militia crushed the remnants of rebellion, the state government drafted a series of regulations for punishing the insurgents. In mid-February, two weeks after Shays' dispersal at Petersham, it issued a stiff Disqualifying Act, offering pardons to privates and noncommissioned officers, but denying them for three years the right to vote, to serve on juries, and to be employed as schoolteachers, innkeepers, or liquor retailers. Massachusetts citizens would thus be shielded from the baneful influence of the Shaysites. Not included in the partial amnesty were the insurgent officers, citizens of other states who had joined the Massachusetts uprising, former state officers or members of the state legislature who had aided the rebels, and persons who had attended regulator conventions. Men in those categories would be tried for treason.

The government's vindictive measures aroused widespread protest, not only from those who had sympathized with the rebel cause but from many of its active opponents as well. General Lincoln, among others, believed that such harsh reprisals would further alienate the discontented, and he observed to General Washington that the disfranchisement of so many people would wholly deprive some towns of their representation in the legislature. New outbreaks, he argued, would then occur in areas that had no other way to voice their grievances. In token concession to its critics, the legislature in March, 1787, appointed a special commission of three men to determine the fate of rebels not covered by the Disqualifying Act. General Lincoln served on the commission, and under his moderating influence it eventually extended pardons to 790 persons. But in the meantime, county courts apprehended and tried whatever rebel leaders they could find. In Hampshire County, with Robert Treat Paine serving as prosecuting attorney, six men were sentenced to death and many others incurred fines or imprisonment. In Berkshire County eight men were sentenced to die for their part in the uprising.

Had the government of 1786–87 remained in office, more than a dozen lives would have been lost to the hangman, hundreds of other men would have suffered disqualifications, and the fundamental causes of Shays' Rebellion might have lingered on to trigger new outbreaks. But however strongly the regulators might complain of the legislative and judicial shortcomings of Massachusetts, they had cause to be thankful that its constitution required annual elections and that the franchise was broad enough to let popular sentiment determine the tenor of government. The result of the April election revealed the breadth and depth of the sympathy in which the regulators were held by the citizens and the extent of popular revulsion at the ineptitude of the government. In the gubernatorial contest, popular John Hancock, recently recovered from an illness that had caused him to resign the governorship early in 1785, overwhelmingly defeated Governor Bowdoin. Only 62 of the 222 members of the legislature and 11 members of the 24-man senate were returned to their seats. In some instances the voters chose men who had actively participated in the rebellion, including Josiah Whitney, who had recently served sixteen days in the Worcester jail.

Within the next few months the new legislature sharply mitigated both the causes of unrest and the punishments assigned to the rebels. It repealed the Disqualifying Act, reprieved all men under sentence of death—some on the very steps of the gallows—and by the following summer it had pardoned even Daniel Shays, though he and a few other leaders were still precluded from holding civil and military offices in the state. Equally important, it enacted long-range reforms—extending the law that permitted the use of certain personal and real property in payment of debts, imposing a lower and more equitable tax schedule, and releasing most debtors from prison.

Now in truth the rebellion was over. Peace, and soon prosperity, returned to the Massachusetts countryside. Differences of opinion still lingered, of course, as was made clear one Sunday when the church at Whately christened two infants—one named after Daniel Shays, the other after Benjamin Lincoln. But the Shaysites made no further trouble for Bay State authorities, and Daniel Shays, the reluctant leader, soon moved on to New York State, where he eked out a skimpy existence on his Revolutionary War pension until his death in 1825.

Americans of the 1780's drew various lessons from the affair in Massachusetts. Some, like Washington and Madison, appear to have misinterpreted the event and ascribed to the rebels a more drastic program than the majority of them had ever advocated. Others, like Mercy Warren, the lady historian, and Joseph

Hawley, the Massachusetts patriot, detected the hand of Great Britain behind the uprising. Still others sensed that the true causes of Shays' Rebellion were local in origin and primarily the fault of the state government. Baron von Steuben had correctly surmised that "when a whole people complains . . . something must be wrong," while Thomas Jefferson, then American Minister to France, thought the rebellion of no dangerous importance and preferred to set it in a broader perspective than had most Americans. "We have had," wrote Jefferson, "13 states independent 11 years. There has been one rebellion. That comes to one rebellion in a century and a half for each state. What country before ever existed a century and a half without a rebellion? And what country can preserve its liberties if their rulers are not warned from time to time that the people preserve the spirit of resistance? . . . The tree of liberty must be refreshed from time to time with the blood of patriots and tyrants." But while observers were drawing these diverse conclusions from the episode in Massachusetts, an increasing number of Americans were concerned with how to make sure it would never happen again.

On May 25, 1787, less than four months after the rout at Petersham, the Constitutional Convention began its deliberations at Independence Hall, Philadelphia. Through a long hot summer the delegates proposed, argued, and compromised as they sought to construct a new and better form of government for the American nation. And among the knottiest problems they faced were several recently emphasized by Shays' Rebellion: problems of currency regulation, of debts and contracts, and of ways to thwart domestic insurrection. As the records of the federal Convention reveal, the recent uprising in Massachusetts lay heavily on the minds of the delegates. Although it is impossible to pinpoint the exact phrases in the final document that owed their wording to the fear of similar revolts, there is no doubt that the Constitution reflected the determination of the Founding Fathers to do all they could to prevent future rebellions and to make it easier for the new government to suppress them if they did occur. Significantly, the new polity forbade the states to issue paper money, strengthened the military powers of the executive branch, and authorized Congress to call up state militiamen to "suppress Insurrections" and enforce the laws of the land. Jefferson's first glimpse of the Constitution convinced him that "our Convention has been too much impressed by the insurrection of Massachusetts. . . ." Jefferson exaggerated, but it is clear that the movement for a stronger central government had gained immense momentum from the "horrid and unnatural Rebellion" of Daniel Shays.

By the summer of 1788 the requisite nine states had ratified the new Constitution, and in the following spring General Washington took the oath of office as President. In the prosperous and dynamic years that followed, the passions generated by the insurrection in Massachusetts were gradually extinguished. But the lesson and the impact of Shays' Rebellion are still with us. Because of it, important changes were made in the government of Massachusetts as well as in the government of the nation, changes that have stood the test of time. Perhaps this episode lends some ironic credence to Thomas Jefferson's suggestion that "the spirit of resistance to government is . . . valuable on certain occasions."

The Constitution: Was It an Economic Document?

Henry Steele Commager

When Charles A. Beard published An Economic Interpretation of the Constitution *in 1913, in which he argued that the personal economic interests of the Founding Fathers played a major role in the shaping of the Constitution, he roused a furor and incidentally triggered a rash of studies designed to show how importantly material interests had influenced people's behavior throughout our history. Beard's line of reasoning was never accepted by all scholars, but for a long time his basic approach came close to dominating the writing of American history. In recent times, however, the Beardian economic interpretation has been subjected to devastating attack (almost line by line) by such historians as Robert E. Brown and Forrest McDonald.*

In this essay Professor Henry Steele Commager of Amherst College takes a fresh look at this controversial subject, offering a thoughtful and objective evaluation of Beard's work and of the motives and actions of the Founding Fathers. Commager, a historian of wide-ranging interests, combines a detailed knowledge of constitutional history with a sensitive perception of the force of ideas in shaping events.

By June 26, 1787, tempers in the Federal Convention were already growing short, for gentlemen had come to the explosive question of representation in the upper chamber. Two days later Franklin moved to invoke divine guidance, and his motion was shunted aside only because there was no money with which to pay a chaplain and the members were unprepared to appeal to Heaven without an intermediary. It was not surprising that when James Madison spoke of representation in the proposed legislature, he was conscious of the solemnity of the occasion. We are, he said, framing a system "which we wish to last for ages" and one that might "decide forever the fate of Republican Government."

It was an awful thought, and when, a few days later, Gouverneur Morris spoke to the same subject he felt the occasion a most solemn one; even the irrepressible Morris could be solemn. "He came here," he observed (so Madison noted),

as a Representative of America; he flattered himself he came here in some degree as a Representative of the whole human race; for the whole human race will be affected by the proceedings of this Convention. He wished gentlemen to extend their views beyond the present moment of time; beyond the narrow limits . . . from which they derive their political origin. . . .

170

> Much has been said of the sentiments of the people. They were unknown.
> They could not be known. All that we can infer is that if the plan we recom-
> mend be reasonable & right; all who have reasonable minds and sound inten-
> tions will embrace it . . .

These were by no means occasional sentiments only. They were sentiments
that occurred again and again throughout the whole of that long hot summer,
until they received their final, eloquent expression from the aged Franklin in that
comment on the rising, not the setting, sun. Even during the most acrimonious
debates members were aware that they were framing a constitution for ages to
come, that they were creating a model for people everywhere on the globe; there
was a lively sense of responsibility and even of destiny. Nor can we now, as we
contemplate that Constitution which is the oldest written national constitution,
and that federal system which is one of the oldest and the most successful in
history, regard these appeals to posterity as merely rhetorical.

That men are not always conscious either of what they do or of the motives
that animate them is a familiar rather than a cynical observation. Some 45 years
ago Charles A. Beard propounded an economic interpretation of the Constitution—an interpretation which submitted that the Constitution was *essentially* (that
is a crucial word) an economic document—and that it was carried through the
Convention and the state ratifying conventions by interested economic groups
for economic reasons. "The Constitution," Mr. Beard concluded, "was essentially an economic document based upon the concept that the fundamental private rights of property are anterior to government and morally beyond the reach
of popular majorities."

*Independence Hall as it appeared in an engraving done just prior to the
Revolution.*

At the time it was pronounced, that interpretation caused something of a sensation, and Mr. Beard was himself eventually to comment with justifiable indignation on the meanness and the vehemence of the attacks upon it—and him. Yet the remarkable thing about the economic interpretation is not the criticism it inspired but the support it commanded. For within a few years it had established itself as the new orthodoxy, and those who took exception to it were stamped either as professional patriots—perhaps secret Sons or Daughters of the Revolution—or naïve academicians who had never learned the facts of economic life.

The attraction that the economic interpretation had for the generation of the twenties and thirties—and that it still exerts—is one of the curiosities of our cultural history, but by no means an inexplicable one. To a generation of materialists Beard's thesis made clear that the stuff of history was material. To a generation disillusioned by the exploitations of big business it discovered that the past, too, had been ravaged by economic exploiters. To a generation that looked with skeptical eyes upon the claims of Wilsonian idealism and all but rejoiced in their frustration, it suggested that all earlier idealisms and patriotisms—even the idealism and patriotism of the framers—had been similarly flawed by selfishness and hypocrisy.

Yet may it not be said of *An Economic Interpretation of the Constitution* that it is not a conclusion but a point of departure? It explains a great deal about the forces that went into the making of the Constitution, and a great deal, too, about the men who assembled in Philadelphia in 1787, but it tells us extraordinarily little about the document itself. And it tells us even less about the historical meaning of that document.

What were the objects of the Federal Convention? The immediate objects were to restore order; to strengthen the public credit; to enable the United States to make satisfactory commercial treaties and agreements; to provide conditions in which trade and commerce could flourish; to facilitate management of the western lands and of Indian affairs. All familiar enough. But what, in the light of history, were the grand objects of the Convention? What was it that gave Madison and Morris and Wilson and King and Washington himself a sense of destiny?

There were two grand objects—objects inextricably interrelated. The first was to solve the problem of federalism, that is, the problem of the distribution of powers among governments. Upon the wisdom with which members of the Convention distinguished between powers of a general and powers of a local nature, and assigned these to their appropriate governments, would depend the success or failure of the new experiment.

But it was impossible for the children of the eighteenth century to talk or think of powers without thinking of power, and this was a healthy realism. No less troublesome—and more fundamental—than the problem of the distribution of powers, was the problem of sanctions. How were they to enforce the terms of the distribution and impose limits upon all the governments involved? It was one thing to work out the ideal distribution of general and local powers. It was another thing to see to it that the states abided by their obligations under the

Articles of Union and that the national government respected the autonomy of states and liberty of individuals.

Those familiar with the Revolutionary era know that the second of these problems was more difficult than the first. Americans had learned how to limit government: the written constitutions, the bills of rights, the checks and balances. They had not yet learned (nor had anyone) how to "substitute the mild magistracy of the law for the cruel and violent magistracy of force." The phrase is Madison's.

Let us return to the *Economic Interpretation.* The correctness of Beard's analysis of the origins and backgrounds of the membership of the Convention, of the arguments in the Convention, and of the methods of assuring ratification, need not be debated. But these considerations are, in a sense, irrelevant and immaterial. For though they are designed to illuminate the document itself, in fact they illuminate only the processes of its manufacture.

The idea that property considerations were paramount in the minds of those assembled in Philadelphia is misleading and unsound and is borne out neither by the evidence of the debates in the Convention nor by the Constitution itself. The Constitution was not *essentially* an economic document. It was, and is, *essentially* a political document. It addresses itself to the great and fundamental question of the distribution of powers between governments. The Constitution was—and is—a document that attempts to provide sanctions behind that distribution; a document that sets up, through law, a standing rule to live by and provides legal machinery for the enforcement of that rule. These are political, not economic functions.

Not only were the principles that animated the framers political rather than economic; the solutions that they formulated to the great questions that confronted them were dictated by political, not by economic considerations.

Here are two fundamental challenges to the Beard interpretation: first, the Constitution is primarily a document in federalism; and second, the Constitution does not in fact confess or display the controlling influence of those who held that "the fundamental private rights of property are anterior to government and morally beyond the reach of popular majorities."

Let us look more closely at these two conventions. The first requires little elaboration or vindication, for it is clear to all students of the Revolutionary era that the one pervasive and over-branching problem of that generation was the problem of imperial organization. How to get the various parts of any empire to work together for common purposes? How to get central control—over war, for example, or commerce or money—without impairing local autonomy? How, on the other hand, to preserve personal liberty and local self-government without impairing the effectiveness of the central government? This was one of the oldest problems in political science—as old as the history of the Greek city-states; as new as the recent debate over Federal aid to education or the Bricker amendment.

The British failed to solve the problem of imperial order; when pushed to the wall they had recourse to the hopelessly doctrinaire Declaratory Act, which was, in fact, a declaration of political bankruptcy; as Edmund Burke observed, no people is going to be argued into slavery. The Americans then took up the

Thomas Rossiter's view of the signing of the Constitution was painted about 1850.

vexatious problem. The Articles of Confederation were satisfactory enough as far as the distribution of powers was concerned, but wholly wanting in sanctions. The absence of sanctions spelled the failure of the Articles—and this failure led to the Philadelphia Convention.

Now it will be readily conceded that many, if not most, of the questions connected with federalism were economic in character. Involved were such practical matters as taxation, the regulation of commerce, coinage, western lands, slavery, and so forth. The problem that presented itself to the framers was not whether government should exercise authority over such matters; it was *which* government should exercise such authority—and how should it be exercised?

There were, after all, no anarchists at the Federal Convention. Everyone agreed that *some* government had to have authority to tax, raise armies, regulate commerce, coin money, control contracts, enact bankruptcy legislation, regulate western territories, make treaties, and do all the things that government must do. But where should these authorities be lodged—with the state governments or with the national government they were about to erect, or with both?

This question was a political, not an economic, one. And the solution at which the framers arrived was based upon a sound understanding of politics, and need not be explained by reference to class attachments or security interests.

Certainly if the framers were concerned primarily or even largely with protecting property against popular majorities, they failed signally to carry out their purposes. It is at this point in our consideration of the *Economic Interpretation of the Constitution* that we need to employ what our literary friends call *explication du texte.* For the weakest link in the Beard interpretation is precisely the crucial one—the document itself. Mr. Beard makes amply clear that those who wrote the Constitution were members of the propertied classes,* and that many of them were personally involved in the outcome of what they were about to do; he makes out a persuasive case that the division over the Constitution was along economic lines. What he does not make clear is how or where the Constitution itself reflects all these economic influences.

Much is made of the contract clause and the paper money clause of the Constitution. No state may impair the obligations of a contract—whatever those words mean, and they apparently did not mean to the framers quite what Chief Justice Marshall later said they meant in *Fletcher v. Peck* or *Dartmouth College v. Woodward.* No state may emit bills of credit or make anything but gold and silver coin legal tender in payment of debts.

These are formidable prohibitions, and clearly reflect the impatience of men of property with the malpractices of the states during the Confederation. Yet quite aside from what the states may or may not have done, who can doubt that these limitations upon the states followed a sound principle—the principle that control of coinage and money belonged to the central, not the local governments, and the principle that local jurisdictions should not be able to modify or overthrow contracts recognized throughout the Union?

What is most interesting in this connection is what is so often overlooked: that the framers did not write any comparable prohibitions upon the United States government. The United States was not forbidden to impair the obligation of its contracts, not at least in the Constitution as it came from the hands of its property-conscious framers. Possibly the Fifth Amendment may have squinted toward such a prohibition; we need not determine that now, for the Fifth Amendment was added by the *states* after the Constitution had been ratified. So, too, the emission of bills of credit and the making other than gold and silver legal tender were limitations on the states, but not on the national government. There was, in fact, a lively debate over the question of limiting the authority of the national government in the matter of bills of credit. When the question came up on August 16, Gouverneur Morris threatened that "The Monied interest will oppose the plan of Government, if paper emissions be not prohibited." In the end the Convention dropped out a specific authorization to emit bills of credit, but pointedly did not prohibit such action. Just where this left the situation troubled Chief Justice Chase's Court briefly three quarters of a century later; the Court recovered its balance, and the sovereign power of the government over money was not again *successfully* challenged.

---

*"A majority of the members were lawyers by profession.

"Most of the members came from towns, on or near the coast, that is, from the regions in which personalty was largely concentrated.

"Not one member represented in his immediate personal economic interests the small farming or mechanic classes.

"The overwhelming majority of members, at least five-sixths, were immediately, directly, and personally interested in the outcome of their labors at Philadelphia, and were to a greater or less extent economic beneficiaries from the adoption of the Constitution." Beard, *An Economic Interpretation of the Constitution.*

Nor were there other specific limitations of an economic character upon the powers of the new government that was being erected on the ruins of the old. The framers properly gave the Congress power to regulate commerce with foreign nations and among the states. The term commerce—as Hamilton and Adair (and Crosskey, too!) have made clear—was broadly meant, and the grant of authority, too, was broad. The framers gave Congress the power to levy taxes and, again, wrote no limitations into the Constitution except as to the apportionment of direct taxes; it remained for the most conservative of Courts to reverse itself, and common sense, and discover that the framers had intended to forbid an income tax! Today, organizations that invoke the very term "constitutional" are agitating for an amendment placing a quantitative limit upon income taxes that may be levied; fortunately, Madison's generation understood better the true nature of governmental power.

The framers gave Congress—in ambiguous terms, to be sure—authority to make "all needful Rules and Regulations respecting the Territory or other Property" of the United States, and provided that "new states may be admitted." These evasive phrases gave little hint of the heated debates in the Convention over western lands. Those who delight to find narrow and undemocratic sentiments in the breasts of the framers never cease to quote a Gouverneur Morris or an Elbridge Gerry on the dangers of the West, and it is possible to compile a horrid catalogue of such statements. But what is significant is not what framers said, but what they did. They did not place any limits upon the disposition of western territory, or establish any barriers against the admission of western states.

The fact is that we look in vain *in the Constitution itself* for any really effective guarantee for property or any effective barriers against what Beard calls "the reach of popular majorities."

It will be argued, however, that what the framers feared was the *states,* and that the specific prohibitions against state action, together with the broad transfer of economic powers from state to nation, were deemed sufficient guarantee against state attacks upon property. As for the national government, care was taken to make that sufficiently aristocratic, sufficiently the representative of the propertied classes, and sufficiently checked and limited so that it would not threaten basic property interests.

It is at this juncture that the familiar principle of limitation on governmental authority commands our attention. Granted the wisest distribution of powers among governments, what guarantee was there that power would be properly exercised? What guarantees were there against the abuse of power? What assurance was there that the large states would not ride roughshod over the small, that majorities would not crush minorities or minorities abuse majorities? What protection was there against mobs, demagogues, dangerous combinations of interests or of states? What protection was there for the commercial interest, the planter interest, the slave interest, the securities interests, the land speculator interests?

It was Madison who most clearly saw the real character of this problem and who formulated its solution. It was not that the people as such were dangerous;

Washington's working copy of a printed draft of the Constitution indicates approval of federal control over coinage and duties in Articles XII and XIII.

"The truth was," he said on July 11, "that all men having power ought to be distrusted to a certain degree." Long before Lord Acton coined the aphorism, the Revolutionary leaders had discovered that power corrupts. They understood, too, the drive for power on the part of individuals and groups. All this is familiar to students of *The Federalist,* No. 10. It should be familiar to students of the debates in Philadelphia, for there, too, Madison set forth his theory and supported it with a wealth of argument. Listen to him on one of the early days of the Convention, June 6, when he is discussing the way to avoid abuses of republican liberty—abuses which "prevailed in the largest as well as the smallest [states] . . ."

> . . . And were we not thence admonished [he continued] to enlarge the sphere as far as the nature of the Government would admit. This was the only defence against the inconveniences of democracy *consistent with the democratic form of Government* [our italics]. All civilized Societies would be divided into different Sects, Factions & interests, as they happened to consist of rich & poor, debtors and creditors, the landed, the manufacturing, the commercial interests, the inhabitants of this district or that district, the followers of this political leader or that political leader, the disciples of this religious Sect or that religious Sect. In all cases where a majority are united by a common interest or passion, the rights of the minority are in danger. . . . In a Republican Govt. The Majority if united have always an opportunity [to oppress the minority. What is the remedy?] The only remedy is to enlarge the sphere, & thereby divide the community into so great a number of interests & parties, that in the first place a majority will not be likely at the same moment to have a common interest separate from that of the whole or of the minority; and in the second place, that in case they should have such an interest, they may not be apt to unite in the pursuit of it. It was incumbent on us then to try this remedy, and . . . to frame a republican system on such a scale & in such a form as will controul all the evils which have been experienced.

This long quotation is wonderfully eloquent of the attitude of the most sagacious of the framers. Madison, Wilson, Franklin, as well as Gerry, Morris, Pinckney, and Hamilton feared power. They feared power whether exercised by a monarch, an aristocracy, an army, or a majority, and they were one in their determination to write into fundamental law limitations on the arbitrary exercise of that power. To assume, as Beard so commonly does, that the fear of the misuse of power by majorities was either peculiar to the Federalists or more ardent with them than with their opponents, is mistaken. Indeed it was rather the anti-Federalists who were most deeply disturbed by the prospect of majority rule; they, rather than the Federalists, were the "men of little faith." Thus it was John Lansing, Jr., of New York (he who left the Convention rather than have any part in its dangerous work) who said that "all free constitutions are formed with two views—to deter the governed from crime, and the governors from tyranny." And the ardent Patrick Henry, who led the attack on the Constitution in the Virginia Convention—and almost defeated it—complained not of too little democracy in that document, but too much.

The framers, to be sure, feared the powers of the majority, as they feared all power unless controlled. But they were insistent that, in the last analysis, there must be government by majority; even conservatives like Morris and Hamilton made this clear. Listen to Hamilton, for example, at the very close of the Convention. Elbridge Gerry, an opponent of the Constitution, had asked for a reconsideration of the provision for calling a constitutional convention, alleging that this opened the gate to a majority that could "bind the union to innovations that may subvert the State-Constitutions altogether." To this Hamilton replied that

> There was no greater evil in subjecting the people of the U.S. to the major voice than the people of a particular State. . . . It was equally desirable now that an easy mode should be established for supplying defects which will probably appear in the New System. . . . There could be no danger in giving this power, as the people would finally decide in the case.

. . . But we need not rely upon what men said; there is too much of making history by quotation anyway. Let us look rather at what men did. We can turn again to the Constitution itself. Granted the elaborate system of checks and balances: the separation of powers, the bicameral legislature, the executive veto, and so forth—checks found in the state constitutions as well, and in our own democratic era as in the earlier one—what provision did the framers make against majority tyranny? What provisions did they write into the Constitution against what Randolph called "democratic licentiousness"?

They granted equality of representation in the Senate. If this meant that conservative Delaware would have the same representation in the upper chamber as democratic Pennsylvania, it also meant that democratic Rhode Island would have the same representation as conservative South Carolina. But the decision for equality of representation was not dictated by considerations either economic or democratic, but rather by the recalcitrance of the small states. Indeed, though it is difficult to generalize here, on the whole it is true that it was the more ardent Federalists who favored proportional representation in both houses.

They elaborated a most complicated method of electing a Chief Executive, a method designed to prevent the easy expression of any majority will. Again the explanation is not simple. The fact was that the framers did not envision the possibility of direct votes for presidential candidates which would not conform to state lines and interests and thus lead to dissension and confusion. Some method, they thought, must be designated to overcome the force of state prejudices (or merely of parochialism) and get an election; the method they anticipated was a preliminary elimination contest by the electoral college and then eventual election by the House. This, said George Mason, was what would occur nineteen times out of twenty.* There is no evidence in the debates that the complicated method finally hit upon for electing a President was designed either to frustrate

---

*It has happened twice: Jefferson vs. Burr (1801) and J. Q. Adams vs. Clay, Jackson, and Crawford (1825).

popular majorities or to protect special economic interests; its purpose was to overcome state pride and particularism.

Senators and Presidents, then, would not be the creatures of democracy. But what guarantee was there that senators would be representatives of property interests, or that the President himself would recognize the "priority of property"? Most states had property qualifications for office holding, but there are none in the Federal Constitution. As far as the Constitution is concerned, the President, congressmen, and Supreme Court justices can all be paupers.

Both General Charles Cotesworth Pinckney and his young cousin Charles, of South Carolina, were worried about this. The latter proposed a property qualification of $100,000 (a tidy sum in those days) for the Presidency, half that for the judges, and substantial sums for members of Congress. Franklin rebuked him. He was distressed, he said, to hear anything "that tended to debase the spirit of the common people." More surprising was the rebuke from that stout conservative, John Dickinson. "He doubted," Madison reports, "the policy of interweaving into a Republican constitution a veneration for wealth. He had always understood that a veneration for poverty & virtue were the objects of republican encouragement." Pinckney's proposal was overwhelmingly rejected.

What of the members of the lower house? When Randolph opened "the main business" on May 29 he said the remedy for the crisis that men faced must be "the republican principle," and two days later members were discussing the fourth resolution, which provided for election to the lower house by the people. Roger Sherman of Connecticut thought that "the people should have as little to do as may be about the Government," and Gerry hastened to agree in words now well-worn from enthusiastic quotation that "The evils we experience flow from the excess of democracy." These voices were soon drowned out, however. Mason "argued strongly for an election . . . by the people. It was to be the grand depository of the democratic principle of the Govt." And the learned James Wilson, striking the note to which he was to recur again and again, made clear that he was for "raising the federal pyramid to a considerable altitude, and for that reason wished to give it as broad a basis as possible." He thought both branches of the legislature—and the President as well, for that matter—should be elected by the people. "The Legislature," he later observed, "ought to be the most exact transcript of the whole Society."

A further observation is unhappily relevant today. It was a maxim with John Adams that "where annual elections end, there tyranny begins," and the whole Revolutionary generation was committed to a frequent return to the source of authority. But the framers put into the Constitution no limits on the number of terms which Presidents or congressmen could serve. It was not that the question was ignored; it received elaborate attention. It was rather that the generation that wrote the Constitution was better grounded in political principles than is our own; that it did not confuse, as we so often do, quantitative and qualitative limitations; and that—in a curious way—it had more confidence in the intelligence and the good will of the people than we seem to have today. It is, in any event, our own generation that has the dubious distinction of writing into the Constitution the first quantitative limitation on the right of the majority to choose their President. It is not the generation of the framers that was undemocratic; it is our generation that is undemocratic.

It is relevant to note, too, that the Constitution contains no property qualification for voting. Most states, to be sure, had such qualifications—in general a freehold or its equivalent—and the Constitution assimilated such qualifications as states might establish. Yet the framers, whether for reasons practical or philosophical we need not determine, made no serious efforts to write any property qualifications for voting into the Constitution itself.

The question of popular control came up clearly in one other connection as well: the matter of ratification. Should the Constitution be ratified by state legislatures, or by conventions? The practical arguments for the two methods were nicely balanced. The decisive argument was not, however, one of expediency but of principle. "To the people with whom all power remains that has not been given up in the Constitutions derived from them" we must resort, said Mason. Madison put the matter on principle, too. "He considered the difference between a system founded on the Legislatures only, and one founded on the people, to be the true difference between a *league* or *treaty* and a *Constitution*." Ellsworth's motion to refer the Constitution to legislatures was defeated by a vote of eight to two, and the resolution to refer it to conventions passed with only Delaware in the negative.

Was the Constitution designed to place private property beyond the reach of majorities? If so, the framers did a very bad job. They failed to write into it the most elementary safeguards for property. They failed to write into it limitations on the tax power, or prohibitions against the abuse of the money power. They failed to provide for rule by those whom Adams was later to call the wise and the rich and the well-born. What they did succeed in doing was to create a system of checks and balances and adjustments and accommodations that would effectively prevent the suppression of most minorities by majorities. They took advantage of the complexity, the diversity, the pluralism, of American society and economy to encourage a balance of interests. They worked out sound and lasting political solutions to the problems of class, interest, section, race, religion, party.

Perhaps the most perspicacious comment on this whole question of the threat from turbulent popular majorities against property and order came, *mirabile dictu,* from the dashing young Charles Pinckney of South Carolina—he of the "lost" Pinckney Plan. On June 25 Pinckney made a major speech and thought it important enough to write out and give to Madison. The point of departure was the hackneyed one of the character of the second branch of the legislature, but the comments were an anticipation of De Tocqueville and Lord Bryce. We need not, Pinckney asserted, fear the rise of class conflicts in America, nor take precautions against them.

> The genius of the people, their mediocrity of situation & the prospects which are afforded their industry in a Country which must be a new one for centuries are unfavorable to the rapid distinction of ranks. . . . If equality is . . . the leading feature of the U. States [he asked], where then are the riches & wealth whose representation & protection is the peculiar province of this permanent

body [the Senate]. Are they in the hands of the few who may be called rich; in the possession of less than a hundred citizens? certainly not. They are in the great body of the people . . . [There was no likelihood that a privileged body would ever develop in the United States, he added, either from the landed interest, the moneyed interest, or the mercantile.] Besides, Sir, I apprehend that on this point the policy of the U. States has been much mistaken. We have unwisely considered ourselves as the inhabitants of an old instead of a new country. We have adopted the maxims of a State full of people . . . The people of this country are not only very different from the inhabitants of any State we are acquainted with in the modern world; but I assert that their situation is distinct from either the people of Greece or of Rome . . .Our true situation appears to me to be this—a new extensive country containing within itself the materials for forming a Government capable of extending to its citizens all the blessings of civil & religious liberty—capable of making them happy at home. This is the great end of Republican Establishments. . . .

Not a government cunningly contrived to protect the interests of property, but one capable of extending to its citizens the blessings of liberty and happiness—was that not, after all, what the framers created?

Washington's Government

James Thomas Flexner

Every American child has learned to think of George Washington as "the father of his country," a title that refers to Washington's wisdom and noble, self-sacrificing character as well as to his service as commander-in-chief of the Continental army and as first president of the United States. What is less generally recognized (though equally appropriate as an indicator of where this view of Washington as a kind of progenitor of the nation came from) is the role he played in setting up the new administration after his inauguration as president. The decisions he made established precedents that determined many of the ways the nation's affairs have been carried on ever since. "I walk on untrodden ground," Washington said in this regard. His acute sense that every decision might shape the course of future leaders and the care and thought he gave to his actions are brought out in detail in this essay by James Thomas Flexner, the author of a Pulitzer Prize–winning biography of Washington and of many other works of history.

Probably because there was so much disagreement at the Constitutional Convention on matters of detail, the Constitution there established was little more than a skeleton. How the government would function in a thousand different particulars remained to be worked out at its beginning.

Only general directions were, for instance, charted for the boundaries between the three great divisions: executive, legislative, and judicial. The government could have ended up, not in its present form, but much closer to the British parliamentary system, with the executive departments subservient to the legislature. Or, had Washington been a different man, the legislative could have become subservient to the executive.

The first session of the new government was thus almost as important to the American future as the Constitutional Convention had been. The Congress and President Washington needed to determine their respective pulls and invent their harnesses while at the same time dragging along the coach of state.

Fortunately the landscape through which they had to move the nation, during that spring and summer of 1789, could not have been more smiling. If Providence was, as Washington liked to believe, watching over the daring American experiment in popular rule, surely that benign power made no greater gift than a period of tranquillity, commercial prosperity, and bountiful harvests during which the government could find internal agreement with no outside interference beyond a few Indian raids on scattered frontiers.

. . . Washington found himself and the Vice President the only members of the executive branch of the new government. He could make no appointments until Congress created the offices to which the appointments would be made. Pending that time, he had to assist him a few holdovers from the organization established under the Articles of Confederation by the defunct Continental Congress. Secretary of War Henry Knox and Secretary for Foreign Affairs John Jay were carrying on as "temporary Secretaries." There were a Treasury Board and a few minor functionaries, a regular army slightly below its authorized strength of 840 men, and a smattering of clerks whose salaries were in arrears. The foreign service consisted principally of Thomas Jefferson in Paris. . . .

Although Jay and Knox were old friends, Washington did not use these holdovers from the old government as such general advisers as he was later to make the members of his own cabinet. He turned for the help he so often desired primarily to the fellow Virginian who had been one of the major architects of the Constitution. He was perpetually summoning James Madison, sending him written requests for advice. Although Madison never became an official spokesman for the administration, his closeness to Washington was well known. The opening of the government thus presented an anomalous picture: the man who was as much of a prime minister as the President was the outstanding member of the House of Representatives.

The provisions in the Constitution concerning what was to become the President's cabinet were indicative of how much was left to be decided. Washington, indeed, first used the word "cabinet" on April 18, 1793, when asking for advice on what steps to take in regard to the war that had just broken out between England and France. The constitutional power of the President to appoint, with the approval of the Senate, all the important nonelective officers included the department heads. However, the only actual authority Washington was given over them was a minor one: he might require of them opinions relating to the duties of their offices. And Congress was given the power to assign directly to the department heads (bypassing the President) the appointment of "inferior Officers."

To secure a single executive rather than a committee, and to have him elected by the people rather than by Congress, had been among the most difficult tasks of the Constitutional Convention. The matter was still undecided two weeks before adjournment. There were many political leaders who still wished the executive limited to putting into effect the will of the legislative, and these saw their opportunity when Congress set up the executive departments. The controversy that developed turned on this question: Who should have the power to discharge the executive officials?

Opponents of a strong President argued that the constitutional provision that the President could appoint only with the approval of the Senate implied he would also have to secure such approval before he could dismiss. This would mean, of course, that a department head who opposed or even blocked the President's policies could be kept in office against the President's wishes by a majority of the Senate. It was argued on the other side that this would prevent the President from being master in his own house.

With Madison laboring mightily in the vineyard, the House of Representatives voted against supporting senatorial interference in presidential dismissals. But the Senate proved so evenly divided that the final vote was a tie, which Adams, as presiding officer, broke by coming out for an independent executive.

Since the matter was so closely contested even with the prestigious Washington in the executive chair, it is hard to doubt that if anyone else had been President, the vote would have gone the other way. This would have resulted in a very different form of government. Since the President's top assistants would have been no more accountable to him than to the Congress, he could have been placed in the position—like that of a modern constitutional monarch—of a figurehead.

Foreign policy having been established in the Constitution as the President's province, Washington did not hesitate to assert his primacy in diplomatic affairs. Thus, when the French king notified "the President and members of the General Congress" that the Dauphin had died, Washington, in sending condolences, pointed out that "the honor of receiving and answering" such communications no longer in any way involved the Congress; it was solely his own.

Concerning treaties, however, the Constitution stipulated that the President had to seek the Senate's "advice and consent." This provision, along with the need for senatorial approval of appointments, required the establishment of lines of communication between the Chief Executive and the Senate. Washington had hardly risen from his sickbed when, with Madison advising him closely, he set out to regularize those lines.

A nineteenth-century engraving of Washington, at left, with his first cabinet: Henry Knox, Secretary of War; Alexander Hamilton, Secretary of the Treasury; Edmund Randolph, Attorney General; and Thomas Jefferson, Secretary of State.

The most important precedent was soon established by a confrontation full of comic overtones. Having drafted instructions for a commission he had appointed, with Senate approval, to negotiate a treaty with the Creeks, Washington went with Secretary Knox to the Senate chamber seeking advice and consent.

The radical senator William Maclay of Pennsylvania scented indignity to the legislature at the very start when the President "took our Vice President's chair" and Knox sat beside him facing the house, while Adams, although he was the Senate's presiding officer, joined the senators below the dais.

Having been handed by Knox the proposed text of the treaty, Adams stood up and started to read it aloud. "Carriages were driving past, and such a noise!" Maclay noted, "I could tell it was something about 'Indians,' but was not master of one sentence of it. Signs were made to the door-keeper to shut down the sashes." It was now possible to hear a little, but the reading had gone on to supplementary documents. This finished, Adams asked for advice and consent to the first section of the treaty instructions.

Robert Morris suggested that the section be read again. It was. Adams asked again for advice and consent. Maclay then rose to say, "The business is new to the Senate. It is of importance. It is our duty to inform ourselves." He requested the reading of some additional papers that had been mentioned. Washington, he felt, was surveying him with "stern displeasure."

The reading of documents began; various members asked to hear others; there was the usual confusion of random discussion; and Washington finally agreed to postpone consideration of the first article. On to the second! A matter came up referring to Georgia, and a member from that state asked that it be postponed till Monday. Maclay was gleefully putting his shoulder to the wheel of confusion, since he "saw no chance of a fair investigation . . . while the President of the United States sat there, with his Secretary of War, to support his opinions and overawe the timid and neutral part of the Senate." However, it was Washington's own crony Morris who moved that the papers brought by the President be submitted to a committee for study.

Washington started up in what Maclay called "a violent fret." He cried, *This defeats every purpose of my coming here!*" He had brought Knox with him to present all the necessary information, "and yet he was delayed and could not go on with the matter!"

Maclay described Washington cooling "by degrees." The President finally agreed to a postponement till Monday. Then he departed "with a discontented air. Had it been any other man than the man whom I wish to regard as the first character in the world, I would have said, with sullen dignity."

On Monday Washington reappeared, well in control of himself. "He was placid and serene, and manifested a spirit of accommodation." Although in the end he achieved his purpose—only minor changes were made in the treaty instructions—Washington had to sit hour after hour, listening to an inconsequential and boring debate. As he finally departed from the Senate chamber, he was overheard to say that "he would be damned if he ever went there again."

The British system, in which the Prime Minister defends his policies before Parliament, demonstrates that it is possible so to set up a government that there can be effective personal meetings between the chief executive and the legislature. But in the United States Washington had forever slammed that door. He never again consulted the Senate in person. No President has ever taken part, in the British manner, in parliamentary debates.

Washington still sometimes sent the secretaries of War or Foreign Affairs to the Senate to deliver documents that would help the senators advise, but the idea seems already to have been growing in his mind that if there were to be any effective foreign negotiations, the prior advice of the Senate would have to be skimped in favor of ultimate consent. Otherwise, the negotiators' hands would be tied before the negotiation started. They might, indeed, be further embarrassed by what seemed a public commitment, since the senators might leak decisions to the newspapers. Concerning the most important foreign negotiations he faced—those with England—Washington resolved to proceed in an unofficial manner that would, among other things, obviate the necessity of consulting the Senate.

England had never fully recognized the victor of the Revolution by appointing a minister to the United States. Since America had retaliated in 1788 by calling John Adams home, official relations between the two nations were in abeyance. However, a British consul, Sir John Temple, appeared in New York and handed to Jay a series of questions from his government concerning American foreign trade, produce, populations, and the matter of whether a new system of justice would aid "the recovery of British debts according to treaty."

Washington did not respond by sending to London a consul bearing any official document. He preferred to inquire informally, through "a special agent," whether the British were willing to change their legislation aimed at curbing American commerce, and whether they would also evacuate the western posts they were holding in violation of the peace treaty. It seemed to Washington natural to select as a personal envoy a personal friend; and one of his closest friends, Gouverneur Morris, was already in Europe.

Washington had first met Morris in New York in 1776, as the General was trying to prepare for the impending onslaught of British armed might. Morris had been sent to him by the local congress as a member of a secret committee. Later, at Valley Forge, Morris appeared as a representative of the Continental Congress and proved immensely helpful in straightening out the desperate supply situation. By then the New York patrician had moved to Philadelphia to become a partner of Robert Morris, who, despite the similarity of names, was no relation. As inflation threatened to wash the cause under, the two Morrises established a little bank that did something to stem the tide. They became Washington's first mentors on the sophistications of finance, as they were also to a much more eager pupil, Alexander Hamilton.

Gouverneur Morris was arrogant, intolerant of fools, and possessed of such a reputation for licentiousness that it was generally believed that the leg he had lost in a carriage accident had come off as the result of an injury he received when jumping out of a lady's window as the husband unexpectedly came upstairs. Boasting that he "never knew the sensations of fear, embarrassment, or inferiority," Morris was as cocksure as he was arrogant. An inveterate prankster, much too elegantly dressed for the taste of simple republicans, he never hesitated to use his quick wit to humiliate men less brilliant than he. Josiah Bartlett of New Hampshire wrote that Morris was "for brass equal to any I am acquainted with."

Despite the objections of Jay and Madison but with the support of Hamilton, Washington entrusted to his mercurial friend the most difficult diplomatic mission of the new government, thereby bringing into the American foreign service (if through the back door) one of the most picturesque and, in the upshot, important characters it was ever to boast. Washington did not notify the Senate, since the Constitution did not require him to do so.

Washington was always careful not to overstep. "Few who are not philosophical spectators," he wrote, "can realize the difficult and delicate part which a man in my situation had to act. . . . I walk on untrodden ground. There is scarcely any part of my conduct wch. may not hereafter be drawn into precedent."

Among Washington's most important contributions to the emerging government was his restraint in exerting his great power beyond what he considered the legitimate province of the executive. Although, like any other citizen, he felt entitled to express his personal opinions to his friends, even if they happened to be legislators, he did not in any official or concerted way use his charisma or his office to influence legislative debates. Nor did he attempt to achieve by executive order any matter that the strictest interpretation of the Constitution could regard as within the legislative domain. The separation of powers has never known a more devoted champion.

Hamilton had explained in *The Federalist* that the veto power was essential to enable the President to protect his office from legislative usurpation. Washington found no such need. Perhaps because he himself so religiously avoided encroaching on the legislative, the effort in the two houses to curb the Presidency collapsed with the effort to give the Senate a hand in executive dismissals. From then on, Congress showered powers and responsibilities on the President.

Not only did the Senate forego its constitutional right to appoint secondary administrative officials, but it threw even such minor appointments as those of lighthouse keepers to the Chief Executive. Washington became so busy he could find no time to deal with his personal correspondence.

"To a man who has no ends to serve, nor friends to provide for," he wrote, "nomination to office is the most irksome part of the Executive trust." Before any offices at all had been created by Congress, the flood of applications stormed in: it crested to between 2,500 and 3,000 appeals. Washington did his best to avoid interviews, but men would appear at his levees to add verbal pleas to the hard-luck stories that came in with every mail. Many applicants, otherwise obviously unsuitable, were veterans who had fought at Washington's side; many were old friends or sons of old friends.

In a manner absolutely contradictory to the aristocratic governments with which the United States was then surrounded, Washington was determined not to be swayed by any personal considerations of blood or friendship. However, in a nation as large as the United States, at a time when travel was so much rarer than now and communications so slow, to identify in a distant state the right man for an office required endless interviews and correspondence. Even John Adams admired Washington's industry and impartiality: "He seeks information from all quarters, and judges more independently than any man I ever knew."

The various great departments were set up in separate bills. Revealing how little the new government, behind its ocean, was concerned with diplomacy, the title of Secretary for Foreign Affairs was changed to Secretary of State, and the duties of the office were expanded to include nearly all domestic operations except war and finance. The War Department was set up much as before. An Attorney General was to serve on a part-time basis as legal adviser for the executive.

It was with establishing the Treasury that Congress went into the most detail. Revealing a typical eighteenth-century respect for the power of the purse, the legislature established connections with the Secretary that did not pass through the Presidency. The Secretary should be directly responsive to Congress for information and should, at the request of the House, "digest and prepare" plans for the improvement and management of revenue. These provisions were intended to enable Congress to lead the Treasury: it was not foreseen that they would work the opposite way. . . .

Congress adjourned on September 29 until January 1, 1790, bringing to a close the initial session of the new government. It had been a time of endless creativity achieved with a minimum of turbulence. As compared with the Constitutional Convention, the session plays a very minor role in the history books; that in itself is a measure of how easy everything was, of how far sentiments had coalesced and how effective had been the leadership.

After Jefferson had finally reached home and then travelled to the capital, he expressed amazement at finding that "the opposition to our new Constitution has almost totally disappeared. . . . If," he added, "the President can be preserved

A crude, heavily satirical cartoon of the era comments on the removal of Congress from New York City to Philadelphia in 1790. The wealthy Senator Robert Morris from Pennsylvania drags his colleagues to their new temporary home.

a few more years, till habits of authority and obedience can be established generally, we have nothing to fear."

The United States was in the modern sense the world's first new nation. There have been many subsequent national births, and these have demonstrated again and again that the national symbol that a new people most naturally seek is what sociologists like to call "a charismatic personality." In the late eighteenth century this universal tendency was further strengthened (and made more frightening) by the still almost totally dominant tradition of royalty. And, to top all, America possessed a man who had been the symbol of national unity for fourteen years. George Washington was, so Madison wrote, the only aspect of the government that had really caught the imagination of the people.

If this made Washington supremely useful, it also made him seem, to men who feared for democratic institutions, extremely dangerous in his extraordinary influence over the people and his power to establish precedents. It seemed as if Washington were a great boulder rising in the streams of American institutions, which could, by the position it occupied, deflect the waters and thus determine the whole future flow of the American government. And entirely apart from his own personal behavior, there was the question of what opportunities a Presidency shaped around Washington might leave to his successors. A tyrant might use its powers for sinister ends.

All intelligent supporters of a strong central government agreed that a first essential was to secure the respect and acceptance of the people. History and existing European example taught that such popular support was, to an important extent, gained through titles and trappings that externalized the function of rulers: to command and be obeyed. Yet many felt that European tradition collided with the possibility—nay, the glorious duty!—of American originality. Was not reflecting European aristocratic behavior in fact the importation of decadence into a fresh Eden which was evolving newer and purer institutions—which the whole world would eventually follow? This gave social behavior a definite political cast.

However much he wanted to do what was expected of him, Washington was no bloodless symbol. Popular attitudes toward his behavior as a President were a maelstrom of myth, of religion and philosophy, of social and economic prejudice. He was a living man, with all the desires and tastes of a powerful individual habituated to controlling his own environment. That strain should result was inevitable.

On his arrival in New York Washington had discovered instantly and unpleasantly that the door of the presidential mansion supplied him with no protection whatsoever. Every person of the least importance felt he had a right to come in and stare, assess the furnishing of the house to see whether it was too grandly aristocratic or too squalidly republican; to utter rotund expressions of admiration and congratulation and then to assess Washington's reply on his own personal gauge for the right mixture of democratic warmth and charismatic grandeur.

Seeking some method of escape that would not only preserve his sanity but enable him to get some work done . . . Washington published in the newspapers that he would receive "visits of compliment" only between the hours of two and three on Tuesdays and Fridays. He would return no visits and accept no invitations "to entertainments." A little later he modified this by establishing two occasions a week when any respectably dressed person could, without introduction, invitation, or any prearrangement, be ushered into his presence. One was the President's "levee," for men only, every Tuesday from three to four. The other was Martha's tea party, for men and women, held on Friday evenings. Washington would also stage dinners on Thursdays at four o'clock in the afternoon. To avoid any charges of favoritism or contests for invitations, only officials and their families would be asked to the dinners, and these in an orderly system of rotation.

His levees exhibited none of the joviality of entertainments at Mount Vernon, nor of the ancient relaxations in army camps. The occasions could hardly have been stiffer. Exposed, as he put it, to "foreign characters, Strangers, and others who from motives of curiosity . . . or any other cause, are induced to call on me," Washington suffered from the same rigid embarrassment that made him so frustrating a sitter for painters. . . .

Perhaps under Martha's urging (which certainly agreed with his own predilections), Washington gradually and inconspicuously loosed his rigorous avoidance of private visits with personal friends—and at the official entertainments Martha shone. She not only soothed the men but charmed the ladies.

Abigail Adams had also arrived late at the capital. Having been told by her husband, John—who sarcastically referred to Washington as "His Majesty"—that hauteur and false grandeur now characterized the Washingtons, she must have been surprised, when she called on Martha, to be received with "great ease and politeness." Martha, she noted, "is plain in her dress, but the plainness is the best of every article. . . . Her hair is white, her teeth beautiful." Abigail even admired Martha's plump figure, considering it better than her own.

Although Washington's levees were usually dull (and criticized for being aristocratically stiff), Martha's weekly tea parties were gay (and criticized for being aristocratically splendid). At the tea parties the General was a different man, since he relaxed in the presence of the fair sex. Female elegance appealed to him, and the ladies of New York (as later in Philadelphia) having no parties more elaborate than these to attend, did not spare the milliners and hairdressers. They wore their hair low, with pearls and bandeaux, *à la grecque,* or rolled moderately skyward, *à la Pompadour.* It was noted that when his duties as a host left him free to circulate, Washington passed the men by and spent all his time with the ladies.

Throughout her tea parties Martha remained seated. Because he did not personally like the Vice President, Washington was all the more meticulous in honoring the office: he saw to it that the seat at Martha's right was assigned to the Vice President's lady. If another lady happened to be sitting there when Abigail Adams arrived, Washington got the interloper to move with a tact that made Abigail comment, "This same President has so happy a faculty to accommodate and yet carry his point, that, if he were really not the best-intentioned man in the world, he might be a very dangerous one." She then launched on a panegyric about Washington that would, had he seen it, have irritated her husband: "He is polite with dignity, affable without familiarity, distant without hautiness, grave without austerity, modest, wise and good."

Servants who stood at the door announced the name of each guest. Then one

In 1796 Gilbert Stuart began a portrait of the first "First Lady," Martha Washington, of which only this head was ever completed.

of Washington's secretaries escorted the ladies to Mrs. Washington. After making a respectful curtsy and engaging in a moment of conversation with Martha, each lady was conducted to a chair where she was supposed to sit "without noticing any of the rest of the company" until the President came up to her. Washington approached and chatted, so noted Abigail—who had been at the Court of St. James's—"with a grace, dignity, and ease that leaves royal George far behind him." The lady was then free to go into the other room, where there were refreshments: ice cream, tea and coffee, cakes, candy, etc.

Martha was capable of breaking up a reception at 9:30 by stating that her husband usually went to bed at 9:00 and that she usually preceded him. Such homey notes (and the lack of liquor) did not keep Martha's teas from figuring luridly in many minds. Newspaper editors who yearned for a high, monarchical society reported the occasions in inflated terms, even referring to the female guests not as "Mrs._____" but as "Lady This" and "Lady That." Republican editors viewed with the utmost alarm: that the servants who ushered in the guests had their hair powdered seemed to threaten the very fabric of the nation.

The Washingtons often went to the theatre, on one occasion taking Senator Maclay, who was horrified that the Chief Magistrate should countenance the exposure of "ladies of character and virtue" to such an "indecent representation" as Sheridan's *School for Scandal*. Maclay also had his turns at Washington's dinner parties.

Despite the restriction of the invitations to officials, the dinners could be gay, since such of Washington's favorite friends as Knox and Robert Morris held office. He often tried to leaven a lump and create a party more like those at Mount Vernon by inviting (as he did with the John Adams family) not only the elders but grown-up sons, daughters, and daughters-in-law. However, there were unsuccessful dinners, and one of these Maclay—who was enough by himself to put a damper on almost any party—reported gleefully for posterity.

As he dressed in preparation, Maclay warned himself that he had to be wary lest his pure republicanism be undermined by the seductions of Washington's aristocratic method of entertaining. He found that the President and Mrs. Washington sat opposite each other at the middle of the dinner table, the ladies being ranged on both sides of Martha, the gentlemen, opposite them, on both sides of George. The dinner began with soup; then fish, various roasted meats, fowls. Dessert consisted of apple pies and pudding followed by ice creams and jellies and then by watermelons, muskmelons, apples, peaches, nuts. Unable to deny that the meal was "the best of the kind" he had ever experienced, Maclay was nonetheless able to find some soothing dissatisfactions: the room was "disagreeably warm," and the food was eaten in solemn silence—"not a health drank."

After the cloth had been removed, the pendulum swung the other way, and there were too many toasts. To Maclay's disgust, the President "drank to the health of every individual by name round the table." The guests then imitated him, "and such a buzz of 'health, sir' and 'health, madam' never had I heard before." Silence, according to Maclay, sank again until the ladies withdrew. Then the President told an anecdote about "a New England clergyman who had lost a hat and wig in passing a river called the Brunks"—which Maclay did not consider funny.

"The President kept a fork in his hand," but instead of using it to open nuts, as Maclay suspected he would, he "played with the fork, striking on the edge of the table with it." Maclay assumed that the President was being pompous and dull, but perhaps Washington was hearing yearningly in his mind's ear laughter on the banks of the Potomac.

Congress decided that it would make a bad precedent to accede to Washington's request that he not be paid a salary but be reimbursed for his expenses: they set the presidential stipend at $25,000 a year. Although they seemed to be

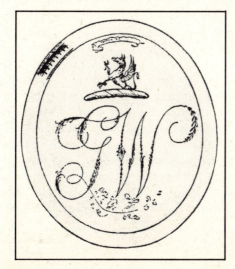

Washington personally designed this pencil sketch of the crest he wanted to adorn the presidential carriage.

brushing aside his self-sacrifice, the decision would have been to Washington's advantage only if his expenses had been less than the $25,000. As it was, he had to supplement his salary each year with some $5,000 from his own pocket. Fortunately, this was not more than he could afford, since the expenses at Mount Vernon, which he now inhabited only for visits, were so much reduced. He was enabled to escape the acute financial embarrassments from which he had suffered on taking office. If he still possessed little fluid cash, he was no longer being dunned for debts.

In 1789 Washington kept fifteen servants around the house and six who were assigned to the stables. He had brought with him seven slaves. However, probably because of the northern objections and his own uneasiness concerning slavery, he hired fourteen white servants, who occupied all the positions that brought them into contact with the public; they included the coachmen, two footmen, and the housemaids. Washington's steward, a well-known tavern owner in New York called Samuel Fraunces, came from the West Indies and must have had a dark complexion, since he was known as Black Sam. He stood at attendance at the dinner table, dressed in a wig and smallclothes, superintending the service. Washington also had a French confectioner and for a time a valet who was probably French—his name was Julian L'Hoste. The valet bought powder for the presidential hair, black silk bags to hold the presidential queue, and the narrow black ribbons known as solitaires that held the queue neatly in place. Although Washington wore black velvet on formal occasions, his favorite suit color was brown. He also wore gray and gray mixtures. The President never appeared in military costume except to receive the members of the Society of the Cincinnati or to review militia.

Washington's dental problems remained forever unsolved, but he tried to take advantage of the superior skills presumably available in New York by hiring still another dentist, John Greenwood, who applied to his empty gums a complete set of new false teeth. The upper portion was a solid piece of sculpture carved from hippopotamus tusk; the base of the lower was made of the same material but had attached to it by gold pivots (in a manner said to have been invented by Greenwood) actual human teeth. The utility was moderate, the comfort small, and Greenwood's devices were a long way from answering the need.

Washington was doing his best to behave in a manner satisfactory both to the world and to his own tastes. In accepting the Presidency, which he had certainly never consciously sought, he had not promised to make himself over into a new man. He could, indeed, reasonably conclude that the nation had come to him because of the kind of man he was. A personal and Virginian brand of elegance had become for him second nature, and thus, although untempted by titles and uneasy with such ceremony as would not be suitable in a private setting, he felt that his normal way of life was correctly aimed "to support propriety of character without partaking of the follies of luxury and ostentation."

Although Washington knew that some republicans thought he was being too aristocratic and Europeanized, he saw on the faces of European aristocratic visitors that they considered his way of life surprisingly plain. Washington believed he was avoiding extremes. His own desires and those of Martha, he wrote, were "limited," and he believed, after he had set up his schedule of levees and teas and dinners, that "our plans of living will now be deemed reasonable by the considerate part of our species."

America, France, and Their Revolutions

Garry Wills

France and the United States have been allies in the two great world wars of this century and with minor exceptions have been on good terms with each other ever since the Civil War. However, for a much longer period (throughout the seventeenth century and for much of the eighteenth) America and France were frequently at war, deadly enemies, divided by religion, competition for land and other forms of wealth, and their respective ties to European power politics.

That long period of enmity ended in the last quarter of the eighteenth century, when the Americans and the French engineered their famous revolutions, both throwing off autocratic monarchs and establishing republics devoted to a common set of principles, what the Americans described as the right of all people to life, liberty, and the pursuit of happiness, the French as liberté, egalité, fraternité. *These revolutions raised the hopes of oppressed people all over the world and inspired many similar revolts.*

It seems safe to say that the common purposes of the two upheavals explain why relations between the two republics have been so harmonious in modern times. But the revolutionary era itself saw sharp fluctuations in the relationship of the two nations because, as Professor Garry Wills of Northwestern University explains in this article, the courses of the two revolutions differed greatly, despite their common objectives.

There were two great revolutions against European monarchs in the late eighteenth century. In the first, the French nation helped Americans achieve their independence from George III. Without that help our revolution could not have succeeded. Yet when the French rebelled against Louis XVI, Americans hailed their action, then hesitated over it, and finally recoiled from it, causing bitterness in France and among some Americans. Why had the "sister republics" not embraced each other when they had the opportunity? Instead of marching together, the revolutions, so similar in their ideals, roots, and principles, passed each other at shouting distance. What began in mutual encouragement ended in mutual misapprehension.

The root of the trouble lay in the equivocal nature of the aid France extended to America in the 1770s. The American Revolution wore two different faces in France, and each was one of the many faces of Benjamin Franklin. On the one hand, Louis XVI was using British colonists to discommode his rival, George III, and Franklin was the courtier who pointed out the advantages of such a course to Louis's ministers. A famous contemporary image of Franklin is the porcelain statuette group by Lemire, in which Franklin bows to the French king, who presents him with the Treaty of 1778, which allied us to France (a document that would be the subject of heated controversy just over a decade later).

A more complex picture of the diplomatic forces at work is the allegorical print by Étienne Pallière, which shows Franklin helping unleash the French Hercules, who bashes with his club Britannia and her cowering lion. . . . (Although the Declaration of Independence had been specifically crafted to bring France into the conflict, Louis responded only after the first substantial defeat of an English army at Saratoga.)

But to the philosophes of the French Enlightenment, Franklin bore quite another face—himself a neoclassical god now, Prometheus, the tamer of lightning and the scourge of tyrants, the scientist and the philosopher of freedom.

Some of the officers who went to serve in the American Revolution—notably Lafayette, Rochambeau, Chastellux, and Admiral d'Estaing—were enlightened critics of their own government as well as supporters of American aspirations, but George Washington never forgot that the motive of King Louis in sending these auxiliaries was not any devotion to antimonarchical principle but a maneuver to

In a 1786 French aquatint that proclaims Louis XVI as America's liberator, Washington's name is misspelled.

regain some of the holdings in the New World he had lost to England after the Seven Years' War.

Washington alone took the measure of French aid in both its aspects. He was a champion of the Enlightenment in areas like his opposition to established churches, but he also had an eye to the practical conditions for exercising freedom. (In the current debates in Congress over Central America, he would definitely agree with those who think free elections mean little to people who cannot feed their own children.) He meant to keep America free from dependence on France as well as from submission to England.

When Lafayette, for example, tried to organize an army to recapture Canada, Washington expressed to Congress his vigorous objections. He wanted to use France, not be used by it. The independence of America could only be maintained by keeping it nonaligned between the great powers. The historian Edmund S. Morgan has convincingly traced Washington's neutrality policy back to the touchiness he felt about accepting French help from a king with his own designs in mind. Washington's caution was justified years later, at the end of the war over the American colonies, when it came out that Louis was negotiating with George III to grant Spain all American territory across the Alleghenies.

But this was a secret war of wills between Washington and King Louis that went on under a surface of amity. Washington did not even confide his misgivings to Lafayette, despite their friendship. After the war diplomatic relations between the two countries, though strained somewhat by French commercial losses in he war, were cordial as a result of Alexander Hamilton's efforts to repay on a regular basis the debts incurred to France. Meanwhile, the leading thinkers in the two countries seemed to form a single community of rational discourse. French visitors to America . . . found models for French social reform in American institutions. American visitors to France—Thomas Jefferson and [the poet] Joel Barlow—saw the stirrings of discontent with the established church and state as natural consequences of the example America had set in its state and federal constitutions. Thomas Paine, having argued for commonsense government in America, went to France to vindicate the rights of man. The French officers who had served with Washington were the only men at Louis XVI's court allowed to wear a foreign decoration—the Order of the Cincinnati eagle, designed by a Frenchman, Pierre Charles L'Enfant.

When the Bastille fell in 1789, Lafayette—recognizing the indebtedness of the French Revolution to Americans, who had shown the way—sent the key of that prison to Washington. Lafayette's face became the first of many that the French Revolution would turn toward America—and a more welcome appearance could not be wished. Jefferson, who had recently returned from France to become Secretary of State—Lafayette was at his farewell dinner in Paris—was actually more enthusiastic about the French Revolution than was France's minister to America, Jean Baptiste de Ternant. Jefferson thought the French experiment would not only confirm the American one but spread irresistibly to all the other enlightened parts of Europe. When the National Assembly in France, conscious of the model offered by the Declaration of Independence, issued a Declaration of the Rights of Man, it was designed to be adaptable to any country.

In this painting by C.E. Mills, Benjamin Franklin signs the 1778 Treaty of Alliance between England and France.

Hamilton, the Secretary of the Treasury, thought, like Jefferson, that French republicanism would spread to other countries—a prospect he feared as destabilizing. He reminded Washington that all treaties had been made with the regime of Louis XVI and that any new government in France would not have the same claim upon America as had the one that actually supplied help to America in its time of crisis. This was Hamilton's way of turning the revolutionary assistance France had given to America against that country's own revolutionary effort. The equivocal nature of Louis XVI's actions was coming back to haunt Franco-American relations.

Jefferson was not convinced. He argued heatedly in cabinet debate that treaties are made with the people who make up a nation and that any people can alter its form of government without forfeiting prior claims upon other nations. Washington agreed with Jefferson that treaty obligations must be met—that, for instance, payments on the war debt should be continued—but he was no more ready to commit America's fortunes to the giant republic of France than to the giant monarchy of France.

While the cabinet debate was going on in private, an international propaganda war broke out in 1790 over the future of the French Revolution. Thomas Paine was at the center of a triangular debate in England, France, and America. The mob's invasion of Versailles, menacing the queen—an attack repulsed by Lafayette—had ruffled the great [English] parliamentarian Edmund Burke's deep sense of historical decorum. Burke wrote his impassioned *Reflections on the Revolution in France* to defend ancient establishments. Paine responded from France with *The Rights of Man,* saying Burke "pities the plumage, but forgets the dying bird" of the French nation. Thomas Jefferson indiscreetly recommended Paine's book to its American publisher as an answer to "heresies" that had arisen in America over the French Revolution—an allusion to John Adams's *Discourses on Davila* (1790), in which Adams denounced French experiments with freedom. When Jefferson's letter was published, he had to apologize for this attack by one member of Washington's administration on the Vice-President of the United States.

Benjamin Franklin is crowned by Liberty in a 1778
allegory that reflects France's hope for its own future.

There was great misunderstanding on all sides because events were moving rapidly in France, though reports of them came slowly to America. In 1792, when news arrived that France had declared war on the alliance of kings that was taking shape in response to the Revolution, Hamilton argued that America's guarantee of French rights in the West Indies was framed in case a *defensive* war should arise, and France had now taken the offensive. Jefferson replied that France was forced to take pre-emptive steps.

But Jefferson's words were being undermined without his knowledge. Lafayette, leading French troops (with Rochambeau) against the Austrians, concluded in 1792 that his home government had reeled out of control. He defected from the army and was soon writing Washington from an Austrian jail, posing delicate problems for the President, who wanted to help his old ally without committing America to either of the two sides Lafayette had already taken. The French Revolution no longer wore a face familiar from America's own fighting days.

. . . Jefferson had written to Lafayette, before his defection, that "we are not to expect to be translated from despotism to liberty in a feather-bed." After

Lafayette's imprisonment Jefferson wrote to his former secretary, William Short: "My own affections have been deeply wounded by some of the martyrs to the cause, but rather than it should have failed, I would have seen half the earth desolated. Were there but an Adam & an Eve left in every country, & left free, it would be better than as it now is."

Jefferson did not know, when he wrote those words, that Louis XVI had been executed on January 21, 1793. Jefferson later wrote that he would have voted, if he were in the French government, for removing the king but not for killing him. That was also Thomas Paine's attitude at the time, and Paine was in a position to do something for the king. Ironically, he tried to arrange to have Louis conducted into exile in America, under the safe-conduct of the new minister about to depart for Philadelphia, Edmond Charles Edouard Genêt. Despite Paine's arguments, Citizen Louis Capet was condemned, and Americans began to realize that revolution meant one thing in a home country deposing its ruler and another in colonies seceding from an empire. There had been no regicide involved in the American Revolution—not even any executions of Loyalists. The death of the king raised the stakes of this second revolution, for its sympathizers as well as its participants.

The famous Tennis Court Oath, by Jacques Louis David, shows the furor of the National Assembly and the tumultuous politics of revolutionary France in 1789.

"Republicans" in America had to rationalize the violence by a harsher definition of what revolution means. As French philosophes had used the American Revolution to change their society, so Jeffersonians out of government argued that the French Revolution, by its logic of antiaristocratic purity, showed that changes were still to be made in American society. If the French Revolution was different from the American, that only meant that the American Revolution should be made to resemble the French more closely. Democratic-Republican Societies were formed not only to support the French Revolution but to import some of its practices. Some Americans began to address each other as "Citizen" and to wear the liberty cap. Bostonians even decided that the proper term for a woman was "Citess."

The aim of all this activity was to push America into open support of France. To prevent this, Washington decided to proclaim the neutrality he had been observing all along. Jefferson argued that he had no power to do this—that only Congress can declare war and that the state of peace when no such declaration has occurred does not need to be proclaimed by the Executive, the department of government that lacks war powers. But Americans were organizing support for a foreign belligerent, and Washington wanted to prevent that. Jefferson at least succeeded in keeping the actual word *neutrality* out of the so-called neutrality proclamation of 1793.

At the very time Washington was proclaiming neutrality in Philadelphia, the new French minister arrived in Charleston. With him, the French Revolution acquired a particular face in America that would prove fatal to hopes for Franco-American unity—the face of Citizen Genêt. Genêt, a young aristocrat . . . , made it his open aim to rally the American citizenry against its own government's stated policy. This was a bracing prospect for people like James Madison, who deplored the President's neutrality in a letter to Jefferson: "The proclamation was in truth a most unfortunate error. It wounds the national honor, by seeming to disregard the stipulated duties to France. It wounds the popular feelings by a seeming indifference to the cause of liberty. . . . If France triumphs, the ill-fated proclamation will be a millstone which would sink any other character [but Washington's] and will force a struggle even on his."

Unfortunately for Genêt, he listened to similar talk from "true Americans," who felt that he must save the President from his own advisers. Hamilton had argued against receiving Genêt at all. Washington overruled him, but Genêt made matters sticky by not bothering to seek a diplomatic reception before he began rallying opinion and money for the French cause. He made a public tour that brought him in a leisurely fashion to the seat of government in Philadelphia.

Jefferson, for as long as he could, nurtured great hopes for the Genêt mission. He was glad to see Ternant, the royal minister, removed, since he thought that remnant of the old regime had been an obstacle to the natural sympathy that would be expressed between the two republics once they understood each other. Jefferson assured his friends that Genêt "offers everything and asks nothing." Genêt had brought with him a personal letter to Jefferson from his old friend Condorcet, which urged that "our republic, founded like yours on reason, on the rights of nature, on equality, ought to be your true ally . . . [that] we ought in some sort to form one people."

This was Jefferson's hope too, but Genêt took the idea of one people so literally that he . . . felt he could speak to all free men without regard for the ceremonies of established governments. He had replaced his own title with the universal "Citizen." He expected American officials to set aside their titles too.

When they did not, Genêt treated them as betrayers of their own revolution. He threatened to appeal over the head of Washington to the people the President claimed to represent. He even attacked Jefferson for the State Department's implementation of the neutrality policy. Jefferson, in his turn, came to realize that Genêt was doing far more damage to the French cause than Ternant ever had. By July 1793 he was writing Madison: "Never in my opinion was so calamitous an appointment made, as that of the present Minister of F[rance] here. Hot-headed, all imagination, no judgment, passionate, disrespectful and even indecent towards the P[resident] in his written as well as verbal communications, talking of appeals from him to Congress, from them to the people, urging the most unreasonable & groundless propositions, & in the most dictatorial style. . . . He renders my position immensely difficult."

Jefferson's only hope of preventing a public reaction against Genêt (and through him against France) was to keep the insulting record of his dealings from publication. But that was made impossible when Genêt went from propagandizing to active war making: he was in touch with Western leaders like George Rogers Clark, who wanted to seize Louisiana form the Spanish. Genêt, an adjutant general of the French army, offered the support of his nation to such a "filibustering" movement. This was all the more embarrassing for Jefferson since Genêt had extracted a letter of recommendation from him introducing Genêt's emissary in this matter to the governor of Kentucky. Genêt, at first a nuisance, had become a disaster.

Yet by the time his recall was demanded, Genêt had to request asylum in this country (where, indeed, he lived out the rest of his long life). During his absence the Jacobins had . . . instituted the Terror. Friends of America like d'Estaing were sent to the guillotine—to which Genêt would undoubtedly have been conducted had he returned to France. Paine, imprisoned by Robespierre, lived in the shadow of the guillotine until its blade fell on Robespierre himself. The Revolution was devouring its own.

America was now a "sister republic" to France only in its own bitter divisions. The ideal accepted by all sides at the beginning of the Washington administration had been a factionless society, in which partisan appeals were to be submitted to impartial consideration. Early divisions had occurred, in the cabinet and in Congress, over matters like the establishment of a federal banking system. But these had not become matters of widespread popular agitation until Genêt made his appeals to the people and Democratic-Republican Societies began staging rallies in imitation of the Parisian mobs. John Adams was no doubt exaggerating when he remembered, late in his life, a time "when ten thousand people in the streets of Philadelphia, day after day threatened to drag Washington out of his house." But there was tumult and disorder of the sort not seen since the demonstrations against George III.

When Washington criticized the Democratic-Republican Societies for introducing faction into American life, he was assailed for suppressing free speech.

Revolutionary soldiers and civilians march to Paris in October, 1789. Spiked loaves of bread signify a food shortage; the impaled heads of the queen's bodyguards signal the furies that would consume the cause.

When Paine published his *Age of Reason* in 1794, it was made the occasion for attacks on the "atheism" of the French Revolution. Jefferson, suffering guilt by association with Paine, would be branded an atheist by his political enemies for the rest of his career. Not only were there public factions now, but one side saw behind the other a despotic foreign conspiracy and the other side saw an anarchic foreign atheism. Each looked through the other at a European specter. Monarchy had had its own odious image before 1789. But after 1794 even republicanism had a horrid aspect when one looked at a France reeling from the Terror.

John Adams's early prediction that force alone would put down the French disruption seemed confirmed by the ascent of Napoleon. The American statesman Stephen Higginson rightly assessed it as something that "drew a red-hot ploughshare through the history of America as well as through that of France. It not merely divided parties, but molded them; gave them their demarcations, their watchwords and their bitterness. The home issues were for a time subordinate, collateral; the real party lines were established on the other side of the Atlantic."

Despite the American Revolution's priority in time, the French Revolution became *the* revolution for all later ages. It is the model, the measure by which other uprisings are judged—the one used, retrospectively, to belittle or enlarge our own earlier rebellion. The Russian Revolution of 1917 was criticized according to its proximity to or departure from the French Revolution—not by its detractors and defenders only, but even by its participants, who were conscious, despite their emphasis on the future, that they were reenacting various stages of that primordial overturn and who looked among themselves for people to play the roles of Danton, Robespierre, and others.

The French Revolution ideologized the modern world. . . . It made the champions of unarticulated loyalties, people like Burke, paradoxically articulate a rationale for such loyalties, laying the basis for conservatism to this very day. Burke did not describe himself as a conservative, since the terms *liberal* and *conservative* were not yet in political use as polar terms. But the Revolution gave us the first lasting expression of such a polarity: the use of *left* and *right* in a political sense—taken from the pro-Revolutionary and anti-Revolutionary parties sitting to the left and right of the speaker in the National Constituent Assembly. . . .

Jefferson, looking back years later on the French Revolution, wrote Adams as one old man to another: "Your prophecies to Dr. Price proved truer than mine; and yet fell short of the fact, for instead of a million, the destruction of 8. or 10. millions of human beings has probably been the effect of these convulsions. I did not, in 89, believe they would have lasted so long nor have cost so much blood. But altho' your prophecy has proved true so far, I hope it does not preclude a better final result."

Jefferson sadly concluded that the French people were not yet "virtuous" enough to accept a sudden republicanism after so many years of superstition and despotism; this was the fear that made him want to limit immigration to America from lands where established churches had corrupted men's outlook. . . . For Jefferson, the past was destroying the Revolution. For Burke, the Revolution was destroying the past. Each was, in his own way, right.

PART FIVE

National Growing Pains

An early nineteenth-century allegory by John A. Woodside is symptomatic of the nationalistic fervor of the period. The triumphant seaman, his fetters broken, treads on England's crown and scepter.

The Frontier and the American Character

Ray Allen Billington

 New ways of looking at the past, called "interpretations," are a constant source of stimulation and controversy among historians. Most interpretations are produced not so much by the discovery of new facts as by present-mindedness; current events cause us to see the past in a new light, or to put it differently, our search for the causes of contemporary events often leads us to change our understanding of the effects of past events.

Of all interpretations of American history, none has been more provocative of research and controversy than Frederick Jackson Turner's "frontier thesis." In a paper published in 1893, Turner argued that the whole character of American civilization had been shaped from earliest colonial times by the existence of undeveloped land and resources and by their exploitation by pioneers. At a time when Americans were becoming aware that the western frontier was disappearing, this idea proved enormously persuasive; for years the Turner thesis dominated the writing of American history. Eventually, however, a new generation of scholars began to uncover its weaknesses and contradictions, and today the interpretation seems only one among many. The role of the frontier is generally accepted as having been important, but it is not seen as "explaining" American development, as Turner suggested.

Ray Allen Billington, a former senior research fellow at the Huntington Library, wrote the definitive biography of Turner. In this essay he sums up and balances the discussion of Turner's ideas that has been going on almost continuously for nearly a century. If this is not the last word that will be written about the effects of the frontier on America, it is the best and fairest general judgment of the subject that we have.

Since the dawn days of historical writing in the United States, historians have labored mightily, and usually in vain, to answer the famous question posed by Hector St. John de Crèvecœur in the eighteenth century: "What then is the American, this new man?" Was that composite figure actually a "new man" with unique traits that distinguished him from his Old World ancestors? Or was he merely a transplanted European? The most widely accepted—and bitterly disputed—answer was advanced by a young Wisconsin historian named Frederick Jackson Turner in 1893. The American was a new man, he held, who owed his distinctive characteristics and institutions to the unusual New World environment—characterized by the availability of free land and an ever-receding frontier—in which his civilization had grown to maturity.

This environmental theory, accepted for a generation after its enunciation, has been vigorously attacked and vehemently defended during the past two decades. How has it fared in this battle of words? Is it still a valid key to the meaning of American history?

Turner's own background provides a clue to the answer. Born in Portage, Wisconsin, in 1861 of pioneer parents from upper New York state, he was reared in a land fringed by the interminable forest and still stamped with the mark of youth. There he mingled with pioneers who had trapped beaver or hunted Indians or cleared the virgin wilderness; from them he learned something of the free and easy democratic values prevailing among those who judged men by their own accomplishments rather than those of their ancestors. At the University of Wisconsin Turner's faith in cultural democracy was deepened, while his intellectual vistas were widened through contact with teachers who led him into that wonderland of adventure where scientific techniques were being applied to social problems, where Darwin's evolutionary hypothesis was awakening scholars to the continuity of progress, and where searchers after truth were beginning to realize the multiplicity of forces responsible for human behavior. The young student showed how well he had learned these lessons in his master's essay on "The Character and Influence of the Fur Trade in Wisconsin"; he emphasized the evolution of institutions from simple to complex forms.

From Wisconsin Turner journeyed to Johns Hopkins University, as did many eager young scholars of that day, only to meet stubborn opposition for the historical theories already taking shape in his mind. His principal professor, Herbert Baxter Adams, viewed mankind's development in evolutionary terms, but held that environment had no place in the equation. American institutions could be understood only as outgrowths of European "germs" that had originated among Teutonic tribes in the forests of medieval Germany. To Turner this explanation was unsatisfactory. The "germ theory" explained the similarities between Europe and America, but what of the many differences? This problem was still much in his mind when he returned to the University of Wisconsin as an instructor in 1889. In two remarkable papers prepared during the next few years he set forth his answer. The first, "The Significance of History," reiterated his belief in what historians call "multiple causation"; to understand man's complex nature, he insisted, one needed not only a knowledge of past politics, but a familiarity with social, economic, and cultural forces as well. The second, "Problems in American History," attempted to isolate those forces most influential in explaining the unique features of American development. Among these Turner believed that the most important was the need for institutions to "adapt themselves to the changes of a remarkably developing, expanding people."

This was the theory that was expanded into a full-blown historical hypothesis in the famous essay on "The Significance of the Frontier in American History," read at a conference of historians held in connection with the World Fair in Chicago, in 1893. The differences between European and American civilization, Turner stated in that monumental work, were in part the product of the distinctive environment of the New World. The most unusual features of that environment were "the existence of an area of free land, its continuous recession, and the advance of American settlement westward." This free land served as a magnet to draw men westward, attracted by the hope of economic gain or adventure. They came as Europeans or easterners, but they soon realized that the wilderness environment was ill-adapted to the habits, institutions, and cultural baggage of the stratified societies they had left behind. Complex political institutions were unnecessary in a tiny frontier outpost; traditional economic practices were useless in an isolated community geared to an economy of self-sufficiency; rigid social customs were outmoded in a land where prestige depended on skill with the axe or rifle rather than on hereditary glories; cultural pursuits were unessential in a land where so many material tasks awaited doing. Hence in each pioneer settlement there occurred a rapid reversion to the primitive. What little government was necessary was provided by simple associations of settlers; each man looked after his family without reliance on his fellows; social hierarchies disintegrated, and cultural progress came to a halt. As the newcomers moved backward along the scale of civilization, the habits and customs of their traditional cultures were forgotten.

Gradually, however, newcomers drifted in, and as the man–land ratio increased, the community began a slow climb back toward civilization. Governmental controls were tightened and extended, economic specialization began, social stratification set in, and cultural activities quickened. But the new society that eventually emerged differed from the old from which it had sprung. The abandonment of cultural baggage during the migrations, the borrowings from the many cultures represented in each pioneer settlement, the deviations natural in separate evolutions, and the impact of the environment all played their parts in creating a unique social organism similar to but differing from those in the East. An "Americanization" of men and their institutions had taken place.

Turner believed that many of the characteristics associated with the American people were traceable to their experience, during the three centuries required to settle the continent, of constantly "beginning over again." Their mobility, their optimism, their inventiveness and willingness to accept innovation, their materialism, their exploitive wastefulness—these were frontier traits; for the pioneer,

Frederick Jackson Turner, photographed about 1890.

accustomed to repeated moves as he drifted westward, viewed the world through rose-colored glasses as he dreamed of a better future, experimented constantly as he adapted artifacts and customs to his peculiar environment, scorned culture as a deterrent to the practical tasks that bulked so large in his life, and squandered seemingly inexhaustible natural resources with abandon. Turner also ascribed America's distinctive brand of individualism, with its dislike of governmental interference in economic functions, to the experience of pioneers who wanted no hindrance from society as they exploited nature's riches. Similarly, he traced the exaggerated nationalism of the United States to its roots among frontiersmen who looked to the national government for land, transportation outlets, and protection against the Indians. And he believed that America's faith in democracy had stemmed from a pioneering experience in which the leveling influence of poverty and the uniqueness of local problems encouraged majority self-rule. He pointed out that these characteristics, prominent among frontiersmen, had persisted long after the frontier itself was no more.

This was Turner's famous "frontier hypothesis." For a generation after its enunciation its persuasive logic won uncritical acceptance among historians, but beginning in the late 1920's, and increasingly after Turner's death in 1932, an avalanche of criticism steadily mounted. His theories, critics said, were contradictory, his generalizations unsupported, his assumptions inadequately based; what empirical proof could he advance, they asked, to prove that the frontier experience was responsible for American individualism, mobility, or wastefulness? He was damned as a romanticist for his claim that democracy sprang from the forest environment of the United States and as an isolationist for failing to recognize the continuing impact of Europe on America. As the "bait-Turner" vogue gained popularity among younger scholars of the 1930's with their international, semi-Marxian views of history, the criticisms of the frontier theory became as irrational as the earlier support given by overenthusiastic advocates.

During the past decade, however, a healthy reaction has slowly and unspectacularly gained momentum. Today's scholars, gradually realizing that Turner was advancing a hypothesis rather than proving a theory, have shown a healthy tendency to abandon fruitless haggling over the meaning of his phrases and to concentrate instead on testing his assumptions. They have directed their efforts primarily toward re-examining his hypothesis in the light of criticisms directed against it and applying it to frontier areas beyond the borders of the United States. Their findings have modified many of the views expressed by Turner but have gone far toward proving that the frontier hypothesis remains one essential tool—albeit not the only one—for interpreting American history.

That Turner was guilty of oversimplifying both the nature and the causes of the migration process was certainly true. He pictured settlers as moving westward in an orderly procession—fur trappers, cattlemen, miners, pioneer farmers, and equipped farmers—with each group playing its part in the transmutation of a wilderness into a civilization. Free land was the magnet that lured them onward, he believed, and this operated most effectively in periods of depression, when the displaced workers of the East sought a refuge from economic storms amidst nature's abundance in the West. "The wilderness ever opened the gate of escape to the poor, the discontented and oppressed," Turner wrote at one time. "If social conditions tended to crystallize in the east, beyond the Alleghenies there was freedom."

No one of these assumptions can be substantiated in the simplified form in which Turner stated it. His vision of an "orderly procession of civilization, marching single file westward" failed to account for deviations that were almost as important as the norm; as essential to the conquest of the forest as trappers or farmers were soldiers, mill-operators, distillers, artisans, storekeepers, merchants, lawyers, editors, speculators, and town dwellers. All played their role, and all contributed to a complex frontier social order that bore little resemblance to the primitive societies Turner pictured. This was especially the case with the early town builders. The hamlets that sprang up adjacent to each pioneer settlement were products of the environment as truly as were the cattlemen or Indian fighters; each evolved economic functions geared to the needs of the primitive area surrounding it, and, in the tight public controls maintained over such essential functions as grist-milling or retail selling, each mirrored the frontiersmen's community-oriented views. In these villages, too, the equalitarian influence of the West was reflected in thoroughly democratic governments, with popularly elected councils supreme and the mayor reduced to a mere figurehead.

The pioneers who marched westward in this disorganized procession were not attracted by the magnet of "free land," for Turner's assumption that before 1862 the public domain was open to all who could pay $1.25 an acre, or that acreage was free after the Homestead Act was passed in that year, has been completely disproved. Turner failed to recognize the presence in the procession to the frontier of that omnipresent profit-seeker, the speculator. Jobbers were always ahead of farmers in the advance westward, buying up likely town sites or appropriating the best farm lands, where the soil was good and transportation outlets available. When the settler arrived his choice was between paying the speculator's price or accepting an inferior site. Even the Homestead Act failed to lessen speculative activity. Capitalizing on generous government grants to railroads and state educational institutions (which did not want to be bothered with sales to individuals), or buying bonus script from soldiers, or securing Indian lands as the reservations were contracted, or seizing on faulty features of congressional acts for the disposal of swampland and timberland, jobbers managed to engross most of the Far West's arable acreage: for every newcomer who obtained a homestead from the government, six or seven purchased farms from speculators.

Those who made these purchases were not, as Turner believed, displaced eastern workers fleeing periodic industrial depressions. Few city-dwelling artisans had the skills or inclination, and almost none the capital, to escape to the frontier. Land prices of $1.25 an acre may seem low today, but they were prohibitive for laborers earning only a dollar a day. Moreover, needed farm machinery, animals, and housing added about $1,000 to the cost of starting a farm in the 1850's, while the cheapest travel rate from New York to St. Louis was about $13 a person. Because these sums were always beyond the reach of factory workers (in bad times they deterred migration even from the rural East), the frontier never served as a "safety valve" for laborers in the sense that Turner employed the term. Instead, the American frontiers were pushed westward largely by younger sons from adjacent farm areas who migrated in periods of prosperity. While these generalizations apply to the pre–Civil War era that was Turner's principal interest, they are even more applicable to the late nineteenth century. During that period the major population shifts were from country to city rather than vice versa; for every worker who left the factory to move to the farm, twenty persons moved from farm to factory. If a safety valve did exist at that time, it was a rural safety valve, drawing off surplus farm labor and thus lessening agrarian discontent during the Granger and Populist eras.

Admitting that the procession to the frontier was more complex than Turner realized, that good lands were seldom free, and that a safety valve never operated to drain the dispossessed and the malcontented from industrial centers, does this mean that his conclusions concerning the migration process have been completely discredited? The opposite is emphatically true. A more divergent group than Turner realized felt the frontier's impact, but that does not minimize the extent of the impact. Too, while lands in the West were almost never free, they were relatively cheaper than those in Europe or the East, and this differential did serve as an attracting force. Nor can pages of statistics disprove the fact that, at least until the Civil War, the frontier served as an indirect safety valve by attracting displaced eastern farmers who would otherwise have moved into industrial cities; thousands who left New England or New York for the Old Northwest in the 1830's and 1840's, when the "rural decay" of the Northeast was beginning, would have sought factory jobs had no western outlet existed.

The effect of their exodus is made clear by comparing the political philosophies of the United States with those of another frontier country, Australia. There, lands lying beyond the coastal mountains were closed to pioneers by the aridity of the soil and by great sheep ranchers who were first on the scene. Australia, as a result, developed an urban civilization and an industrialized population relatively sooner than did the United States; and it had labor unions, labor-dominated governments, and political philosophies that would be viewed as radical in America. Without the safety valve of its own West, feeble though it may have been, such a course might have been followed in the United States.

Frederick Jackson Turner's conclusions concerning the influence of the frontier on Americans have also been questioned, debated, and modified since he advanced his hypothesis, but they have not been seriously altered. This is true even of one of his statements that has been more vigorously disputed than any other: "American democracy was born of no theorist's dream; it was not carried in the *Susan Constant* to Virginia, nor in the *Mayflower* to Plymouth. It came out of the American forest, and it gained a new strength each time it touched a new frontier." When he penned those oft-quoted words, Turner wrote as a propagandist against the "germ theory" school of history; in a less emotional and more thoughtful moment, he ascribed America's democratic institutions not to "imitation, or simple borrowing," but to "the evolution and adaptation of organs in response to changed environment." Even this moderate theory has aroused critical venom. Democracy, according to anti-Turnerians, was well advanced in

Europe and *was* transported to America on the *Susan Constant* and the *Mayflower;* within this country democratic practices have multiplied most rapidly as a result of eastern lower-class pressures and have only been imitated in the West. If, critics ask, some mystical forest influence was responsible for such practices as manhood suffrage, increased authority for legislatures at the expense of executives, equitable legislative representation, and women's political rights, why did they not evolve in frontier areas outside the United States—in Russia, Latin America, and Canada, for example—exactly as they did here?

The answer, of course, is that democratic theory and institutions were imported from England, but that the frontier environment tended to make them, in practice, even more democratic. Two conditions common in pioneer communities made this inevitable. One was the wide diffusion of land ownership; this created an independent outlook and led to a demand for political participation on the part of those who had a stake in society. The other was the common social and economic level and the absence, characteristic of all primitive communities, of any prior leadership structure. The lack of any national or external controls made self-rule a hard necessity, and the frontiersmen, with their experience in community co-operation at cabin-raisings, logrollings, corn-huskings, and road or school building, accepted simple democratic practices as natural and inevitable. These practices, originating on the grass roots level, were expanded and extended in the recurring process of government-building that marked the westward movement of civilization. Each new territory that was organized—there were 31 in all—required a frame of government; this was drafted by relatively poor recent arrivals or by a minority of upper-class leaders, all of whom were committed to democratic ideals through their frontier community experiences. The result was a constant democratization of institutions and practices as constitution-makers adopted the most liberal features of older frames of government with which they were familiar.

This was true even in frontier lands outside the United States, for wherever there were frontiers, existing practices were modified in the direction of greater equality and a wider popular participation in governmental affairs. The results were never identical, of course, for both the environment and the nature of the imported institutions varied too greatly from country to country. In Russia, for instance, even though it promised no democracy comparable to that of the United States, the eastward-moving Siberian frontier, the haven of some seven million peasants during the nineteenth and early twentieth centuries, was notable for its lack of guilds, authoritarian churches, and all-powerful nobility. An official visiting there in 1910 was alarmed by the "enormous, rudely democratic country" evolving under the influence of the small homesteads that were the normal living units; he feared that czarism and European Russia would soon be "throttled" by the egalitarian currents developing on the frontier.

That the frontier accentuated the spirit of nationalism and individualism in the United States, as Turner maintained, was also true. Every page of the country's history, from the War of 1812 through the era of Manifest Destiny to today's bitter conflicts with Russia, demonstrates that the American attitude toward the world has been far more nationalistic than that of non-frontier countries and that

A contemporary etching of a wagon train encampment along the Laramie River.

this attitude has been strongest in the newest regions. Similarly, the pioneering experience converted settlers into individualists, although through a somewhat different process than Turner envisaged. His emphasis on a desire for freedom as a primary force luring men westward and his belief that pioneers developed an attitude of self-sufficiency in their lone battle against nature have been questioned, and with justice. Hoped-for gain was the magnet that attracted most migrants to the cheaper lands of the West, while once there they lived in units where co-operative enterprise—for protection against the Indians, for cabin-raising, law enforcement, and the like—was more essential than in the better established towns of the East. Yet the fact remains that the abundant resources and the greater social mobility of frontier areas did instill into frontiersmen a uniquely American form of individualism. Even though they may be sheeplike in following the decrees of social arbiters or fashion dictators, Americans today, like their pioneer ancestors, dislike governmental interference in their affairs. "Rugged individualism" did not originate on the frontier any more than democracy or nationalism did, but each concept was deepened and sharpened by frontier conditions.

His opponents have also cast doubt on Turner's assertion that American inventiveness and willingness to adopt innovations are traits inherited from pioneer ancestors who constantly devised new techniques and artifacts to cope with an unfamiliar environment. The critics insist that each mechanical improvement needed for the conquest of the frontier, from plows to barbed-wire fencing, originated in the East; when frontiersmen faced such an incomprehensible task as conquering the Great Plains they proved so tradition-bound that their advance halted until eastern inventors provided them with the tools needed to subdue grasslands. Unassailable as this argument may be, it ignores the fact that the recurring demand for implements and methods needed in the frontier advance did put a premium on inventiveness by Americans, whether they lived in the East and West. That even today they are less bound by tradition than other peoples is due in part to their pioneer heritage.

The anti-intellectualism and materialism which are national traits can also be traced to the frontier experience. There was little in pioneer life to attract the timid, the cultivated, or the aesthetically sensitive. In the boisterous western borderlands, book learning and intellectual speculation were suspect among those dedicated to the material tasks necessary to subdue a continent. Americans today reflect their background in placing the "intellectual" well below the "practical businessman" in their scale of heroes. Yet the frontiersman, as Turner recognized, was an idealist as well as a materialist. He admired material objects not only as symbols of advancing civilization but as the substance of his hopes for a better future. Given economic success he would be able to afford the aesthetic and intellectual pursuits that he felt were his due, even though he was not quite able to appreciate them. This spirit inspired the cultural activities—literary societies, debating clubs, "thespian groups," libraries, schools, camp meetings—that thrived in the most primitive western communities. It also helped nurture in the pioneers an infinite faith in the future. The belief in progress, both material and intellectual, that is part of modern America's creed was strengthened by the frontier experience.

Frederick Jackson Turner, then, was not far wrong when he maintained that frontiersmen did develop unique traits and that these, perpetuated, form the principal distinguishing characteristics of the American people today. To a degree unknown among Europeans, Americans do display a restless energy, a versatility, a practical ingenuity, an earthly practicality. They do squander their natural resources with an abandon unknown elsewhere; they have developed a mobility both social and physical that marks them as a people apart. In few other lands is the democratic ideal worshiped so intensely, or nationalism carried to such extremes of isolationism or international arrogance. Rarely do other peoples display such indifference toward intellectualism or aesthetic values; seldom in comparable cultural areas do they cling so tenaciously to the shibboleth of rugged individualism. Nor do residents of non-frontier lands experience to the same degree the heady optimism, the rosy faith in the future, the belief in the inevitability of progress that form part of the American creed. These are pioneer traits, and they have become a part of the national heritage.

Yet if the frontier wrought such a transformation within the United States, why did it not have a similar effect on other countries with frontiers? If the pioneering experience was responsible for our democracy and nationalism and individualism, why have the peoples of Africa, Latin America, Canada, and Russia failed to develop identical characteristics? The answer is obvious: in few nations of the world has the sort of frontier that Turner described existed. For he saw the frontier not as a borderland between unsettled and settled lands, but as an accessible area in which a low man–land ratio and abundant natural resources provided an unusual opportunity for the individual to better himself. Where autocratic governments controlled population movements, where resources were lacking, or where conditions prohibited ordinary individuals from exploiting nature's virgin riches, a frontier in the Turnerian sense could not be said to exist.

The areas of the world that have been occupied since the beginning of the age of discovery contain remarkably few frontiers of the American kind. In Africa the few Europeans were so outnumbered by relatively uncivilized native inhabitants that the need for protection transcended any impulses toward democracy or individualism. In Latin America the rugged terrain and steaming jungles restricted areas exploitable by individuals to the Brazilian plains and the Argentine pampas; these did attract frontiersmen, although in Argentina the prior occupation of most good lands by government-favored cattle growers kept small farmers out until railroads penetrated the region. In Canada the path westward was blocked by the Laurentian Shield, a tangled mass of hills and sterile, brush-choked soil covering the country north and west of the St. Lawrence Valley. When railroads finally penetrated this barrier in the late nineteenth century, they carried pioneers directly from the East to the prairie provinces of the West; the newcomers, with no prior pioneering experience, simply adapted to their new situation the eastern institutions with which they were familiar. Among the world's frontier nations only Russia provided a physical environment comparable to that of the United States, and there the pioneers were too accustomed to rigid feudal and monarchic controls to respond as Americans did.

Further proof that the westward expansion of the United States has been a powerful formative force has been provided by the problems facing the nation in the present century. During the past fifty years the American people have been adjusting their lives and institutions to existence in a frontierless land, for while the superintendent of the census was decidedly premature when he announced in 1890 that the country's "unsettled area has been so broken into by isolated bodies of settlement that there can hardly be said to be a frontier line" remaining, the era of cheap land was rapidly drawing to a close. In attempting to adjust the country to its new, expansionless future, statesmen have frequently called upon the frontier hypothesis to justify everything from rugged individualism to the welfare state, and from isolationism to world domination.

Political opinion has divided sharply on the necessity of altering the nation's governmental philosophy and techniques in response to the changed environment. Some statesmen and scholars have rebelled against what they call Turner's "Space Concept of History," with all that it implies concerning the lack of opportunity for the individual in an expansionless land. They insist that modern technology has created a whole host of new "frontiers"—of intensive farming, electronics, mechanics, manufacturing, nuclear fission, and the like—which offer such diverse outlets to individual talents that governmental interference in the nation's economic activities is unjustified. On the other hand, equally competent spokesmen argue that these newer "frontiers" offer little opportunity to the individual—as distinguished from the corporation or the capitalist—and hence cannot duplicate the function of the frontier of free land. The government, they insist, must provide the people with the security and opportunity that vanished when escape to the West became impossible. This school's most eloquent spokesman, Franklin D. Roosevelt, declared: "Our last frontier has long since been reached. . . . Equality of opportunity as we have known it no longer exists. . . . Our task now is not the discovery or exploitation of natural resources or necessarily producing more goods. It is the sober, less dramatic business of administering resources and plants already in hand, of seeking to re-establish foreign markets for our surplus production, of meeting the problem of under-consumption, of adjusting production to consumption, of distributing wealth and products more equitably, of adapting existing economic organizations to the service of the people. The day of enlightened administration has come." To Roosevelt, and to thousands like him, the passing of the frontier created a new era in history which demanded a new philosophy of government.

Diplomats have also found in the frontier hypothesis justification for many of their moves, from imperialist expansion to the restriction of immigration. Harking back to Turner's statement that the perennial rebirth of society was necessary to keep alive the democratic spirit, expansionists have argued through the twentieth century for an extension of American power and territories. During the Spanish-American War imperialists preached such a doctrine, adding the argument that Spain's lands were needed to provide a population outlet for a people who could no longer escape to their own frontier. Idealists such as Woodrow Wilson could agree with materialists like J. P. Morgan that the extension of American authority abroad, either through territorial acquisitions or economic penetration, would be good for both business and democracy. Later, Franklin D. Roosevelt favored a similar expansion of the American democratic ideal as a necessary prelude to the better world that he hoped would emerge from World War II. His successor, Harry Truman, envisaged his "Truman Doctrine" as a device to extend and defend the frontiers of democracy throughout the globe. While popular belief in the superiority of America's political institutions was far older than Turner, that belief rested partly on the frontier experience of the United States.

These practical applications of the frontier hypothesis, as well as its demonstrated influence on the nation's development, suggest that its critics have been unable to destroy the theory's effectiveness as a key to understanding American history. The recurring rebirth of society in the United States over a period of three hundred years did endow the people with characteristics and institutions that distinguish them from the inhabitants of other nations. It is obviously untrue that the frontier experience alone accounts for the unique features of American civilization; that civilization can be understood only as the product of the interplay of the Old World heritage and New World conditions. But among those conditions none has bulked larger than the operation of the frontier process.

Marbury v. Madison

John A. Garraty

One of the most remarkable aspects of the Constitution of the United States (and the secret of its longevity) is its flexibility. A form of government designed to deal with the problems of a handful of farmers, merchants, and craftsmen scattered along a thousand miles of coastline, separated from one another by acres of forest, and facing the trackless western wilderness has endured with a minimum of changes through nearly two centuries, in which the nation has occupied a continental domain and become an urban-industrial behemoth.

A major reason for the flexibility of the Constitution has been the system of judicial review, which exists in the document largely by implication but has nonetheless functioned with enormous effectiveness. The following essay deals with one of the great landmarks in the development of the power of the Supreme Court to interpret the meaning of the Constitution and thus define the powers of both the federal government and the states. The case of Marbury v. Madison, *like so many controversies that crucially affected the Constitution, was in itself of no importance. A minor federal official deprived of his office by a technicality was seeking redress from the Court. But in deciding his fate, the Court laid down a principle that altered the whole future of the country, shaping events that neither Marbury, nor Madison, nor the framers of the Constitution could possibly have anticipated.*

I t was the evening of March 3, 1801, his last day in office, and President John Adams was in a black and bitter mood. Assailed by his enemies, betrayed by some of his most trusted friends, he and his Federalist party had gone down to defeat the previous November before the forces of Thomas Jefferson. His world seemed to have crumbled about his doughty shoulders.

Conservatives of Adams' persuasion were deeply convinced that Thomas Jefferson was a dangerous radical. He would, they thought, in the name of individual liberty and states' rights, import the worst excesses of the French Revolution, undermine the very foundations of American society, and bring the proud edifice of the national government, so laboriously erected under Washington and Adams, tumbling to the ground. Jefferson was a "visionary," Chief Justice Oliver Ellsworth had said. With him as President, "there would be no national energy." Ardent believers in a powerful central government like Secretary of State John Marshall feared that Jefferson would "sap the fundamental principles of government." Others went so far as to call him a "howling atheist."

Adams himself was not quite so disturbed as some, but he was deeply troubled. "What course is it we steer?" he had written despairingly to an old friend after the election. "To what harbor are we bound?" Now on the morrow Jefferson was to be inaugurated, and Adams was so disgruntled that he was unwilling to remain for the ceremonies, the first to be held in the new capital on the Potomac. At the moment, however, John Adams was still President of the United States, and not yet ready to abandon what he called "all virtuous exertion" in the pursuit of his duty. Sitting at his desk in the damp, drafty, still-unfinished sandstone mansion soon to be known as "the White House," he was writing his name on official papers in his large, quavering hand.

The documents he was signing were mostly commissions formally appointing various staunch Federalists to positions in the national judiciary, but the President did not consider his actions routine. On the contrary: he believed he was saving the republic itself. Jefferson was to be President and his Democratic-Republicans would control the Congress, but the courts, thank goodness, would be beyond his control: as soon as the extent of Jefferson's triumph was known, Adams had determined to make the judiciary a stronghold of Federalism. Responding enthusiastically to his request for expansion of the courts, the lame-duck Congress had established sixteen new circuit judgeships (and a host of marshals, attorneys, and clerks as well). It had also given Adams blanket authority to create as many justices of the peace for the new District of Columbia as he saw fit, and—to postpone the evil day when Jefferson would be able to put one of his sympathizers on the Supreme Court—it provided that when the next vacancy occurred, it should not be filled, thus reducing the Court from six justices to five. (The Constitution says nothing about the number of justices on the Court; its size is left to Congress. Originally six, the membership was enlarged to seven in 1807. The justices first numbered nine in 1837. Briefly during the Civil War the bench held ten; the number was set at seven again in 1866 and in 1869 returned to nine, where it has remained.)

In this same period between the election and the inauguration of the new President, Chief Justice Ellsworth, who was old and feeble, had resigned, and Adams had replaced him with Secretary of State Marshall. John Marshall was primarily a soldier and politician; he knew relatively little of the law. But he had a powerful mind, and, as Adams reflected, his "reading of the science" was "fresh in his head." He was also but forty-five years of age, and vigorous. Clearly a long life lay ahead of him, and a more forceful opponent of Jeffersonian principles would have been hard to find.

Marshall had been confirmed by the Senate on January 27, and without resigning as Secretary of State he had begun at once to help Adams strengthen the judicial branch of the government. They had worked rapidly, for time was short. The new courts were authorized by Congress on February 13; within two weeks Adams had submitted a full slate of officials for confirmation by the Senate. The new justices of the peace for the District of Columbia were authorized on February 27; within three days Adams had submitted for confirmation the names of no less than forty-two justices for the sparsely populated region. The Federalist Senate had done its part nobly, pushing through the various confirmations with great dispatch. Now, in the lamplight of his last night in Washington, John Adams was affixing his signature to the commissions of these "midnight justices," as the last-minute appointees were to become derisively known.

Working with his customary puritanical diligence, Adams completed his work by nine o'clock, and when he went off to bed for the last time as President of the United States, it was presumably with a clear conscience. The papers were carried to the State Department, where Secretary Marshall was to affix the Great Seal of the United States to each, and see to it that the commissions were then dispatched to the new appointees. But Marshall, a Virginian with something of the southerner's easygoing carelessness about detail, failed to complete this routine task.

All the important new circuit judgeships were taken care of, and most of the other appointments as well. But in the bustle of last-minute arrangements, the commissions of the new justices of the peace for the District of Columbia went astray. As a result of this trivial slip-up, and entirely without anyone's having planned it, a fundamental principle of the Constitution—affecting the lives of countless millions of future Americans—was to be established. Because *Secretary of State* Marshall made his last mistake, *Chief Justice* Marshall was soon to make one of the first—and in some respects the greatest—of his decisions.

It is still not entirely clear what happened to the missing commissions on the night of March 3. To help with the rush of work, Adams had borrowed two State Department clerks, Jacob Wagner and Daniel Brent. Brent prepared a list of the forty-two new justices and gave it to another clerk, who filled in the blank commissions. As fast as batches of these were made ready, Brent took them to Adams' office, where he turned them over to William Smith Shaw, the President's private secretary. After they were signed, Brent brought them back to the State Department, where Marshall was supposed to affix the Great Seal. Evidently he did seal these documents, but he did not trouble to make sure that they were delivered to the appointees. As he later said: "I did not send out the commissions because I apprehended such . . . to be completed when signed & sealed." Actually, he admitted, he would have sent them out in any case "but for the extreme hurry of the time & the absence of Mr. Wagner who had been called on by the President to act as his private secretary."

March 4 dawned and Jefferson, who apparently had not yet digested the significance of Adams' partisan appointments, prepared to take the oath of office and deliver his inaugural address. His mood, as the brilliant speech indicated, was friendly and conciliatory. He even asked Chief Justice Marshall, who administered the inaugural oath, to stay on briefly as Secretary of State while the new administration was getting established. That morning it would still have been possible to deliver the commissions. As a matter of fact, a few actually were delivered, although quite by chance.

Marshall's brother James (whom Adams had just made circuit judge for the District of Columbia) was disturbed by rumors that there was going to be a riot in Alexandria in connection with the inaugural festivities. Feeling the need of some justices of the peace in case trouble developed, he went to the State Department and personally picked up a number of the undelivered commissions. He signed a receipt for them, but "finding that he could not conveniently carry the whole," he returned several, crossing out the names of these from the receipt.

Among the ones returned were those appointing William Harper and Robert Townsend Hooe. By failing to deliver these commissions, Judge James M. Marshall unknowingly enabled Harper and Hooe, obscure men, to win for themselves a small claim to legal immortality.

The new President was eager to mollify the Federalists, but when he realized the extent to which Adams had packed the judiciary with his "most ardent political enemies," he was indignant. Adams' behavior, he said at the time, was an "outrage on decency," and some years later, when passions had cooled a little, he wrote sorrowfully: "I can say with truth that one act of Mr. Adams' life, and one only, ever gave me a moment's personal displeasure. I did consider his last appointments to office as personally unkind." When he discovered the justice-of-the-peace commissions in the State Department, he decided at once not to allow them to be delivered.

James Madison, the Secretary of State, was not yet in Washington. Jefferson called in his Attorney General, a Massachusetts lawyer named Levi Lincoln, whom he had designated Acting Secretary. Giving Lincoln a new list of justices of the peace, he told him to put them "into a general commission" and notify the men of their selection.

In truth, Jefferson acted with remarkable forbearance. He reduced the number of justices to thirty, fifteen for the federal District, fifteen for Alexandria County. But only seven of his appointees were his own men; the rest he chose from among the forty-two names originally submitted by Adams. Lincoln prepared two general commissions, one for each area, and notified the appointees. Then, almost certainly, he destroyed the original commissions signed by Adams.

For some time thereafter Jefferson did very little about the way Adams had packed the judiciary. Indeed, despite his much-criticized remark that office holders seldom die and never resign, he dismissed relatively few persons from the government service. For example, the State Department clerks, Wagner and Brent, were permitted to keep their jobs. The new President learned quickly how hard it was to institute basic changes in a going organization. "The great machine of society" could not easily be moved, he admitted, adding that it was impossible "to advance the notions of a whole people suddenly to ideal right." Soon some of his more impatient supporters, like John Randolph of Roanoke, were grumbling about the President's moderation.

But Jefferson was merely biding his time. Within a month of the inauguration he conferred with Madison at Monticello and made the basic decision to try to abolish the new system of circuit courts. Aside from removing the newly appointed marshals and attorneys, who served at the pleasure of the Chief Executive, little could be done until the new Congress met in December. Then, however, he struck. In his first annual message he urged the "contemplation" by Congress of the Judiciary Act of 1801. To direct the lawmakers' thinking, he submitted a statistical report showing how few cases the federal courts had been called upon to deal with since 1789. In January, 1802, a repeal bill was introduced; after long debate it passed early in March, thus abolishing the jobs of the new circuit judges.

Some of those deposed petitioned Congress for "relief," but their plea was

Thomas Jefferson, by Gilbert Stuart.

coldly rejected. Since these men had been appointed for life, the Federalists claimed that the repeal act was unconstitutional, but to prevent the Supreme Court from quickly so declaring, Congress passed another bill abolishing the June term of the Court and setting the second Monday of February, 1803, for its next session. By that time, the Jeffersonians reasoned, the old system would be dead beyond resurrection.

This powerful assault on the courts thoroughly alarmed the conservative Federalists; to them the foundations of stable government seemed threatened if the "independence" of the judiciary could be thus destroyed. No one was more disturbed than the new Chief Justice, John Marshall, nor was anyone better equipped by temperament and intellect to resist it. Headstrong but shrewd, contemptuous of detail and of abstractions but a powerful logician, he detested Jefferson (to whom he was distantly related), and the President fully returned his dislike.

In the developing conflict Marshall operated at a disadvantage that in modern times a Chief Justice would not have to face. The Supreme Court had none of the prestige and little of the accepted authority it now possesses. Few cases had come before it, and few of these were of any great importance. Before appointing Marshall, Adams had offered the Chief Justiceship to John Jay, the first man to hold the post, as an appointee of President Washington. Jay had resigned from the Court in 1795 to become governor of New York. He refused the reappointment, saying that the Court lacked "energy, weight, and dignity." A prominent newspaper of the day referred to the Chief Justiceship, with considerable truth, as a "sinecure." One of the reasons Marshall had accepted the post was his belief that it would afford him ample leisure for writing the biography of his hero, George Washington. Indeed, in the grandiose plans for the new capital, no thought had been given to housing the Supreme Court, so that when Marshall took office in 1801 the justices had to meet in the office of the clerk of the Senate, a small room on the first floor of what is now the north wing of the Capitol.

Nevertheless, Marshall struck out at every opportunity against the power and authority of the new President; but the opportunities were pitifully few. In one case, he refused to allow a presidential message to be read into the record on the ground that this would bring the President into the Court, in violation of the principle of separation of powers. In another, he ruled that Jefferson's decision in a prize case involving an American privateer was illegal. But these were matters of small importance.

When he tried to move more boldly, his colleagues would not sustain him. He was ready to declare the judicial repeal act unconstitutional, but none of the deposed circuit court judges would bring a case to court. Marshall also tried to persuade his associates that it was unconstitutional for Supreme Court justices to ride the circuit, as they were forced again to do by the abolishment of the lower courts. But although they agreed with his legal reasoning, they refused to go along—because, they said, years of acquiescence in the practice lent sanction to the old law requiring it. Thus frustrated, Marshall was eager for any chance to attack his enemy, and when a case that was to be known as *Marbury* v. *Madison* came before the Court in December, 1801, he took it up with gusto.

William Marbury, a forty-one-year-old Washingtonian, was one of the justices of the peace for the District of Columbia whose commissions Jefferson had held up. Originally from Annapolis, he had moved to Washington to work as an aide to the first Secretary of the Navy, Benjamin Stoddert. It was probably his service to this staunch Federalist that earned him the appointment by Adams. Together with one Dennis Ramsay and Messrs. Harper and Hooe, whose commissions James Marshall had *almost* delivered, Marbury was asking the Court to issue an order (a writ of mandamus) requiring Secretary of State Madison to hand over their "missing" commissions. Marshall willingly assumed jurisdiction and issued an order calling upon Madison to show cause at the next term of the Supreme Court why such a writ should not be issued. Here clearly was an opportunity to get at the President through one of his chief agents, to assert the authority of the Court over the executive branch of the government.

This small controversy quickly became a matter of great moment both to the administration and to Marshall. The decision to do away with the June term of the Court was made in part to give Madison more time before having to deal with Marshall's order. The abolition of the circuit courts and the postponement of the next Supreme Court session to February, 1803, made Marshall even more determined to use the Marbury case to attack Jefferson. Of course Marshall was personally and embarrassingly involved in this case, since his carelessness was the cause of its very existence. He ought to have disqualified himself, but his fighting spirit was aroused, and he was in no mood to back out.

On the other hand, the Jeffersonians used every conceivable means to obstruct judicial investigation of executive affairs. Madison ignored Marshall's order. When Marbury and Ramsay called on the Secretary to inquire whether their commissions had been duly signed (Hooe and Harper could count on the testimony of James Marshall to prove that theirs had been attended to), Madison gave them no satisfactory answer. When they asked to *see* the documents, Madison referred them to the clerk, Jacob Wagner. He, in turn, would only say that the commissions were not then in the State Department files.

Unless the plaintiffs could prove that Adams had appointed them, their case would collapse. Frustrated at the State Department, they turned to the Senate for help. A friendly senator introduced a motion calling upon the Secretary of the Senate to produce the record of the action in executive session on their nominations. But the motion was defeated, after an angry debate, on January 31, 1803. Thus, tempers were hot when the Court finally met on February 9 to deal with the case.

In addition to Marshall, only Justices Bushrod Washington (a nephew of the first President) and Samuel Chase were on the bench, and the Chief Justice dominated the proceedings. The almost childishly obstructive tactics of administration witnesses were no match for his fair but forthright management of the hearing. The plaintiffs' lawyer was Charles Lee, an able advocate and brother of "Light-Horse Harry" Lee; he had served as Attorney General under both Washington and Adams. He was a close friend of Marshall, and his dislike of Jefferson had been magnified by the repeal of the Judiciary Act of 1801, for he was another of the circuit court judges whose "midnight" appointments repeal had cancelled.

Lee's task was to prove that the commissions had been completed by Adams and Marshall, and to demonstrate that the Court had authority to compel Madison to issue them. He summoned Wagner and Brent, and when they objected to being sworn because "they were clerks in the Department of State, and not bound to disclose any facts relating to the business or transactions in the office," Lee argued that in addition to their "confidential" duties as agents of the President, the Secretary and his deputies had duties "of a public nature" delegated to them by Congress. They must testify about these public matters just as, in a suit involving property, a clerk in the land office could be compelled to state whether or not a particular land patent was on file.

Marshall agreed, and ordered the clerks to testify. They then disclosed many of the details of what had gone on in the presidential mansion and in the State Department on the evening of March 3, 1801, but they claimed to be unsure of what had become of the plaintiffs' commissions.

Next Lee called Attorney General Levi Lincoln. He too objected strenuously to testifying. He demanded that Lee submit his questions in writing so that he might consider carefully his obligations both to the Court and to the President before making up his mind. He also suggested that it might be necessary for him to exercise his constitutional right (under the Fifth Amendment) to refuse to give evidence that might, as he put it, "criminate" him. Lee then wrote out four questions. After studying them, Lincoln asked to be excused from answering, but the justices ruled against him. Still hesitant, the Attorney General asked for time to consider his position further, and Marshall agreed to an overnight adjournment.

The next day, the tenth of February, Lincoln offered to answer all Lee's questions but the last: What had he done with the commissions? He had seen "a considerable number of commissions" signed and sealed, but could not remember—he claimed—whether the plaintiffs' were among them. He did not know if Madison had ever seen these documents, but was certain that *he* had not given them to the Secretary. On the basis of this last statement, Marshall ruled that the embarrassing question as to what Lincoln had done with the commissions was irrelevant; he excused Lincoln from answering it.

Despite these reluctant witnesses, Lee was able to show conclusively through affidavits submitted by another clerk and by James Marshall that the commissions had been signed and sealed. In his closing argument he stressed the significance of the case as a test of the principle of judicial independence. "The emoluments or the dignity of the office," he said, "are no objects with the applicants." This was undoubtedly true; the positions were unimportant, and two years of the five-year terms had already expired. As Jefferson later pointed out, the controversy itself had become "a moot case" by 1803. But Marshall saw it as a last-ditch fight against an administration campaign to make lackeys of all federal judges, while Jefferson looked at it as an attempt by the Federalist-dominated judiciary to usurp the power of the executive.

In this controversy over principle, Marshall and the Federalists were of neces-

John Marshall, by Chester Harding.

sity the aggressors. The administration boycotted the hearings. After Lee's summation, no government spokesman came forward to argue the other side, Attorney General Lincoln coldly announcing that he "had received no instructions to appear." With his control over Congress, Jefferson was content to wait for Marshall to act. If he overreached himself, the Chief Justice could be impeached. If he backed down, the already trifling prestige of his Court would be further reduced.

Marshall had acted throughout with characteristic boldness; quite possibly it was he who had persuaded the four aggrieved justices of the peace to press their suit in the first place. But now his combative temperament seemed to have driven him too far. As he considered the Marbury case after the close of the hearings, he must have realized this himself, for he was indeed in a fearful predicament. However sound his logic and just his cause, he was on very dangerous ground. Both political partisanship and his sense of justice prompted him to issue the writ sought by Marbury and his fellows, but what effect would the mandamus produce? Madison almost certainly would ignore it, and Jefferson would back him up. No power but public opinion could make the executive department obey an order of the Court. Since Jefferson was riding the crest of a wave of popularity, to issue the writ would be a futile act of defiance; it might even trigger impeachment proceedings against Marshall that, if successful, would destroy him and reduce the Court to servility.

Yet what was the alternative? To find against the petitioners would be to abandon all principle and surrender abjectly to Jefferson. This a man of Marshall's character could simply not consider. Either horn of the dilemma threatened utter disaster; that it was disaster essentially of his own making could only make the Chief Justice's discomfiture the more complete.

But at some point between the close of the hearings on February 14 and the announcement of his decision on the twenty-fourth, Marshall found a way out. It was an inspired solution, surely the cleverest of his long career. It provided a perfect escape from the dilemma, which probably explains why he was able to persuade the associate justices to agree to it despite the fact that it was based on the most questionable legal logic. The issue, Marshall saw, involved a conflict between the Court and the President, the problem being how to check the President without exposing the Court to his might. Marshall's solution was to state vigorously the justice of the plaintiffs' cause and to condemn the action of the Chief Executive, but to deny the Court's power to provide the plaintiffs with relief.

Marbury and his associates were legally entitled to their commissions, Marshall announced. In withholding them Madison was acting "in plain violation" of the law of the land. But the Supreme Court could not issue a writ of mandamus, because the provision of the Judiciary Act of 1789 authorizing the Court to issue such writs was unconstitutional. In other words, Congress did not have the legal right to give that power to the Court.

So far as it concerned the Judiciary Act, modern commentators agree that Marshall's decision was based on a very weak legal argument. Section 13 of the Act of 1789 stated that the Supreme Court could issue the writ to "persons holding office under the authority of the United States." This law had been framed by experts thoroughly familiar with the Constitution, including William Paterson, one of Marshall's associate justices. The Court had issued the writ in earlier cases without questioning Section 13 for a moment. But Marshall now claimed that the Court could not issue a mandamus except in cases that came to it *on appeal* from a lower court, since the Constitution, he said, granted original jurisdiction to the Court only in certain specified cases—those "affecting ambassadors, other public ministers and consuls, and those in which a state shall be a party." The Marbury case had *originated* in the Supreme Court; since it did not involve a diplomat or a state, any law that gave the Court the right to decide it was unauthorized.

This was shaky reasoning because the Constitution does not necessarily *limit* the Supreme Court's original jurisdiction to the cases it specifies. And even accepting Marshall's narrow view of the constitutional provision, his decision had a major weakness. As the Court's principal chronicler, Charles Warren, has written, "It seems plain, at the present time, that it would have been possible for Marshall, if he had been so inclined, to have construed the language of [Section 13 of the Act of 1789] which authorized writs of mandamus, in such a manner as to have enabled him to escape the necessity of declaring the section unconstitutional."

Marshall was on more solid ground when he went on to argue cogently the theory that "the constitution controls any legislative act repugnant to it," which he called "one of the fundamental principles of our society." The Constitution is "the *supreme* law of the land," he emphasized. Since it is the "duty of the judicial department to say what the law is," the Supreme Court must overturn any law of Congress that violates the Constitution. "A law repugnant to the Constitution," he concluded flatly, "is void." By this reasoning, Section 13 of the Act of 1789 simply ceased to exist, and without it the Court could not issue the writ of mandamus. By thus denying himself authority, Marshall found the means to flay his enemies without exposing himself to their wrath.

Although this was the first time the Court had declared an act of Congress unconstitutional, its right to do so had not been seriously challenged by most authorities. Even Jefferson accepted the principle, claiming only that the executive as well as the judiciary could decide questions of constitutionality. Jefferson was furious over what he called the "twistifications" of Marshall's gratuitous opinion in *Marbury* v. *Madison,* but his anger was directed at the Chief Justice's stinging criticisms of his behavior, not at the constitutional doctrine Marshall had enunciated.

Even in 1803, the idea of judicial review, which Professor E. S. Corwin has called "the most distinctive feature of the American constitutional system," had had a long history in America. The concept of natural law (the belief that certain principles of right and justice transcend the laws of mere men) was thoroughly established in American thinking. It is seen, for example, in Jefferson's statement in the immortal Declaration that men "are endowed by their Creator" with "unalienable" rights. Although not a direct precedent for Marshall's decision, the colonial practice of "disallowance," whereby various laws had been ruled void on the ground that local legislatures had exceeded their powers in passing them, illustrates the American belief that there is a limit to legislative power and that courts may say when it has been overstepped.

More specifically, Lord Coke, England's chief justice under James I, had declared early in the seventeenth century that "the common law will controul acts of Parliament." One of the American Revolution's chief statesmen and legal apologists, James Otis, had drawn upon this argument a century and a half later in his famous denunciation of the Writs of Assistance. And in the 1780's, courts in New Jersey, New York, Rhode Island, and North Carolina had exercised judicial review over the acts of local legislatures. The debates at the Constitutional Convention and some of the Federalist Papers (especially No. 78) indicated that most of the Founding Fathers accepted the idea of judicial review as already established. The Supreme Court, in fact, had considered the constitutionality of a law of Congress before—when it upheld a federal tax law in 1796—and it had encountered little questioning of its right to do so. All these precedents—when taken together with the fact that the section of the Act of 1789 nullified by Marshall's decision was of minor importance—explain why no one paid much attention to this part of the decision.

Thus the "Case of the Missing Commissions" passed into history, seemingly a fracas of but slight significance. When it was over, Marbury and his colleagues returned to the obscurity whence they had arisen.* In the partisan struggle for power between Marshall and Jefferson, the incident was of secondary importance. The real showdown came later—in the impeachment proceedings against Justice Chase and the treason trial of Aaron Burr. In the long run, Marshall won his fight to preserve the independence and integrity of the federal judiciary, but generally speaking, the courts have not been able to exert as much influence over the appointive and dismissal powers of the President as Marshall had hoped to win for them in *Marbury* v. *Madison*. Even the enunciation of the Supreme Court's power to void acts of Congress wrought no immediate change in American life. Indeed, it was more than half a century before another was overturned.

Nevertheless, this trivial squabble over a few petty political plums was of vital importance for later American history. For with the expansion of the federal government into new areas of activity in more recent times, the power of the Supreme Court to nullify acts of Congress has been repeatedly employed, with profound effects. At various times legislation concerning the income tax, child labor, wages and hours, and many other aspects of our social, economic, and political life have been thrown out by the Court, and always, in the last analysis, its right to do so has depended upon the decision John Marshall handed down to escape from a dilemma of his own making.

---

*What happened to Marbury? According to his descendants, he became president of a Georgetown bank in 1814, reared a family, and died, uncommissioned, in 1835.

Was Jackson Wise to Dismantle the Bank?

Bray Hammond

 The conflict waged by President Andrew Jackson against the Second Bank of the United States, one of the most dramatic political confrontations in American history, has produced over the years a wide variety of reactions. Jackson's Whig enemies presented him as a ruthless, dictatorial ignoramus striking out at the Bank in order to increase his own power; his friends described him as a noble crusader destroying the "monster," a monopolistic economic colossus that was extracting profits for its wealthy stockholders from "the people's money." In later years historians tended to accept one or the other of these views, usually without much understanding of the financial questions around which the "bank war" raged.

This was the situation when the late Bray Hammond, then a retired governor of the Federal Reserve Board, wrote the following essay. In the 1940s a liberal young historian, Arthur M. Schlesinger, Jr., had published The Age of Jackson, *a widely read book that took an extremely pro-Jackson position in the controversy. Hammond, whose knowledge of banking and finance enabled him to grasp and explain the issues involved, disagreed with Schlesinger's interpretation. His research also led to the uncovering of a great deal of new evidence about the attitudes and actions of Nicholas Biddle, president of the Bank, and of many of the state bankers who opposed him. Although the subject, like nearly all important historical questions, is still being debated, Hammond's thesis represents the dominant view at the present time.*

"Relief, Sir!" interrupted the President. "Come not to me, sir! Go to the monster. It is folly, sir, to talk to Andrew Jackson. The government will not bow to the monster. . . . Andrew Jackson yet lives to put his foot upon the head of the monster and crush him to the dust."

The monster, "a hydra of corruption," was known also as the Second Bank of the United States, chartered by Congress in 1816 as depository of the federal government, which was its principal stockholder and customer. The words were reported by a committee which called on President Jackson in the spring of 1834 to complain because he and Secretary of the Treasury Roger Taney had removed the federal deposits from the federal depository into what the Jacksonians called "selected banks" and others called "pet banks." The President was disgusted with the committee.

"Andrew Jackson," he exclaimed in the third person as before, "would never recharter that monster of corruption. Sooner than live in a country where such a power prevailed, he would seek an asylum in the wilds of Arabia."

In effect, he had already put his foot on the monster and crushed him in the dust. He had done so by vetoing a new charter for the Bank and removing the federal accounts from its books. So long as the federal Bank had the federal accounts, it had been regulator of the currency and of credit in general. Its power to regulate had derived from the fact that the federal Treasury was the largest single transactor in the economy and the largest bank depositor. Receiving the checks and notes of local banks deposited with it by government collectors of revenue, it had had constantly to come back on the local banks for settlements of the amounts which the checks and notes called for. It had had to do so because it made those amounts immediately available to the Treasury, wherever desired. Since settlement by the local banks was in specie, i.e. silver and gold coin, the pressure for settlement automatically regulated local bank lending; for the more the local banks lent, the larger the amount of their notes and checks in use and the larger the sums they had to settle in specie. This loss of specie reduced their power to lend.

All this had made the federal Bank the regulator not alone of the currency but of bank lending in general, the restraint it had exerted being fully as effective as that of the twelve Federal Reserve Banks at present, though by a different process. With its life now limited to two more years and the government accounts removed from its books, it was already crushed but still writhing.

The Jacksonian attack on the Bank is an affair respecting which posterity seems to have come to an opinion that is half hero worship and half discernment. In the words of Professor William G. Sumner, the affair was a struggle "between the democracy and the money power." Viewed in that light, Jackson's victory was a grand thing. But Sumner also observed—this was three quarters of a century ago—that since Jackson's victory the currency, which previously had owned no superior in the world, had never again been so good. More recently Professor Lester V. Chandler, granting the Bank's imperfections, has said that its abolition without replacement by something to take over its functions was a "major blunder" which "ushered in a generation of banking anarchy and monetary disorder." So the affair stands, a triumph and a blunder.

During Andrew Jackson's lifetime three things had begun to alter prodigiously the economic life of Americans. These were steam, credit, and natural resources.

Steam had been lifting the lids of pots for thousands of years, and for a century or so it had been lifting water from coal mines. But only in recent years had it been turning spindles, propelling ships, drawing trains of cars, and multiplying incredibly the productive powers of man. For thousands of years money had been lent, but in most people's minds debt had signified distress—as it still did in Andrew Jackson's. Only now was its productive power, long known to merchants as a means of making one sum of money do the work of several, becoming popularly recognized by enterprising men for projects which required larger sums than could be assembled in coin. For three centuries or more America's resources had been crudely surmised, but only now were their variety, abundance, and accessibility becoming practical realities. And it was the union of these three, steam, credit, and natural resources, that was now turning Anglo-Saxon America from the modest agrarian interests that had preoccupied her for two centuries of European settlement to the dazzling possibilities of industrial exploitation.

In the presence of these possibilities, the democracy was becoming transformed from one that was Jeffersonian and agrarian to one that was financial and industrial. But it was still a democracy: its recruits were still men born and reared on farms, its vocabulary was still Jeffersonian, and its basic conceptions changed insensibly from the libertarianism of agrarians to that of *laissez faire.* When Andrew Jackson became President in 1829, boys born in log cabins were already becoming businessmen but with no notion of surrendering as bankers and manufacturers the freedom they might have enjoyed as farmers.

There followed a century of exploitation from which America emerged with the most wealthy and powerful economy there is, with her people the best fed, the best housed, the best clothed, and the best equipped on earth. But the loss and waste have long been apparent. The battle was only for the strong, and millions who lived in the midst of wealth never got to touch it. The age of the Robber Barons was scarcely a golden age. It was scarcely what Thomas Jefferson desired.

It could scarcely have been what Andrew Jackson desired either, for his ideals were more or less Jeffersonian by common inheritance, and the abuse of credit was one of the things he abominated. Yet no man ever did more to encourage the abuse of credit than he. For the one agency able to exert some restraint on credit was the federal Bank. In destroying it, he let speculation loose. Though a hard-money devotee who hated banks and wanted no money but coin, he fostered the formation of swarms of banks and endowed the country with a filthy and depreciated paper currency which he believed to be unsound and unconstitutional and from which the Civil War delivered it in the Administration of Abraham Lincoln thirty years later.

This, of course, was not Andrew Jackson's fault, unless one believes he would have done what he did had his advisers been different. Though a resolute and decisive person, he also relied on his friends. He had his official cabinet, largely selected for political expediency, and he had his "kitchen cabinet" for informal counsel. Of those advisers most influential with him, all but two were either businessmen or closely associated with the business world. The two exceptions were Major William B. Lewis, a planter and neighbor from Tennessee who came to live with him in the White House; and James K. Polk, also of Tennessee, later President of the United States. These two, with Jackson himself, constituted the agrarian element in the Jacksonian Administration. Several of the others, however, were agrarian in the sense that they had started as poor farm boys.

Martin Van Buren, probably the ablest of Jackson's political associates, was a lawyer whose investments had made him rich. Amos Kendall, the ablest in a business and administrative sense, later made the telegraph one of the greatest of American business enterprises and himself a man of wealth. He provided the Jacksonians their watchword, "The world is governed too much." He said, "our countrymen are beginning to demand" that the government be content with "protecting their persons and property, leaving them to direct their labor and capital as they please, within the moral law; getting rich or remaining poor as may result from their own management or fortune." Kendall's views may be sound, but they are not what one expects to hear from the democracy when struggling with the money power.

Roger Taney, later Chief Justice, never got rich, but he liked banks and was a modest investor in bank stock. "There is perhaps no business," he said as Jackson's secretary of the treasury, "which yields a profit so certain and liberal as the business of banking and exchange; and it is proper that it should be open as far as practicable to the most free competition and its advantages shared by all classes of society." His own bank in Baltimore was one of the first of the pets in which he deposited government money.

David Henshaw, Jacksonian boss of Massachusetts, was a banker and industrialist whose advice in practical matters had direct influence in Washington. Henshaw projected a Jacksonian bank to take the place of the existing institution but to be bigger. (A similar project was got up by friends of Van Buren in New York and one of the two was mentioned favorably by Jackson in his veto message as a possible alternative to the existing United States Bank.) Samuel Ingham, Jackson's first secretary of the treasury, was a paper manufacturer in Pennsylvania and later a banker in New Jersey. Churchill C. Cambreleng, congressional leader of the attack on the Bank, was a New York businessman and former agent of John Jacob Astor. These are not all of the Jacksonians who were intent on the federal Bank's destruction, but they are typical.

There was a very cogent reason why these businessmen and their class generally wanted to kill the Bank of the United States. It interfered with easy money; it kept the state banks from lending as freely as they might otherwise and businessmen from borrowing.

New York, for example, was now the financial and commercial center of the country and its largest city, which Philadelphia formerly had been. The customs duties collected at its wharves and paid by its businessmen were far the largest of any American port, and customs duties were then the principal source of federal income. These duties were paid by New York businessmen with checks on New York banks. These checks were deposited by the federal collectors in the New York office of the Bank of the United States, whose headquarters were in Philadelphia and a majority of whose directors were Philadelphia businessmen. This, Amos Kendall observed, was a "wrong done to New York in depriving her of her natural advantages."

It was not merely a matter of prestige. As already noted, the United States Bank, receiving the checks of the New York businessmen, made the funds at once available to the secretary of the treasury. The Bank had therefore to call on the New York banks for the funds the checks represented. This meant that the New York banks, in order to pay the federal Bank, had to draw down their reserves; which meant that they had less money to lend; which meant that the New York businessmen could not borrow as freely and cheaply as they might otherwise. All this because their money had gone to Philadelphia.

Jackson slays the Bank, "the hydra of corruption," assisted by Van Buren (center) and a popular cartoon character of the day (right). Bank President Biddle is in the top hat.

Actually the situation was not so bad as my simplified account makes it appear. For one thing, the goods imported at New York were sold elsewhere in the country, and more money came to New York in payment for them than went out of the city in duties paid the government. But I have described it in the bald, one-sided terms that appealed to the local politicians and to the businessmen prone to grumbling because money was not so easy as they would like. There was truth in what they said, but less than they made out.

New York's grievance was special because her customs receipts were so large and went to a vanquished rival. Otherwise the federal Bank's pressure on the local banks—all of which were state banks—was felt in some degree through the country at large. Wherever money was paid to a federal agency—for postage, for fines, for lands, for excise, for import duties—money was drawn from the local banks into the federal Bank. The flow of funds did not drain the local banks empty and leave them nothing to do, though they and the states' rights politicians talked as if that were the case. The federal Bank was simply their principal single creditor.

And though private business brought more money to New York and other commercial centers than it took away, the federal government took more away than it brought. For its largest payments were made elsewhere—to naval stations, army posts, Indian agents, owners of the public debt, largely foreign, and civilians in the government service throughout the country. In the normal flow of money payments from hand to hand in the economy, those to the federal government and consequently to the federal Bank were so large and conspicuous that the state banks involved in making them were disagreeably conscious of their size and frequency.

These banks, of course, were mostly eastern and urban rather than western and rural, because it was in eastern cities that the federal government received most of its income. Accordingly, it was in the eastern business centers, Boston, New York, Baltimore, and Charleston, that resentment against Philadelphia and the federal Bank was strongest. This resentment was intensified by the fact that the federal Bank's branch offices were also competitors for private business in these and other cities, which the present Federal Reserve Banks, very wisely, are not.

General Jackson's accession to the presidency afforded an opportunity to put an end to the federal Bank. Its charter would expire in seven years. The question of renewal was to be settled in that interval. Jackson was popular and politically powerful. His background and principles were agrarian. An attack on the Bank by him would be an attack "by the democracy on the money power." It would have, therefore, every political advantage.

The realities behind these words, however, were not what the words implied. The democracy till very recently had been agrarian because most of the population was agricultural. But the promoters of the assault on the Bank were neither agrarian in their current interests nor representative of what democracy implied.

In the western and rural regions, which were the most democratic in a traditional sense, dislike of the federal Bank persisted, though by 1829 it had less to feed on than formerly. Years before, under incompetent managers, the Bank had lent unwisely in the West, had been forced to harsh measures of self-preservation, and had made itself hated, with the help, as usual, of the state banks and states' rights politicians. But the West needed money, and though the Bank never provided enough it did provide some, and in the absence of new offenses disfavor had palpably subsided by the time Jackson became President.

There were also, in the same regions, vestiges or more of the traditional agrarian conviction that all banks were evil. This principle was still staunchly held by Andrew Jackson. He hated all banks, did so through a long life, and said so time after time. He thought they all violated the Constitution. But he was led by the men around him to focus his aversion on the federal Bank, which being the biggest must be the worst and whose regulatory pressure on the state banks must obviously be the oppression to be expected from a great, soulless corporation.

However, not all agrarian leaders went along with him. For many years the more intelligent had discriminated in favor of the federal Bank, recognizing that its operations reduced the tendency to inflation which, as a hard-money party, the agrarians deplored. Altogether, it was no longer to be expected that the agrarian democracy would initiate a vigorous attack on the federal Bank, though it was certainly to be expected that such an attack would receive very general agrarian support.

It was in the cities and within the business world that both the attack on the

Bank and its defense would be principally conducted. For there the Bank had its strongest enemies and its strongest friends. Its friends were the more conservative houses that had dominated the old business world but had only a minor part in the new. It was a distinguished part, however, and influential. This influence, which arose from prestige and substantial wealth, combined with the strength which the federal Bank derived from the federal accounts to constitute what may tritely be called a "money power." But it was a disciplined, conservative money power and just what the economy needed.

But it was no longer *the* money power. It was rivaled, as Philadelphia was by New York, by the newer, more vigorous, more aggressive, and more democratic part of the business world.

The businessmen comprising the latter were a quite different lot from the old. The Industrial Revolution required more men to finance, to man, and manage its railways, factories, and other enterprises than the old business world, comprising a few rich merchants, could possibly provide. The Industrial Revolution was set to absorb the greater part of the population.

Yet when the new recruits, who yesterday were mechanics and farmers, offered themselves not only as laborers but as managers, owners, and entrepreneurs requiring capital, they met a response that was not always respectful. There was still the smell of the barnyard on their boots, and their hands were better adapted to hammer and nails than to quills and ink. The aristocrats were amused. They were also chary of lending to such borrowers; whereupon farmers' and mechanics' banks began to be set up. These banks found themselves hindered by the older banks and by the federal Bank. They and their borrowers were furious. They resisted the federal Bank in suits, encouraged by sympathetic states' rights politicians, and found themselves blocked by the federal courts.

Nor were their grievances merely material. They disliked being snubbed. Even when they became wealthy themselves, they still railed at "the capitalists" and "the aristocrats," as David Henshaw of Massachusetts did, meaning the old families, the Appletons and Lawrences whom he named, the business counterparts of the political figures that the Jacksonian revolution had replaced. Henshaw and his fellow Jacksonian leaders were full of virtue, rancor, and democracy. Their struggle was not merely to make money but to demonstrate what they already asserted, that they were as good as anyone, or more so. In their denunciation of the federal Bank, one finds them calling it again and again "an aristocracy" and its proprietors, other than the federal government, "aristocrats."

The Jacksonians, as distinct from Jackson himself, wanted a world where *laissez faire* prevailed; where, as Amos Kendall said, everyone would be free to get rich; where, as Roger Taney said, the benefits of banks would be open to all classes; where, as the enterprising exploiters of the land unanimously demanded, credit would be easy. To be sure, relatively few would be rich, and a good many already settling into an urban industrial class were beginning to realize it. But that consideration did not count with the Jacksonian leaders. They wanted a new order; they achieved the age of the Robber Barons.

The attack on the old order took the form of an attack on the federal Bank for a number of reasons which may be summed up in political expediency. A factor in the success of the attack was that the president of the Bank, Nicholas Biddle, was the pampered scion of capitalists and aristocrats. He was born to wealth and prominence. He was elegant, literary, intellectual, witty, and conscious of his own merits. When at the age of 37 he became head of the largest moneyed corporation in the world he was wholly without practical experience. In his new duties he had to rely on brains, self-confidence, and hard work. With these he did extraordinarily well. He had a remarkable grasp of productive and financial inter-relations in the economy. The policies he formulated were sound. His manage-ment of the Bank, despite his inexperience, was efficient. His great weakness was naïveté, born of his ignorance of strife. . . .

Nicholas Biddle's response to the Jacksonian attack was inept. He was slow in recognizing that an attack was being made and ignored the warnings of his more astute friends. He expected the public to be moved by careful and learned explanations of what the Bank did. He broadcast copies of Jackson's veto mes-sage, one of the most popular and effective documents in American political history, with the expectation that people in general would agree with him that it was a piece of hollow demagogy. He entered a match for which he had no aptitude, impelled by a quixotic sense of duty and an inability to let his work be derogated. He engaged in a knock-down-drag-out fight with a group of experts as relentless as any American politics has ever known. The picture he presents is that of Little Lord Fauntleroy, lace on his shirt and good in his heart, running into those rough boys down the alley.

In his proper technical responsibilities Nicholas Biddle was a competent central banker performing a highly useful and beneficial task. It is a pity he had to be interrupted, both for him and for the economy. For him it meant demorali-zation. He lost track of what was going on in the Bank, he made blundering mistakes, he talked big. These things his opponents used tellingly against him. He turned from able direction of the central banking process to the hazardous business of making money, of which he knew nothing and for which his only knack lay in an enthusiastic appraisal of America's great economic future. In the end his Bank of the United States broke, he lost his fortune, he was tried on criminal charges (but released on a technicality), and he died a broken man.

This was personal misfortune, undeserved and severe. The more important victim was the American people. For with destruction of the United States Bank there was removed from an overexcitable economy the influence most effective in moderating its booms and depressions.

Andrew Jackson had vetoed recharter in 1832 and transferred the federal accounts to the pet banks in 1833 and 1834. The Bank's federal charter expired in 1836, though Nicholas Biddle obtained a charter from Pennsylvania and con-tinued the organization as a state bank. The period was one of boom. Then in 1837 there was panic, all the banks in the country suspended, prices fell, and business collapsed. It was all Andrew Jackson's fault, his opponents declared, for killing the federal Bank. This was too generous. Jackson was not to blame for everything. The crisis was world-wide and induced by many forces. It would have happened anyway. Yet certainly Jackson's destruction of the Bank did not help.

Instead it worsened the collapse. Had the Bank been allowed to continue the salutary performance of the years immediately preceding the attack upon it, and had it been supported rather than undermined by the Administration, the wild inflation which culminated in the collapse would have been curbed and the disaster diminished. Such a course would have been consistent with Jackson's convictions and professions. Instead he smote the Bank fatally at the moment of its best performance and in the course of trends against which it was needed most. Thereby he gave unhindered play to the speculation and inflation that he was always denouncing.

To a susceptible people the prospect was intoxicating. A continent abounding in varied resources and favorable to the maintenance of an immense population in the utmost comfort spread before the gaze of an energetic, ambitious, and clever race of men, who to exploit its wealth had two new instruments of miraculous potency: steam and credit. They rushed forward into the bright prospect, trampling, suffering, succeeding, failing. There was nothing to restrain them. For about a century the big rush lasted. Now it is over. And in a more critical mood we note that a number of things are missing or have gone wrong.

That critical mood was known to others than Jackson. Emerson, Hawthorne, and Thoreau felt it. So did an older and more experienced contemporary of theirs, Albert Gallatin, friend and aide in the past to Thomas Jefferson, and now president of a New York bank but loyal to Jeffersonian ideals.

"The energy of this nation," he wrote to an old friend toward the end of Andrew Jackson's Administration, "is not to be controlled; it is at present exclusively applied to the acquisition of wealth and to improvements of stupendous magnitude. Whatever has that tendency, and of course an immoderate expansion of credit, receives favor. The apparent prosperity and the progress of cultivation, population, commerce, and improvement are beyond expectation. But it seems to me as if general demoralization was the consequence; I doubt whether general happiness is increased; and I would have preferred a gradual, slower, and more secure progress. I am, however, an old man, and the young generation has a right to govern itself. . . ."

In these last words, Mr. Gallatin was echoing the remark of Thomas Jefferson that "the world belongs to the living." Neither Gallatin nor Jefferson, however, thought it should be stripped by the living. Yet nothing but the inadequacy of their powers seems to have kept those nineteenth-century generations from stripping it. And perhaps nothing else could.

But to the extent that credit multiplies man's economic powers, curbs upon credit extension are a means of conservation, and an important means. The Bank of the United States was such a means. Its career was short and it had imperfections. Nevertheless it worked. The evidence is in the protest of the bankers and entrepreneurs, the lenders and the borrowers, against its restraints. Their outcry against the oppressor was heard, and Andrew Jackson hurried to their rescue. Had he not, some other way of stopping its conservative and steadying influence could doubtless have been found. The appetite for credit is avid, as Andrew

Jackson knew in his day and might have foretold for ours. But because he never meant to serve it, the credit for what happened goes rather to the clever advisers who led the old hero to the monster's lair and dutifully held his hat while he stamped on its head and crushed it in the dust.

Meanwhile, the new money power had curled up securely in Wall Street, where it has been at home ever since.

Andrew Jackson and the Annexation of Texas

Robert V. Remini

 Andrew Jackson is generally considered one of our great presidents, though, for reasons this essay makes abundantly clear, he was also one of our most controversial chief executives. Whether some of his more belligerent and indeed irrational statements were contrived rather than heartfelt is a matter of debate among historians, but there is no doubt that he was an extremely colorful person and as shrewd a politician as ever lived.

The desire to see Texas added to the United States was one of the major fixations of Jackson's remarkable career. How he pursued that objective, relentlessly and with every political weapon he could command, during and after his two terms as president, is the subject of this article. The author, Robert V. Remini of the University of Illinois at Chicago, is the leading contemporary authority on Jackson; his three–volume biography of Old Hickory won both an American Book Award and a Pulitzer Prize.

From the moment he entered the White House in March 1829, Andrew Jackson of Tennessee turned a cold and calculating eye on Texas. Sitting in his study on the second floor of the mansion, maps strewn around the room, the white-haired, sharp-featured, cadaverous President breathed a passion for Texas that was soon shared by other Americans.

Old Hickory always believed—or so he said—that Texas had been acquired by the United States as part of the Louisiana Purchase in 1803 and then had been recklessly thrown away when "that old scamp J. Q. Adams" negotiated the Florida treaty with Spain in 1819 and agreed to the Sabine River as the western boundary of the country. The claim was questionable at the very least, but many Southerners, outraged by Northern reaction to the slavery issue during the debates over the admission of Missouri and chagrined over the institution's prohibition in the Louisiana Territory north of 36° 30′, decided to press it anyway.

The loss of Texas by virtue of the Florida treaty dismayed some Americans. It infuriated Jackson. "How infatuated must have been our councils who gave up the rich country of Texas," he wrote. Such action, in his mind, verged on treason. And why had it happened? "It surely must have been with the view to keep the political ascendence in the North, and east," he fumed, "& cripple the rising greatness of the West." No matter. He would attend to it at the first opportunity. And indeed he did—or tried to. "I have long since been aware of the importance of Texas to the United States," he wrote a friend just a few months after taking office as President, "and of the real necessity of extending our boundary west of the Sabine. . . . I shall keep my eye on this object & the first propitious moment make the attempt to regain the Territory as far south & west as the great Desert."

All his attempts at acquiring Texas proved feeble, however, mostly because he had assigned a freewheeling, fast-talking, double-dealing incompetent to represent the United States in Mexico. Col. Anthony Butler made numerous "diplomatic" efforts to purchase Texas from Mexico, and when those failed, he turned to bribery. "I have just had a very singular conversation with a Mexican," he wrote Jackson in October of 1833, and this Mexican "has much influence with the Presidt. Genl. St. Anna." The Mexican had bluntly asked Butler, "Have you command of Money?"

"Yes, I have money," Butler responded.

The price would be high, said the Mexican, in excess of half a million dollars. The Mexican himself required two or three hundred thousand, and Butler allowed that "there are others amongst whom it may become necessary to distribute 3 or 4 Hundred thousand more."

"Can you command that Sum?" the Mexican demanded.

"Yes," Butler assured him.

He was wrong. "I have read your confidential letter with care, and astonishment," a furious Jackson replied, ". . . astonishment that you would entrust such a letter, without being in cypher, to the mail." Moreover, wrote Jackson, he was astounded by Butler's presumption that "my instructions authorized you to apply to corruption, when nothing could be farther from my intention than to convey such an idea."

At length Jackson had to recall Butler. The President was discouraged not only by the diplomatic failure and the shady operations of his minister but also by the resistance of the Mexicans to his assurance that a "natural boundary" at the Rio Grande River would work to the mutual benefit of both nations. Such a boundary, Jackson insisted, would eliminate "collisions" that two peoples of "conflicting laws, habits and interests" were bound to have. Moreover, it would provide the Mexicans with needed cash to bolster their economy: the President was willing to go as high as five million dollars to purchase the territory. Failure of the sale was sure to encourage the many Americans who had moved to Texas over the previous ten years to establish an independent republic. And such a turn of events, the President feared, would sever the "bonds of amity and good understanding" between the United States and Mexico.

Since the early 1820s, Americans had been migrating to Texas, particularly from the South and West. Motivated to a large extent by the hard times generated by the Panic of 1819, they sought relief in Texas because the Mexicans encouraged them to settle there. Led by Moses Austin and his son Stephen F., they established an American colony in Texas and accepted Mexican authority. Slave owners from Alabama, Mississippi, and Tennessee were particularly attracted to this haven. By 1830 over twelve thousand Americans had emigrated to Texas, and Mexico, alarmed, eventually prohibited all immigration from the north.

Many Texans desired immediate annexation by the United States, especially after 1829, when slavery was forbidden throughout Mexican territory. The blatant and hostile intentions of these Texans naturally provoked the Mexicans, and Jackson's fumbling efforts to purchase the territory only exacerbated an already worsening situation. Despite his passion for Texas, the President wanted neither war with Mexico nor domestic strife over the wisdom of adding what might become another slave state. Still, he would not abandon his dream of territorial expansion. "The boundary between the U. States and Mexico," he jotted into his private memorandum book, ". . . must be altered."

Jackson's apprehensions deepened when he learned that his old friend and protégé, Sam Houston, late governor of Tennessee, had fled to Texas after a disastrous marriage and reportedly "would conquer Mexico or Texas, & be worth two millions in two years." These were the "efusions of a distempered brain," said Jackson; Houston would never place millions before the welfare of his country, but that did not guarantee a peaceful resolution to the problem.

Perhaps, given Mexico's stiff opposition to territorial dismemberment, no one in the United States possessed the diplomatic skill to bring about the peaceful acquisition of this valuable and strategically important landmass. But certainly Jackson botched what little chance he may have had by appointing Butler and then keeping him long after Jackson had reason to believe that his minister was a scoundrel. Gen. Antonio López de Santa Anna was convinced that the United States had acted dishonorably and had violated its neutrality laws by encouraging filibustering expeditions into Texas and by arming Americans to instigate revolution.

The failure of American diplomacy did indeed spur the Texans to take matters into their own hands. A war party was formed at the same time that the Mexican government was moving to centralize control over all parts of the Mexican republic, including Texas. The struggle for independence ignited in October 1835 and roared to its climax when General Santa Anna marched into Texas at the head of a five-thousand-man army. Texas proclaimed its independence on March 2, 1836, and on April 21 a Texan army commanded by Sam Houston defeated Santa Anna at the Battle of San Jacinto. Santa Anna himself was captured and forced to sign a treaty (later repudiated) recognizing Texan independence.

No American doubted that annexation by the United States would soon follow. Some Texans might have preferred to remain a republic, but probably many more desired eventual statehood.

The Mexican minister to the United States, Manuel Eduardo de Gorostiza, peppered President Jackson with angry protests. He raged against American treachery and ultimately demanded his passports. Relations between Mexico and the United States rapidly deteriorated, and within two months it appeared that war between the two countries would break out momentarily. The secretary of the Navy, Mahlon Dickerson, reported at a cabinet meeting that Com Alexander J. Dallas had notified him that the American consul and residents at Tampico had suffered innumerable "indignities" at the hands of Mexican authorities. Moreover, American armed vessels in the area had been refused water, and their officers had been denied permission to go ashore. Worse, these authorities had threatened to put to death all Americans in Tampico in retaliation for the capture of Santa Anna.

Dickerson concluded his report. [Attorney General] Benjamin Butler, in a letter to his wife, explained what happened next. Jackson "broke out in his most impassioned manner." He jumped to his feet, gesticulated wildly, and shook his fist at invisible enemies. It was one of the most frightening displays of the President's anger that the cabinet had ever witnessed. The members sat frozen, staring; nobody dared interrupt the wild outburst.

Then, wrote Butler, Old Hickory barked, "Write immediately to Commodore Dallas & order him to *blockade* the harbour of Tampico, & to suffer nothing to enter till they allow him to land and obtain his supplies of water & communicate with the Consul, & if they touch the hair of the head of one of our citizens, tell him *to batter down & destroy their town & exterminate the inhabitants from the face of the earth!*"

The cabinet sucked in its collective breath, but said nothing. Could he be serious?

Finally, Jackson addressed his secretary of state, John Forsyth. "Have you rec[eived] any information on this subject?"

Forsyth shook his head.

"Then let the Secy of the Navy furnish you the papers," Jackson ordered, "& do you write immediately to Mr. Gorostiza informing him of the orders we have given to Commodore Dallas, & that we shall not permit a jot or tittle of the treaty to be violated, or a citizen of the United States to be injured without taking immediate redress."

Fortunately, cooler heads on both sides prevented the extermination of the citizens of Tampico, but American-Mexican relations continued to deteriorate: Texans were doing everything possible to force U.S. recognition of their independence and eventual annexation. Commissioners dispatched to lobby in Washington were all warmly received by the President. During one such meeting Jackson turned to Special Commissioner Samuel Carson and said. "Is it true, Mr. Carson, that your Government has sent Santa Anna back to Mexico?" Carson responded that Santa Anna was indeed expected to depart shortly to assist in winning ratification of the treaty recognizing the independence of Texas.

"Then I tell you, Sir," said Jackson, "if ever he sets foot on Mexican ground, your Government may whistle; he, Sir, will give you trouble, if he escapes, which you dream not of."

Then there would be war, Carson said.

"Where is your means, Sir, to carry on an offensive war against Mexico?"

"In the enthusiasms of the American people," said Carson happily, "their devotion to the cause of Liberty are the ways and means, to defray the expenses of the War."

Jackson blanched. It was one thing for the President of the United States to threaten war, quite another for "outsiders" from Texas to presume they could manipulate this country into one. The United States had a treaty with Mexico, and the annexation of Mexican territory would most certainly be viewed around the world as a betrayal. Civilized countries would label it a brutal and aggressive act, a violation of the "law of nations." The "Texians," as Jackson frequently called them, must realize that annexation would take time and careful planning. Thus, when Stephen F. Austin sent him an impassioned letter requesting assistance, Jackson wrote the following endorsement: "[Austin] does not reflect that we have a treaty with Mexico, and our national faith is pledged to support it. The Texians before they took the step to declare themselves Independent, which has aroused and united all Mexico against them ought to have pondered well, it was a rash and premature act. our nutrality must be faithfully maintained."

And there were other problems. Abolitionists, for one. These troublemakers would exploit any issue to attack slavery, said Jackson, even if it ruptured relations between the North and South. They intended to oppose the admission of Texas because it represented the continued expansion of slavery. Texas, therefore, posed a possible threat to the Union, which hobbled Jackson's efforts to negotiate a swift treaty of admission. His passion for Texas could never match his passion for the Union. "Prudence," he later wrote, seemed to dictate that "we should stand aloof" and see how things would develop. No doubt he was also fearful of jeopardizing the election of his hand-picked successor to the Presidency, Martin Van Buren.

At this juncture Sam Houston decided to send Santa Anna to Washington to meet Jackson in the hope that their talks together would help the cause of Texas annexation. Houston released the Mexican, presented him with a handsome horse, and headed him (under armed escort) to the capital. Santa Anna arrived on January 17, 1837.

At the moment, Old Hickory was recovering from a severe "hemorrhage of the lungs" that had almost ended his life. For months he remained in his room, not daring to expose himself to a relapse by needless movement around the White House. In fact, he left his room only four times during the final six months of his administration. Still, on state occasions, Jackson could muster great presence and exude the appearance of enormous strength. For his part, Santa Anna, despite his long trip, looked refreshed and relaxed. He was amused and rather pleased by the notoriety that his arrival in the capital had provoked. Many assumed he would look malevolent. They were surprised to find him a gracious and cultivated man of impeccable manners and dress.

On Thursday, January 19, 1837, the Mexican general was escorted into the presence of the American general at the White House. The two men greeted one another politely and with a degree of dignified reserve. Always the gentleman, Old Hickory assured his guest that he was most welcome in Washington and expressed pleasure in meeting him at long last. "General Andrew Jackson greeted me warmly," Santa Anna later wrote, "and honored me at a dinner attended by notables of all countries." Jackson treated him not as an enemy but as a head of state, even though Santa Anna had been succeeded in Mexico by Anastasio Bustamante.

The official greeting, reception, and dinner went extremely well, but the conversations involved nothing of substance. Not until the following day did the two men turn to the matter that had brought them together.

Santa Anna began by proposing the cession of Texas for a "fair consideration." The United States, responded Jackson, could do nothing about a cession until the "disposition of the Texians" was resolved. "Until Texas is acknowledged

Independent," said the President, this nation could make no official move. At some point in the conversation, Jackson outlined a proposal for the Mexican to take back to his country. Beginning with the supposition that Mexico would officially acknowledge the independence of Texas at some point early on, Jackson suggested that the boundary of the United States be extended to include Texas and northern California—in effect, this would run the "line of the U. States to the Rio grand—up that stream to latitude 38 north & then to the pacific including north California." In return the United States would compensate Mexico with $3,500,000. "But before we promise anything," Jackson continued, "Genl Santana must say that he will use his influence to suspend hostilities." The President assured his visitor that the principal objective of the United States was not territorial acquisition or the further embarrassment of the Mexican Republic, but rather to "secure peace & tranquility on our respective borders & lay the foundation of a permanent tranquility between the U.S. and Mexico."

The interview ended on a polite but indefinite note. President Jackson provided Santa Anna with a warship to carry him to Veracruz, and the Mexican had nothing but gratitude for his treatment.

A little later Jackson mentioned his conversation with Santa Anna to William Wharton, recently arrived in Washington to represent Texas. Wharton protested: Texan independence was an accomplished fact achieved through her own military power, and Mexico had no right to make a treaty that in any way bound her. What the United States must do, insisted Wharton, was to recognize Texan independence; then the nation could move on to the question of possible annexation.

Jackson grimaced. Perhaps, suggested the President to Wharton, as a way of quieting the sectional rivalry that recognition was sure to provoke, Texas might claim California in order to "paralyze" Northern opposition to annexation. Acquisition of California along with Texas meant the continuation of representational balance in the Senate between free and slave states. The suggestion did not elicit much enthusiasm from Wharton. Texas could never legitimately claim California or undertake a war to assert its claim. California was simply not on the negotiating table.

Congress, however, responded to the wishes of the "Texians" without grappling with the sectional consequences and, during the final days of Jackson's administration, recognized the independence of the Texas Republic. The President quickly appointed Alcée Louis La Branche of Louisiana as chargé d'affaires to Texas, and the Senate confirmed the nomination only hours before the final adjournment of Congress. Around midnight, when word came that La Branche had been confirmed, Jackson met with Wharton and a few others to celebrate. They lifted their glasses in a single toast: Texas!

But Jackson returned home defeated in his one great effort to reach the Rio Grande. He rightly feared his failure might jeopardize the integrity and tranquillity of the Union.

The more he thought about it, as he sat in his study at the Hermitage reading the reports that arrived daily from Washington, the more he convinced himself that the security of the United States demanded the acquisition of Texas. Never mind the machinations of abolitionists. They were nothing compared with the danger posed by foreign enemies: Great Britain, for example.

If Britain should decide to reenter the continent through Texas and attempt a linkup with Canada, then war would be inevitable. "The safety of the republic being the supreme law, and Texas having offered us the key to the safety of our country from all foreign intrigues and diplomacy," Jackson wrote, "I say accept the key . . . and bolt the door at once." If England concluded an alliance with the "Texians"—which seemed under way at that very moment—then she would most likely move "an army from canady, along our western frontier," march through Arkansas and Louisiana, seize New Orleans, "excite the negroes to insurrection," "arouse the Indians on our west to war," and "throw our whole west into flames that would cost oceans of blood & hundreds of millions of money to quench, & reclaim. . . ." As he wrote these words, Jackson worked himself into a passion. "Texas must be ours," he raged. "Our safety requires it." Later he repeated his demand with a little less passion but with the same determination. We must have Texas, "peaceably if we can, forcibly if we must."

Despite strong Northern pressure, the new President, John Tyler, obtained a treaty of annexation signed by representatives of Texas and the United States in April 1844 and submitted it to the Senate for ratification. It was accompanied by an extraordinary letter to the British minister to Washington, Richard Pakenham, written by the secretary of state, John C. Calhoun. In it Calhoun contended that the treaty had been signed for the express purpose of protecting American slavery from British attempts to bring about universal emancipation. The extension of the American slave interests into Texas, he said, would nullify that "reprehensible" goal.

Friends of annexation groaned when they read copies of Calhoun's provocative letter. The secretary had placed annexation *"exclusively* upon the ground of *protection of Slavery* in the *Southern States!"* and the senators from the nonslaveholding states who favored annexation were furious because "it would be death to them, politically, if they were to vote for the Treaty based on such principles."

Why had Calhoun done it? Why had he jeopardized the treaty by the gratuitous mention of slavery? Maj. William B. Lewis, one of Jackson's oldest friends, claimed to know. The secretary of state meant to kill the treaty, he wrote, in order to "drive off every Northern man from the reannexation" and thereby give him a "pretext to unite the whole South upon himself as the Champion of its cause." Put simply, he meant to divide the Union, create a Southern confederacy, and make himself the "great man of this fragment which he expects to tear from the embrace of our glorious Govt." Like abolitionists, Lewis added, Southern hotheads were determined to disrupt the Union to achieve their own selfish objectives. Unfortunately, Texas had become a pawn in the fatal game of personal ambition. As far as Jackson was concerned, between "that arch fiend, J. Q. Adams" and that *"Cateline,"* John C. Calhoun, they were tearing the Union apart.

So the treaty failed. And shortly thereafter the ostensible Whig and Democratic candidates for the Presidency in the next election, Henry Clay and Martin Van Buren, publicly announced their opposition to annexation. Clay (himself a slave owner) regarded annexation as dangerous to the country because it might provoke a war with Mexico, excite sectional passions over slavery, and prove financially disastrous, since the $10 million Texas debt would have to be assumed by the United States. Van Buren was especially concerned over the sectional rancor and possibility of war.

Jackson "shed tears of regret" when he read the letter of his old friend Martin Van Buren. "I would to god I had been at Mr. V. B. elbow when he closed his letter. I would have brought to his view *the proper conclusion.*" The only course of action left was to dump Van Buren as a presidential candidate and nominate someone else, someone who "is an annexation man," he wrote, "and from the Southwest." Other Democrats agreed, and at the national nominating convention in Baltimore, they "arranged" to replace Van Buren with James K. Polk.

Clay and Polk ran a close race. Among other things, Polk promised to "reannex" Texas, claiming like Jackson that it was part of the Louisiana Purchase and had been shamefully surrendered by that "crazy old man, John Quincy Adams." In the election, he won 170 electoral votes to Clay's 105. The popular vote was even closer: 1,337,243 to 1,299,062. Polk defeated Clay by a 1.4 percent margin. "A mere *Tom Tit,*" growled John Quincy Adams, had triumphed over the "old Eagle. The partial associations of Native Americans, Irish Catholics, abolition societies, liberty party, the Pope of Rome, the Democracy of the sword, and the dotage of a ruffian [Andrew Jackson] are sealing the fate of this nation, which nothing less than the interposition of Omnipotence can save."

Between the time of his election and inauguration, Polk met several times with Jackson at the Hermitage. Old Hickory instructed his friend on the necessity of annexing Texas in order to "put to rest the vexing question of abolitionism, the dangerous rock to our Union, and put at defiance all combined Europe, if combined to invade us." But Polk needed no instruction. Upon his arrival in Washington, he was queried by many members of Congress about his plans and goals. "He is for Texas, Texas, Texas," reported Sen. Willie P. Mangum of North Carolina, "& talks of but little else."

The outgoing President, John Tyler, saw his opportunity to capitalize on Polk's victory, and he helped arrange a joint resolution of annexation for both houses of Congress. After considerable politicking the House and Senate gave their approval, and Tyler signed the resolution on March 1, 1845, just three days before he was to leave office. A messenger was immediately dispatched to Texas with the "glorious" news.

"Texas is ours," trumpeted the newspapers. "The Union is safe." A feeble old man who had only a few months to live added his voice to the general acclaim. Andrew Jackson thanked God that he had lived to see this happy day. "I . . . congratulate my beloved country [that] Texas is reannexed," he wrote, "and the safety, prosperity, and the greatest interest of the whole Union is secured by this . . . great and important national act."

But others expressed more disturbing views. They feared that the admission of Texas would lead inevitably to war with Mexico and possibly civil war. And their direst predictions proved correct. Texas ratified annexation on July 4 and was admitted into the Union as a slave state on December 29, 1845. The following spring—on May 11, 1846—the United States declared war against Mexico. Later the North and South submitted their dispute over slavery to a frightful test of arms. Within twenty years the Union cracked apart, and to weld it back together did indeed take "oceans of blood & hundreds of millions of money."

PART SIX

Antebellum Society

William Sidney Mount was a founder of the American school of genre art. In The Rustic Dance *(1830, detail), he portrayed antebellum society with lighthearted candor.*

Religion on the Frontier

Bernard A. Weisberger

The following essay illustrates how exotic and colorful historical material can be presented in all its vigor without the historian surrendering the obligation to analyze and explain the significance of the subject he or she is describing. Indeed, in this case the discussion of the "meaning" of a backwoods revivalism adds greatly to the verisimilitude of the strange events themselves. Portraits of the emotionally charged religious camp meetings of the nineteenth-century frontier easily degenerate into caricature. Bernard A. Weisberger studiously avoids this trap both by showing that the meetings were complex affairs (to which many kinds of people, driven by differing urges, came) and by pointing out the rational bases for the meetings and the emotional excesses they generated. He takes a relatively narrow subject, frontier religion, and relates it to a wide range of larger questions: American democracy; east-west conflicts; the nature of nationalism; human nature itself.

Dr. Weisberger, formerly a professor of history at Chicago, Rochester, and other universities, is currently devoting himself full time to historical research and writing. Among his books are They Gathered at the River, *a study of revivalism,* The American Newspaperman, *and* The New Industrial Society.

T he great revival in the West, or the Kentucky Revival of 1800, as it was sometimes called, was a landmark in American history. It was not some accidental outburst of religious hysteria that crackled through the clearings. Rather, it was one of many answers to a question on which America's destiny hung during Thomas Jefferson's Presidency. Which way would the West go? It was filling up fast in 1800, and yet it still remained isolated behind the mountain barriers, only thinly linked to the nation by a cranky, awkward, and dangerous transportation "system" of trails and rivers. Could it be held within the bounds of American institutions as they had developed over 175 colonial years? Would its raw energies pull it into some new orbit—say, an independent confederation? Or, if it stayed in the Union, would it send representatives swarming back eastward to crush old patterns under the weight of numbers?

No group asked this question more anxiously than eastern clergymen. For, in 1800, they saw that their particular pattern was being abandoned on the frontier. From Kentucky, Tennessee, the western Carolinas, and Virginia, reports came back of a world that was shaggy, vicious, and churchless. The hard-living men and women of the forest clearings were not raising temples to God. Their morals (to eastern eyes) were parlous. Corn liquor flowed freely; marriages were celebrated long after children had arrived; gun and rope settled far too many legal disputes. The West was crowded with Sabbath-breakers and profane swearers, thieves, murderers, and blasphemers, with neither courts of law nor public opinion to raise a rebuke. The whole region seemed "hair-hung and breeze-shaken" over Hell's vault. And this was a matter of life-or-death seriousness to the churches. It was clear even then that America's future lay beyond the mountains. And if the West grew up Godless, then the entire nation would one day turn from His ways, to its destruction. It was no wonder that pious folk of the seaboard dug into their pocketbooks to scrape up funds for "home missionary" societies aimed at paying the way of parsons traveling westward. Or that church assemblies warned of crises ahead and called for special days of fasting, humiliation, and prayer for the West.

Yet, for a fact, the easterners were wrong. They misjudged their pioneers. Western people wanted and needed the church just as badly as the church needed their support for survival. Religion had a part to play in the hard-driven lives of the frontier settlers. It was more than a mere foundation for morality. It offered the hope of a bright future, shining beyond the dirt-floored, hog-and-hominy present. It offered an emotional outlet for lives ringed with inhibition. It was a social thing, too, furnishing occasions on which to lay aside axe and gun and skillet and gather with neighbors, to sing, to weep, to pray, or simply to talk with others. The West had to have religion—but religion of its own special kind. The West was not "lost" in 1800, but on the verge of being saved. Only it was going to be saved the same way it did everything else: on its own individualistic terms.

The East found this hard to understand. The East had trouble taking stock of such a man as the father of the western revival, James McGready. McGready was an angular, black-eyed Scotch-Irishman, born on the Pennsylvania frontier. He came of a hard-working and pious stock that had filled the western stretches of the Colonies in the sixty years before the Revolution. McGready was true to the spirit of his Highland Calvinistic ancestors, who worked, prayed, and fought heartily. He grew to adolescence without becoming a swearer, drinker, or Sabbath-breaker, which made him something of a God-fearing rarity among frontier youth. So his family sent him to a private school conducted by a minister, where he wrestled with Scripture in the morning and did farm chores in the afternoon for his "tuition." In 1788, he was licensed to preach, and came down to western North Carolina's Guilford County, where his family had moved. Thus, McGready was a product of western Presbyterianism.

That was important. In the 1790's, the religious picture in the United States already showed considerable (and characteristic) variety. Episcopalianism was solidly rooted among the landed gentry of the South. The Dutch Reformed Church carried on the heritage established when the flag of Holland flapped over New York. Various shoots of Lutheranism pushed up out of the soil of German settlements. Baptism and Methodism were small but growing faiths. There were little wedges in the pie of church membership labeled "Quaker," "Catholic," and "Jewish." A few bold souls called themselves Deists. A few more were on the way to becoming Unitarians. American worship wore a coat of many colors. But in New England and the mid-Atlantic states, the Presbyterian and Congregational bodies were unquestionably in the forefront. Both were rooted in the preceding century's Puritanism. Both officially believed in "predestination" and "limited election"—God had chosen a few individuals to be saved from general damnation, and the list, made up from the beginning of eternity, was unchangeable. These chosen "saints" were born in sin, but in His own way God would convert them to holiness during their lifetimes. Meanwhile, the laws of God must be interpreted and explained to mankind. In order to do this, the Presbyterians and Congregationalists had raised up colleges to train their ministers, the most famous among them by 1800 being Harvard, Yale, and Princeton. Graduates of these schools thundered of Jehovah's wrath to their congregations in two-hour sermons rich with samples of their learning. During the week they warmed their study chairs ten hours a day, writing black-bound volumes of theology.

Religion of this sort lacked appeal for the Scotch-Irish migrants pushing into the frontier regions. They were Presbyterians in name. But their wild surroundings did something to them. They came to resent authority—whether exercised by excise collectors, land speculators, lawyers, or, finally, ministers. What was more, they wanted a little stronger assurance of salvation than a strict reading of limited election gave them. There was a need, in this fur-capped, bewhiskered Christian world, for more promise in life, and more passion too. Learned lectures might do for townspeople, but not for pioneers.

Among common folk, both East *and* West, a ferment of resentment against the "aristocratic" notion of election was at work. In the 1740's it had exploded in a revival called the Great Awakening. Baptist, Presbyterian, Congregationalist, Anglican, and Dutch-Reformed Christians were caught up in a common whirlwind of handclapping, shouting, and hosannaing. A good many new leaders, and a number of unpleasant schisms, had risen out of this storm. And in western Pennsylvania, revival-minded Presbyterians had founded a number of little academies to train their preachers. Derisively dubbed "log colleges" by the learned, they took the name proudly. Their graduates were short on Greek and exegesis but long on zeal. When the Great Awakening sputtered out before the Revolution, these colleges remained, helping to keep the sparks alive. Now, with the new nation established, the fire was ready to blaze again. McGready, himself a log-college graduate, was one of the first to blow on it.

McGready got to grips with the powers of darkness in North Carolina without wasting any time. He began to preach against the "formality and deadness" of the local churches. Besides that, he demanded some concrete testimony of good living from his flock, and the particular evidence he asked for was highly exacting. The new preacher insisted that strong drink was a slippery path to Hell. In Guilford County this did not sit well. Frontiersmen saw no harm in lightening a hard life with a dram or two, and they wanted no lectures on the subject from men of the cloth. In point of fact, there was no cloth. Pioneer ministers wore buckskin, and took their turn with the next man at hoeing corn or splitting kindling. McGready got nowhere—at least nowhere in North Carolina. After a futile battle, he left to seek a more promising future in Kentucky—some said by request of the congregation.

In Kentucky, circumstances were riper for him. Despite eastern concern, a

Anabaptists of Hudson Falls, New York, attend a convert's immersion in the Hudson River.

new Christian community was taking shape in that rugged, bear-and-savage-haunted wilderness province, where crude living went along with high dreaming. It was a community ready to be stirred into life, and McGready was the man to seize the stick. In Logan County, in the southwestern part of the state—a region well-known for unregenerate doings—he had three small congregations: at Red River, Gasper River, and Muddy River. He began to preach to these congregations, and he did not deal with such recondite matters as the doctrines contained in Matthew, or their applications. Instead he would "so describe Heaven" that his listeners would "see its glories and long to be there." Then he went on to "array hell and its horrors" so that the wicked would "tremble and quake, imagining a lake of fire and brimstone yawning to overwhelm them." With that brimstone smoking away in the background, McGready struck for bedrock. The whole point of Christianity, for him, was in the conversion of sinners to saints assured of eternal bliss. His question of questions was dagger-sharp: "If I were converted, would I feel it and know it?" A McGready parishioner was not going to be allowed to rest in self-satisfaction merely because he attended worship and avoided the grosser forms of indecency.

Under such spurring, results began to show among the faithful. In 1799, during a service at Gasper River, many fell to the ground and lay "powerless, groaning, praying and crying for mercy." Women began to scream. Big, tough men sobbed like hysterical children. What could explain this? Simply the fact that belly-deep fear was taking over. For it is well to remember that in those days conversion was the *only* token of salvation. No matter how young one was, no matter how blameless a life he had led, until the moment of transformation one was a sinner, bound for torment. If death stepped in before conversion was completed, babes and grandsires alike sank screaming into a lake of burning pitch—a lake that was not metaphorical, not symbolical, but *real* and eternal. And death on the frontier was always around the corner—in the unexpected arrow, the milk sickness, the carelessly felled tree, the leap of the wounded grizzly. Frontiersmen bottled up their fear. It was the price of sanity and survival. But when a religious service provided an acceptable excuse for breaking down the barriers, it was no wonder that men shivered and wept.

After shaking up the dry bones of the Gasper River settlement, McGready moved on in June of 1800 to Red River. He meant to hold a sacramental service, at the end of which church members would take the Lord's Supper together. What he got was something more uncontrolled. In a meetinghouse of undressed logs McGready shared his pulpit with three other Presbyterian ministers. A Methodist preacher was also present. That was not unusual. Frontier preachers were a small band. They knew each other well. A service was a social occasion, and therefore a treat, and several ministers often took part in order to draw it out.

The Presbyterian shepherds did their preaching, and what they said has not come down to us, but they must have dragged a harrow through the congregation's feelings. When John McGee, the Methodist, arose, an awesome hush had fallen on the house. McGee faced a problem. The Methodists were relative newcomers to America, officially on the scene only since 1766. They were frowned on by more established groups, mainly because they gave emotion free rein in their worship. It was not unusual at a Methodist meeting for women to faint, men to shout in strange tongues, and the minister himself to windmill his arms and bawl himself red-faced. For the more formal Presbyterians, such conduct was out of bounds. McGee knew this, and wanted to mind his ecclesiastical manners. But he knew a ripe audience when he saw one, too, and after an apparent debate with himself, he made his move. Rising, he shouted that everyone in the house should submit to "the Lord Omnipotent." Then he began to bounce from backless bench to backless bench, pleading, crying, shouting, shaking, and exhorting, "with all possible energy and ecstasy."

That broke the dam. The sinners of Red River had spent a lonely winter with pent-up terrors gnawing at them. McGee's appeal was irresistible. In a moment the floor was "covered with the slain; their screams for mercy pierced the heavens." Cursers, duelers, whiskey-swillers, and cardplayers lay next to little children of ten and eleven, rolling and crying in "agonies of distress" for salvation. It was a remarkable performance for a region "destitute of religion." When it was through, a new harvest of souls had been gathered for the Lord.

Word of the Red River meeting whisked through the territory. When McGready got to Muddy River, his next congregation, new scenes of excitement were enacted. During the meeting, sinners prayed and cried for mercy once again, and some of them, overwhelmed by feeling, bolted from the house and rushed in agony into the woods. Their cries and sobs could be heard ringing through the surrounding trees. And when this meeting had yielded up its quota of saved, the Kentucky Revival was not only a fact, but a well-known one. McGready announced another sacramental meeting for Gasper River, and before long, dozens, perhaps hundreds, of Kentuckians who did not belong to his district were threading the trails on their way to the service. Some came as far as a hundred miles, a hard week's trip in the back country. In wagons, on horseback, and on foot came the leathershirted men, rifles balanced on their shoulders, and their pinched-looking, tired women, all looking for blessed assurance and a washing away of their sins.

At Gasper River, history was made. The cabins of the neighborhood could not hold the influx of visitors, so the newcomers came prepared to camp out. They brought tents—some of them—and cold pork, roasted hens, slabs of corn bread, and perhaps a little whiskey to hold them up through the rigors of a long vigil. The Gasper River meetinghouse was too small for the crowd, so the men got out their educated axes, and in a while the clop-clop of tree-felling formed an overture to the services. Split-log benches were dragged into place outdoors, and the worshipers adjourned to God's first temple. What was taking place was an outdoor religious exercise, meant to last two or three days, among people who camped on the spot. This was the camp meeting. Some claimed that Gasper River sheltered the very first of them. That claim has been challenged in the court of historical inquiry. But whether it stands up or not, the Gasper River meeting was something new in worship. It took its form from its western surroundings. Outsiders were a long time in understanding it, because they saw its crude outside and not its passionate heart.

The outside was raw enough. Once again McGready exhorted, and once again sinners fell prostrate to the ground. Night came on; inside the meetinghouse, candlelight threw grotesque, waving shadows on the walls, Outside, the darkness deepened the sense of mystery and of eternity's nearness. Preachers grew hoarse and exhausted, but insatiable worshipers gathered in knots to pray together, and to relieve their feelings by telling each other of "the sweet wonders which they saw in Christ." Hour followed hour, into dawn. For people who had to rise (and generally retire) with the sun each day of their lives, this alone was enough to make the meeting memorable for the rest of their lives. Lightheaded and hollow-eyed, the "mourners," or unconverted, listened alternately to threats of sulphur and promises of bliss, from Saturday until Monday. On Tuesday, after three throbbing days, they broke it up. Forty-five had professed salvation. Satan had gotten a thorough gouging.

Now the tide of camp-meeting revivalism began to roll northward. One of the visitors at the Logan County meetings was a young Presbyterian clergyman whose life was something of a copy of McGready's. Barton Warren Stone too had learned on the frontier to revere God Almighty and to farm well. He too had studied religion in a log college. But more than this, he was one of McGready's own converts, having fallen under the power of the older man's oratory in North Carolina. Stone liked what he observed in Logan County, and he took

McGready's preaching methods and the camp-meeting idea back to his own congregations in Bourbon County, well to the north and east. Soon he too had imitators, among them Richard McNemar, who had small Presbyterian charges across the river in Ohio.

But it was Stone himself who touched off the monster camp meeting of the region's history. He set a sacramental service for August 6, 1801, at Cane Ridge, not far from the city of Lexington. Some undefinable current of excitement running from cabin to cabin brought out every Kentuckian who could drop his earthly concerns and move, by horseflesh or shoe leather, toward the camp-ground. Later on, some people estimated that 25,000 were on hand, but that figure is almost too fantastic for belief. In 1800, Kentucky had only a quarter of a million residents, and Lexington, the largest town, numbered under two thousand. But even a crowd of three or four thousand would have overwhelmed anything in the previous experience of the settlers.

Whatever the actual number, there was a sight to dazzle the eyes of the ministers who had come. Technically the meeting was Presbyterian, but Baptist and Methodist parsons had come along, and there was room for them, because no one man could hope to reach such a mob. Preaching stands built of logs were set up outdoors. One man remembered a typical scene—a crowd spilling out of the doors of the one meetinghouse, where two Presbyterian ministers were alternately holding forth, and three other groups scattered within a radius of a hundred yards. One cluster of sinners was gathered at the feet of a Presbyterian preacher, another gave ear to a Methodist exhorter, and lastly, a knot of Negroes was attending on the words of some orator of their own race. All over the campground, individual speakers had gathered little audiences to hear of *their* experiences. One observer said that there were as many as three hundred of these laymen "testifying."

So Cane Ridge was not really a meeting, but a series of meetings that gathered and broke up without any recognizable order. One Methodist brother who could not find a free preaching-stand ventured up the slanting trunk of a partly fallen tree. He found a flat spot, fifteen feet off the ground, and he spoke from this vantage point while a friend on the ground held up an umbrella on a long pole to shelter him from the weather. Within a few moments, this clergyman claimed, he had gathered an audience of thousands. Undoubtedly they stayed until lured away by some fresh address from a stump or the tail of a wagon. For the crowds were without form as they collected, listened, shouted "Amen!" and "Hallelujah!" and drifted off to find neighbors or refreshments or more preaching. The din can only be guessed at. The guilty were groaning and sometimes screaming at the top of their lungs, and those who felt that they were saved were clapping their hands, shouting hymns, and generally noising out their exultation. There were always hecklers at the meetings too, and some of them were no doubt shouting irreverent remarks at the faithful. Crying children added their bit, and tethered horses and oxen stamped, bawled, and whinnied to make the dissonance complete. Someone said that the meeting sounded from afar like the roar of Niagara. At night the campfires threw weird shadow-patterns of trees across the scene, and the whole moving, resounding gathering appeared to be tossing on the waves of some invisible storm. As if to etch the experience into men's memories, there were real rainstorms, and the drenched participants were thrown into fresh waves of screaming as thunder and lightning crashed around them.

All in all, a memorable enough episode. And yet still stranger things happened to put the brand of the Lord's sponsorship on Cane Ridge's mass excitement. Overwhelmed with their sensations, some men and women lay rigid and stiff on the ground for hours in a kind of catalepsy. One "blasphemer" who had come to scoff at the proceedings tumbled from his saddle unconscious and remained so for a day and a half. There was something incredibly compelling in what was going on. One remembered testimony came from a reasonably hard-headed young man named James Finley. Later in life Finley became a Methodist preacher, but in 1801 he was, except for a better-than-average education, a typical frontiersman. He had a small farm, a new wife, and a vigorous love of hunting. He had come to the Cane Ridge meeting out of curiosity, but as he looked on, he was taken with an uncontrollable trembling and feelings of suffocation. He left the campground, found a log tavern, and put away a glass of brandy to steady his nerves. But they were beyond steadying. All the way home he kept breaking out in irrational fits of laughter or tears. Many a spirit, returning from Cane Ridge, must have been moved in the same near-hysterical way.

A holy frenzy seemed to have taken hold of the West. Throughout the frontier communities, the ecstasy of conversion overflowed into the nervous system. At Cane Ridge, and at a hundred subsequent meetings, the worshipers behaved in ways that would be unbelievable if there were not plenty of good testimony to their truth. Some got the "jerks," a spasmodic twitching of the entire body. They were a fearful thing to behold. Some victims hopped from place to place like bouncing balls. Sometimes heads snapped from side to side so rapidly that faces became a blur, and handkerchiefs whipped off women's heads. One preacher saw women taken with the jerks at table, so that teacups went flying from their hands to splash against log walls. Churchmen disagreed about the meaning of these symptoms. Were they signs of conversion? Or demonstrations of the Lord's power, meant to convince doubters? Peter Cartwright, a famous evangelist of a slightly later era, believed the latter. He told of a skeptic at one of his meetings who was taken with the jerks and in a particularly vicious spasm snapped his neck. He died, a witness to the judgment of Omnipotence but gasping out to the last his "cursing and bitterness." Besides the jerks, there were strange seizures in which those at prayer broke into uncontrollable guffaws or intoned weird and wordless melodies or barked like dogs.

It was wild and shaggy, and very much a part of life in the clearings. Westerners wanted to feel religion in their bones. In their tough and violent lives intellectual exercises had no place, but howls and leaps were something that men who were "half-horse and half-alligator" understood. It was natural for the frontier to get religion with a mighty roar. Any other way would not have seemed home-like to people who, half in fun and half in sheer defensiveness, loved their brag, bluster, and bluff.

Yet there was something deeper than mere excitement underneath it all. Something fundamental was taking place, some kind of genuine religious revolution, bearing a made-in-America stamp. The East was unhappy with it. For one thing, camp-meeting wildness grated on the nerves of the educated clergy. All of this jigging and howling looked more like the work of Satan than of God. There were ugly rumors too, about unsanctified activities at the meetings. Some candidates for salvation showed up with cigars between their teeth. Despite official condemnation, liquor flowed free and white-hot on the outskirts of the gatherings. It might be that corn did more than its shares in justifying God's ways to man. Then there were stories that would not down which told how, in the shadows around the clearing, excited men and women were carried away in the hysteria and, as the catch phrase had it, "begot more souls than were saved" at the meeting. All these tales might have had some partial truth, yet in themselves they did not prove much about frontier religion. As it happened, a part of every camp-meeting audience apparently consisted of loafers and rowdies who came for the show and who were quite capable of any sin that a Presbyterian college graduate was likely to imagine.

Yet it was not the unscrubbed vigor of the meetings that really bothered conservatives in the Presbyterian Church. Their fundamental problem was in adjusting themselves and their faith to a new kind of democratic urge. Enemies of the revivals did not like the success of emotional preaching. What would happen to learning, and all that learning stood for, if a leather-lunged countryman with a gift for lurid word pictures could be a champion salvationist? And what would happen—what *had* happened—to the doctrine of election when the revival preacher shouted "Repent!" at overwrought thousands, seeming to say that any Tom, Dick, or Harry who felt moved by the Spirit might be receiving the promise of eternal bliss? Would mob enthusiasm replace God's careful winnowing of the flock to choose His lambs? The whole orderly scheme of life on earth, symbolized by a powerful church, an educated ministry, and a straight and narrow gate of salvation, stood in peril.

Nor were the conservatives wrong. In truth, when the McGreadys and Stones struck at "deadness" and "mechanical worship" in the older churches, they were going beyond theology. They were hitting out at a view of things that gave a plain and unlettered man little chance for a say in spiritual affairs. A church run by skilled theologians was apt to set rules that puzzled simple minds. A church which held that many were called, but few chosen, *was* aristocratic in a sense. The congregations of the western evangelists did not care for rules, particularly rules that were not immediately plain to anyone. In their view, the Bible alone was straightforward enough. Neither would they stand for anything resembling aristocracy, whatever form it might take. They wanted cheap land and the vote, and they were getting these things. They wanted salvation as well—or at least free and easy access to it—and they were bound to have that too. If longer-established congregations and their leaders back east did not like that notion, the time for a parting of the ways was at hand. In politics, such a parting is known as a revolution; in religion, it is schism. Neither word frightened the western revivalists very much.

The trouble did not take long to develop. In McGready's territory, a new Cumberland Presbytery, or subgroup, was organized in 1801. Before long it was

With the help of the Word, and sometimes of the bottle, frontier camp meetings went on for days and reaped rich harvests of converts.

in a battle with the Kentucky Synod, the next highest administrative body in the hierarchy. The specific issue was the licensing of certain "uneducated" candidates for the ministry. The root question was revivalism. The battle finally went up to the General Assembly, for Presbyterians a sort of combined Congress and Supreme Court. In 1809 the offending revivalistic presbytery was dissolved. Promptly, most of its congregations banded themselves into the separate Cumberland Presbyterian Church. Meanwhile, Barton Stone, Richard McNemar, and other members of the northern Kentucky wing of camp-meeting Presbyterianism were also in trouble. They founded a splinter group known as the "New Lights," and the Kentucky Synod, as might have been foreseen, lost little time in putting the New Lights out, via heresy proceedings. Next, they formed an independent Springfield Presbytery. But like all radicals, they found it easier to keep going than to apply the brakes. In 1804 the Springfield Presbytery fell apart. Stone and some of his friends joined with others in a new body, shorn of titles and formality, which carried the magnificently simple name of the Christian Church. Later on, Stone went over to the followers of Thomas and Alexander Campbell, who called themselves Disciples of Christ. Richard McNemar, after various spiritual adventures, became a Shaker. Thus, ten years after Cane Ridge, the score was depressing for Presbyterians. Revivalism had brought on innumerable arguments, split off whole presbyteries, and sent ministers and congregations flying into the arms of at least four other church groups. That splintering was a stronger indictment than any conservative could have invented to bring against Cane Ridge, or against its western child, the camp meeting.

A dead end appeared to have been reached. But it was only a second-act curtain. In the first act, religion in the West, given up for lost, had been saved by revivalism. In the second, grown strong and rambunctious, it had quarreled with its eastern parents. Now the time was at hand for a third-act resolution of the drama. Both sides would have to back down and compromise. For the lesson of history was already plain. In religious matters, as in all matters, East and West, metropolis and frontier, were not really warring opposites. Each nourished the other, and each had an impact on the other. Whatever emerged as "American" would carry some of the imprint of both, or it would perish.

On the part of the West, the retreat consisted of taming the camp meeting. Oddly enough, it was not the Presbyterians who did that. By 1812 or so, they had drawn back from it, afraid of its explosive qualities. But the Methodists were in an excellent position to make use of revivalism and all its trappings. They had, at that time at least, no educated conservative wing. They welcomed zealous backwood preachers, even if they were grammatically deficient. In fact, they worked such men into their organization and sent them, under the name of "circuit-riders," traveling tirelessly on horseback to every lonely settlement that the wilderness spawned. The result was that the Methodists were soon far in the lead in evangelizing the frontier. They did not have to worry about the claims of limited election either. Their formal theology did not recognize it. With a plain-spoken and far-reaching ministry freely offering salvation to all true believers, Methodism needed only some kind of official harvest season to count and bind together the converts. The camp meeting was the perfect answer. By 1811, the

Methodists had held four or five hundred of them throughout the country; by 1820, they had held a thousand—by far the majority of all such gatherings in the nation.

But these meetings were not replicas of Cane Ridge. They were combed, washed, and made respectable. Permanent sites were picked, regular dates chosen, and preachers and flocks given ample time to prepare. When meeting time came, the arriving worshipers in their wagons were efficiently taken in charge, told where to park their vehicles and pasture their teams, and given a spot for their tents. Orderly rows of these tents surrounded a preaching area equipped with sturdy benches and preaching stands. The effect was something like that of a formal bivouac just before a general's inspection. Tight scheduling kept the worship moving according to plan—dawn prayers, eight o'clock sermons, eleven o'clock sermons, dinner breaks, afternoon prayers and sermons, meals again, and candlelight services. Years of experience tightened the schedules, and camp-meetings manuals embodied the fruits of practice. Regular hymns replaced the discordant bawling of the primitive era. Things took on a generally homelike look. There were Methodist ladies who did not hesitate to bring their best feather beds to spread in the tents, and meals tended to be planned and ample affairs. Hams, turkeys, gravies, biscuits, preserves, and melons produced contented worshipers and happy memories.

There were new rules to cope with disorderliness as well. Candles, lamps, and torches fixed to trees kept the area well lit and discouraged young converts from amorous ways. Guards patrolled the circumference of the camp, and heroic if sometimes losing battles were fought to keep whiskey out. In such almost decorous surroundings jerks, barks, dances and trances became infrequent and finally nonexistent.

Not that there was a total lack of enthusiasm. Hymns were still yelled and stamped as much as sung. Nor was it out of bounds for the audience to pepper the sermon with ejaculations of "Amen!" and "Glory!" Outsiders were still shocked by some things they saw. But they did not realize how far improvement had gone.

Eastern churchmen had to back down somewhat, too. Gradually, tentatively, they picked up the revival and made it part of their religious life. In small eastern towns it became regularized into an annual season of "ingathering," like the harvest or the election. Yet it could not be contained within neat, white-painted meetinghouses. Under the "sivilized" clothing, the tattered form of Twain's Pap Finn persisted. Certain things were taken for granted after a time. The doctrine of election was bypassed and, in practice, allowed to wither away.

Moreover, a new kind of religious leader, the popular evangelist, took the stage. Men like Charles G. Finney in the 1830's, Dwight L. Moody in the 1870's, and Billy Sunday in the decade just preceding the First World War flashed into national prominence. Their meetings overflowed church buildings and spilled into convention halls, auditoriums, and specially built "tabernacles." As it happened, these men came from lay ranks into preaching. Finney was a lawyer, Moody a shoe salesman, and Sunday a baseball player. They spoke down-to-earth language to their massed listeners, reduced the Bible to basic axioms, and drew their parables from the courtroom, the market, and the barnyard. They made salvation the only goal of their service, and at the meeting's end they beckoned the penitents forward to acknowledge the receipt of grace. In short, they carried on the camp-meeting tradition. By the closing years of the nineteenth century, however, the old campgrounds for the most part were slowly abandoned. Growing cities swallowed them up, and rapid transportation destroyed the original reason for the prolonged camp-out. But the meetings were not dead. Mass revivalism had moved them indoors and made them a permanent part of American Protestantism.

All of this cost something in religious depth, religious learning, religious dignity. Yet there was not much choice. The American churches lacked the support of an all-powerful state or of age-old traditions. They had to move with the times. That is why their history is so checkered with schismatic movements—symptoms of the struggle to get in step with the parade. Hence, if the West in 1800 could not ignore religion, the rest of the country, in succeeding years, could not ignore the western notion of religion. One student of the camp meeting has said that it flourished "side by side with the militia muster, with the cabin raising and the political barbecue." That was true, and those institutions were already worked deeply into the American grain by 1840. They reflected a spirit of democracy, optimism, and impatience that would sweep us across a continent, sweep us into industrialism, sweep us into a civil war. That spirit demanded some religious expression, some promise of a millennium in which all could share.

The camp meeting was part of that religious expression, part of the whole revival system that channeled American impulses into church-going ways. In the home of the brave, piety was organized so that Satan got no breathing spells. Neither, for that matter, did anyone else.

The Education of Women

Elaine Kendall

 The great contemporary interest in the position of women in American society has led to many historical investigations in an attempt to throw light on how the current situation came to be. Much of this work has centered around the long struggle of feminists to obtain equal treatment before the law: the vote, equal pay for equal work, even such basic rights as that of married women to own property in their own names and to make wills without their husbands' approval. But historical attention has also been focused on other aspects of women's place—on such interesting questions as family structure and function in different periods and, as in the following essay, on female education. The author, Elaine Kendall, traces the history of how girls were educated in America from colonial times to the middle of the nineteenth century. This is a story of progress, but of limited progress, one that helps explain both the strength of the feminists' demands for reform and the slowness with which these demands were achieved. Kendall is the author of a history of women's education, appropriately titled, as readers of her essay here will understand, Peculiar Institutions.

"Could I have died a martyr in the cause, and thus ensured its success, I could have blessed the faggot and hugged the stake." The cause was state support for female education, the would-be Saint Joan was Emma Willard, and the rhetorical standards of the 1820's were lofty and impassioned. The most militant feminists rarely scale such heights today. For one thing, dogged effort has finally reduced the supply of grand injustices; and today's preference for less florid metaphor has deprived the movement of such dramatic images. Comparatively speaking, the rest of the struggle is a downhill run, leading straight to twenty-four-hour daycare centers, revised and updated forms of marriage, free access to the executive suite, and rows of "Ms's" on Senate office doors. Glorying in our headway, we easily forget that leverage comes with literacy, and literacy for women is a relative novelty.

Long before the Revolution, American males already had Harvard, Yale, and Princeton, as well as a full range of other educational institutions—grammar schools, academies, seminaries, and numerous smaller colleges. American girls had only their mother's knee. By 1818, the year in which Emma Willard first introduced her *Plan for the Improvement of Female Education*, the gap was almost as wide as ever. Public schooling was a local option, quite whimsically interpreted. The towns could provide as much or as little as they wished, extending or restricting attendance as they saw fit. Ms. Willard presented her novel proposals to the New York State legislature, which dealt with the question by putting it repeatedly at the bottom of the agenda until the session was safely over. Lavish tributes to

Emma Willard.

Mother's Knee filled the halls of Albany. In the opinion of the senators, M.'s K. not only outshone our men's colleges but also Oxford, Cambridge, and Heidelberg as an institution of female edification. Despite the support of De Witt Clinton, John Adams, and Thomas Jefferson, it was three more years—when a building and grounds were offered independently by the town of Troy—before the Willard Seminary actually got under way. The academy still flourishes and claims to "mark the beginning of higher education for women in the United States." Since that is not precisely the same as being the first such school and the rival contenders have either vanished or metamorphosed into other sorts of institutions entirely, there is no reason to dispute it. The pre-Revolutionary South did have a few early convents, including one at New Orleans that was established by the Ursuline order in 1727 and taught religion, needlework, and something of what was called basic skills. Other religious groups, particularly the Moravians and Quakers, supported female seminaries during the eighteenth century, but these places did not really attempt to offer advanced education—a commodity for which there was little market in an era when girls were unwelcome in elementary schools. A few New England clergymen opened small academies for girls during the first decade of the nineteenth century, but these noble and well-intentioned efforts were ephemeral, never outlasting their founders. Until Emma Willard succeeded in extracting that bit of real estate from Troy, public and private support for such ventures was virtually nonexistent.

Some few ambitious and determined girls did succeed in learning to read and write in colonial America, but hardly ever at public expense and certainly not in comfort. Their number was pitifully small, and those who gained more than the rudiments of literacy would hardly have crowded a saltbox parlor. . . .

As the grip of Puritanism gradually relaxed, the image of a learned female improved infinitesimally. She was no longer regarded as a disorderly person or a heretic but merely as a nuisance to her husband, family, and friends. A sensible woman soon found ways to conceal her little store of knowledge or, if hints of it should accidentally slip out, to disparage or apologize for it. Abigail Adams, whose wistful letters show a continuing interest in women's education, described her own with a demurely rhymed disclaimer:

> The little learning I have gained
> Is all from simple nature drained.

In fact, the wife of John Adams was entirely self-educated. She disciplined herself to plod doggedly through works of ancient history whenever her household duties permitted, being careful to do so in the privacy of her boudoir. In her letters she deplored the fact that it was still customary to "ridicule female learning" and even in the "best families" to deny girls more than the barest rudiments.

The prevailing colonial feeling toward female education was still so unanimously negative that it was not always thought necessary to mention it. Sometimes this turned out to be a boon. A few villages, in their haste to establish schools for boys, neglected to specify that only males would be admitted. From the beginning they wrote their charters rather carelessly, using the loose generic term "children." This loophole was nearly always blocked as soon as the risks became apparent, but in the interim period of grace girls were occasionally able to pick up a few crumbs of knowledge. They did so by sitting outside the schoolhouse or on its steps, eavesdropping on the boys' recitations. More rarely, girls were tolerated in the rear of the schoolhouse behind a curtain, in a kind of makeshift seraglio. This Levantine arrangement, however, was soon abandoned as inappropriate to the time and place, and the attendance requirements were made unambiguous. New England winters and Cape Cod architecture being what they are, the amount of learning that one could have acquired by these systems was necessarily scanty. Still it was judged excessive. The female scholars in the yard and on the stairs seemed to suffer disproportionately from pleurisy and other respiratory ailments. Further proof of the divine attitude toward the educating of women was not sought. Girls were excluded for their own good, as well as to ensure the future of the Colonies.

After the Revolution the atmosphere in the New England states did become considerably more lenient. Here and there a town council might vote to allow girls inside the school building from five to seven in the morning, from six to eight at night, or, in a few very liberal communities, during the few weeks in summer when the boys were at work in the fields or shipyards. This was a giant step forward and would have been epochal if teachers had always appeared at these awkward times. Unfortunately the girls often had to muddle through on their own without benefit of faculty. The enlightened trend, moreover, was far from general. In 1792 the town of Wellesley, Massachusetts, voted "not to be at any expense for schooling girls," and similarly worded bylaws were quite usual throughout the northern states until the 1820's. In the southern Colonies, where distances between the great estates delayed the beginnings of any public schooling even longer, wealthy planters often imported tutors to instruct their sons in academic subjects. If they could afford the additional luxury, they might also engage singing and dancing masters for the daughters, who were not expected to share their brothers' more arduous lessons. In a pleasant little memoir of the South, *Colonial Days and Dames,* Anne Wharton, a descendant of Thomas Jefferson, noted that "very little from books was thought necessary for a girl. She was trained to domestic matters . . . the accomplishments of the day . . . to play upon the harpsichord or spinet, and to work impossible dragons and roses upon canvas."

Although the odds against a girl's gaining more than the sketchiest training during this era seem to have been overwhelming, there were some remarkable exceptions. The undiscouraged few included Emma Willard herself; Catherine and Harriet Beecher, the clergyman's daughters, who established an early academy at Hartford; and Mary Lyon, who founded the college that began in 1837 as Mount Holyoke Seminary. Usually, however, the tentative and halfhearted experiments permitted by the New England towns served only to give aid and comfort to the opposition. They seemed to show that the female mind was not inclined to scholarship and the female body was not strong enough to withstand exposure—*literal* exposure, in many cases—to it. By 1830 or so primary education had been grudgingly extended to girls almost everywhere, but it was nearly impossible to find anyone who dared champion any further risks. Boston had actually opened a girls' high school in 1826 only to abolish it two years later. . . .

Public schools obviously were not the only route to learning or most female American children up through colonial times would have been doomed to total ignorance. Fathers, especially clergymen fathers, would often drill their daughters in the Bible and sometimes teach them to read and do simple sums as well. Nothing that enhanced an understanding of the Scriptures could be entirely bad, and arithmetic was considered useful in case a woman were to find herself the sole support of her children. Brothers would sometimes lend or hand down their old school books, and fond uncles might help a favorite and clever niece with her sums. The boys' tutor was often amenable to a pretty sister's pleas for lessons. For those girls not fortunate enough to be the daughters of foresighted New England parsons or wealthy tobacco and cotton factors, most colonial towns provided dame schools. These catered to boys as well as to girls of various ages. They offered a supplement to the curriculum at Mother's Knee, but only just. Because these schools were kept by women who had acquired their own learning haphazardly, the education they offered was motley at best. The solitary teacher could impart no more than she herself knew, and that rarely exceeded the alphabet, the shorter catechism, sewing, knitting, some numbers, and perhaps a recipe for baked beans and brown bread. The actual academic function of these early American institutions seems to have been somewhat exaggerated and romanticized by historians. Dame schools were really no more than small businesses, managed by impoverished women who looked after neighborhood children and saw to it that idle little hands did not make work for the devil. The fees (tuition is too grand a word) were tiny, with threepence a week per child about par. That sum could hardly have paid for a single hornbook for the entire class. The dame school itself was an English idea, transplanted almost intact to the Colonies. Several seem to have been under way by the end of the seventeenth century. . . .

As the country became more affluent, schoolkeeping gradually began to attract more ambitious types. Older girls were still being excluded from the town seminaries and in many places from the grammar schools as well. A great many people quickly realized that there was money to be made by teaching the children of the new middle class and that they could sell their services for far more than pennies. No special accreditation or qualification was required, and there was no competition from the state. Toward the end of the eighteenth century and at the beginning of the nineteenth, platoons of self-styled professors invaded American towns and cities, promising to instruct both sexes and all ages in every known art, science, air, and grace. These projects were popularly known as adventure schools, a phrase that has a pleasant modern ring to it, suggesting open classrooms, free electives, and individual attention.

That, however, is deceptive. The people who ran such schools were usually adventurers in the not very admirable sense of the word: unscrupulous, self-serving, and of doubtful origins and attainments. Many simply equipped themselves with false diplomas and titles from foreign universities and set up shop. The schools continued to operate only as long as they turned a profit. When enrollment dropped, interest waned, or fraud became obvious, the establishment would simply fold and the proprietors move to another town for a fresh start. The newer territories were particularly alluring to the worst of these entrepreneurs, since their reputations could neither precede nor follow them there. A new name, a new prospectus, an ad in the gazette, and they were in business again until scandal or mismanagement obliged them to move on. Such "schools" were not devised for the particular benefit of girls; but because they were independent commercial enterprises, no solvent person was turned away. Thousands of young women did take advantage of the new opportunity and were, in many cases, taken advantage of in return. For boys the adventure schools were an alternative to the strict classicism and religiosity of the academies and seminaries, but for girls they were the only educational possibility between the dame school and marriage.

There was little effort to devise a planned or coherent course of study, though elaborately decorated certificates were awarded upon completion of a series of lessons. The scholar could buy whatever he or she fancied from a mind-bending list. One could take needlework at one place, languages at another, dancing or "ouranology" at a third. (It was a pompous era, and no one was fonder of polysyllables than the professors. Ouranology was sky-watching, but it sounded impressive.) There were no minimum or maximum course requirements, though the schoolmasters naturally made every effort to stock the same subjects offered by the competition, in order to reduce the incidence of school-hopping. . . .

Many of the adventure schools hedged their financial risks by functioning as a combination store and educational institution, selling fancywork, "very good Orange-Oyl," sweetmeats, sewing notions, painted china, and candles along with lessons in dancing, foreign languages, geography, penmanship, and spelling. Usually they were mama-and-papa affairs, with the wife instructing girls in "curious works" and the husband concentrating upon "higher studies." Curious works covered a great deal of ground—the making of artificial fruits and flowers, the "raising of paste," enamelling, japanning, quilting, fancy embroidery, and in at least one recorded case "flowering on catgut," an intriguing accomplishment that has passed into total oblivion, leaving no surviving examples.

The adventure schools advertised heavily in newspapers and journals of the period, often in terms indicating that teaching was not an especially prestigious profession. One Thomas Carroll took several columns in a May, 1765, issue of the New York *Mercury* to announce a curriculum that would have taxed the entire faculty of Harvard and then proceeded to explain that he "was not under the necessity of coming here to teach, he had views of living more happy, but some unforeseen, and unexpected events have happened since his arrival here . . . ," thus reducing this Renaissance paragon to schoolkeeping and his lady to teaching French knots and quilting.

While they lasted adventure schools attempted to offer something for everyone, including adults, and came in all forms, sizes, and price ranges. They met anywhere and everywhere: "at the Back of Mr. Benson's Brew-House," in rented halls, in borrowed parlors, at inns, and from time to time in barns or open fields. The adventurer was usually available for private lessons as well, making house calls "with the utmost discretion," especially in the case of questionable studies like dancing or French verbs. The entire physical plant usually fitted into a carpetbag. . . .

The pretentious and empty promises of the adventure schools eventually aroused considerable criticism. Americans may not yet have appreciated the value of female education, but they seem always to have known the value of a dollar. It was not long before the public realized that flowering on catgut was not so useful an accomplishment for their daughters as ciphering or reading. The more marginal operators began to melt away, and those schoolmasters who hung on were obliged to devote more attention to practical subjects and eliminate many of the patent absurdities. . . .

Certain religious groups, particularly the Moravians and the Quakers, had always eschewed frippery and pioneered in the more realistic education of women. Friends' schools were organized as soon as the size and prosperity of the settlements permitted them. This training emphasized housewifery but did include the fundamentals of literacy. Many of the earliest eighteenth-century Quaker primary schools were co-educational, though access to them was limited to the immediate community. Because these were concentrated in the Philadelphia area, girls born in Pennsylvania had a much better chance of acquiring some education than their contemporaries elsewhere. The Moravians (who also settled in the southeastern states) quickly recognized the general lack of facilities in the rest of the Colonies and offered boarding arrangements in a few of their schools. The student body soon included intrepid and homesick girls from New England and even the West Indies. These institutions were purposeful and rather solemn, the antithesis of superficiality. The Moravians insisted upon communal household chores as well as domestic skills, and in the eighteenth century these obligations could be onerous; dusting, sweeping, spinning, carding, and weaving came before embroidery and hemstitching. These homely lessons were enlivened by rhymes celebrating the pleasure of honest work. Examples survive in the seminary archives and supply a hint of the uplifting atmosphere:

> *I've spun seven cuts, dear companions allow*
> *That I am yet little, and know not right how;*
>
> *Mine twenty and four, which I finished with joy,*
> *And my hands and my feet did willing employ.*

Though the teaching sisters in these sectarian schools seem to have been kind and patient, the life was rigorous and strictly ordered, a distinct and not always popular alternative to pleasant afternoons with easygoing adventure masters. In an era when education for women was still widely regarded as a luxury for the upper classes, the appeal of the pioneering religious seminaries tended to be somewhat narrow. If a family happened to be sufficiently well-off to think of educating their girls, the tendency was to make fine ladies of them. As a result there were many young women who could carry a tune but not a number, who could model a passable wax apple but couldn't read a recipe, who had memorized the language of flowers but had only the vaguest grasp of English grammar. There seemed to be no middle ground between the austerities of the religious schools and the hollow frivolities offered by commercial ventures. Alternatives did not really exist until the 1820's, when the earliest tentative attempts were made to found independent academies and seminaries.

Catherine and Harriet Beecher, who were among the first to open a school designed to bridge the gulf, believed almost as strongly as the Moravians in the importance of domestic economy. They were, however, obliged by public demand to include a long list of dainty accomplishments in their Hartford curriculum. Many girls continued to regard the new secular seminaries as they had the adventure schools—as rival shops where they could browse or buy at will, dropping in and out at any time they chose. To the despair of the well-intentioned founders few students ever stayed to complete the course at any one place. Parents judged a school as if it were a buffet table, evaluating it by the number and variety of subjects displayed. In writing later of the difficult beginnings of the Hartford Seminary, Catherine Beecher said that "all was perpetual haste, imperfection, irregularity, and the merely mechanical commitment of words to memory, without any chance for imparting clear and connected ideas in a single branch of knowledge. The review of those days is like the memory of a troubled and distracting dream."

Public opinion about the education of girls continued to be sharply (if never clearly) divided until after the Civil War. Those who pioneered in the field were at the mercy of socially ambitious and ambivalent parents, confused and unevenly prepared students, and constantly shifting social attitudes. In sudden and disconcerting switches "the friends" of women's education often turned out to be less than wholehearted in their advocacy. Benjamin Rush, whose *Thoughts Upon Female Education,* written in 1787, influenced and inspired Emma Willard, Mary Lyon, and the Beecher sisters, later admitted that his thoughtful considerations had finally left him "not enthusiastical upon the subject." Even at his best, Rush sounds no more than tepid; American ladies, he wrote, "should be qualified to a certain degree by a peculiar and suitable education to concur in instructing their sons in the principles of liberty and government." During her long editorship of *Godey's Lady's Book* Sarah Josepha Hale welcomed every new female seminary and academy but faithfully reminded her readers that the sanctity of the home came first: ". . . on what does social well-being rest but in our homes . . . ?" "Oh, spare our homes!" was a constant refrain, this chorus coming from the September, 1856, issue. *Godey's Lady's Book* reflects the pervasive nineteenth-century fear that the educated woman might be a threat to the established and symbiotic pattern of American family life. The totally ignorant woman, on the other hand, was something of an embarrassment to the new nation. The country was inundated by visiting European journalists during this period, and they invariably commented upon the dullness of our social life and the disappointing vacuity of the sweet-faced girls and handsome matrons they met. Though Americans themselves seemed to feel safer with a bore than with a bluestocking, they were forced to give the matter some worried thought.

"If all our girls become philosophers," the critics asked, "who will darn our stockings and cook the meals?" It was widely, if somewhat irrationally, assumed that a maiden who had learned continental stichery upon fine lawn might heave to and sew up a shirt if necessary, but few men believed that a woman who had once tasted the heady delights of Shakespeare's plays would ever have dinner ready on time—or at all.

The founders of female seminaries were obliged to cater to this unease by modifying their plans and their pronouncements accordingly. The solid academic subjects were so generally thought irrelevant for "housewives and helpmates" that it was usually necessary to disguise them as something more palatable. The Beechers taught their girls chemistry at Hartford but were careful to assure parents and prospective husbands that its principles were applicable in the kitchen. The study of mathematics could be justified by its usefulness in running a household. Eventually the educators grew more daring, recommending geology as a means toward understanding the Deluge and other Biblical mysteries and suggesting geography and even history as suitable because these studies would "enlarge women's sphere of thought, rendering them more interesting as companions to men of science." There is, however, little evidence that many were converted to this extreme point of view. The average nineteenth-century American man was not at all keen on chat with an interesting companion, preferring a wife like the one in the popular jingle *"who never learnt the art of schooling/Untamed with the itch of ruling."* The cliché of the period was "woman's sphere." The phrase was so frequently repeated that it acquires almost physical qualities. Woman's Sphere—the nineteenth-century woman was fixed and sealed within it like a model ship inside a bottle. To tamper with the arrangement was to risk ruining a complex and fragile structure that had been painstakingly assembled over the course of two centuries. Just one ill-considered jolt might make matchwood of the entire apparatus.

In 1812 the anonymous author of *Sketches of the History, Genius, and Disposition of the Fair Sex* wrote that women are "born for a life of uniformity and dependence. . . . Were it in your power to give them genius, it would be almost always a useless and very often a dangerous present. It would, in general, make them regret the station which Providence has assigned them, or have recourse to unjustifiable ways to get from it." The writer identified himself only as a "friend of the sex" (not actually specifying which one).

This century's feminists may rage at and revel in such quotes, but the nineteenth-century educators were forced to live with this attitude and work within and around it. In order to gain any public or private support for women's secondary schools they had to prove that a woman would not desert her husband and children as soon as she could write a legible sentence or recite a theorem. That fear was genuine, and the old arguments resurfaced again and again. What about Saint Paul's injunction? What about the sanctity of the home? What about the health of the future mothers of the race? What about supper?

Advocates of secondary education for women, therefore, became consummate politicians, theologians, hygienists, and, when necessary, apologists. "It is desirable," wrote Mary Lyon in 1834 of her Mount Holyoke Female Seminary project, "that the plans relating to the subject should not seem to originate with us but with benevolent *gentlemen.* If the object should excite attention there is danger that many good men will fear the effect on society of so much female influence and what they will call female greatness." New and subtle counterarguments were presented with great delicacy. God had entrusted the tender minds of children to women; therefore women were morally obliged to teach. The home would be a holier place if the chatelaine understood religious principles and could explain them. The founders of Abbot Academy proclaimed that "to form the immortal mind to habits suited to an immortal being, and to instill principles of conduct and form the character for an immortal destiny, shall be subordinate to no other care." All that harping on immortality went down smoothly in the evangelistic atmosphere of the 1820's. A thick coating of religion was applied to every new educational venture. The parents of prospective students were assured that their daughters would not only study religion in class but would have twice-daily periods of silent meditation, frequent revival meetings, and a Sunday that

13
HORIZONTAL BAR.

14
THE TRIANGLE.

15
STOOPING FORWARD.

16
BENDING BACKWARD.

A series of genteel exercises for genteel young ladies from Godey's Lady's Book. *How the young ladies managed to perform much, if any, serious exercise swathed in those voluminous skirts remains something of a mystery.*

included all of these. In reading the early seminary catalogues, one finds it hard to see where secular studies could have fit in at all. To the religious guarantees were appended promises of careful attention to health. The educators lost no time in adding the new science of calisthenics to their curricula. They had the medical records of their students compared to that of the public at large and published the gratifying results in newspapers and magazines. Domestic work was also to be required of girls who attended the new seminaries, partly for economy's sake but mainly so that they would not forget their ultimate destiny.

All of this was calming and persuasive, but nothing was so effective as simple economics. By the 1830's most states had begun a program of primary public education. As the West followed suit the need for teachers became acute and desperate. Men were not attracted to the profession because the pay was wretched, the living conditions were lonely, and the status of a schoolmaster was negligible if not downright laughable. Saint Paul was revised, updated, and finally reversed. He had not, after all, envisioned the one-room schoolhouses of the American prairies, the wages of three dollars a month, or the practice of "boarding around."

Within an astonishingly short time fears for female health subsided. The first women teachers proved amazingly durable, able to withstand every rigor of frontier life. In a letter to her former headmistress one alumna of the Hartford Seminary described accommodations out west:

> I board where there are eight children, and the parents, and only two rooms in the house. I must do as the family do about washing, as there is but one basin, and no place to go to wash but out the door. I have not enjoyed the luxury of either lamp or candle, their only light being a cup of grease with a rag for a wick. Evening is my only time to write, but this kind of light makes such a disagreeable smoke and smell, I cannot bear it, and do without light, except the fire. I occupy a room with three of the children and a niece who boards here. The other room serves as a kitchen, parlor, and bedroom for the rest of the family. . . .

Other graduates were just as stoical and often no more comfortable:

> I board with a physician, and the house has only two rooms. One serves as kitchen, eating, and sitting room; the other, where I lodge, serves also as the doctor's office, and there is no time, night or day, when I am not liable to interruption.
>
> My school embraces both sexes, and all ages from five to seventeen, and not one can read intelligibly. They have no idea of the proprieties of the schoolroom or of study. . . . My furniture consists now of . . . benches, a single board put up against the side of the room for a writing desk, a few bricks for andirons, and a stick of wood for shovel and tongs.

These letters were collected by Catherine Beecher in her book *True Remedy for the Wrongs of Women*, which advanced the cause of women's education by showing the worthwhile uses to which it could be put. Delighted with the early results, several states quickly set up committees to consider training women teachers on a larger scale. Their findings were favorable, though couched in oddly ambiguous language. New York's group reported that women seemed to be "endued with peculiar faculties" for the occupation. "While man's nature is rough, stern, impatient, ambitious, hers is gentle, tender, enduring, unaspiring." That was most encouraging, but the gentlemen also generously acknowledged that "the habits of female teachers are better and their morals purer; they are much more apt to be content with, and continue in, the occupation of teaching."

A Michigan report stated in 1842 that "an elementary school, where the rudiments of an English education only are taught, such as reading, spelling, writing, and the outlines barely of geography, arithmetic, and grammar, requires a female of practical common sense with amiable and winning manners, a patient spirit, and a tolerable knowledge of the springs of human action. A female thus qualified, carrying with her into the schoolroom the gentle influences of her sex, will do more to inculcate right morals and prepare the youthful intellect for the severer discipline of its after years, than the most accomplished and learned male teacher." Far from objecting to these rather condescending statements, the founders of the struggling seminaries were more than happy to hear them. Even the miserable wages offered to teachers could be regarded as an advantage, since they provided the single most effective argument for more female academies. "But where are we to raise such an army of teachers as are required for this great work?" asked Catherine Beecher in the same book that contained the letters from her ex-students. "Not from the sex which finds it so much more honorable, easy, and lucrative, to enter the many roads to wealth and honor open in this land. . . . It is WOMAN who is to come [forth] at this emergency, and meet the demand—woman, whom experience and testimony have shown to be the best, as well as the cheapest guardian and teacher of childhood, in the school as well as the nursery."

Teaching became a woman's profession by default and by rationalization. Clergymen and theologians suddenly had nothing but praise for women teachers. God must have meant them to teach because he made them so good at it. They would work for a half or a third of the salary demanded by a man. What, after all, was a schoolroom but an extension of the home, woman's natural sphere? And if females had to have schools of their own to prepare them for this holy mission, then so be it. Future American generations must not be allowed to suffer for want of instruction when a Troy, Hartford, or Mount Holyoke girl asked no more than three dollars a month, safe escort to the boondocks, and a candle of her own.

Everyday Life Before the Civil War

Jack Larkin

Some of the most difficult things to learn about the past are not the things that were obscure and unusual but those that were so obvious that the people of the time did not think them worth mentioning. Matters that historians have had the greatest difficulty discovering are often ones that at the time almost no one thought worth describing because they were common knowledge. Much that we know about life in early America we know because foreign travelers were struck by manners and customs of the people that to them seemed different from those of their native lands. But the very reason the behavior seemed notable to an outsider—that it was characteristic of the society—often meant that to the Americans it was ordinary or "normal," something "everyone" already knew. Similarly, while people naturally take care of and preserve fine jewelry and expensive furniture, "everyday" objects central to their existence tend to get used up and discarded and thus are rare and hard to find in later years.

Of course everyday objects and attitudes can be discovered and recovered, and from them historians can learn an enormous amount about why people did the "unimportant" things that interest us today and why they held the beliefs that led to those actions. Jack Larkin, Chief Historian at Old Sturbridge Village restoration in Massachusetts, presents in this essay a miscellany of information about early nineteenth-century life, information that Americans of those years would have taken for granted but that to modern readers is fascinating.

Contemporary observers of early-nineteenth-century America left a fragmentary but nonetheless fascinating and revealing picture of the manner in which rich and poor, Southerner and Northerner, farmer and city dweller, freeman and slave presented themselves to the world. To begin with, a wide variety of characteristic facial expressions, gestures, and ways of carrying the body reflected the extraordinary regional and social diversity of the young republic.

When two farmers met in early-nineteenth-century New England, wrote Francis Underwood, of Enfield, Massachusetts, the author of a pioneering 1893 study of small-town life, "their greeting might seem to a stranger gruff or surly, since the facial muscles were so inexpressive, while, in fact, they were on excellent terms." In courtship and marriage, countrymen and women were equally constrained, with couples "wearing all unconsciously the masks which custom had prescribed; and the onlookers who did not know the secret . . . would think them cold and indifferent."

A runaway pig creates mayhem on a city street.

The Yankees, however, were not the stiffest Americans. Even by their own impassive standards, New Englanders found New York Dutchmen and Pennsylvania German farmers "clumsy and chill" or "dull and stolid." But the "wild Irish" stood out in America for precisely the opposite reason. They were not "chill" or "stolid" enough, but loud and expansive. Their expressiveness made Anglo-Americans uncomfortable.

The seemingly uncontrolled physical energy of American blacks left many whites ill at ease. Of the slaves celebrating at a plantation ball, it was "impossible to describe the things these people did with their bodies," Frances Kemble Butler, an English-born actress who married a Georgia slave owner, observed, "and above all with their faces. . . ." Blacks' expressions and gestures, their preference for rhythmic rather than rigid bodily motion, their alternations of energy and rest made no cultural sense to observers who saw only "antics and

A dour face of the early 1800s.

frolics," "laziness," or "savagery." Sometimes perceived as obsequious, childlike, and dependent, or sullen and inexpressive, slaves also wore masks—not "all unconsciously" as Northern farm folk did, but as part of their self-protective strategies for controlling what masters, mistresses, and other whites could know about their feelings and motivations.

American city dwellers, whose daily routines were driven by the quicker pace of commerce, were easy to distinguish from "heavy and slouching" farmers attuned to slow seasonal rhythms. New Yorkers, in particular, had already acquired their own characteristic body language. The clerks and commercial men who crowded Broadway, intent on their business, had a universal "contraction of the brow, knitting of the eyebrows, and compression of the lips . . . and a hurried walk." It was a popular American saying in the 1830s, reported Frederick Marryat, an Englishman who traveled extensively in the period, that "a New York merchant always walks as if he had a good dinner before him, and a bailiff behind him."

Early-nineteenth-century Americans lived in a world of dirt, insects, and pungent smells. Farmyards were strewn with animal wastes, and farmers wore manure-spattered boots and trousers everywhere. Men's and women's working clothes alike were often stiff with dirt and dried sweat, and men's shirts were often stained with "yellow rivulets" of tobacco juice. The locations of privies were all too obvious on warm or windy days. Unemptied chamber pots advertised their presence. Wet baby "napkins," today's diapers, were not immediately washed but simply put by the fire to dry. . . .

Densely populated, but poorly cleaned and drained, America's cities were often far more noisome than its farmyards. Horse manure thickly covered city streets, and few neighborhoods were free from the spreading stench of tanneries

Freely moving pigs gorged themselves on refuse and trash.

and slaughterhouses. New York City accumulated so much refuse that it was generally believed the actual surfaces of the streets had not been seen for decades. During her stay in Cincinnati, the English writer Frances Trollope followed the practice of the vast majority of American city housewives when she threw her household "slops"—refuse food and dirty dishwater—out into the street. An irate neighbor soon informed her that municipal ordinances forbade "throwing such things at the sides of the streets" as she had done; "they must just all be cast right into the middle and the pigs soon takes them off." In most cities hundreds, sometimes thousands, of free-roaming pigs scavenged the garbage; one exception was Charleston, South Carolina, where buzzards patrolled the streets. By converting garbage into pork, pigs kept city streets cleaner than they would otherwise have been, but the pigs themselves befouled the streets and those who ate their meat—primarily poor families—ran greater than usual risks of infection.

The most visible symbols of early American sanitation were privies or "necessary houses." But Americans did not always use them; many rural householders simply took to the closest available patch of woods or brush. However, in more densely settled communities and in regions with cold winters, privies were in widespread use. They were not usually put in out-of-the-way locations. The fashion of some Northern farm families, according to Robert B. Thomas's *Farmer's Almanack* in 1826, had long been to have their "necessary planted in a garden or other conspicuous place." Other countryfolk went even further in

Chamber pots were dumped in the streets.

turning human wastes to agricultural account and built their outhouses "within the territory of a hog yard, that the swine may root and ruminate and devour the nastiness thereof." Thomas was a long-standing critic of primitive manners in the countryside and roundly condemned these traditional sanitary arrangements as demonstrating a "want of taste, decency, and propriety." . . .

Sleeping accommodations in American country taverns were often dirty and insect-ridden. The eighteenth-century observer of American life Isaac Weld saw "filthy beds swarming with bugs" in 1794; in 1840 Charles Dickens noted "a sort of game not on the bill of fare." Complaints increased in intensity as travelers went south or west. Tavern beds were uniquely vulnerable to infestation by whatever insect guests travelers brought with them. The bedding of most American households was surely less foul. Yet it was dirty enough. New England farmers were still too often "tormented all night by bed bugs," complained *The Farmer's Almanack* in 1837, and books of domestic advice contained extensive instructions on removing them from feather beds and straw ticks.

Journeying between Washington and New Orleans in 1828, Margaret Hall, a well-to-do and cultivated Scottish woman, became far more familiar with intimate insect life than she had ever been in the genteel houses of London or Edinburgh. Her letters home, never intended for publication, gave a graphic and unsparing account of American sanitary conditions. After sleeping in a succession of beds with the "usual complement of fleas and bugs," she and her party had themselves become infested: "We bring them along with us in our clothes and when I undress I find them crawling on my skin, nasty wretches." New and distasteful to her, such discoveries were commonplace among the ordinary folk with whom she lodged. The American children she saw on her Southern journey were "kept in such a state of filth," with clothes "dirty and slovenly to a degree," but this was "nothing in comparison with their heads . . . [which] are absolutely

Insects infested many American beds.

crawling!" In New Orleans she observed women picking through children's heads for lice, "catching them according to the method depicted in an engraving of a similar proceeding in the streets of Naples."

Americans were not "clean and decent" by today's standards, and it was virtually impossible that they should be. The furnishings and use of rooms in most American houses made more than the most elementary washing difficult. In a New England farmer's household, wrote Underwood, each household member would "go down to the 'sink' in the lean-to, next to the kitchen, fortunate if he had not to break ice in order to wash his face and hands, or more fortunate if a little warm water was poured into his basin from the kettle swung over the kitchen fire." Even in the comfortable household of the prominent minister Lyman Beecher in Litchfield, Connecticut, around 1815, all family members washed in the kitchen, using a stone sink and "a couple of basins."

Southerners washed in their detached kitchens or, like Westerners in warm weather, washed outside, "at the doors . . . or at the wells" of their houses. Using basins and sinks outdoors or in full view of others, most Americans found anything more than "washing the face and hands once a-day," usually in cold water, difficult, even unthinkable. Most men and women also washed without soap, reserving it for laundering clothes; instead they used a brisk rubbing with a coarse towel to scrub the dirt off their skins.

Gradually the practice of complete bathing spread beyond the topmost levels of American society and into smaller towns and villages. This became possible as families moved washing equipment out of kitchens and into bedchambers, from shared space to space that could be made private. As more prosperous households furnished one or two of their chambers with washing equipment—a washstand, a basin, and a ewer, or large-mouthed pitcher—family members could shut the chamber door, undress, and wash themselves completely. The daughters of the Larcom family, living in Lowell, Massachusetts, in the late 1830s, began to bathe in a bedchamber in this way; Lucy Larcom described how her oldest sister started to take "a full cold bath every morning before she went to her work . . . in a room without a fire," and the other young Larcoms "did the same whenever we could be resolute enough." By the 1830s better city hotels and even some country taverns were providing individual basins and pitchers in their rooms.

At a far remove from "primitive manners" and "bad practices" was the genteel ideal of domestic sanitation embodied in the "chamber sets"—matching basin and ewer for private bathing, a cup for brushing the teeth, and a chamber pot with cover to minimize odor and spillage—that American stores were beginning to stock. By 1840 a significant minority of American households owned chamber sets and washstands to hold them in their bedchambers. For a handful there was the very faint dawning of an entirely new age of sanitary arrangements. In 1829 the new Tremont House hotel in Boston offered its patrons indoor plumbing: eight chambers with bathtubs and eight "water closets." In New York City and Philadelphia, which had developed rudimentary public water systems, a few wealthy households had water taps and, more rarely, water closets by the 1830s. For all others flush toilets and bathtubs remained far in the future. . . .

Davy Crockett, like many Americans, preferred to wash himself in the great outdoors.

In the early part of the century America was a bawdy, hard-edged, and violent land. We drank more than we ever had before or ever would again. We smoked and chewed tobacco like addicts and fought and quarreled on the flimsiest pretexts. The tavern was the most important gateway to the primarily male world of drink and disorder: in sight of the village church in most American communities, observed Daniel Drake, a Cincinnati physician who wrote a reminiscence of his Kentucky boyhood, stood the village tavern, and the two structures "did in fact represent two great opposing principles."

The great majority of American men in every region were taverngoers. The printed street directories of American cities listed tavernkeepers in staggering numbers, and even the best-churched parts of New England could show more "licensed houses" than meetinghouses. In 1827 the fast-growing city of Rochester, New York, with a population of approximately eight thousand, had nearly one hundred establishments licensed to sell liquor, or one for every eighty inhabitants.

America's most important centers of male sociability, taverns were often the scene of excited gaming and vicious fights and always of hard drinking, heavy smoking, and an enormous amount of alcohol-stimulated talk. City men came to their neighborhood taverns daily, and "tavern haunting, tippling, and gaming," as Samuel Goodrich, a New England historian and publisher, remembered, "were the chief resources of men in the dead and dreary winter months" in the countryside.

A REGULAR ROW IN THE BACKWOODS.

Backwoodsmen have a "knock down" in this 1841 woodcut from Crockett's Almanack.

City taverns catered to clienteles of different classes: sordid sailors' grog-shops near the waterfront were rife with brawling and prostitution; neighborhood taverns and liquor-selling groceries were visited by craftsmen and clerks; well-appointed and relatively decorous places were favored by substantial merchants. Taverns on busy highways often specialized in teamsters or stage passengers, while country inns took their patrons as they came.

Taverns accommodated women as travelers, but their barroom clienteles were almost exclusively male. Apart from the dockside dives frequented by prostitutes, or the liquor-selling groceries of poor city neighborhoods, women rarely drank in public. . . .

By almost any standard, Americans drank not only nearly universally but in large quantities. Their yearly consumption at the time of the Revolution has been estimated at the equivalent of three and one-half gallons of pure two-hundred-proof alcohol for each person. After 1790 American men began to drink even more. By the late 1820s their imbibing had risen to an all-time high of almost four gallons per capita.

Along with drinking went fighting. Americans fought often and with great relish. York, Pennsylvania, for example, was a peaceable place as American communities went, but the Miller and Weaver families had a long-running quarrel. It had begun in 1800 when the Millers found young George Weaver stealing apples in their yard and punished him by "throwing him over the fence," injuring him painfully. Over the years hostilities broke out periodically. Lewis Miller remembered walking down the street as a teenaged boy and meeting Mrs. Weaver, who drenched him with the bucket of water she was carrying. He retaliated by "turning about and giving her a kick, laughing at her, this is for your politeness." Other York households had their quarrels too; in "a general fight on Beaver Street," Mistress Hess and Mistress Forsch tore each other's caps from their heads. Their husbands and then the neighbors interfered and "all of them had a knock down." . . .

. . . White Southerners lived with a pervasive fear of the violent potential of their slaves, and the Nat Turner uprising in Virginia in 1831, when a party of slaves rebelled and killed whites before being overcome, gave rise to tighter and harsher controls. But in daily reality slaves had far more to fear from their masters.

Margaret Hall was no proponent of abolition and had little sympathy for black Americans. Yet in her travels south she confronted incidents of what she ironically called the "good treatment of slaves" that were impossible to ignore. At a country tavern in Georgia, she summoned the slave chambermaid, but "she could not come" because "the mistress had been whipping her and she was not fit to be seen. Next morning she made her appearance with her face marked in several places by the cuts of the cowskin and her neck handkerchief covered with spots of blood."

Southern stores were very much like Northern ones, Francis Kemble Butler observed, except that they stocked "negro-whips" and "mantraps" on their shelves. A few slaves were never beaten at all, and for most, whippings were not a daily or weekly occurrence. But they were, of all Americans, by far the most vulnerable to violence. All slaves had, as William Wells Brown, an ex-slave him-

A white master takes a baby from its mother.

self, said, often "heard the crack of the whip, and the screams of the slave" and knew that they were never more than a white man's or woman's whim away from a beating. . . .

Although it remained a powerful force in many parts of the United States, the American way of drunkenness began to lose ground as early as the mid-1820s. The powerful upsurge in liquor consumption had provoked a powerful reaction, an unprecedented attack on all forms of drink that gathered momentum in the Northeast. Some New England clergymen had been campaigning in their own communities as early as 1810, but their concerns took on organized impetus with the founding of the American Temperance Society in 1826. Energized in part by a concern for social order, in part by evangelical piety, temperance reformers popularized a radically new way of looking at alcohol. The "good creature" became "demon rum"; prominent physicians and writers on physiology, like Benjamin Rush, told Americans that alcohol, traditionally considered healthy and fortifying, was actually a physical and moral poison. National and state societies distributed anti-liquor tracts, at first calling for moderation in drink but increasingly demanding total abstinence from alcohol.

To a surprising degree these aggressive temperance campaigns worked. By 1840 the consumption of alcohol had declined by more than two-thirds, from close to four gallons per person each year to less than one and one-half. Country storekeepers gave up the sale of spirits, local authorities limited the number of tavern licenses, and farmers even abandoned hard cider and cut down their apple orchards. The shift to temperance was a striking transformation in the everyday habits of an enormous number of Americans. "A great, though silent change," in Horace Greeley's words, had been "wrought in public sentiment."

But although the "great change" affected some Americans everywhere, it had a very uneven impact. Organized temperance reform was sharply delimited by geography. Temperance societies were enormously powerful in New England and western New York, and numerous in eastern New York, New Jersey, and Pennsylvania. More than three-fourths of all recorded temperance pledges came from these states. In the South and West, and in the laborers' and artisans' neighborhoods of the cities, the campaign against drink was much weaker. In many places drinking ways survived and even flourished, but as individuals and families came under the influence of militant evangelical piety, their "men of business and sobriety" increased gradually in number. . . .

Whipping and the pillory, with their attentive audiences, began to disappear from the statute book, to be replaced by terms of imprisonment in another new American institution, the state penitentiary. Beginning with Pennsylvania's abolition of flogging in 1790 and Massachusetts's elimination of mutilating punishments in 1805, several American states gradually accepted John Hancock's view of 1796 that "mutilating or lacerating the body" was less an effective punishment than "an indignity to human nature." Connecticut's town constables whipped petty criminals for the last time in 1828.

Slaveholding states were far slower to change their provisions for public punishment. The whipping and mutilation of blacks may have become a little less

A popular temperance print of 1826 shows a drunkard's progress from a morning dram to the loss of his home.

ferocious over the decades, but the whip remained the essential instrument of punishment and discipline. "The secret of our success," thought a slave owner, looking back after emancipation, had been "the great motive power contained in that little instrument." Delaware achieved notoriety by keeping flogging on the books for whites and blacks alike through most of the twentieth century.

Although there were important stirrings of sentiment against capital punishment, all American states continued to execute convicted murderers before the mid-1840s. Public hangings never lost their drawing power. But a number of American public officials began to abandon the long-standing view of executions as instructive communal rituals. They saw the crowd's holiday mood and eager participation as sharing too much in the condemned killer's own brutality. Starting with Pennsylvania, New York, and Massachusetts in the mid-1830s, several state legislatures voted to take executions away from the crowd, out of the public realm. Sheriffs began to carry out death sentences behind the walls of the jailyard, before a small assembly of representative onlookers. Other states clung much longer to tradition and continued public executions into the twentieth century.

Early-nineteenth-century Americans were more licentious than we ordinarily imagine them to be.

"On the 20th day of July" in 1830, Harriet Winter, a young woman working as a domestic in Joseph Dunham's household in Brimfield, Massachusetts, "was gathering raspberries" in a field west of the house. "Near the close of day," Charles Phelps, a farm laborer then living in the town, "came to the field where she was," and in the gathering dusk they made love—and, Justice of the Peace Asa Lincoln added in his account, "it was the Sabbath." American communities did not usually document their inhabitants' amorous rendezvous, and Harriet's tryst with Charles was a commonplace event in early-nineteenth-century America. It escaped historical oblivion because she was unlucky, less in becoming pregnant than in Charles's refusal to marry her. Asa Lincoln did not approve of Sabbath evening indiscretions, but he was not pursuing Harriet for immorality. He was concerned instead with economic responsibility for the child. Thus he interrogated Harriet about the baby's father—while she was in labor, as was the long-customary practice—in order to force Charles to contribute to the maintenance of the child, who was going to be "born a bastard and chargeable to the town."

Some foreign travelers found that the Americans they met were reluctant to admit that such things happened in the United States. They were remarkably straitlaced about sexual matters in public and eager to insist upon the "purity" of their manners. But to take such protestations at face value, the unusually candid Englishman Frederick Marryat thought, would be "to suppose that human nature is not the same everywhere."

The well-organized birth and marriage records of a number of American communities reveal that in late-eighteenth-century America pregnancy was frequently the prelude to marriage. The proportion of brides who were pregnant at the time of their weddings had been rising since the late seventeenth century and peaked in the turbulent decades during and after the Revolution. In the 1780s and 1790s nearly one-third of rural New England's brides were already with child. The frequency of sexual intercourse before marriage was surely higher, since some couples would have escaped early pregnancy. For many couples sexual relations were part of serious courtship. Premarital pregnancies in late-eighteenth-century Dedham, Massachusetts, observed the local historian Erastus Worthington in 1828, were occasioned by "the custom then prevalent of females admitting young men to their beds, who sought their company in marriage."

Pregnancies usually simply accelerated a marriage that would have taken place in any case, but community and parental pressure worked strongly to assure it. Most rural communities simply accepted the "early" pregnancies that marked so many marriages, although in Hingham, Massachusetts, tax records suggest that the families of well-to-do brides were considerably less generous to couples who had had "early babies" than to those who had avoided pregnancy. . . .

Most Americans—and the American common law—still did not regard abortion as a crime until the fetus had "quickened" or began to move perceptibly in the womb. Books of medical advice actually contained prescriptions for bringing on delayed menstrual periods, which would also produce an abortion if the woman happened to be pregnant. They suggested heavy doses of purgatives that created violent cramps, powerful douches, or extreme kinds of physical activity, like the "violent exercise, raising great weights . . . strokes on the belly . . . [and] falls" noted in William Buchan's *Domestic Medicine,* a manual read widely through the 1820s. Women's folklore echoed most of these prescriptions and added others, particularly the use of two American herbal preparations—savin, or the extract of juniper berries, and Seneca snakeroot—as abortion-producing drugs. They were dangerous procedures but sometimes effective.

Starting at the turn of the nineteenth century, the sexual lives of many Americans began to change, shaped by a growing insistence on control: reining in the passions in courtship, limiting family size, and even redefining male and female sexual desire.

Bundling was already on the wane in rural America before 1800; by the 1820s it was written about as a rare and antique custom. It had ceased, thought an elderly man from East Haddam, Connecticut, "as a consequence of education and refinement." Decade by decade the proportion of young women who had conceived a child before marriage declined. In most of the towns of New England the rate had dropped from nearly one pregnant bride in three to one in five or six by 1840; in some places prenuptial pregnancy dropped to 5 percent. For many young Americans this marked the acceptance of new limits on sexual behavior, imposed not by their parents or other authorities in their communities but by themselves.

These young men and women were not more closely supervised by their parents than earlier generations had been; in fact, they had more mobility and greater freedom. The couples that courted in the new style put a far greater emphasis on control of the passions. For some of them—young Northern merchants and professional men and their intended brides—revealing love letters have survived for the years after 1820. Their intimate correspondence reveals that they did not give up sexual expression but gave it new boundaries, reserving sexual intercourse for marriage. Many of them were marrying later than their parents, often living through long engagements while the husband-to-be strove to establish his place in the world. They chose not to risk a pregnancy that would precipitate them into an early marriage.

Many American husbands and wives were also breaking with tradition as they began to limit the size of their families. Clearly, married couples were renegotiating the terms of their sexual lives together, but they remained resolutely silent about how they did it. In the first two decades of the nineteenth century, they almost certainly set about avoiding childbirth through abstinence; coitus interruptus, or male withdrawal; and perhaps sometimes abortion. These contraceptive techniques had long been traditional in preindustrial Europe, although previously little used in America.

As they entered the 1830s, Americans had their first opportunity to learn, at least in print, about more effective or less self-denying forms of birth control. They could read reasonably inexpensive editions of the first works on contraception published in the United States: Robert Dale Owen's *Moral Physiology* of 1831 and Dr. Charles Knowlton's *The Fruits of Philosophy* of 1832. Both authors frankly described the full range of contraceptive techniques, although they solemnly rejected physical intervention in the sexual act and recommended only douching after intercourse and coitus interruptus. Official opinion, legal and religious, was deeply hostile. Knowlton, who had trained as a physician in rural Massachusetts, was prosecuted in three different counties for obscenity, convicted once, and imprisoned for three months.

But both works found substantial numbers of Americans eager to read them. By 1839 each book had gone through nine editions, putting a combined total of twenty to thirty thousand copies in circulation. . . .

Everyone smokes and some chew in America," wrote Isaac Weld in 1795. Americans turned tobacco, a new and controversial stimulant at the time of colonial settlement, into a crucially important staple crop and made its heavy use a commonplace—and a never-ending source of surprise and indignation to visi-

On the home front: a smoker indulges.

tors. Tobacco use spread in the United States because it was comparatively cheap, a homegrown product free from the heavy import duties levied on it by European governments. A number of slave rations described in plantation documents included "one hand of tobacco per month." Through the eighteenth century most American smokers used clay pipes, which are abundant in colonial archeological sites, although some men and women dipped snuff or inhaled powdered tobacco.

Where the smokers of early colonial America "drank" or gulped smoke through the short, thick stems of their seventeenth-century pipes, those of 1800 inhaled it more slowly and gradually; from the early seventeenth to the late eighteenth century, pipe stems became steadily longer and narrower, increasingly distancing smokers from their burning tobacco.

In the 1790s cigars, or "segars," were introduced from the Caribbean. Prosperous men widely took them up; they were the most expensive way to consume tobacco, and it was a sign of financial security to puff away on "longnines" or "principe cigars at three cents each" while the poor used clay pipes and much cheaper "cut plug" tobacco. After 1800 in American streets, barrooms, stores, public conveyances, and even private homes it became nearly impossible to avoid tobacco chewers. Chewing extended tobacco use, particularly into workplaces; men who smoked pipes at home or in the tavern barroom could chew while working in barns or workshops where smoking carried the danger of fire.

"In all the public places of America," wrote Charles Dickens, multitudes of men engaged in "the odious practice of chewing and expectoration," a recreation practiced by all ranks of American society. Chewing stimulated salivation and gave rise to a public environment of frequent and copious spitting, where men every few minutes were "squirting a mouthful of saliva through the room."

Spittoons were provided in the more meticulous establishments, but men often ignored them. The floors of American public buildings were not pleasant to contemplate. A courtroom in New York City in 1833 was decorated by a "mass of abomination" contributed to by "judges, counsel, jury, witnesses, officers, and audience."

The Americans of 1820 would have been more recognizable to us in the informal and egalitarian way they treated one another. The traditional signs of deference before social superiors—the deep bow, the "courtesy," the doffed cap, lowered head, and averted eyes—had been a part of social relationships in colonial America. In the 1780s, wrote the American poetess Lydia Huntley Sigourney in 1824, there were still "individuals . . . in every grade of society" who had grown up "when a bow was not an offense to fashion nor . . . a relic of monarchy." But in the early nineteenth century such signals of subordination rapidly fell away. It was a natural consequence of the Revolution, she maintained, which, "in giving us liberty, obliterated almost every vestige of politeness of the 'old school.' " Shaking hands became the accustomed American greeting between men, a gesture whose symmetry and mutuality signified equality. Frederick Marryat found in 1835 that it was "invariably the custom to shake hands" when he was introduced to Americans and that he could not carefully grade the acknowledgment he would give to new acquaintances according to their signs of wealth and breeding. He found instead that he had to "go on shaking hands here, there and everywhere, and with everybody." Americans were not blind to inequalities of economic and social power, but they less and less gave them overt physical expression. Bred in a society where such distinctions were far more clearly spelled out, Marryat was somewhat disoriented in the United States; "it is impossible to know who is who," he claimed, "in this land of equality."

Well-born British travelers encountered not just confusion but conflict when they failed to receive the signs of respect they expected. Margaret Hall's letters home during her Southern travels outlined a true comedy of manners. At every stage stop in the Carolinas, Georgia, and Alabama, she demanded that country tavernkeepers and their households give her deferential service and well-prepared meals; she received instead rancid bacon and "such an absence of all kindness of feeling, such unbending frigid heartlessness." But she and her family had a far greater share than they realized in creating this chilly reception. Squeezed between the pride and poise of the great planters and the social debasement of the slaves, small Southern farmers often displayed a prickly insolence, a considered lack of response, to those who too obviously considered themselves their betters. Greatly to their discomfort and incomprehension, the Halls were experiencing what a British traveler more sympathetic to American ways, Patrick Shirreff, called "the democratic rudeness which assumed or presumptuous superiority seldom fails to experience."

In the seventeenth century white American colonials were no taller than their European counterparts, but by the time of the Revolution they were close to their late-twentieth-century average height for men of slightly over five feet eight inches. The citizens of the early republic towered over most Europeans. Americans' early achievement of modern stature—by a full century and more—was a striking consequence of American abundance. Americans were taller because they were better nourished than the great majority of the world's peoples.

Yet not all Americans participated equally in the nation's abundance. Differences in stature between whites and blacks, and between city and country dwellers, echoed those between Europeans and Americans. Enslaved blacks were a full inch shorter than whites. But they remained a full inch taller than European peasants and laborers and were taller still than their fellow slaves eating the scanty diets afforded by the more savagely oppressive plantation system of the West Indies. And by 1820 those who lived in the expanding cities of the United States— even excluding immigrants whose heights would have reflected European, not American, conditions—were noticeably shorter than the people of the countryside, suggesting an increasing concentration of poverty and poorer diets in urban places.

Across the United States almost all country households ate the two great American staples: corn and "the eternal pork," as one surfeited traveler called it, "which makes its appearance on every American table, high and low, rich and poor." Families in the cattle-raising, dairying country of New England, New York, and northern Ohio ate butter, cheese, and salted beef as well as pork and made

Possum and other game were dietary staples.

their bread from wheat flour or rye and Indian corn. In Pennsylvania, as well as Maryland, Delaware, and Virginia, Americans ate the same breadstuffs as their Northern neighbors, but their consumption of cheese and beef declined every mile southward in favor of pork.

Farther to the south, and in the West, corn and corn-fed pork were truly "eternal"; where reliance on them reached its peak in the Southern uplands, they were still the only crops many small farmers raised. Most Southern and Western families built their diets around smoked and salted bacon, rather than the Northerners' salt pork, and, instead of wheat or rye bread, made cornpone or hoecake, a coarse, strong bread, and hominy, pounded Indian corn boiled together with milk.

Before 1800, game—venison, possum, raccoon, and wild fowl—was for many American households "a substantial portion of the supply of food at certain seasons of the year," although only on the frontier was it a regular part of the diet. In the West and South this continued to be true, but in the Northeast game became increasingly rare as forests gave way to open farmland, where wild animals could not live. . . . The old ways, so startlingly unfamiliar to the modern reader, gradually fell away. Americans changed their assumptions about what was proper, decent, and normal in everyday life in directions that would have greatly surprised most of the men and women of the early republic. Some aspects of their "primitive manners" succumbed to campaigns for temperance and gentility, while others evaporated with the later growth of mass merchandising and mass communications.

Important patterns of regional, class, and ethnic distinctiveness remain in American everyday life. But they are far less powerful, and less central to understanding American experience, than they once were. Through the rest of the nineteenth century and into the twentieth, the United States became ever more diverse, with new waves of Eastern and Southern European immigrants joining the older Americans of Northern European stock. Yet the new arrivals—and even more, their descendants—have experienced the attractiveness and reshaping power of a national culture formed by department stores, newspapers, radios, movies, and universal public education. America, the developing nation, developed into us. And perhaps our manners and morals, to some future observer, will seem as idiosyncratic and astonishing as this portrait of our earlier self.

Prison "Reform" in America

Roger T. Pray

One of the puzzles about American society is the fact that while throughout its history the country has been one of the richest and most free in the world, a land of opportunity and a happy place where (in Jefferson's words) there was enough land to support "a thousand generations" of future citizens, it has also had a reputation for lawlessness, home to an extremely large number of criminals. It has also, as Roger T. Pray points out in this essay, been a country where much attention has been devoted to the search for ways to prevent crime, showing criminals the error of their ways by locking them up and attempting to reform them.

As early as the 1830s American methods of treating criminals were famous. One of the greatest European students of American society, the Frenchman Alexis de Tocqueville developed his understanding of America while on an official mission to examine American prison systems.

Roger T. Pray is a prison psychologist, currently a researcher with the Utah Department of Correction.

Prisons are a fact of life in America. However unsatisfactory and however well-concealed they may be, we cannot imagine doing without them. They remain such a fundamental bulwark against crime and criminals that we now keep a larger portion of our population in prisons than any other nation except the Soviet Union and South Africa, and for terms that are longer than in many countries. Furthermore, we Americans invented the prison.

It was created by humanitarians in Philadelphia in 1790 and spread from there to other cities in the United States and Europe. The stubborn questions that perplex us today about how prisons can and should work—what they can achieve and how they might fail—began to be asked almost as soon as the first one opened. The history of prisons in America is the history of a troubled search for solutions.

Before there were prisons, serious crimes were almost always redressed by corporal or capital punishment. Institutions like the Bastille and the Tower of London mainly held political prisoners, not ordinary criminals. Jails existed, but primarily for pretrial detention. The closest thing to the modern prison was the workhouse, a place of hard labor almost exclusively for minor offenders, derelicts, and vagrants. Once a felon was convicted, he was punished bodily or fined but not incarcerated. Today's system, where imprisonment is a common penalty for a felony, is a historical newcomer.

The colonists did not have prisons. Until the Revolution they were required to follow the British criminal code, which depended heavily on corporal and capital punishment. The code applied to religious offenses as well as secular ones, and it was sometimes hard to tell the difference. A condemned man about to be executed commonly had to face his coffin while a clergyman exhorted the congregation to avoid this soul's plight. Crimes that didn't warrant the death penalty were dealt with by fines (especially for the rich) or "sanguinary" punishments, such as flogging and mutilation (more often for the less well-off).

Many colonial punishments were designed to terrorize offenders and hold them up to ridicule. The ducking stool, the stocks and the pillory, branding of the hand or forehead, and public flogging were all commonplace.

Many crimes were punishable by death. In Pennsylvania between 1718 and 1776, under the British penal code, execution could be prescribed for high treason, petty treason, murder, burglary, rape, sodomy, buggery, malicious maiming, manslaughter by stabbing, witchcraft by conjuration, and arson. All other felonies were capital on a second conviction. The death penalty was usually carried out by hanging, although stoning, breaking on the rack, and burning at the stake were not unknown.

Toward the end of the 1700s people began to realize that cruel physical retribution did little to curb crime; more important, society was experiencing changes that would profoundly affect penology. The nation's population began to increase dramatically. As people began to move around more frequently and easily, the effectiveness of ridicule naturally declined. People began to perceive the old penal code and its punishments as not only obsolete and barbaric but also foreign, left over from the hated British. A more just American solution should and could be developed.

Ironically the search for new punishments was to rely heavily on new ideas imported from Europe in the writings of such social thinkers of the Enlightenment as the baron de Montesquieu, Voltaire, Thomas Paine, and Cesare Beccaria. Whereas the Calvinists of colonial times had regarded man as basically depraved, these thinkers saw him as essentially good. It followed that a criminal could be rehabilitated. And since all men now were held to be born free and equal, even the worst were entitled to certain elementary rights to life, ultimate liberty, and at least some chance to pursue happiness.

The European theorizer who had the most direct influence upon penology was Beccaria, the Italian author of an influential 1764 essay, *On Crimes and Punishments.* Beccaria, a nobleman, had become deeply concerned about the deplorable treatment of criminals in his country. His work had a profound effect on criminal punishment the world over.

Beccaria wrote that "the purpose of punishment is not to torment a sensible being, or to undo a crime [but] is none other than to prevent the criminal from doing further injury to society and to prevent others from committing the like offense." He urged that accused criminals be treated humanely prior to trial and be afforded every opportunity to present evidence in their own behalf. Trials should be speedy, and secret accusations and torture to extract confessions abolished. He also wrote that overly harsh and inequitably applied laws caused more

The prison at Walnut Street, in Philadelphia, was the first in the world. It was established in 1790; by 1817 conditions had so deteriorated that it was considered a failure and described as a "seminar for vice."

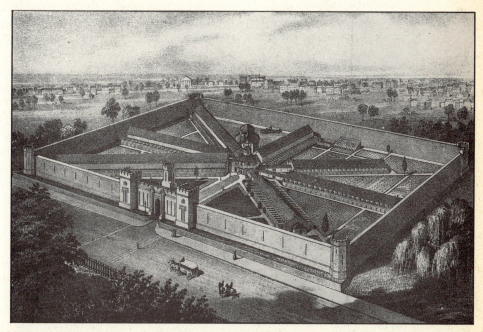

Cherry Hill State Prison at Philadelphia, 1855, was the model prison of what became known as the Pennsylvania system, the first system to separate prisoners by placing them into individual cells.

problems than they alleviated. "The severity of the punishment," he wrote, "of itself emboldens men to commit the very wrongs it is supposed to prevent. They are driven to commit additional crimes to avoid the punishment for a single one. . . . The certainty of a punishment, even if it be moderate, will always make a stronger impression than the fear of another which is more terrible but combined with the hope of impunity."

Beccaria believed the answer was to make punishments fit specific crimes. His writings had such enormous impact in this country that by the early 1800s most states had amended their criminal codes and strictly limited the death penalty to a few of the most serious crimes.

The largest ground swell for reform in America came from Quakers, and they played a crucial role in inventing the prison. Most of them lived in Pennsylvania and western New Jersey—in and around the nation's most important city, Philadelphia—and they were the only significant religious group to find brutal criminal punishments irreconcilable with their Christian beliefs. Toward the end of the eighteenth century, as new ideas about punishment spread, the Quakers set about to transform penal practices.

First, in 1786 they persuaded the Pennsylvania legislature to limit the death penalty to murder, treason, rape, and arson. People convicted of robbery, burglary, sodomy, or buggery would now have to give up their possessions and be imprisoned for up to ten years; if convicted of larceny, they could have to make double restitution (half to the state) and spend up to three years in prison. Next, the Quakers took on the terrible conditions in jails. Philadelphia jails locked up men and women in the same rooms at night. Inmates were thrown together with no regard for age, seriousness of offense, or ability to defend themselves. Liquor was sold on the premises. And detainees had to pay a fee to underwrite their own incarcerations, even if they were found innocent of any crime.

In 1787 the Quakers and their sympathizers formed the Philadelphia Society for Alleviating the Miseries of Public Prisons. Many prominent citizens took up the banner. In March, Dr. Benjamin Rush gave a lecture at the home of Benjamin Franklin in which he recommended dividing a large house into apartments for convicts, with special cells for the solitary confinement of troublesome inmates.

The Philadelphia Society soon persuaded the Pennsylvania legislature to convert a jail on Walnut Street into a prison for the confinement of convicted criminals from across the state. It was designed for two classes of inmates: serious offenders would be housed in sixteen solitary cells; less hardened ones would sleep in large rooms and would work together in shops. This became the first prison as we know it.

The creation of the Walnut Street prison in 1790 elicited tremendous enthusiasm in Philadelphia. It promised a vast improvement in the treatment of jailed offenders. And the initial results were very promising. Yearly commitments dropped from 131 in 1789 to just 45 in 1793. Burglars and pickpockets seemed to disappear from Philadelphia, and few discharged prisoners were caught committing new crimes. The Pennsylvania legislature was so impressed that it again amended the law in 1794 to reduce the number of crimes calling for capital punishment to just one: first-degree murder.

Prisoners work at the laundry at Sing Sing, in New York, in 1878. Many prisons not only used inmates for internal prison work, as shown here, but also hired them out to private contractors as laborers.

When society began putting into practice the new theories of penology, Americans became confident that a rational system of certain but humane punishment would vastly reduce crime. If colonial laws had contributed to crime, new laws would deter it. The prison was necessary, but the focus was on the laws, not on the nature of the prison. No one was yet arguing that life inside a prison would improve anybody.

The Walnut Street prison, the first in the world, served as the prototype for all other prisons built in this country over the next thirty years. But just as the Walnut Street Prison represented a dramatic departure from colonial practices, so developments in New York and Pennsylvania in the 1820s represented another departure of even greater magnitude—one that was to make even Europe vitally interested in the course of American penology. Before that happened, things went to pieces in Walnut Street.

Despite the initial enthusiasm over the prison, conditions soon became dreadful. As yet no one had very clear ideas about what prisons should look like or how they should be run. Between 1790 and 1820 they tended to be like houses where all prisoners not in solitary confinement lived in common rooms and ate in large dining halls. It was difficult to avoid putting more and more offenders in the large rooms, and this caused overcrowding and management problems.

Moreover, it was hard to make inmates work. Difficulties with uncooperative prisoners led to a gradual resurrection of the very corporal punishments the prison had been created to eliminate, although some prisons did try using isolation and the withholding of rations to control inmates.

By the early 1800s Walnut Street and other prisons were gruesome places. The early prison historian Richard Phelps described the prison established in 1790 in an abandoned copper mine at Simsbury, Connecticut—one of the first after Walnut Street: "The passage down the shaft into the cavern was upon a ladder fastened upon one side and resting on the bottom. At the foot of this passage commences a gradual descent for a considerable distance, all around being solid rock or ore. . . . On the sides, in the niches of the cavern, platforms were built of boards for the prisoners, on which straw was placed for their beds. The horrid gloom of this dungeon can scarcely be realized. The impenetrable vastness supporting the awful mass above impending as if ready to crush one to atoms; the dripping water trickling like tears from its sides; the unearthly echoes, all conspired to strike aghast with amazement and horror. A bell summoning the prisoners to work brought them up from the cavern beneath through a trapdoor, in regular numbers, two or three together. . . . The prisoners were heavily ironed and secured by fetters and being therefore unable to walk made their way by jumps and hops. On entering the smithy some went to the side of the forges where collars dependent by iron chains from the roof were fastened around their necks and others were chained in pairs to wheelbarrows. The attendants delivered pickled pork to the prisoners for dinner at their forges, a piece for each thrown on the floor and left to be washed and boiled in the water used for cooling the iron wrought at the forges. Meat was distributed in a similar manner for breakfast."

By 1817 the Philadelphia Society acknowledged that Walnut Street had so degenerated that as many as forty prisoners were being housed in an eighteen-by-eighteen-foot room, that it was now no different from a European jail, and that it had become a virtual "seminary for vice." As a remedy the society persuaded the Pennsylvania legislature to build two new prisons—one in eastern and one in western Pennsylvania. These were to be built with only single cells, so that every inmate could be kept alone, eliminating all the problems of congregate living.

The criminal justice situation in New York before the 1790s had been similar to that in Pennsylvania: many crimes called for capital punishment, and corporal punishment was extensive. In 1794 reformers from New York visited Philadelphia and decided to emulate Walnut Street. New York reduced its list of capital crimes to just murder and treason, and two prisons were built—one at Albany and one in Greenwich Village. As in Pennsylvania, they soon became overcrowded. Conditions so degenerated that in 1816 a third and very different prison was authorized, at Auburn.

The Auburn prison followed a new scheme: the worst offenders went into solitary confinement; but a second class was put in separate cells three days a week, and minor offenders were allowed to work together six days a week. By 1823 most of the Auburn inmates serving long terms in solitary had suffered mental breakdowns. Isolation was discontinued, and the governor pardoned most of the remaining isolated inmates. The Auburn system was now revamped to allow congregate work by day for all (with a rule of total silence) and solitary confinement by night. This was essentially a compromise between total group living, which had led to such horrendous conditions earlier, and total isolation, which bred insanity.

These developments in Pennsylvania and New York became the basis for a tremendous thirty-five-year rivalry between what were seen as the two basic forms of the prison: the individual system, represented by Pennsylvania, and the congregate system, represented by Auburn. The supporters of the Pennsylvania system (the Philadelphia Society) called Auburn a cheap imitation. Auburn's defenders (the Boston Prison Discipline Society) called the individual system extravagant and claimed it led to death and insanity while failing to eliminate interaction between inmates, since heat ducts and water pipes still allowed clandestine communication.

As various states contemplated prison construction, they moved firmly into one camp or the other. The Reverend Louis Dwight, self-styled spokesman for the Boston Prison Discipline Society, made sure that state legislatures contemplating building prisons received copies of his annual reports. He promoted the Auburn system with religious zeal and regarded any opposition as heretical. His reports were quite misleading—as were those promulgated by advocates of the individual system—but he was very effective in encouraging other states to emulate Auburn.

Prison reformers in both camps agreed that the great mistake of the 1790s had been the failure to keep inmates from associating with one another. The only issue was whether they should labor and eat silently in groups or remain alone in their cells. For this reason prison architecture—the layout of cells, eating and sleeping arrangements, and work facilities—became a vital concern.

Attitudes had already changed drastically since the prison's first years. Whereas the focus had been on more humane laws, which were supposed to eliminate crime from society, now it was believed that laws had failed but the internal routine of the prison could reform offenders before returning them to society. In 1829 and 1830 inspectors at the Auburn prison interviewed inmates about to be released in hope of uncovering clues to the origins of their criminality. It emerged that most of them had come from broken or otherwise unwholesome homes. The inspectors concluded that a lack of rigorous childhood training in discipline and obedience was, along with exposure to vice, a major cause of crime. If so, order and discipline in the penitentiary should inculcate criminals with proper values and work habits, and isolation from evil influences should allow the basic goodness in man to emerge.

So much effort was expended to isolate inmates from the evils of society that even newspapers were banned from one prison. Correspondence with one's family was typically either forbidden or limited to one letter during the whole confinement. The occasional visitor had to be of unquestioned moral character. The warden of Sing Sing (established in 1824) told inmates in 1826: "It is true that while confined here you can have no intelligence concerning relatives or friends. . . . You are to be literally buried from the world."

The Pennsylvania system isolated the inmate for his entire stay. He was to leave the institution as ignorant of his fellow convicts as when he arrived. A convict arriving at Pennsylvania's Eastern Penitentiary was examined by a physician and then given a hot bath and some clothes. Later he was blindfolded and led to a central rotunda, where the superintendent explained the rules and operation of the prison. Then, still blindfolded, he was taken to his cell, whose number became his name. He was allowed to exercise in the little yard next to his cell only when the inmates in the adjoining yards were not present. He was left alone except when brought meals. After a few days he was asked if he would like some work—an offer usually accepted because of boredom. If he behaved, he would be allowed a Bible. So isolated were the prisoners that they did not hear for months about a cholera epidemic that decimated Philadelphia, and not one inmate caught the disease.

At Auburn prisoners slept alone in their cells at night but worked and ate in groups. They were forbidden to converse or even to exchange glances with other inmates. Strict routines were established to maintain this silence. Since Auburn officials couldn't have inmates casually walking from place to place, they invented the lockstep. Standing immediately behind one another, each looking over the shoulder of the man ahead, with faces turned down and to the right to prevent conversation, prisoners shuffled along in unison. The lockstep survived until the 1930s.

The routine at Auburn was described graphically, if uncritically, in an 1826 report of the Boston Prison Discipline Society: "The unremitted industry, the entire subordination, and subdued feeling among the convicts, has probably no parallel among any equal number of convicts. In their solitary cells, they spend the night with no other book than the Bible, and at sunrise they proceed in military order, under the eye of the turnkey, in solid columns, with the lock march to the workshops, thence in the same order at the hour of breakfast, to the common hall, where they partake of their wholesome and frugal meal in silence. Not even a whisper might be heard through the whole apartment.

"Convicts are seated in single file, at narrow tables with their backs toward the center, so that there can be no interchange of signs. If one has more food than he wants, he raises his left hand, and if another has less, he raises his right hand, and the waiter changes it. . . . There is the most perfect attention to business from morning till night, interrupted only by the time necessary to dine—and never by the fact that the whole body of prisoners have done their tasks and the time is now their own, and they can do as they please.

"At the close of the day, a little before sunset, the work is all laid aside, at once, and the convicts return in military order, to the silent cells where they partake of their frugal meal, which they are permitted to take from the kitchen, where it is furnished for them, as they returned from the shop. After supper, they can, if they choose, read the scriptures, undisturbed, and can reflect in silence on the error of their lives. They must not disturb their fellow prisoners by even a whisper."

Many important Europeans came to visit these institutions with the hope of applying the new systems at home. In fact, the typical distinguished foreigner would no more have passed up a chance to visit a prison than he would have missed seeing a Southern plantation or a Lowell, Massachusetts, textile mill. Alexis de Tocqueville's second main objective during his visit, after studying our form of government, was the examination of our prisons. He found strengths and weaknesses in both systems. In his view, inmates at Auburn were treated more harshly, but at Pennsylvania they were more unhappy. He concluded that seclusion was physically unhealthy but morally effective; and that although the Pennsylvania system was more expensive to construct and operate, it was easier to administer. . . .

Theories were one thing; in actual practice and with the passage of time, the new prison systems deteriorated. By the mid-1800s prisons everywhere scarcely reflected the designs that had been so fiercely debated. The rigorous routine at Auburn and the solitary confinement of Pennsylvania both had been virtually abandoned.

The major reason was overcrowding. Sentences were extremely long and of fixed duration. With no provisions for early release or parole, prisons filled up fast. Overcrowding led to a relaxation of rules, and this in turn enabled inmates to mix freely. Prisons again began to experience the old problems of congregate living. Part of the trouble was that prisoners were not segregated by age or criminal record, and rules and regulations were geared to the worst offenders.

It had originally been anticipated that inmates would read the Bible, talk with and emulate those exemplary outsiders approved to enter their institution, and contemplate their sins in silence. But most inmates couldn't read and had no use

A nineteenth-century discipline device: the iron-basket helmet.

for do-gooders. Whereas the fathers of the penitentiary had expected inmates to be amenable to change, most were hardened criminals serving long sentences and had little to lose by making trouble or trying to escape. So wardens concentrated on maintaining order, and almost every form of brutality found its way back into the penitentiary. Floggings were so common that the public became appalled when it found out about them. At Sing Sing in 1843 as many as three thousand lashes per month were administered.

Many of the punishments had a medieval cast. Prisoners were tied up by their hands with their toes barely touching the floor. They were strapped on their backs to boards or bars for twenty days at a time. They were placed in sweatboxes—unventilated cells on either side of a fireplace. Alcohol was poured on epileptics having seizures and then ignited to detect shamming. New Jersey investigators in 1829 discovered a fourteen-year-old boy who had been imprisoned with hardened criminals and also physically restrained because he could fit through the gratings in prison doors. Prison officials had placed an iron yoke around his head and fastened his hands to it twenty inches apart at shoulder level.

The distressing aspects of the penitentiary did not stop at the prison walls. In the 1830s inmate labor was often leased to private contractors. Its low price meant a valuable competitive advantage, and the awarding of contracts for it unavoidably invited graft and corruption. Some states began to restrict the use of inmate labor by the mid-1840s.

By the last half of the nineteenth century, citizens had lost faith in the idea that a properly structured environment could cure society's crime problem.

Samuel Slater Imports a Revolution

Arnold Welles

The transition of the United States from an agricultural to a predominantly industrial nation was one of the most important and, by the end of the period, most obvious developments of the nineteenth century. When Washington became president, there was not a true factory in the entire country; when Theodore Roosevelt became president, the United States was already the leading industrial nation of the world. Industrialization and the factory system are not absolutely synonymous terms, but factories are the basic structures in which the industrial process operates most effectively. And Samuel Slater, a young English immigrant, was the man who designed and built the first factory in America. What Slater did, a remarkable personal story as well as one of the key events in the economic and social history of the United States, is told in this essay by one of his great-great-grandsons, Arnold Welles, a successful businessman who is also a fine historian.

Feats of memory, particularly of the kind of memory derided as "photographic"—for all the cornucopias of wealth they sometimes pour over television contestants—are looked down on in modern times, but they have their role in history. Consider, for example, the story of Samuel Slater. It would be impolite to call him a spy, for he would not have considered himself one. Furthermore, he was a man of peace. Yet in his own time this cotton spinner's apprentice achieved with his prodigious memory an effect as great as or greater than any successful military espionage has brought about in our own. For he successfully transplanted the infant Industrial Revolution, which was in many ways an English monopoly, across an ocean to a new country.

To understand Slater's feat, one must look back to the economic situation of England and America in the days directly after the Colonies had achieved their independence. If Britain no longer ruled her former colonies, she clung tenaciously to her trade with them. Thanks to her flourishing new textile industry, she was able to sell large quantities of cotton goods in the United States at prices so low there was little incentive left for making cloth over here by the old-fashioned hand methods. To maintain this favorable dependency as long as possible, England went to fantastic lengths to guard the secrets that had mechanized her cotton industry, and so effective were these measures that America might well have continued solely as an agricultural nation for years, had it not been for Samuel Slater.

Slater was born in 1768 on his family's property, Holly House, in Derbyshire, England. His father, William Slater, was an educated, independent farmer and timber merchant, the close friend and neighbor of Jedediah Strutt, successively farmer, textile manufacturer, and partner of England's famous inventor, Sir Richard Arkwright, whose spinning frame had revolutionized the manufacture of cotton yarn. Three years after Samuel Slater's birth, Strutt had financed Arkwright's factory at Cromford—the world's earliest authentic cotton mill—where water power replaced humans and animals in moving the machinery, and where the whole operation of spinning yarn could be accomplished for the first time automatically under one roof. Within five years Arkwright's mills were employing over 5,000 workers, and England's factory system was launched.

It was in this atmosphere of industrial revolution that young Slater grew up. He showed signs of his future mechanical bent at a tender age by making himself a polished steel spindle with which to help wind worsted for his mother, and whenever he had the chance, he would walk over to nearby Cromford or Belper on the Derwent River to see the cotton mills which Strutt and Arkwright owned. In 1782 Strutt began to erect a large hosiery factory at Milford, a mile from the Slater property, and he asked William Slater's permission to engage his eldest son as clerk. Slater, who had noticed the ability and inclinations of his younger son, Samuel, recommended him instead, observing that he not only "wrote well and was good at figures" but was also of a decided mechanical bent.

Thus, at the age of fourteen, Samuel Slater went to live and work with Strutt. When William Slater died shortly afterward, in 1783, young Samuel Slater signed his own indenture to learn cotton spinning as an apprentice in Strutt's factory until the age of 21.

During the early days of his term the boy became so engrossed in the business that he would go for six months without seeing his family, despite the fact that they lived only a mile away, and he would frequently spend his only free day, Sunday, experimenting alone on machinery. In those days millowners had to build all their own machinery, and Slater acquired valuable experience in its design, as well as its operation, and in the processes of spinning yarn. Even before completing his term of indenture he was made superintendent of Strutt's new hosiery mill.

But Slater had become concerned about the chances for an independent career in England. Arkwright's patents having expired, factories had sprung up everywhere, and Slater could see that to launch out on his own he would need more and more capital to stay ahead of the technical improvements constantly taking place. His attention had been drawn to the United States by an article in a Philadelphia paper saying that a bounty of £100 had been granted by the Pennsylvania legislature to a man who had designed a textile machine. Young Slater made up his mind that he would go to the United States and introduce the Arkwright methods there. As his first step, even before his term with Strutt expired, Slater obtained his employer's permission to supervise the erection of the new cotton works Arkwright was then starting, and from this experience he gained valuable knowledge for the future.

There were, it was true, grave risks to consider. Britain still strictly forbade the export of textile machinery or the designs for it. With France entering a period of revolution which might unsettle the economy of the Old World, it was even more important that the large American market be safeguarded for British commerce. As a result, the Arkwright machines and technique were nowhere in use in America at the time, and various attempts—in Pennsylvania, Massachusetts, Connecticut, Maryland, and South Carolina—to produce satisfactory cotton textiles had borne little fruit. Without Arkwright's inventions it was impossible to make cotton yarn strong enough for the warps needed in hand-loom weaving.

Enterprising Yankees undertook all kinds of ingenious attempts to smuggle out modern machines or drawings. Even the American minister to France was involved in some of them: machinery would be quietly purchased in England, dismantled, and sent in pieces to our Paris legation for transshipment to the United States in boxes labeled "glassware" or "farm implements." British agents and the Royal Navy managed to intercept almost all such shipments, however, and skilled workers who attempted to slip away with drawings or models were apprehended on the high seas and brought back. Passengers leaving England for American ports were thoroughly searched by customs agents before boarding ship.

Slater knew of these handicaps and determined to take along nothing in writing save his indenture papers. . . . But he was carrying with him in a very remarkable memory the complete details of a modern cotton mill.

This portrait of an eminently successful Samuel Slater includes in the background a view of his first cotton-spinning mill.

After a passage of 66 days, Slater's ship reached New York. He had originally intended to go to Philadelphia, but when he learned of the existence of the New York Manufacturing Company on Vesey Street in downtown Manhattan, he showed his indenture and got a job there instead. The company had recently been organized to make yarns and cloth, but the yarn was linen and the machinery, hand-operated, was copied from antiquated English models. This was a far cry from the factories Slater had supervised in Derbyshire.

Fortunately, about this time, the newcomer happened to meet the captain of a packet sailing between New York and Providence, Rhode Island, and from him learned of the interest in textile manufacturing shown by a wealthy, retired merchant of Providence, Moses Brown, later to become one of the founders of Brown University. A converted Quaker and a man of large imagination and business acumen, Brown had invested considerable cash in two rough, hand-operated spinning frames and a crude carding machine as well as in a couple of obsolete "jennies." But all his attempts to produce cotton yarns had ended in failure, and he could find little use for his expensive machinery. Such was the situation when he received a letter from Slater:

New York, December 2d, 1789

Sir,—

A few days ago I was informed that you wanted a manager of *cotton spinning,* etc., in which business I flatter myself that I can give the greatest satisfaction, in making machinery, making good yarn, either for *stockings* or *twist,* as any that is made in England; as I have had opportunity, and an oversight of Sir Richard Arkwright's works, and in Mr. Strutt's mill upwards of eight years. If you are not provided for, should be glad to serve you; though I am in the New York manufactory, and have been for three weeks since I arrived from England. But we have but *one card, two machines,* two spinning jennies, which I think are not worth using. *My intention* is to erect a *perpetual card and spinning.* (Meaning the Arkwright patents). If you please to drop a line respecting the amount of encouragement you wish to give, by favor of Captain Brown, you will much oblige, sir, your most obedient humble servant.

SAMUEL SLATER

N.B.—Please to direct to me at No. 37, Golden Hill, New York.

Slater's letter fired the shrewd Quaker's imagination, and he hastened to reply, declaring that he and his associates were "destitute of a person acquainted with water-frame spinning" and offering Slater all the profits from successful operation of their machinery over and above interest on the capital invested and depreciation charges. His invitation concluded: "If the present situation does not come up to what thou wishes, and, from thy knowledge of the business, can be ascertained of the advantages of the mills, so as to induce thee to come and work ours, and have the *credit* as well as the advantage of perfecting the first water-mill in America, we should be glad to engage thy care so long as they can be made profitable to both, and we can agree."

Tempted and flattered, and assuming that the Providence operation needed only an experienced overseer to make it a success, Slater decided to accept. He took a boat in January, 1790, reached Providence on the eighteenth of the month, and immediately called on Moses Brown.

The two men were in striking contrast. Slater, only 21, was nearly six feet tall and powerfully built, with ruddy complexion and fair hair. Moses Brown, in his soft, broad-brimmed Quaker hat, was well past middle age, of small stature, with a pair of bright, bespectacled eyes set in a benevolent face framed by flowing gray locks. Satisfied from a glance at the Strutt indenture that his young caller was bona fide, Brown took Slater in a sleigh to the little hamlet of Pawtucket, a community consisting of a dozen or so cottages on both sides of the Blackstone River, just outside Providence. They stopped at a small clothier's shop on the river's bank, close by a bridge which linked Rhode Island and Massachusetts. Here was assembled Brown's ill-assorted machinery.

Slater took one look and shook his head, his disappointment obvious. Compared to Strutt's splendid mill this was almost a caricature. He spoke bluntly: "These will not do; they are good for nothing in their present condition, nor can they be made to answer." Brown urged him to reconsider, to give the machines a try, but the young Englishman was not to be persuaded. At last, in desperation, the old merchant threw Slater a challenge:

"Thee said thee could make machinery. Why not do it?"

Reluctantly, Slater finally agreed to build a new mill, using such parts of the old as would answer, but only on one condition: that Brown provide a trusted mechanic to make the machinery which Slater would design and that the man be put under bond neither to disclose the nature of the work nor to copy it.

"If I don't make as good yarn as they do in England," Slater declared, "I will have nothing for my services, but will throw the whole of what I have attempted over the bridge!" Brown agreed, arranging in addition to pay Slater's living expenses.

Then the old merchant took his visitor to the cottage of Oziel Wilkinson, an ingenious ironmaster, with whom Slater could board. Wilkinson, also a Quaker, operated a small anchor forge using water power from the river, and there he turned out ships' chandlery, shovels, scythes, and other tools. As the young Englishman entered the Wilkinson home, his host's younger daughter shyly scampered out of sight, but Hannah, the elder, lingered in the doorway to look at the stranger. Slater fell in love with her. (Within two years they would be married, and Hannah Slater would later acquire fame in her own right as the discoverer of cotton sewing thread, which she first produced from the fine yarns her husband manufactured.) In the Wilkinson household young Slater found new parents who helped him overcome his homesickness and encouraged him in the first difficult months.

Part of that winter he spent experimenting with Moses Brown's crude carding machine, and he was able to improve the quality of cotton fleece it turned out. This, when spun by hand on the jennies, produced a better yarn, but one which was still too weak and uneven to be used as warp in the hand-weaving of cloth. Slater was downhearted; he realized that he must build everything from scratch.

The rest of the winter he spent assembling the necessary materials for constructing the Arkwright machines and processes. He lacked even the tools with which to make the complicated equipment, and he was forced to make many of them himself before any building could commence. Furthermore, without models to copy, he had to work out his own computations for all measurements. One of the most ingenious elements of the Arkwright inventions was the variation in speeds of various parts of the machines. Mathematical tables for these were not available anywhere save in England; Slater had to rely on his own extraordinary memory. Nevertheless, by April, 1790, he was ready to sign a firm partnership agreement to build two carding machines, a drawing and roving frame, and two spinning frames, all to be run automatically by water power. He was to receive one dollar a day as wages, half-ownership in the machinery he built, and, in addition, one half of the mill's net profits after it was in operation. Moses Brown had turned over the supervision of his textile investments to William Almy, his son-in-law, and Smith Brown, his cousin, and these two men became Slater's new partners.

Now, behind shuttered windows in the little clothier's building on the river-bank, young Slater began to design the first successful cotton mill in America. As he drew the plans with chalk on wood, Sylvanus Brown, an experienced local wheelwright, cut out the parts from sturdy oak and fastened them together with wooden dowels. Young David Wilkinson, Slater's future brother-in-law and like his father a skilled ironworker, forged shafts for the spindles, rollers for the frames, and teeth in the cards which Pliny Earle, of Leicester, Massachusetts, prepared for the carding machines. Before iron gearwheels and card rims could be made, Slater and Wilkinson had to go to Mansfield, Massachusetts, to find suitable castings. By autumn, working sixteen hours a day, Slater had more than fulfilled his agreement: he had built not two but three carding machines, as well as the drawing and roving frame and the two spinning frames. At last he was ready for a trial.

Taking up a handful of raw cotton, Slater fed it into the carding machine, cranked by hand for the occasion by an elderly Negro. This engine was one of the most important elements of the Arkwright system, for in it the raw cotton was pulled across leather cards studded with small iron teeth which drew out and straightened the fibers, laid them side by side, and formed them into a long, narrow fleece called an "end," or "sliver." This was then placed on the drawing and roving frame to be further stretched, smoothed, and then twisted before being spun into yarn on the spinning frame. Before the cotton was run through the cards, the fibers lay in every direction, and it was essential that the carding be successful if the "end" was to be suitable for the subsequent steps. But when Slater fed the test cotton into his machine it only piled up on the cards. . . .

After a number of sleepless nights, Slater determined that the trouble arose from a faulty translation of his design into reality, for Pliny Earle had never before made cards of that description. Slater decided that the teeth stood too far apart, and that under pressure of the raw cotton they fell back from their proper places instead of standing firm and combing the cotton as it moved past. He pointed out the defect to Earle, and together, using a discarded piece of grindstone, they beat the teeth into the correct shape. Another test was made and the machine worked satisfactorily.

The final stage was now at hand. Almost a year had passed in preparation for this moment. Would the machinery operate automatically by water power? That was the miracle of the Arkwright techniques, which gave them their name, "perpetual spinning." A connection was made to the small water wheel which had been used by the clothier in whose little shop Slater's new machinery now stood. It was deep winter, and the Blackstone River was frozen over, so that Slater was obliged to crawl down and break up the ice around the wheel. When the wheel turned over, his machinery began to hum.

On December 20, 1790, Samuel Slater's mill produced the first cotton yarn ever made automatically in America. It was strong and of good quality, suitable for sheetings and other types of heavy cotton goods; soon Slater was turning out yarn fine enough to be woven into shirtings, checks, ginghams, and stockings, all of which had until then been imported from Europe. Good cotton cloth woven at home from English yarn had cost from forty to fifty cents per yard, but soon Slater brought the cost down as low as nine cents. For the remainder of that first winter, unable to get anyone else to do the job, Slater spent two or three hours each morning before breakfast breaking the river ice to start the water wheel. Daily it left him soaking wet and numb from exposure; his health was affected for the rest of his life.

The little mill started with four employees, but by the end of one month Slater had nine hands at work, most of them children. In this he was following the practice in England, where entire families were employed in the mills. Early English millowners had found children more agile and dexterous than adults, their quick fingers and small hands tending the moving parts more easily. Slater, like other pioneer millowners dealing with small working forces, was able to

About 1812 an unknown artist portrayed Slater's first mill, on Rhode Island's Blackstone River.

maintain a paternalistic attitude toward the young persons in his charge; until the coming of the factory system and absentee ownership, child labor was not the evil it later became. Slater introduced a number of social customs he had learned in the Arkwright and Strutt mills. For his workers he built the first Sunday school in New England and there provided instruction in reading, writing, and arithmetic, as well as in religion. Later he promoted common day schools for his mill hands, often paying the teachers' wages out of his own pocket.

Proudly Slater sent a sample of his yarn back to Strutt in Derbyshire, who pronounced it excellent. Yet Americans hesitated to use it, preferring traditional hand-spun linen yarn or machine-made cotton yarn imported from England. Within four months Moses Brown was writing to the owners of a little factory in Beverly, Massachusetts, run by a relative, proposing a joint petition to Congress: Why not raise the duties on imported cotton goods? Some of the proceeds could be given to southern cotton farmers as a bounty for upgrading their raw cotton, and some could be presented to the infant textile industry as a subsidy.

Next, Brown arranged to transmit to Alexander Hamilton, secretary of the treasury and already known as a supporter of industry, a sample of Slater's yarn and of the first cotton check made from it, along with various suggestions for encouraging the new textile manufacturers. He reported to Hamilton that within a year machinery and mills could be erected to supply enough yarn for the entire nation. Two months later, when Hamilton presented to Congress his famous *Report on Manufacturers,* he mentioned "the manufactory at Providence [which] has the merit of being the first in introducing into the United States the celebrated cotton mill."

By the end of their first ten months of operations, Almy, Brown & Slater had sold almost 8,000 yards of cloth produced by home weavers from their yarns. After twenty months the factory was turning out more yarn than the weavers in its immediate vicinity could use; a surplus of 2,000 pounds had piled up. Desperately, Moses Brown appealed to Slater, "Thee must shut down thy gates or thee will spin all my farms into cotton yarn."

It was at this point that the full force of Slater's revolutionary processes began to become apparent. To dispose of their surplus the partners began to employ agents in Salem, New York, Baltimore, and Philadelphia, and so encouraging were the sales that it became obvious to them that their potential market was enormous. In 1791, therefore, they closed the little mill and built nearby a more efficient factory designed to accommodate all the processes of yarn manufacturing under one roof. It was opened in 1793. (Now the Old Slater Mill Museum, the building still stands today.)

As of December, 1792, the partners' ledgers had shown a credit in Slater's name of £882, representing his share of the proceeds from the sale of yarn spun by his mill. From then on both he and the infant industry he had helped to create prospered rapidly. The factory was no longer a neighborhood affair but sought its markets in a wider world. When the War of 1812 had ended, there were 165 mills in Rhode Island, Massachusetts, and Connecticut alone, many of them started by former employees of Slater who had gone into business for themselves. By this time Slater, too, had branched out; he owned at least seven mills, either outright or in partnership. An important mill town in Rhode Island already bore the name of Slatersville. Around three new cotton, woolen, and thread mills which he built in Massachusetts, a new textile center sprang up which became the town of Webster. Later, his far-reaching enterprise carried him to Amoskeag Falls on the Merrimac River; in 1822 he bought an interest in a small mill already established there, and in 1826 erected a new mill which became the famous Amoskeag Manufacturing Company, hub of an even greater textile center— Manchester, New Hampshire.

President James Monroe had come to Pawtucket in 1817 to visit the "Old Mill," which was then the largest cotton mill in the nation, containing 5,170 spindles. It had started with 72. Slater himself conducted his distinguished visitor through the factory and proudly showed him his original spinning frame, still running after 27 years. Some years later another President, Andrew Jackson, visited Pawtucket, and when he was told that Slater was confined to his house by rheumatism brought on from that first winter of breaking the ice on the Blackstone, Old Hickory went to pay his respects to the invalid. Courteously addressing Slater as "the Father of American Manufactures," General Jackson said:

"I understand you taught us how to spin, so as to rival Great Britain in her manufactures; you set all these thousands of spindles to work, which I have been delighted in viewing, and which have made so many happy, by a lucrative employment."

Slater thanked his visitor politely and with the dry wit for which he was well known replied:

"Yes, Sir, I suppose that I gave out the psalm, and they have been singing to the tune ever since."

By the time he died in 1835, Slater had become generally recognized as the country's leading textile industrialist. The industry he had founded 45 years earlier had shown phenomenal growth. In 1790 the estimated value of all American manufactured goods barely exceeded $20,000,000, and the domestic cotton crop was about 2,000,000 pounds. By 1835 cotton manufactured goods alone were valued in excess of $47,000,000, and that single industry was consuming almost 80,000,000 pounds of cotton annually. Few men in our history have lived to see such tremendous economic changes wrought in one lifetime by their own efforts.

The social changes which Samuel Slater witnessed and helped to further were even more far-reaching. When he arrived in 1789 America was a nation of small farmers and artisans. By the time he died, and to a considerable extent because of his accomplishments, many artisans had become mill hands.

Three years after Slater's mill began operations, a young Yale graduate named Eli Whitney, visiting a Georgia plantation, devised the cotton gin, and this, in combination with English cotton mills and American ones like Slater's in New England, enormously stimulated the cotton economy (and the slave-labor system) of the South. Simultaneously, and paradoxically, Slater and Whitney helped fasten on the North an industrial economy which would defeat the South when the long-standing economic conflict between the two sections flared out at last in civil war.

The Black Slave Driver

Randall M. Miller

To be a slave must indeed have been a terrible experience. The hard labor in the service of another, the loss of liberty, the constant possibility of arbitrary punishment, the absence of the hope of much improvement in one's situation made life hard to bear for those caught up in the South's "peculiar institution." The system was so fundamentally unfair that the modern mind finds it difficult to understand how supposedly civilized people could have created and maintained it.

Because of the gap between our point of view toward slavery and that of Americans only a century and a quarter ago, and because of the obvious connection between the long existence of slavery in America and so many modern social problems, historians have devoted a great deal of effort to studying the institution. What has emerged from their research is a system far more complicated than appears on the surface. Slavery was a cruel form of exploitation for all its victims, but it affected these victims in many different ways. Almost as wide a variety of work patterns and human relations developed among the slaves and between the slaves and their masters as developed between workers and employers in those parts of the United States where slavery did not exist. In the following article Professor Randall M. Miller of St. Joseph's University describes the role of one "elite" slave type—the black slave driver. Professor Miller is the author of "Dear Master": Letters of a Slave Family.

Wise planters of the ante-bellum South never relaxed their search for talent among their slaves. The ambitious, intelligent, and proficient were winnowed out and recruited for positions of trust and responsibility. These privileged bondsmen—artisans, house servants, foremen—served as intermediaries between the master and the slave community; they exercised considerable power; they learned vital skills of survival in a complex, often hostile world. Knowing, as they did, the master's needs and vulnerabilities, they were the most dangerous of slaves; but they were also the most necessary.

None of these men in the middle has been more misunderstood than the slave driver, policeman of the fields and the quarters. To enforce discipline and guarantee performance in the fields, planters enlisted slave foremen or drivers. On large plantations they worked as assistants to the white overseers; on smaller units they served immediately under the master. Generally, they were of an imposing physical presence capable of commanding respect from the other slaves. Ex-slaves described the drivers as, for example, "a great, big cullud man," "a large tall, black man," "a burly fellow . . . severe in the extreme." Armed with a whip and outfitted in high leather boots and greatcoat, all emblematic of plantation authority, the driver exuded an aura of power.

The English traveler, Basil Hall, thought the driver had power more symbolic than real. The slaves knew better. With hardly repressed anger, ex-slave Adelaine Marshall condemned the black foremen at the Brevard plantation in Texas for "all de time whippin' and stroppin' de niggers to make dem work harder." Many other former slaves echoed this theme of driver brutality; accounts of mutilations, lacerations, burnings, and whippings fill the pages of the slave narratives. But physical coercion alone never moved slaves to industry. The drivers, therefore, were selected as men able to bargain, bribe, cajole, flatter, and only as a last resort, to flog the slaves to perform their tasks and refrain from acts destructive of order in the quarters.

Masters often conferred with their black slave drivers on matters of farming, or on social arrangements in the quarters, and often deferred to their advice. As the driver matured and became more knowledgeable, his relationship with his master became one of mutual regard, in sharp contrast to the master's less settled and more transient relationship with white overseers.

White overseers as well were frequently governed by the driver's counsel, although the relationship between these two species of foreman was sometimes strained. The overseer's insistence on steady work from the slaves, and the driver's interest in protecting his people from white abuses, placed the driver in the agonizing dilemma of torn loyalties and interest. In this conflict the driver often appealed to the master and won his support. A chorus of complaint from white Southern overseers alleged that planters trusted the black driver more than the overseer. The charge seems to have been justified. John Hartwell Cocke of Virginia regarded his driver as his "humble friend," but held overseers at arm's length. The astute agricultural reformer and planter, James H. Hammond, unabashedly acknowledged that he disregarded his overseer's testimony in many instances and instead heeded his driver, whom Hammond considered a "confidential servant" especially enjoined to guard against "any excesses or omissions of the overseer." Planters dismissed overseers as an expendable breed, and, indeed, overseers rarely lasted more than two or three seasons with any single master. The driver, however, stayed on indefinitely as the master's man, and some masters came to depend on him to an extraordinary degree.

Through the driver, the planter sought to inculcate the "proper" standards of work and behavior in his slaves. A few carefully enumerated the driver's duties, leaving him little discretion; but for most, formal rules were unknown, and broad policy areas were left to the driver's judgment. Although an overseer reviewed his work on large farms, the driver made many of the day-to-day decisions on farming as well as meting out rewards and punishments. By blowing on a bugle or horn, he woke up the slaves each morning. He determined the work pace; he directed the marling, plowing, terracing, planting, hoeing, picking, and innumerable other farming operations; he encouraged the slaves in their religious instruction and sometimes led devotions; he mediated family disputes. His duties varied from disciplinarian to family counselor or hygienist. The quick-witted driver who amputated the finger of a woman slave who had been bitten by a rattlesnake saved her life. More than this, he took over the function of the master as protector by making slaves instinctively look to him for aid in times of crisis. So, too, did the driver who held the keys to the plantation stores and parceled out the weekly rations to the slaves. Whatever changes might occur in white management, the basic daily functions of the plantation routine continued unbroken under the driver.

The slave driver had power. For favorites he might sneak extra rations or wink at minor indiscretions; for recalcitrants he might ruthlessly pursue every violation of the plantation code of conduct. But he wielded power only to a point, for when the driver's regime became tyrannical or overly dependent on brute force, he ceased to serve his purpose for the master or the slaves. Planters wanted stability and profits, not discord. Slaves wanted peace in the quarters and a minimum of white intrusion into their lives. A factious slave population sabotaged farming arrangements, ran off, or dissembled in countless ways. To ensure his continued rule, the driver had to curry favor in both camps, black and white. His justice must remain evenhanded, and his discipline rooted in something more enduring than the lash—namely community approbation.

In exchange for the driver's services, the planter compensated him with privileges, even offers of freedom. More immediately, planters tried to encourage the driver in a variety of small ways—with bits of praise, pats on the back, presents. They gave material rewards such as double rations, superior housing, and gifts for the driver's family. Some masters allowed their drivers to marry women "off the plantation," and a few drivers had more than one wife. Planters often set aside extra land for the driver's personal use, and allowed him to draft other slaves to tend his garden and cotton patch. He was usually permitted to sell the produce of his own garden in town for cash. Drivers also went to town to purchase supplies for the master, to do errands, and to transact business for the slaves. They often received cash payments of ten to several hundred dollars a year as gifts, or even wages. During winter months some drivers hired themselves out to earn extra money, and others learned trades with which to build personal estates. Conspicuous consumption heightened the driver's standing and gave sanction to his authority.

Who were these men, and how did they rise in the plantation hierarchy? A collective portrait of the slave driver drawn from slave narratives and planters' accounts yields little support for the generalized charge that drivers were brutish and isolated from their fellow slaves. Although some were kinfolks of other privileged bondsmen, many came from more humble origins. Few slaves were bred to be drivers, and fewer still were purchased for that reason. Most important, no pronounced sense of caste developed in the South to set off drivers from the rest of the slave community.

The awkward attempts of some planters to put distance between slave elites and field hands, by means of special clothes and indulgences, fooled no one. Drivers, after all, took their meals in the quarters, married and raised their families there, worshiped there, and frolicked there. The location of the driver's cabin at the head of the row, midway between the Big House and the quarters, placed the driver closest to the master symbolically, but his place remained in the quarters. Rather than suffer a driver with a puffed-up ego who had little rapport with the slaves, a master might even administer a whipping to him in front of the

In the early 1830s the Englishman Captain Basil Hall sketched these two black slave drivers as illustrations for his book of travel reminiscences.

others. Lashings, demotions, and other humiliations provided ample reminders that the driver was more slave than free.

Drivers were generally in their late thirties or early forties when appointed, and they usually held long tenures. Yet there were a few in their twenties and at least one in his teens. If the candidate was, as one planter wrote, "honest, industrious, not too talkative (which is a necessary qualification), a man of good sense, a good hand himself, and has been heretofore faithful in the discharge of whatever may have been committed to his care," he would do nicely. Whatever the strictures on verbosity, planters chose articulate men capable of communicating the master's wishes and values to the slaves with a minimum of distortion and at the same time able to relay accurately the messages and impulses of the slaves to the master. Thus one planter sent the driver along with a boatload of slaves divided from the rest by sale so that the driver could "jolly the negroes and give them confidence" and explain the master's side.

In reading black and white accounts of bondage, one is struck by the repeated references to the master's confidence in his black slave driver. He left his family alone with the driver, entrusted his comfort and well-being to his care, and gave the driver free rein in ordering the private affairs of his other slaves. One rice planter, R.F.W. Allston, a shrewd student of slave psychology, confirmed his driver in an impressive, formal ceremony of investiture blessed by a clergyman. William S. Pettigrew of North Carolina often reminded his drivers that their good "credit" depended on their faithful duty during his absence. This call for reciprocity worked in subtle ways to compel the driver to uphold the master's interest. Former driver Archer Alexander described his entrapment. He justified his loyalty to his master, who once sold two of his children away from him, by explaining that the master "trusted me every way, and I couldn't do no other than what was right."

Ambiguities of the driver's relationship with the master and the slaves are best illustrated in the one area he could not readily conceal from the overseer or the master—work. All masters demanded frequent performance reports from their drivers. Masters knew the slaves' minimal capacities, and they could corroborate the driver's testimony with private inspections of the field and with their own crop tallies after harvest. Aware of these facts, slaves conceded the driver's need to keep them moving, and forgave occasional excesses of zeal.

In assigning tasks or setting the work pace, the driver could push the slaves relentlessly to impress the master, apply the slaves' time to his private purposes, or manipulate the system to reward favorites and punish enemies. Those members of the driver's family who toiled in the fields usually drew light chores; as a rule they also escaped the lash. So did lovers. A slave woman who spurned a driver's advances, however, might find herself isolated in a remote section of the field, and thus vulnerable to the driver's amorous assaults, or assigned impossible tasks so that the vengeful driver could punish her under the guise of sound labor management.

In the face of driver abuses, however, no slave was wholly defenseless. If the driver unduly imposed on him, he might run to the master or overseer for relief. Enlightened planters advised against punishing a slave beyond the limits of reasonable service, because hard treatment brought forth scant improvement and much dissatisfaction. Drivers usually marked out tasks for each slave according to ability, and remained on the ground until everyone finished. Even the cruel driver had little personal interest in overmeasuring tasks, since unfinished work kept him in the fields. Moreover, unrealistic work demands might prompt a general flight to the swamps, sabotage, or worse.

As the lead man in the gang labor system, a thoughtful driver would set a steady pace—singing, shouting, cracking his whip, or working at the head of the gang. In this way the slaves could do their work in a manner that would both satisfy the master and reduce the driver's need to whip or embarrass the weaker, slower slaves. Slave accounts tell of men like Moses Bell, a driver on a wheat farm in Virginia, who helped one woman "cause she wasn't very strong"; or like the driver who countermanded his master's orders and sent a nursing mother back to her cabin because she was "too sick to work." Like any champion of the weak, the driver acquired stature in the eyes of the oppressed. Young slaves appreciated drivers like July Gist, who eased their transition to fieldwork and taught them how to avoid punishment. Gist stressed careful husbandry and never rushed the young slaves as they adapted to the rigors of plowing, hoeing, and picking from sunup to sundown.

Unwritten rules governed the driver's conduct. He must not whip with malice or without cause, for example. The driver who exceeded his authority and surpassed whites in viciousness produced bitterness and recalcitrance. Jane Johnson of South Carolina considered the driver "de devil setting' cross-legged for de rest of us on de plantation," and she could not believe that her master intended "for dat nigger to treat us like he did. He took 'vantage of his [the master] bein' 'way and talk soft when he come again." Slaves reserved special enmity for such drivers. After witnessing a driver lash his mother and aunt, Henry Cheatem swore "to kill dat nigger iffen it was de las' thing I eber done." Mary Reynolds despised Solomon for his savage whippings, and even more because he disrupted the slaves' "frolickin'" and religious meetings in the quarters. In her old age she consoled herself with the assurance that the driver was "burnin' in hell today, and it pleasures me to know it."

If masters or informal community pressures did not check abusive drivers, the slaves resorted to more direct remedies. For example, a host of Florida slaves plotted a mass escape from the driver Prince's blows. When discovered, several of the conspirators preferred incarceration to further subservience to Prince. Some slaves refused to be whipped or to have their families mistreated in any manner, and a driver who challenged them risked violent resistance. According to an Alabama driver who tried to correct an alleged shirker, the slave "flong down his cradle and made a oath and said that he had as live [lief] die as to live and he then tried to take the whip out of my hand." The slaves could return cruelty with cruelty. One group of Louisiana slaves murdered a driver by placing crushed glass in his food, and another killed their driver and cut him into small pieces to conceal the crime.

Many slaves, however, recognized that the driver whipped out of duty rather than desire. Moses Grandy, for example, refused to condemn harsh drivers because he understood that they must whip with "sufficient severity" to retain their posts and keep the lash off their own backs. Slaves would grant the driver that much provided that he showed no taste for it and did not whip when he was not obligated to do so. Many drivers deluded their masters by putting on grand exhibitions of zeal in the white men's presence. Some developed the art, as driver Solomon Northup described it, of "throwing the lash within a hair's breadth of the back, the ear, the nose, without, however, touching either of them." When his master was out of sight, "Ole" Gabe of Virginia whipped a post instead of the slaves while the ostensible victims howled for the master's benefit. He once cracked the post so loudly that his master yelled for him to desist lest he kill the slave, who then bolted screaming from the barn with berry juice streaming down his back. This so horrified the master that he threatened Gabe with a thrashing equal to the one he gave the slave.

The successful driver did not tattle on his people and he kept the white folks out of the slaves' private lives as much as possible. In the letters written by literate drivers to their masters, the drivers remained remarkably reticent on life in the quarters: the masters knew little about what went on there from sundown to sunup because the drivers, their principal agents, did not tell them. To be sure, severe fighting among the slaves and egregious crimes were impossible to conceal. By and large, however, the drivers successfully contained the breakdowns of plantation authority, and received sufficient cooperation from the slaves so that they would not be called upon to explain and to punish.

The conscientious driver widened his circle of friends by doing favors, overlooking faults, never breaking a promise, avoiding confrontations whenever possible, and working through the informal group structure to resolve disputes and problems. If clashes occurred—and they were inevitable in the elemental world of the plantation—the driver gave his opponents an opportunity to save face rather than shaming them. Sometimes he fattened the slaves' larder by pilfering for them from the plantation smokehouse, or arranged passes for them, ostensibly to attend religious meetings or to do chores, but in fact to visit relatives and friends on other plantations. In the quarters he left the correction of a wayward child to the child's parents, respected the slaves' religious leaders, mediated marital squabbles, and protected the weak from thieves and bullies. Slaves applauded the driver who broke up a boisterous, quarrelsome couple by placing them in separate cabins, thus restoring quiet to the quarters and saving the couple from sale at the hands of an irritated master. In brief, the driver acted the way any responsible community leader would act to keep his community intact and safe. He earned the slaves' trust. Ex-slave Billy Stammper summed up the feelings of many slaves toward the driver: "Cullud folks don' min' bein' bossed by er cullud man if he's smart an' good to em," which is to say, if he was smart enough to be good to them.

More than any other event, the Civil War tested the driver's loyalty and expanded his opportunities for self-aggrandizement and to help his people. With the menfolk away during the war, the Southern white lady and the black slave drivers assumed control of the plantations. Frustrated in their efforts to engage white overseers, masters ignored the laws and left their plantations in the hands

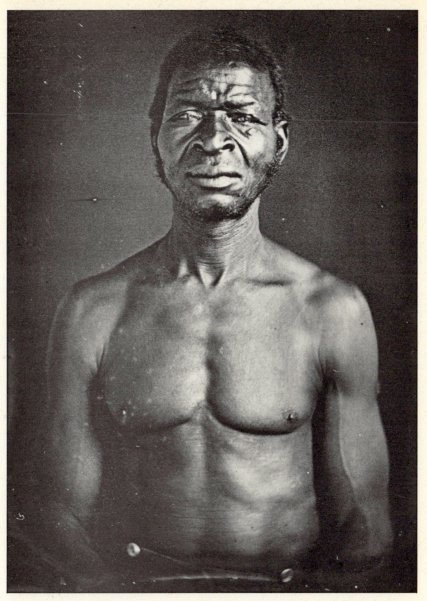

A rare early daguerrotype of "Jack (driver) Guinea, Plantation of B. F. Taylor, Esq." in Columbia, S. C. The picture was taken in 1852 by J. T. Zealy, who had been commissioned by Louis Agassiz, the prominent Harvard zoologist, to make a study of African-born slaves.

of house servants, older privileged bondsmen, or drivers of long service—men they could trust not to ravage their land or their women during their absence. In their diaries and later in their histories, planters congratulated themselves that they had not misplaced their trust. However romanticized, the stories of faithful retainers hiding the family silver and shielding the planter's family and homestead from Yankee depredations are legion.

But planters who wanted universal, unfeigned loyalty from their drivers asked for too much. In the midst of unraveling planter hegemony, slave foremen looked to their own interest. Some, like Edmund Ruffin's "faithful and intelligent" Jem Sykes, simply absconded. Some went alone; others inspired a general stampede. If they remained on the plantations, they sometimes took part in raids on the master's cellar and storehouse. In the absence of a strong white power the slaves neglected the upkeep of the farm and equipment and idled away their days as much as possible. Apparently, drivers could not or would not push their people under such circumstances. The worst excesses occurred in the sugar parishes of Louisiana, where drivers had commanded unusually harsh regimes. The Union advance in 1863 excited many slaves to flee the plantations, but not before they murdered some of their overseers and masters. One Rapides Parish planter wrote that the presence of Federal troops "turned the negroes crazy . . . and everything like subordination and restraint was at an end." The slaves slaughtered livestock and plundered furiously. In this, the drivers "everywhere have proved the worst negroes," perhaps in a bid to retain their leadership through exaggerated displays of violence.

Most drivers, however, remained calm. Conservative men by temperament, they were not about to launch a premature, perhaps suicidal, revolution. On the Chesnut plantation, for example, the drivers early expressed enthusiasm for the Confederate side, thus satisfying their master of their loyalty. In 1864, however, they declined an offer to fight for the Confederacy in exchange for freedom because, as Mrs. Chesnut sagely observed, "they are pretty sure of having it anyway."

Many masters found their drivers "much changed" by emancipation. An embittered Mary Jones of Georgia wrote of the metamorphosis of the driver Cato who headed up a black delegation demanding land: "Cato has been to me a most insolent, indolent, and dishonest man; I have not a shadow of confidence in him, and will not wish to retain him on the place." The Edmonstons of South Carolina found that with freedom their Henry, for fifteen years the master's "right-hand man," dropped his "affection and cheerful simplicity" and became "grasping" in his "exorbitant demands" for land. Where they remained as foremen over hired gangs of freedmen, they ingratiated themselves with their charges by easing up on work requirements and stealing for the hands. Much of their authority disappeared with emancipation. When Mrs. R. F. W. Allston visited the plantation of her brother-in-law in April, 1865, she confronted a sullen and insolent group of former slaves who had recently completed their plunder of the plantation provision houses. Mrs. Allston called for Jacob, the head man and sole manager of the estate during the war, and ordered him to give the keys to her. A "huge man" then stepped forward to warn Jacob that if he complied, "blood'll flow." Mrs. Allston departed without the keys.

The paternalistic order of the past was rapidly disrupted by impersonal economic forces in the prostrate postwar South. Planters attempted to lock their former slaves into long-term labor contracts, and looked to the drivers to hold the people on the farms. But neither drivers nor slaves would stay under such conditions. Some owners, short of capital, divided their holdings into tenant parcels and installed a black family on each, sharing the crops of each parcel with the tenant after the harvest. There was, however, no room in this arrangement for the driver.

But with the possible exception of the former slave artisans, the former driver was the most qualified freedman to survive on his own. Indeed, for devotees of Horatio Alger, some former drivers provided inspiring, if somewhat scaled-down, models of success. The story of Limus, a former driver on the sea islands of South Carolina, is a case in point. A "black Yankee" in habits and values, the fifty-year-old freedman started with his one-half acre plot and a beaten-down horse, and raised vegetables and poultry for the Hilton Head market nearby. He also hunted and fished to supplement his income and his family's diet. With two wives and two families to support, he could hardly afford to relax. He worked fourteen acres of cotton on abandoned land to the three to six acres of his fellow freedmen. He also purchased a large boat on which he transported passengers and produce to Hilton Head. His prior marketing experience as a driver stood him in good stead as he negotiated contracts with whites and blacks alike, and he established himself as the principal supplier for the Union troops stationed in the area. By practicing ruthless underconsumption and efficient management, he saved almost five hundred dollars in his first year of freedom, money which he plowed back into his enterprises.

Some drivers had received gifts of cash and land during slavery from which they could build their estates in freedom; they were able to exploit old relationships for credit; they had learned marketing skills and how to deal with whites in a cash economy, so that they were not so easily cheated or overawed by whites after the war; they understood every level of farm management and practice; and with the artisans they were the slaves most likely to have imbibed the Protestant work ethic of self-denial and persevering labor. If alert and lucky, they could turn the limited opportunities of freedom to their pecuniary gain, provided they did not alienate their benefactors. Recognizing this continued dependence on white aid, one driver warned his fellow freedmen to ignore carpetbagger blandishments, for the "outsiders" would "start a graveyard" if they persuaded blacks to "sass" whites. Even in freedom the former driver straddled two worlds.

The experience of the slave driver should remind us that slavery affected each slave differently—that to fathom the complexities and subtleties of the peculiar institution and those trapped within it, we must take into account each slave's occupational role, his place in the slave and plantation hierarchy, his manner of interaction with the white and black communities, his self-image, to name the most obvious factors. Slave drivers have not fared well in our histories of American Negro slavery. The prevailing neo-abolitionist historiography has limned a portrait of the driver as an unscrupulous, brutal, even sadistic betrayer of his race. He was nothing of the sort. While the driver's behavior was sometimes extreme, it strikingly exemplified the ambiguities and paradoxes of the slave system. Drivers did not brood in self-pity or guilt over their miserable condition and the heavy demands made on them from above and below. They took their world for granted and made the best out of a bad situation. They had to do so. Both white and black depended on the man in the middle.

PART SEVEN

Civil War and Reconstruction

Quite innocent of war, these Confederate volunteers struck bold poses before the First Battle of Bull Run in 1861.

Soldiering in the Civil War

Bruce Catton

 Surely one of the most "popular" of American historians was Bruce Catton, the first editor of American Heritage *magazine, whose books about the Civil War have been read and enjoyed by hundreds of thousands of persons. Yet Catton based his books on meticulous research in archives and old attics, and his analyses of events and individuals have been widely praised by Civil War scholars.*

One of the reasons for Catton's success was his ability to understand the Civil War both in broad strategic terms and also as a human conflict, full of tragedy, bravery, and humor. This essay provides us with a graphic portrait of the ordinary soldier, Union and Confederate. From dozens of anecdotes and small details one gathers a general impression, vivid yet with a sense of its universal applicability, of what it was like to fight in that epic struggle. At the same time—and it is one of the infallible marks of a good historian—Catton saw the "G.I." of the 1860s from a modern perspective and was thus able to explain why he acted and believed as he did.

T he volunteer soldier in the American Civil War used a clumsy muzzle-loading rifle, lived chiefly on salt pork and hardtack, and retained to the very end a loose-jointed, informal attitude toward the army with which he had cast his lot. But despite all of the surface differences, he was at bottom blood brother to the G.I. Joe of modern days.

Which is to say that he was basically, and incurably, a civilian in arms. A volunteer, he was still a soldier because he had to be one, and he lived for the day when he could leave the army forever. His attitude toward discipline, toward his officers, and toward the whole spit-and-polish concept of military existence was essentially one of careless tolerance. He refused to hate his enemies—indeed, he often got along with them much better than with some of his own comrades—and his indoctrination was often so imperfect that what was sometimes despairingly said of the American soldier in World War II would apply equally to him: he seemed to be fighting chiefly so that he could some day get back to Mom's cooking.

What really set the Civil War soldier apart was the fact that he came from a less sophisticated society. He was no starry-eyed innocent, to be sure—or, if he was, the army quickly took care of that—but the America of the 1860's was less highly developed than modern America. It lacked the ineffable advantages of radio, television, and moving pictures. It was still essentially a rural nation; it had growing cities, but they were smaller and somehow less urban than today's cities;

a much greater percentage of the population lived on farms or in country towns and villages than is the case now, and there was more of a backwoods, hay-seed-in-the-hair flavor to the people who came from them.

For example: every war finds some ardent youngsters who want to enlist despite the fact that they are under the military age limit of eighteen. Such a lad today simply goes to the recruiting station, swears that he is eighteen, and signs up. The lad of the 1860's saw it a little differently. He could not swear that he was eighteen when he was only sixteen; in his innocent way, he felt that to lie to his own government was just plain wrong. But he worked out a little dodge that got him into the army anyway. He would take a bit of paper, scribble the number *18* on it, and put it in the sole of his shoe. Then, when the recruiting officer asked him how old he was, he could truthfully say: "I am *over* eighteen." That was a common happening, early in the Civil War; one cannot possibly imagine it being tried today.

Similarly, the drill sergeants repeatedly found that among the raw recruits there were men so abysmally untaught that they did not know left from right, and hence could not step off on the left foot as all soldiers should. To teach these lads how to march, the sergeants would tie a wisp of hay to the left foot and a wisp of straw to the right; then, setting the men to march, they would chant, "Hay-foot, straw-foot, hay-foot, straw-foot"—and so on, until everybody had caught on. A common name for a green recruit in those days was "strawfoot."

On the drill field, when a squad was getting basic training, the men were as likely as not to intone a little rhythmic chant as they tramped across the sod—thus:

March! March! March old soldier march!
Hayfoot, strawfoot,
Belly-full of bean soup—
March old soldier march!

Because of his unsophistication, the ordinary soldier in the Civil War, North and South alike, usually joined up with very romantic ideas about soldiering. Army life rubbed the romance off just as rapidly then as it does now, but at the start every volunteer went into the army thinking that he was heading off to high adventure. Under everything else, he enlisted because he thought army life was going to be fun, and usually it took quite a few weeks in camp to disabuse him of this strange notion. Right at the start, soldiering had an almost idyllic quality; if this quality faded rapidly, the memory of it remained through all the rest of life.

Early days in camp simply cemented the idea. An Illinois recruit, writing home from training camp, confessed: "It is fun to lie around, face unwashed, hair uncombed, shirt unbuttoned and everything uneverythinged. It sure beats clerking." Another Illinois boy confessed: "I don't see why people will stay at home when they can get to soldiering. A year of it is worth getting shot for to any man." And a Massachusetts boy, recalling the early days of army life, wrote that "Our drill, as I remember it, consisted largely of running around the Old Westbury town hall, yelling like Devils and firing at an imaginary foe." One of the commonest discoveries that comes from a reading of Civil War diaries is that the chief worry, in training camp, was a fear that the war would be over before the ardent young recruits could get into it. It is only fair to say that most of the diarists looked back on this innocent worry, a year or so afterward, with rueful amusement.

There was a regiment recruited in northern Pennsylvania in 1861—13th Pennsylvania Reserves officially, known to the rest of the Union Army as the Bucktails because the rookies decorated their caps with strips of fur from the carcass of a deer that was hanging in front of a butcher shop near their camp—and in mid-spring these youthful soldiers were ordered to rendezvous at Harrisburg. So they marched cross-country (along a road known today as the Bucktail Trail) to the north branch of the Susquehanna, where they built rafts. One raft, for the colonel, was made oversized with a stable; the colonel's horse had to ride, too. Then the Bucktails floated down the river, singing and firing their muskets and having a gay old time, camping out along the bank at night, and finally they got to Harrisburg; and they served through the worst of the war, getting badly shot up and losing most of their men to Confederate bullets, but they never forgot the picnic air of those first days of army life, when they drifted down a river through the forests, with a song in the air and the bright light of adventure shining just ahead. Men do not go to war that way nowadays.

Discipline in those early regiments was pretty sketchy. The big catch was that most regiments were recruited locally—in one town, or one county, or in one part of a city—and everybody more or less knew everybody else. Particularly, the privates knew their officers—most of whom were elected to their jobs by the enlisted men—and they never saw any sense in being formal with them. Within reasonable limits, the Civil War private was willing to do what his company commander told him to do, but he saw little point in carrying it to extremes.

So an Indiana soldier wrote: "We had enlisted to put down the Rebellion, and had no patience with the red-tape tomfoolery of the regular service. The boys recognized no superiors, except in the line of legitimate duty. Shoulder straps waived, a private was ready at the drop of a hat to thrash his commander—a thing that occurred more than once." A New York regiment, drilling on a hot parade ground, heard a private address his company commander thus: "Say, Tom, let's quit this darn foolin' around and go over to the sutler's and get a drink." There was very little of the "Captain, sir" business in those armies. If a company or regimental officer got anything especial in the way of obedience, he got it because the enlisted men recognized him as a natural leader and superior and not just because he had a commission signed by Abraham Lincoln.

Odd rivalries developed between regiments. (It should be noted that the Civil War soldier's first loyalty went usually to his regiment, just as a navy man's loyalty goes to his ship; he liked to believe that his regiment was better than all others, and he would fight for it, any time and anywhere.) The army legends of those days tell of a Manhattan regiment, camped near Washington, whose nearest neighbor was a regiment from Brooklyn, with which the Manhattanites nursed a deep rivalry. Neither regiment had a chaplain; and there came to the Manhattan colonel one day a minister, who volunteered to hold religious services for the men in the ranks.

The colonel doubted that this would be a good idea. His men, he said, were

A haunting face from a lost generation: Georgia Private Edwin Jennison, killed at Malvern Hill.

rather irreligious, not to say godless, and he feared they would not give the reverend gentlemen a respectful hearing. But the minister said he would take his chances; after all, he had just held services with the Brooklyn regiment, and the men there had been very quiet and devout. That was enough for the colonel. What the Brooklyn regiment could do, his regiment could do. He ordered the men paraded for divine worship, announcing that any man who talked, laughed, or even coughed would be summarily court-martialed.

So the clergyman held services, and everyone was attentive. At the end of the sermon, the minister asked if any of his hearers would care to step forward and make public profession of faith; in the Brooklyn regiment, he said, fourteen men had done this. Instantly the New York colonel was on his feet.

"Adjutant!" he bellowed. "We're not going to let that damn Brooklyn regiment beat us at anything. Detail twenty men and have them baptized at once!"

Each regiment seemed to have its own mythology, tales which may have been false but which, by their mere existence, reflected faithfully certain aspects of army life. The 48th New York, for instance, was said to have an unusually large number of ministers in its ranks, serving not as chaplains but as combat soldiers. The 48th, fairly early in the war, found itself posted in a swamp along the South Carolina coast, toiling mightily in semitropical heat, amid clouds of mosquitoes, to build fortifications, and it was noted that all hands became excessively profane, including the one-time clergymen. A visiting general, watching the regiment at work one day, recalled the legend and asked the regiment's lieutenant colonel if he himself was a minister in private life.

"Well, no, General," said the officer apologetically. "I can't say that I was a regularly ordained minister. I was just one of these————local preachers."

Another story was hung on this same 48th New York. A Confederate ironclad gunboat was supposed to be ready to steam through channels in the swamp and attack the 48th's outposts, and elaborate plans were made to trap it with obstructions in the channel, a tangle of ropes to snarl the propellers, and so on. But it occurred to the colonel that even if the gunboat was trapped the soldiers could not get into it; it was sheathed in iron, all its ports would be closed, and men with axes could never chop their way into it. Then the colonel had an inspiration. Remembering that many of his men had been recruited from the less savory districts of New York City, he paraded the regiment and (according to legend) announced:

"Now men, you've been in this cursed swamp for two weeks—up to your ears in mud, no fun, no glory and blessed poor pay. Here's a chance. Let every man who has had experience as a cracksman or a safeblower step to the front." To the last man, the regiment marched forward four paces and came expectantly to attention.

Not unlike this was the reputation of the 6th New York, which contained so many Bowery toughs that the rest of the army said a man had to be able to show that he had done time in prison in order to get into the regiment. It was about to leave for the South, and the colonel gave his men an inspirational talk. They were going, he said, to a land of wealthy plantation owners, where each Southerner had riches of which he could be despoiled; and he took out his own gold watch and held it up for all to see, remarking that any deserving soldier could easily get one like it, once they got down to plantation-land. Half an hour later, wishing to see what time it was, he felt for his watch . . . and it was gone.

If the Civil War army spun queer tales about itself, it had to face a reality which, in all of its aspects, was singularly unpleasant. One of the worst aspects had to do with food.

From first to last, the Civil War armies enlisted no men as cooks, and there were no cooks' and bakers' schools to help matters. Often enough, when in camp, a company would simply be issued a quantity of provisions—flour, pork, beans, potatoes, and so on—and invited to prepare the stuff as best it could. Half a dozen men would form a mess, members would take turns with the cooking, and everybody had to eat what these amateurs prepared or go hungry. Later in the war, each company commander would usually detail two men to act as cooks for the company, and if either of the two happened to know anything about cooking the company was in luck. One army legend held that company officers usually detailed the least valuable soldiers to this job, on the theory that they would do less harm in the cook shack than anywhere else. One soldier, writing after the war, asserted flatly: "A company cook is a most peculiar being; he generally knows less about cooking than any other man in the company. Not being able to learn the drill, and too dirty to appear on inspection, he is sent to the cook house to get him out of the ranks."

When an army was on the march, the ration issue usually consisted of salt pork, hardtack, and coffee. (In the Confederate Army the coffee was often missing, and the hardtack was frequently replaced by corn bread; often enough the meal was not sifted, and stray bits of cob would appear in it.) The hardtack was good enough, if fresh, which was not always the case; with age it usually got infested with weevils, and veterans remarked that it was better to eat it in the dark.

In the Union Army, most of the time, the soldier could supplement his rations (if he had money) by buying extras from the sutler—the latter being a civilian merchant licensed to accompany the army, functioning somewhat as the regular post exchange functions nowadays. The sutler charged high prices and specialized in indigestibles like pies, canned lobster salad, and so on; and it was noted that men who patronized him regularly came down with stomach upsets. The Confederate Army had few sutlers, which helps to explain why the hungry Confederates were so delighted when they could capture a Yankee camp: to seize a sutler's tent meant high living for the captors, and the men in Lee's army were furious when, in the 1864 campaign, they learned that General Grant had ordered the Union Army to move without sutlers. Johnny Reb felt that Grant was really taking an unfair advantage by cutting off this possible source of supply.

If Civil War cooking arrangements were impromptu and imperfect, the same applied to its hospital system. The surgeons, usually, were good men by the standards of that day—which were low since no one on earth knew anything about germs or about how wounds became infected, and antisepsis in the operating room was a concept that had not yet come into existence; it is common to read of a surgeon whetting his scalpel on the sole of his shoe just before operating.

But the hospital attendants, stretcher-bearers, and the like were chosen just as the company cooks were chosen; that is, they were detailed from the ranks, and the average officer selected the most worthless men he had simply because he wanted to get rid of men who could not be counted on in combat. As a result, sick or wounded men often got atrocious care.

A result of all of this—coupled with the fact that many men enlisted without being given any medical examinations—was that every Civil War regiment was suffered a constant wastage from sickness. On paper, a regiment was supposed to have a strength ranging between 960 and 1,040 men; actually, no regiment ever got to the battlefield with anything like that strength, and since there was no established system for sending in replacements a veteran regiment that could must 350 enlisted men present for duty was considered pretty solid. From first to last, approximately twice as many Civil War soldiers died of disease—typhoid, dysentery, and pneumonia were the great killers—as died in action; and in addition to those who died a great many more got medical discharges.

In its wisdom, the Northern government set up a number of base hospitals in Northern states, far from the battle fronts, on the theory that a man recovering from wounds or sickness would recuperate better back home. Unfortunately, the hospitals thus established were under local control, and the men in them were no longer under the orders of their own regiments or armies. As a result, thou-

A drawing of Confederate soldiers carousing in camp typifies the casual discipline of both Northern and Southern soldiers.

sands of men who were sent north for convalescence never returned to the army. Many were detailed for light work at the hospitals, and in these details they stayed because nobody had the authority to extract them and send them back to duty. Others, recovering their health, simply went home and stayed there. They were answerable to the hospital authorities, not to the army command, and the hospital authorities rarely cared very much whether they returned to duty or not. The whole system was ideally designed to make desertion easy.

On top of all of this, many men had very little understanding of the requirements of military discipline. A homesick boy often saw nothing wrong in leaving the army and going home to see the folks for a time. A man from a farm might slip off to go home and put in a crop. In neither case would the man look on himself as a deserter; he meant to return, he figured he would get back in time for any fighting that would take place, and in his own mind he was innocent of any wrongdoing. But in many cases the date of return would be postponed from week to week; the man might end as a deserter, even though he had not intended to be one when he left.

This merely reflected the loose discipline that prevailed in Civil War armies, which in turn reflected the underlying civilian-mindedness that pervaded the rank and file. The behavior of Northern armies on the march in Southern territory reflected the same thing—and, in the end, had a profound effect on the institution of chattel slavery.

Armies of occupation always tend to bear down hard on civilian property in enemy territory. Union armies in the Civil War, being imperfectly disciplined to begin with—and suffering, furthermore, from a highly defective rationing system—bore down with especial fervor. Chickens, hams, cornfields, anything edible that might be found on a Southern plantation, looked like fair game, and the loose fringe of stragglers that always trailed around the edges of a moving Union army looted with a fine disregard for civilian property rights.

This was made all the more pointed by the fact that the average Northern soldier, poorly indoctrinated though he was, had strong feelings about the evils of secession. To his mind, the Southerners who sought to set up a nation of their own were in rebellion against the best government mankind had ever known. Being rebels, they had forfeited their rights; if evil things happened to them that (as the average Northern soldier saw it) was no more than just retribution. This meant that even when the army command tried earnestly to prevent looting and individual foraging the officers at company and regimental levels seldom tried very hard to carry out the high command's orders.

William Tecumseh Sherman has come down in history as the very archetype of the Northern soldier who believed in pillage and looting; yet during the first years of the war Sherman resorted to all manner of ferocious punishments to keep his men from despoiling Southern property. He had looters tied up by the thumbs, ordered courtsmartial, issued any number of stern orders—and all to very little effect. Long before he adopted the practice of commandeering or destroying Southern property as a war measure, his soldiers were practicing it against his will, partly because discipline was poor and partly because they saw nothing wrong with it.

It was common for a Union colonel, as his regiment made camp in a Southern state, to address his men, pointing to a nearby farm, and say: "Now, boys, that barn is full of nice fat pigs and chickens. I don't want to see any of you take any of them"—whereupon he would fold his arms and look sternly in the opposite direction. It was also common for a regimental commander to read, on parade, some ukase from higher authority forbidding foraging, and then to wink solemnly—a clear hint that he did not expect anyone to take the order seriously. One colonel, punishing some men who had robbed a chicken house, said angrily: "Boys, I want you to understand that I am not punishing you for stealing but for getting caught at it."

It is more than a century since that war was fought, and things look a little different now than they looked at the time. At this distance, it may be possible to look indulgently on the wholesale foraging in which Union armies indulged; to the Southern farmers who bore the brunt of it, the business looked very ugly indeed. Many a Southern family saw the foodstuffs needed for the winter swept away in an hour by grinning hoodlums who did not need and could not use a quarter of what they took. Among the foragers there were many lawless characters who took watches, jewels, and any other valuable they could find; it is recorded that a squad would now and then carry a piano out to the lawn, take it apart, and use the wires to hang pots and pans over the campfire. . . . The Civil War was really romantic only at a considerable distance.

Underneath his feeling that it was good to add chickens and hams to the army ration, and his belief that civilians in a state of secession could expect no better

Combat artist Alfred Waud made this sketch of the results of a foraging expedition by Northern troops in Virginia.

fate, the Union soldier also came to believe that to destroy Southern property was to help win the war. Under orders, he tore up railroads and burned warehouses; it was not long before he realized that anything that damaged the Confederate economy weakened the Confederate war effort, so he rationalized his looting and foraging by arguing that it was a step in breaking the Southern will to resist. It is at this point that the institution of human slavery enters the picture.

Most Northern soldiers had very little feeling against slavery as such, and very little sympathy for the Negro himself. They thought they were fighting to save the Union, not to end slavery, and except for New England troops most Union regiments contained very little abolition sentiment. Nevertheless, the soldiers moved energetically and effectively to destroy slavery, not because they especially intended to but simply because they were out to do all the damage they could do. They were operating against Southern property—and the most obvious, important, and easily removable property of all was the slave. To help the slaves get away from the plantation was, clearly, to weaken Southern productive capacity, which in turn weakened Confederate armies. Hence the Union soldier, wherever he went, took the peculiar institution apart, chattel by chattel.

As a result, slavery had been fatally weakened long before the war itself came to an end. The mere act of fighting the war killed it. Of all institutions on earth, the institution of human slavery was the one least adapted to survive a war. It could not survive the presence of loose-jointed, heavy-handed armies of occupation. It may hardly be too much too say that the mere act of taking up arms in slavery's defense doomed slavery.

Above and beyond everything else, of course, the business of the Civil War soldier was to fight. He fought with weapons that look very crude to modern eyes, and he moved by an outmoded system of tactics, but the price he paid when he got into action was just as high as the price modern soldiers pay despite the almost infinite development of firepower since the 1860's.

Standard infantry weapon in the Civil War was the rifled Springfield—a muzzle-loader firing a conical lead bullet, usually of .54 caliber.

To load was rather laborious, and it took a good man to get off more than two shots a minute. The weapon had a range of nearly a mile, and its "effective range"—that is, the range at which it would hit often enough to make infantry fire truly effective—was figured at about 250 yards. Compared with a modern Garand, the old muzzle-loader is no better than a museum piece; but compared with all previous weapons—the weapons on which infantry tactics in the 1860's were still based—it was a fearfully destructive and efficient piece.

For the infantry of that day still moved and fought in formations dictated in the old days of smoothbore muskets, whose effective range was no more than 100 yards and which were wildly inaccurate at any distance. Armies using those weapons attacked in solid mass formations, the men standing, literally, elbow to elbow. They could get from effective range to hand-to-hand fighting in a very short time, and if they had a proper numerical advantage over the defensive line they could come to grips without losing too many men along the way. But in the Civil War the conditions had changed radically; men would be hit while the rival lines were still half a mile apart, and to advance in mass was simply to invite wholesale

Winslow Homer's sketch of Union troops on the firing line portrays the kind of mass formations vulnerable to the Civil War's improved weaponry.

destruction. Tactics had not yet been adjusted to the new rifles; as a result, Civil War attacks could be fearfully costly, and when the defenders dug entrenchments and got some proteciton—as the men learned to do, very quickly—a direct frontal assault could be little better than a form of mass suicide.

It took the high command a long time to revise tactics to meet this changed situation, and Civil War battles ran up dreadful casualty lists. For an army to lose 25 per cent of its numbers in a major battle was by no means uncommon, and in some fights—the Confederate army at Gettysburg is an outstanding example—the percentage of loss ran close to one third of the total number engaged. Individual units were sometimes nearly wiped out. Some of the Union and Confederate regiments that fought at Gettysburg lost up to 80 per cent of their numbers; a regiment with such losses was usually wrecked, as an effective fighting force, for the rest of the war.

The point of all of which is that the discipline which took the Civil War soldier into action, while it may have been very sketchy by modern standards, was nevertheless highly effective on the field of battle. Any armies that could go through such battles as Antietam, Stone's River, Franklin or Chickamauga and come back for more had very little to learn about the business of fighting.

Perhaps the Confederate General D. H. Hill said it, once and for all. The battle of Malvern Hill, fought on the Virginia peninsula early in the summer of 1862, finished the famous Seven Days campaign, in which George B. McClellan's Army of the Potomac was driven back from in front of Richmond by Robert E. Lee's Army of Northern Virginia. At Malvern Hill, McClellan's men fought a rear-guard action—a bitter, confused fight which came at the end of a solid week of wearing, costly battles and forced marches. Federal artillery wrecked the Confederate assault columns, and at the end of the day Hill looked out over the battlefield, strewn with dead and wounded boys. Shaking his head, and reflecting on the valor in attack and in defense which the two armies had displayed, Hill never forgot about this. Looking back on it, long after the war was over, he declared, in substance:

"Give me Confederate infantry and Yankee artillery and I'll whip the world!"

The South's Inner Civil War

Eric Foner

That the Civil War divided the nation is a commonplace, but it involved divisions far more complicated than the obvious split between North and South. In both the Union and the Confederacy, the people were far from unanimous in their support of the conflict. Opposition to the war in the North has been studied at length, but most people and indeed many historians have assumed that the Southerners, fighting to defend not only their way of life but their homes against northern "invaders," were united in support of the Confederacy. The decision of Colonel Robert E. Lee, who despite his devotion to the United States and his dislike of slavery resigned his commission and offered his services to the Confederacy when his state, Virginia, seceded, has been seen as typical.

That the South was in fact badly divided by the conflict is convincingly demonstrated by this essay by Professor Eric Foner of Columbia University. In addition to pointing out what should have been obvious, that black Southerners were overwhelmingly pro-Union, Foner shows that large elements in the white population also opposed first secession and then the vigorous conduction of the war. Professor Foner's book, Reconstruction: America's Unfinished Revolution, 1863–1877, *won a Bancroft Prize and many other honors.*

A mericans tend to think of the Civil War as a titanic struggle between two regions of the country, one united in commitment to the Union, the other equally devoted to its own nationhood. Yet neither North nor South was truly unified. Lincoln was constantly beset by draft resistance, peace sentiment, and resentment of the immense economic changes unleashed by the war. Internal dissent was, if anything, even more widespread in the wartime South. Not only did the four million slaves identify with the Union cause, but large numbers of white Southerners came to believe that they had more to lose from a continuation of the war than from a Northern victory. Indeed, scholars today consider the erosion of the will to fight as important a cause of Confederate defeat as the South's inferiority in manpower and industrial resources. Even as it waged a desperate struggle for independence, the Confederacy was increasingly divided against itself.

This was a matter of conflict more than simple warweariness. The South's inner civil war reflected how wartime events and Confederate policies eventually reacted upon the region's distinctive social and political structure. Like a massive earthquake, the Civil War and the destruction of slavery permanently altered the landscape of Southern life, exposing and widening fault lines that had lain barely visible just beneath the surface. The most profound revolution, of course, was the destruction of slavery. But white society after the war was transformed no less fully than black.

From the earliest days of settlement, there had never been a single white South. In 1860 a majority of white Southerners lived not in the plantation belt but in the upcountry, an area of small farmers and herdsmen who owned few slaves or none at all. Self-sufficiency remained the primary goal of these farm families, a large majority of whom owned their land. Henry Warren, a Northerner who settled in Leake County in Mississippi's hill country after the war, recalled white families attending church "dressed in homespun cloth, the product of the spinning wheel and hand loom, with which so many of the log cabins of that section were at that time equipped." This economic order, far removed from the lavish world of the great planters, gave rise to a distinctive subculture that celebrated mutuality, egalitarianism (for whites), and proud independence. But so long as slavery and planter rule did not interfere with the yeomanry's self-sufficient agriculture and local independence, the latent class conflict among whites failed to find coherent expression.

It was in the secession crisis and subsequent Civil War that upcountry yeomen discovered themselves as a political class. The elections for delegates to secession conventions in the winter of 1860–61 produced massive repudiations of disunion in yeoman areas. Once the war had begun, most of the South's white population rallied to the Confederate cause. But from the outset disloyalty was rife in the Southern mountains. Virginia's western counties seceded from the Old Dominion in 1861 and two years later reentered the Union as a separate state.

In East Tennessee, long conscious of its remoteness from the rest of the state, supporters of the Confederacy formed a small minority. This mountainous area contained a quarter of the state's population but had long been overshadowed economically and politically by the wealthier, slave-owning counties to the west. A majority of Tennessee's white opposed secession, although once war had begun a popular referendum supported joining the Confederacy. But East Tennessee still voted, by a two-to-one margin, to remain within the Union. Indeed, a convention of mountain Unionists declared the state's secession null and void and "not binding" on "loyal citizens." The delegates called for the region's secession from the state (an idea dating back to the proposed state of Franklin in the 1780s). Andrew Johnson, who had grown to manhood there, was the only United States senator from a seceding state to remain at his post in Washington once the war had begun, and in August 1861 East Tennessee voters elected three Unionists to represent them in the federal Congress.

Meanwhile, almost every county in the region saw Unionist military companies established to disrupt the Confederate war effort. In July 1861 the local political leader William B. Carter traveled to Washington, where he proposed to President Lincoln that Unionists try to cut East Tennessee off from the rest of the Confederacy by burning railroad bridges. Carter later claimed that Gen. George B. McClellan promised that once this had been done, a Federal army would liberate the area.

Carter's plan proved to be a disaster for East Tennessee Unionists. Four bridges were in fact burned, but others proved too heavily guarded. In one case

The Unionist William Brownlow became governor of Tennessee.

Unionists overpowered the Confederate guards only to discover that they had misplaced their matches. And it was a Confederate army, not a Union one, that invaded East Tennessee in force after these incidents. Several men were seized and summarily executed, and hundreds of Unionists were thrown in jail. The result was a massive flight of male citizens from the region. Many who made their way through the mountains to safety subsequently returned as members of the Union army. Felix A. Reeve, for example, one of the earliest exiles, reentered East Tennessee in 1863 at the head of the 8th Regiment of Tennessee Infantry. All told, some thirty-one thousand white Tennesseans eventually joined the Union army. Tennessee was one of the few Southern states from which more whites than blacks enlisted to fight for the Union.

Throughout the war East Tennessee remained the most conspicuous example of discontent within the Confederacy. But other mountain counties also rejected secession from the outset. One citizen of Winston County in the northern Alabama hill country believed yeomen had no business fighting for a planter-dominated Confederacy: "all tha want is to git you . . . to fight for their infurnal negroes and after you do their fightin' you may kiss their hine parts for o tha care." On July 4, 1861, a convention of three thousand residents voted to take Winston out of the Confederacy; if a state could withdraw from the Union, they declared, a county had the same right to secede from a state. Unionists here carried local elections and formed volunteer military bands that resisted Confederate enlistment officers and sought to protect local families from harassment by secessionists.

Georgia's mountainous Rabun County was "almost a unit against secession." As one local resident recalled in 1865, "You cannot find a people who were more averse to secession than were the people of our county. . . . I canvassed the county in 1860–61 myself and I know that there were not exceeding twenty men in this county who were in favor of secession." Secret Union organizations also flourished in the Ozark Mountains of northern Arkansas. More than one hundred members of the Peace and Constitutional Society were arrested late in 1861 and given the choice of jail or enlisting in the Confederate army. As in East Tennessee, many residents fled, and more than eight thousand men eventually served in Union regiments.

Discontent developed more slowly outside the mountains. It was not simply devotion to the Union but the impact of the war and the consequences of Confederate policies that awakened peace sentiment and social conflict. In any society war demands sacrifice, and public support often rests on the conviction that sacrifice is equitably shared. But the Confederate government increasingly molded its policies in the interest of the planters.

Within the South the most crucial development of the early years of the war was the disintegration of slavery. War, it has been said, is the midwife of revolution, and whatever politicians and military commanders might decree, slaves saw the conflict as heralding the end of bondage. Three years into the conflict Gen. William T. Sherman encountered a black Georgian who summed up the slaves' understanding of the war from its outset: "He said . . . he had been looking for the 'angel of the Lord' ever since he was knee-high, and, though we professed to be fighting for the Union, he supposed that slavery was the cause, and that our success was to be his freedom." On the basis of this conviction, the slaves took actions that not only propelled the reluctant North down the road to emancipation but severely exacerbated the latent class conflict within the white South.

As the Union army occupied territory on the periphery of the Confederacy, first in Virginia, then in Tennessee, Louisiana, and elsewhere, slaves by the thousands headed for the Union lines. Long before the Emancipation Proclamation slaves grasped that the presence of occupying troops destroyed the coercive power of both the individual master and the slaveholding community. On Magnolia Plantation in Louisiana, for example, the arrival of the Union army in 1862 sparked a work stoppage and worse. "We have a terrible state of affairs here," reported one planter. "Negroes refusing to work. . . . The negroes have erected a gallows in the quarters and [say] they must drive their master . . . off the plantation hang their master etc. and that then they will be free."

Even in the heart of the Confederacy, far from Federal troops, the conflict undermined the South's "peculiar institution." Their "grapevine telegraph" kept many slaves remarkably well informed about the war's progress. And the drain of white men into military service left plantations under the control of planters' wives and elderly and infirm men, whose authority slaves increasingly felt able to challenge. Reports of "demoralized" and "insubordinate" behavior multiplied throughout the South. Slavery, Confederate Vice-President Alexander H. Stephens proudly affirmed, was the cornerstone of the Confederacy. Accordingly, slavery's disintegration compelled the Confederate government to take steps to save the institution, and these policies, in turn, sundered white society.

The impression that planters were not bearing their fair share of the war's burdens spread quickly in the upcountry. Committed to Southern independence, most planters were also devoted to the survival of plantation slavery, and when these goals clashed, the latter often took precedence. After a burst of Confederate patriotism in 1861, increasing numbers of planters resisted calls for a shift from cotton to food production, even as the course of the war and the drain of manpower undermined the subsistence economy of the upcountry, threatening soldiers' families with destitution. When Union forces occupied New Orleans in 1862 and extended their control of the Mississippi Valley in 1863, large numbers of planters, merchants, and factors salvaged their fortunes by engaging in cotton traffic with the Yankee occupiers. Few demonstrated such unalloyed self-interest as James L. Alcorn, Mississippi's future Republican governor, who, after a brief stint in the Southern army, retired to his plantation, smuggled contraband cotton into Northern hands, and invested the profits in land and Union currency. But it was widely resented that, as a Richmond newspaper put it, many "rampant cotton and sugar planters, who were so early and furiously in the field of secession," quickly took oaths of allegiance during the war and resumed raising cotton "in partnership with their Yankee *protectors.*" Other planters resisted the impressment of their slaves to build military fortifications and, to the end, opposed calls for the enlistment of blacks in the Confederate army, afraid, an Alabama newspaper later explained, "to risk the loss of their property."

Even more devastating for upcountry morale, however, were policies of the Confederate government. The upcountry became convinced that it bore an unfair share of taxation; it particularly resented the tax in kind and the policy of impressment that authorized military officers to appropriate farm goods to feed the army. Planters, to be sure, now paid a higher proportion of their own income in taxes than before the war, but they suffered far less severely from such seizures, which undermined the yeomanry's subsistence agriculture. By the middle of the war, Lee's army was relying almost entirely upon food impressed from farms and plantations in Georgia and South Carolina.

The North Georgia hill counties suffered the most severely. "These impressments," Georgia's governor Joseph E. Brown lamented in 1863, "have been ruinous to the people of the northeastern part of the State, where . . . probably not half a supply of provisions [is] made for the support of the women and children. One man in fifty may have a surplus, and forty out of the fifty may not have half enough. . . . Every pound of meat and every bushel of grain, carried out of that part of the State by impressing officers, must be replaced by the State at public expense or the wives and children of soldiers in the army must starve for food." The impressment of horses and oxen for the army proved equally disastrous, for it made it almost impossible for some farm families to plow their fields or transport their produce to market. These problems were exacerbated by the South's rampant inflation.

During the war poverty descended upon thousands of upcountry families, especially those with men in the army. Food riots broke out in Virginia and North Carolina. In 1864 a group of farmers in Randolph County, Alabama, sent a poignant petition to Confederate President Jefferson Davis describing conditions in their "poor and mountainous" county: "There are now on the rolls of the Probate court, 1600 indigent families to be Supported; they average 5 to each family; making a grand total of 8000 persons. Deaths from Starvation have absolutely occurred. . . . Women riots have taken place in Several parts of the County in which Govt wheat and corn has been seized to prevent Starvation of themselves and families. Where it will end unless relief is afforded we cannot tell."

But above all, it was the organization of conscription that convinced many yeomen the struggle for Southern independence had become "a rich man's war and a poor man's fight." Beginning in 1862, the Confederacy enacted the first conscription laws in American history, including provisions that a draftee could avoid service by producing a substitute and that one able-bodied white male would be exempted for every twenty slaves. This legislation was deeply resented in the upcountry, for the cost of a substitute quickly rose far beyond the means of most white families, while the "twenty Negro" provision—a direct response to the decline of discipline on the plantations—allowed many overseers and planters' sons to escape military service. Even though the provision was subsequently repealed, conscription still bore more heavily on the yeomanry, which depended on the labor of the entire family for subsistence, than on planter families supported by the labor of slaves.

In large areas of the Southern upcountry, disillusionment eventually led to outright resistance to Confederate authority—a civil war within the Civil War. Beginning in 1863, desertion became a "crying evil" for the Confederate army. By war's end more than one hundred thousand men had fled. "The deserters," reported one Confederate army officer, "belong almost entirely to the poorest class of non slaveholders whose labor is indispensable to the daily support of their families. . . . When the father, husband or son is forced into the service, the suffering at home with them is inevitable. It is not in the nature of these men to remain quiet in the ranks under such circumstances."

Poverty, not disloyalty, this officer believed, produced most desertions. But in many parts of the upcountry, the two became intimately interrelated. In the hill counties and piney woods of Mississippi, bands of deserters hid from Confederate authorities, and organizations like Choctaw County's Loyal League worked, said one contemporary observer, to "break up the war by advising desertion, robbing the families of those who remained in the army, and keeping the Federal authorities advised" of Confederate military movements. Northern Alabama, generally enthusiastic about the Confederacy in 1861, was the scene two years later of widespread opposition to conscription and the war. "The condition of things in the mountain districts," wrote John A. Campbell, the South's assistant secretary of war, "menaces the existence of the Confederacy as fatally as . . . the armies of the United States."

Campbell's fears were amply justified by events in Jones County, Mississippi. Although later claims that Jones "seceded" from the Confederacy appear to be exaggerated, disaffection became endemic in this piney woods county. Newton Knight, a strongly pro-Union subsistence farmer, was drafted early in the war and chose to serve as a hospital orderly rather than go into combat against the Union. When his wife wrote him that Confederate cavalry had seized his horse under the impressment law and was mistreating their neighbors, Knight deserted, returned home, and organized Unionists and deserters to "fight for their rights and the freedom of Jones County." In response, Confederate troops seized and hanged one of Knight's brothers, but the irregular force of Unionists subsequently fought a successful battle against a Confederate cavalry unit.

Outside of East Tennessee the most extensive antiwar organizing took place in western and central North Carolina, whose residents had largely supported the Confederacy in 1861. Here the secret Heroes of America, numbering perhaps ten thousand men, established an "underground railroad" to enable Unionists to escape to Federal lines. The Heroes originated in North Carolina's Quaker Belt, a group of Piedmont counties whose Quaker and Moravian residents had long harbored pacifist and antislavery sentiments. Unionists in this region managed to elect "peace men" to the state legislature and a member of the Heroes as the local sheriff. By 1864 the organization had spread into the North Carolina mountains, had garnered considerable support among Raleigh artisans, and was even organizing in plantation areas (where there is some evidence of black involvement in its activities).

One of the Heroes' key organizers was Dr. John Lewis Johnson, a Philadelphia-born druggist and physician. After serving in the Confederate army early in the war and being captured—probably deliberately—he returned home to form bands of Union sympathizers. In 1864 he fled to the North, whereupon his wife was arrested and jailed in Richmond, resulting in the death of their infant son. For the remainder of the war, Johnson lived in Cincinnati with another son, who had deserted from the Confederate army.

North Carolina's Confederate governor Zebulon Vance dismissed the Heroes of America as "altogether a low and insignificant concern." But by 1864 the organization was engaged in espionage, promoting desertion, and helping escaped Federal prisoners reach Tennessee and Kentucky. It was also deeply involved in William W. Holden's 1864 race for governor as a peace candidate. Holden was decisively defeated, but in Heroes' strongholds like Raleigh he polled nearly half the vote.

Most of all, the Heroes of America helped galvanize the class resentments rising to the surface of Southern life. Alexander H. Jones, a Hendersonville newspaper editor and leader of the Heroes, pointedly expressed their views: "This great national strife originated with men and measures that were . . . opposed to a democratic form of government. . . . The fact is, these *bombastic, high-falutin* aristocratic fools have been in the habit of driving negroes and poor helpless white people until they think . . . that they themselves are superior; [and] hate, deride and suspicion the poor."

As early as 1862 Joshua B. Moore, a North Alabama slaveholder, predicted that Southerners without a direct stake in slavery "are not going to fight through a long war to save it—never. They will tire of it and quit." Moore was only half right. Nonslaveholding yeomen supplied the bulk of Confederate soldiers as well as the majority of deserters and draft resisters. But there is no question that the war was a disaster for the upcountry South. Lying at the war's strategic cross-roads, portions of upcountry Tennessee, Alabama, and Mississippi were laid waste by the march of opposing armies. In other areas marauding bands of deserters plundered the farms and workshops of Confederate sympathizers, driving off livestock and destroying crops, while Confederate troops and vigilantes routed Union families from their homes. Kinship ties were shredded as brother fought brother and neighbor battled neighbor not only on Civil War battlefields but in what one contemporary called the South's "vulgar internecine warfare."

No one knows how many Southerners perished in this internal civil war. Atrocities were committed by both sides, but since the bulk of the upcountry remained within Confederate lines, Unionists suffered more severely. After April 1862, when President Davis declared martial law in East Tennessee and suspended the writ of habeas corpus, thousands of Unionists saw their property seized. In Shelton Laurel, a remote valley in Appalachian North Carolina, Confederate soldiers in January 1863 murdered thirteen Unionist prisoners in cold blood. Solomon Jones, the "Union patriarch" of the South Carolina mountains, was driven from his farm, forced to live in the woods, and eventually jailed by Confederate authorities. Throughout the upcountry Unionists abandoned their homes to hide from the conscription officers and Confederate sheriffs who hunted them, as they had once hunted runaway slaves, with bloodhounds; some found refuge in the very mountain caves that had once sheltered fugitives from bondage.

For Southerners loyal to the Union, the war left deep scars. Long after the end of fighting, bitter memories of persecution would remain, and tales would be told and retold of the fortitude and suffering of Union families. "We could fill a book with facts of wrongs done to our people . . . ," an Alabama Unionist told a congressional committee in 1866. "You have no idea of the strength of principle and devotion these people exhibited towards the national government." A Mississippi Unionist later recalled how the office of James M. Jones, editor of the Corinth *Republican,* "was surrounded by the infuriated rebels, his paper was suppressed, his person threatened with violence, he was broken up and ruined forever, all for advocating the Union of our fathers." Jones later fled the state and enlisted in the Union army (one of only five hundred white Mississippians to do so). A Tennessean told a similar story: "They were driven from their homes . . . persecuted like wild beasts by the rebel authorities, and hunted down in the mountains; they were hanged on the gallows, shot down and robbed. . . . Perhaps no people on the face of the earth were ever more persecuted than were the loyal people of East Tennessee."

Thus the war permanently redrew the economic and political map of the white South. Military devastation and the Confederacy's economic policies plunged much of the upcountry into poverty, thereby threatening the yeomanry's economic independence and opening the door to the postwar spread of cotton cultivation and tenant farming. Yeoman disaffection shattered the political hegemony of the planters, separating "the lower and uneducated class," according to one Georgia planter, "from the more wealthy and more enlightened portion of our population."

The war ended the upcountry's isolation, weakened its localism, and awakened its political self-consciousness. Out of the Union opposition would come many of the most prominent white Republican leaders of Reconstruction. Edward Degener, a German-born San Antonio grocer who had seen his two sons executed for treason by the Confederacy, served as a Republican congressman after the war. The party's Reconstruction Southern governors would include Edmund J. Davis, who during the war raised the 1st Texas Cavalry for the Union Army; William W. Holden, the unsuccessful "peace" candidate of 1864; William H. Smith and David P. Lewis, organizers of a Peace Society in Confederate Alabama; and William G. Brownlow, a circuit-riding Methodist preacher and Knoxville, Tennessee, editor.

Perhaps more than any other individual, Brownlow personified the changes wrought by the Civil War and the bitter hatred of "rebels" so pervasive among Southern Unionists. Before 1860 he had been an avid defender of slavery. The peculiar institution, he declared, would not be abolished until "the angel Gabriel sounds the last loud trump of God." (His newspaper also called Harriet Beecher Stowe a "deliberate liar" for her portrayal of slavery in *Uncle Tom's Cabin,* adding that she was "as ugly as Original sin" to boot.)

With secession, Brownlow turned his caustic pen against the Confederacy. In October 1861 he was arrested and sent North, and his paper was closed. He returned to Knoxville two years later, when Gen. Ambrose E. Burnside occupied the city. Now he was a firm defender of emancipation and an advocate of reprisals against pro-Confederate Southerners. He would, Brownlow wrote in 1864, arm "every wolf, panther, catamount, and bear in the mountains of America . . . every rattlesnake and crocodile . . . every devil in Hell, and turn them loose upon the Confederacy" in order to win the war.

The South's inner civil war not only helped weaken the Confederate war effort but bequeathed to Reconstruction explosive political issues, unresolved questions, and broad opportunities for change. The disaffected regions would embrace the Republican party after the Civil War; some remained strongholds well into the twentieth century. The war experience goes a long way toward explaining the strength of Republican voting in parts of the Reconstruction upcountry. To these "scalawags" the party represented, first and foremost, the inheritor of wartime Unionism.

Their loyalty first to the Union and then to Republicanism did not, however, imply abolitionist sentiment during the war or a commitment to the rights of blacks thereafter, although they were perfectly willing to see slavery sacrificed to preserve the Union. Indeed, the black-white alliance within the Reconstruction Republican party was always fragile, especially as blacks aggressively pursued demands for a larger share of political offices and far-reaching civil rights legislation. Upcountry Unionism was essentially defensive, a response to the undermining of local autonomy and economic self-sufficiency rather than a coherent program for the social reconstruction of the South. Its basis, the Northern reporter

Sidney Andrews discovered in the fall of 1865, was "hatred of those who went into the Rebellion" and of "a certain ruling class" that had brought upon the region the devastating impact of war.

Although recent writing has made Civil War scholars aware of the extent of disaffection in the Confederacy, the South's inner civil war remains largely unknown to most Americans. Perhaps this is because the story of Southern Unionism challenges two related popular mythologies that have helped shape how Americans think about that era: the portrait of the Confederacy as a heroic "lost cause" and of Reconstruction as an ignoble "tragic era."

For much of this century historians who sympathized with the Confederate struggle minimized the extent of Southern discontent and often castigated the region's Unionists as "Tories," traitors analogous to Americans who remained loyal to George III during the Revolution. And many Northern writers, while praising Unionists' resolve, found it difficult to identify enthusiastically with men complicitous in the alleged horrors of Reconstruction. Yet as the smoke of these historiographical battles clears, and a more complex view of the war and Reconstruction emerges, it has become abundantly clear that no one can claim to fully understand the Civil War era without coming to terms with the South's Unionists, the persecution they suffered, and how they helped determine the outcome of our greatest national crisis.

How Lincoln Freed the Slaves

Stephen B. Oates

The story of how Abraham Lincoln "freed" the slaves by signing the Emancipation Proclamation is one of the most familiar and least understood events in American history. When he became president, Lincoln was not an abolitionist, though his hatred of slavery was profound. How he gradually developed his policy toward the institution during the Civil War is the subject of this article by Stephen B. Oates, professor of history at the University of Massachusetts.

Like all presidents, Lincoln had to react to many kinds of political pressures. Like only a few presidents, he had at the same time to deal with military problems, the mishandling of which might cost the lives of thousands of men. Like no other president, on his decisions depended the very existence of the Union. Professor Oates is the author of With Malice Toward None: The Life of Abraham Lincoln, *books on the Nat Turner rebellion and the life of John Brown, and other works.*

When the cold, fastidious Mississippian rose to speak, a hush fell over the crowded Senate chamber. It was January 21, 1861, and Jefferson Davis and four other senators from the Deep South were here this day to announce their resignations. Over the winter, five Southern states had seceded from the Union, contending that Abraham Lincoln's election as President doomed the white man's South, that Lincoln and his fellow Republicans were abolitionist fanatics out to eradicate slavery and plunge Dixie into racial chaos. Though the Republicans had pledged to leave the peculiar institution alone where it already existed, Deep Southerners refused to believe them and left the Union to save their slave-based society from Republican aggression.

For his part, Jefferson Davis regretted that Mississippi had been obliged to secede, and he had spent a sleepless night, distressed about the breakup of the Union and fearful of the future. To be sure, he loved the idea of a Southern confederacy; and he had warned Republicans that if the South could not depart in peace, a war would begin, the likes of which man had never seen before. But today, as he gave his valedictory in the Senate, Davis was sad and forlorn, his voice quavering. He bore his Republican adversaries no hostility, he said, and wished them and their people well. He apologized if in the heat of debate he had offended anybody—and he forgave those who had insulted him. "Mr. President and Senators," he said with great difficulty, "having made the announcement which the occasion seemed to me to require, it only remains for me to bid you a final adieu."

Several senators were visibly moved, and there were audible sobs in the

347

galleries. As Davis made his exit, with Southern ladies waving handkerchiefs and crying out in favor of secession, Republicans stared grimly after him, realizing perhaps for the first time that the South was in earnest, the Union was disintegrating.

As Lincoln's inauguration approached and more Southern congressmen resigned to join the Confederacy, Republicans gained control of both houses and voted to expel the secessionists as traitors. Senator Lyman Trumbull of Illinois pronounced them all mad, and Charles Sumner of Massachusetts exhorted the free states to stand firm in the crisis. Michigan's Zachariah Chandler vowed to whip the South back into the Union and preserve the integrity of the government. And Ben Wade of Ohio predicted that secession would bring about the destruction of slavery, the very thing Southerners dreaded most. "The first blast of civil war," he had thundered at them, "is the death warrant of your institution."

After the events at Fort Sumter, Wade, Chandler, and Sumner called repeatedly at the White House and spoke with Lincoln about slavery and the rebellion. Sumner was a tall, elegant bachelor, with rich brown hair, a massive forehead, blue eyes, and a rather sad smile. He had traveled widely in England, where his friends included some of the most eminent political and literary figures. A humorless, erudite Bostonian, educated at Harvard, Sumner even looked English, with his tailored coats, checkered trousers, and English gaiters. He was so conscious of manners "that he never allowed himself, even in the privacy of his own chamber, to fall into a position which he would not take in his chair in the Senate. 'Habit,' he said, 'is everything.' " Sumner spoke out with great courage against racial injustice and was one of the few Republicans who advocated complete Negro equality. Back in 1856 Representative Preston Brooks of South Carolina

Senator Charles Sumner in a steel-engraved portrait made during the early 1860s.

had beaten him almost to death in the Senate Chamber for his "Crime Against Kansas" speech, and Sumner still carried physical and psychological scars from that attack. The senator now served as Lincoln's chief foreign policy adviser, often accompanied him on his carriage rides, and became the President's warm personal friend.

Zachariah Chandler was a Detroit businessman who had amassed a fortune in real estate and dry goods. Profane, hard-drinking, and eternally grim, Chandler had been one of the founders of the national Republican party and had served on the Republican National Committee in 1856 and 1860. Elected to the Senate in 1857, he had plunged into the acrimonious debates over slavery in the West, exhorting his colleagues not to surrender another inch of territory to slaveholders. When Southerners threatened to murder Republicans, brandishing pistols and bowie knives in the Senate itself, Chandler took up calisthenics and improved his marksmanship in case he had to fight. Once civil war commenced, he demanded that the government suppress the "armed traitors" of the South with all-out warfare.

Now serving his second term in the Senate, Benjamin Franklin Wade was short and thick chested, with iron-gray hair, sunken black eyes, and a square and beardless face. He was blunt and irascible, known as "Bluff Ben" for his readiness to duel with slaveowners, and he told more ribald jokes than any other man in the Senate, but he also had a charitable side: once when he spotted a destitute neighbor robbing his corncrib, Wade moved out of sight in order not to humiliate the man. Once the war began, he was determined that Congress should have an equal voice with Lincoln in shaping Union war policies. According to diplomat Rudolf Schleiden, Wade was "perhaps the most energetic personality in the entire Congress." "That queer, rough, but intelligent-looking man," said one Washington observer, "is old Senator Wade of Ohio, who doesn't care a pinch of snuff whether people like what he says or not." Wade hated slavery as Sumner and Chandler did. But like most whites of his generation, he was prejudiced against blacks: he complained about their "odor," growled about all the "Nigger" cooks in Washington, and insisted that he had eaten food "cooked by Niggers until I can smell and taste the Nigger . . . all over." Like many Republicans, he thought the best solution to America's race problem was to ship all Negroes back to Africa.

As far as the Republican party was concerned, the three senators belonged to a loose faction inaccurately categorized as "radicals," a misnomer that has persisted through the years. These "more advanced Republicans," as the Detroit *Post* and *Tribune* referred to them, were really progressive, nineteenth-century liberals who felt a powerful kinship with English liberals like John Bright and Richard Cobden. What advanced Republicans wanted was to reform the American system—to bring their nation into line with the Declaration's premise—by ridding it of slavery and the South's ruling planter class. But while the advanced Republicans supported other social reforms, spoke out forthrightly against the crime and anachronism of slavery, and refused to compromise with the "Slave Power," they desired no radical break from basic American ideals and liberal institutions. Moreover, they were often at odds with one another on such issues as currency, the tariff, and precisely what rights black people should exercise in American white society.

Before secession, the advanced Republicans had endorsed the party's hands-off policy about slavery in the South: they all agreed that Congress had no constitutional authority to menace slavery as a state institution; all agreed, too, that the federal government could only abolish slavery in the national capital and outlaw it in the national territories, thus containing the institution in the South where they hoped it would ultimately perish. But civil war had removed their constitutional scruples about slavery in the Southern states, thereby bringing about the first significant difference between them and the more "moderate" and "conservative" members of the party. While the latter insisted that the Union must be restored with slavery intact, the advanced Republicans argued that the national government could now remove the peculiar institution by the war powers, and they wanted the President to do it in his capacity as Commander-in-Chief. This was what Sumner, Wade, and Chandler came to talk about with Lincoln. They respected the President, had applauded his nomination, campaigned indefatigably in his behalf, and cheered his firm stand at Fort Sumter. Now they urged him to destroy slavery as a war measure, pointing out that this would maim and cripple the Confederacy and hasten an end to the rebellion. Sumner flatly asserted that slavery and the rebellion were "mated" and would stand or fall together.

Lincoln seemed sympathetic. He detested human bondage as much as they did, and he wanted to stay on good terms with advanced Republicans on Capitol Hill, for he needed their support in prosecuting the war. Moreover, he respected the senators and referred to men like Sumner as the conscience of the party.

Yet to the senators' dismay, he would not free the slaves, could not free them. For one thing, he had no intention of alienating moderate and conservative Republicans—the majority of the party—by issuing an emancipation decree. For another, emancipation would almost surely send the loyal slave states—Delaware, Maryland, Kentucky, and Missouri—spiraling into the Confederacy, something that would be calamitous to the Union. Then, too, Lincoln was waging a bipartisan war with Northern Democrats and Republicans alike enlisting in his armies. An abolition policy, Lincoln feared, would splinter that coalition, perhaps even cause a new civil war behind Union lines.

Though deeply disappointed, the three senators at first acquiesced in Lincoln's policy because they wanted to maintain Republican unity in combating the rebellion. Sumner told himself that at bottom Lincoln was "a deeply convinced and faithful anti-slavery man" and that the sheer pressure of war would force him to strike at Negro bondage eventually.

On July 4, 1861, the Thirty-seventh Congress convened with a rebel army entrenched less than thirty miles away. Republicans controlled both houses, and the advanced Republicans quickly gained positions of leadership out of proportion to their numbers. Many had been in Congress for years, and their uncompromising stand against slavery expansion and concessions to secessionists had won them accolades from all manner of Republicans. Like Chandler, several advanced Republicans had helped establish the national party; all were prominent in their state parties. Their prestige, skill, and energy—Chandler, for example, routinely put in eighteen-hour workdays—had helped bring them to position of power on Capitol Hill.

In the Senate, advanced Republicans chaired nearly all the crucial committees. Sumner ran the committee on foreign relations, Chandler the committee on commerce, and Wade the committee on territories. In addition, Lyman Trumbull of Illinois, a dry, logical speaker with sandy hair and gold-rimmed spectacles, headed the judiciary committee. Henry Wilson, Sumner's Massachusetts colleague, a stout, beardless, red-faced businessman who had once been a shoemaker's apprentice, held Jefferson Davis's old job as chairman of the committee on military affairs. William Pitt Fessenden of Maine, impeccably dressed in his black jackets and black silk ties, famous for his forensic duels with Stephen A. Douglas before the war, chaired the finance committee and cooperated closely with Salmon Chase, Lincoln's Secretary of the Treasury. Fessenden had been born out of wedlock—a terrible stigma in that time—and the awful, unspoken shame of his illegitimacy had made him proud and quick to take offense, intolerant of human failings in others as well as himself. He and Sumner had once been friends, had called one another "my dear Sumner" and "my dear Fessenden," and often entered the Senate arm in arm. But Fessenden had taken umbrage at what he thought were Sumner's haughty airs, and their friendship had changed to bristling animosity. Fessenden remained "old friends" with Wade and Chandler, though, and also hobnobbed with Jacob Collamer of Vermont, a Republican conservative.

Advanced Republicans were equally prominent in the House. There was James Ashley of Ohio, an emotional, dramatic man with a curly brown mane, who chaired the committee on territories. There was George Washington Julian from Indiana, protégé of Joshua "Old War Horse" Giddings and a contentious, frowning individual who proved himself a formidable anti-slavery legislator. There was portly, unkempt Owen Lovejoy of Illinois, brother of Elijah, the abolitionist martyr; an eloquent anti-slavery orator, he headed the committee on agriculture. Like Sumner, Lovejoy was a close friend of Lincoln's—"the *best* friend I had in Congress," the President once remarked—and strove to sustain administration policies while simultaneously pushing the main cause of emancipation.

Finally there was sixty-nine-year-old Thaddeus Stevens of Pennsylvania, who controlled the nation's purse strings as chairman of the powerful committee on ways and means. Afflicted with a clubfoot, Stevens was a grim, sardonic bachelor with a cutting wit ("I now yield to Mr. B.," he once said, "who will make a few feeble remarks") and a fondness for gambling that took him almost nightly to Washington's casinos. To the delight of his colleagues, he indulged in witticisms so off color that they had to be deleted from the *Congressional Globe.* A wealthy ironmaster with a Jekyll-and-Hyde personality, he had contributed generously to charities and causes, crusaded for public schools in Pennsylvania, and defended fugitive slaves there. Crippled, as Fawn Brodie has noted, Stevens spoke of bondage "in terms of shackled limbs and a longing for freedom to dance." He lived with his mulatto housekeeper, Lydia Smith, and there is strong evidence that they were lovers. Antimiscegenation laws made marriage impossible, and their liaison not only generated malicious gossip but probably kept Stevens from becoming what he most wanted to be—a United States senator. He liked to quote the Bible that "He hath made of one blood all nations of men," yet he never championed complete equality for blacks—"not equality in all things," he once asserted, "simply before the laws, nothing else." Serving a fourth term as congressman, this bitter, intimidating, high-minded man was to rule the Civil War House and become "the master-spirit," said Alexander McClure, "of every aggressive movement in Congress to overthrow the rebellion and slavery.

As the session progressed that summer, congressional Republicans demonstrated remarkable harmony. They all wanted to preserve the Union and help the President fight the war through to a swift and successful conclusion. In agreement with Lincoln's slave policy, congressional Republicans also voted for the so-called Crittenden-Johnson resolutions, which declared that the sole purpose of the war was to restore the Union. For the sake of party unity, most advanced Republicans reluctantly supported the resolutions, too. But they agreed with Congressman Albert Riddle of Ohio that slavery ought to be destroyed. "You all believe that it is to go out, when it does, through convulsion, fire and blood," Riddle stormed on the House floor. "That convulsion is upon us. The man is a delirious ass who does not see it and realize this. For me, I mean to make a conquest of it; to beat it to extinction under the iron hoofs of our war horses."

For the advanced Republicans, the first chance to strike at slavery came late in July, after the Union rout at Bull Run. Observing that rebel forces used slaves to carry weapons and perform other military tasks, the advanced Republicans vigorously championed a confiscation bill, which authorized the seizure of any slave employed in the Confederate war effort, and they mustered almost unanimous Republican support in pushing the measure through Congress. Border-state Democrats like John J. Crittenden of Kentucky complained that the bill was unconstitutional, but most Republicans agreed with Henry Wilson that "if traitors use bondmen to destroy this country, my doctrine is that the Government shall at once convert those bondmen into men that cannot be used to destroy our country." In war, Republicans contended, the government had every right to confiscate enemy property—including slave property—as legitimate contraband. Though the bill was hardly a general emancipation act, advanced Republicans hailed its passage as an important first step. They were glad indeed when Lincoln signed the bill into law and commanded his armies to enforce it. At last the President appeared to be coming around to their views.

But they had misunderstood him. When General John Charles Frémont, commander of the Western Department, ordered that the slaves of all rebels in Missouri be "declared freemen," Lincoln pronounced this a dangerous and unauthorized political act that would alienate the loyal border and commanded Frémont to modify his order so that it accorded strictly with the congressional confiscation act. Though border Unionists applauded Lincoln, advanced Republicans were dismayed that he had overruled Frémont's emancipation decree. Sumner declared that Lincoln "is now a dictator." Wade charged that Lincoln's opinions on slavery "could only come of one, born of 'poor white trash' and educated in a slave State." And Fessenden denounced the President for his "weak and unjustifiable concession to the Union men of the border States."

Still, the Frémont episode did not cause an irreparable split between Lincoln and the advanced Republicans, as some writers have claimed. In fact, when Lincoln subsequently removed the general from command, Trumbull, Chandler, and Lovejoy sustained the President, conceding that the celebrated Pathfinder and first standard-bearer of their party was a maladroit administrator. But in the fall and winter of 1861, advanced Republicans did mount an all-out campaign to make the obliteration of slavery a Union war objective. One after another they came to the White House—Wade, Chandler, and Trumbull, Sumner, Julian, and Lovejoy—and implored and badgered the President to issue an emancipation proclamation on military grounds. With the war dragging on, they insisted that slavery must be attacked in order to weaken the Confederate ability to fight.

Moreover, they argued, slavery had caused the conflict and was now the cornerstone of the Confederacy. It was absurd to fight a war without removing the thing that had brought it about. Should Lincoln restore the Union with slavery preserved, Southerners would just start another war whenever they thought the institution threatened, so that the present struggle would have been in vain. If Lincoln really wanted to salvage the Union, he must hurl his armies at the heart of the rebellion. He must tear slavery out root and branch and smash the South's arrogant planters—those mischievous men the advanced Republicans believed had masterminded secession and fomented war. The annihilation of slavery, Julian asserted, was "not a debatable and distant alternative, but a pressing and absolute necessity." So what if most of the country opposed emancipation lest it result in an exodus of Southern blacks into the North? "It was the duty of the President," he said "to lead, not follow public opinion."

Sumner, as Lincoln's foreign policy adviser, also linked emancipation to opinion overseas. There was a strong possibility that Britain would recognize the Confederacy as an independent nation—potentially disastrous for the Union since the Confederacy could then form alliances and seek mediation, perhaps even armed intervention. But, Sumner argued, if Lincoln made the destruction of slavery a Union war aim, Britain would balk at recognition and intervention because of her own anti-slavery tradition. And whatever powerful Britain did, the rest of Europe was sure to follow.

Also, as Sumner kept saying, emancipation would break the chains of several million oppressed human beings and right America at last with her own ideals. Lincoln and the Republican party could no longer wait to remove slavery. The President must do it by the war powers. The rebellion, monstrous and terrible though it was, had given him the opportunity.

But Lincoln still did not agree. "I think Sumner and the rest of you would upset our applecart altogether if you had your way," he told some advanced Republicans one day. "We didn't go into the war to put down slavery, but to put the flag back; and to act differently at this moment would, I have no doubt, not only weaken our cause, but smack of bad faith. . . . This thunderbolt will keep." And in his message to Congress in December of 1861, the President declared that he did not want the war degenerating into "a violent and remorseless revolutionary struggle." He was striving, he said, "to keep the integrity of the Union prominent as the primary object of the contest."

Advanced Republicans were deeply aggrieved. Fessenden thought the President had lost all hold on Congress, and Wade complained that not even a galvanic battery could inspire Lincoln to "courage, decision and enterprise." "He means well," wrote Trumbull, "and in ordinary times would have made one of the best of Presidents, but he lacks confidence in himself and the *will* necessary in this great emergency."

By year's end, though, Lincoln's mind had begun to change. He spoke with Sumner about emancipation and assured the senator that "the only difference between you and me on this subject is a difference of a month or six weeks in time." And he now felt, he said, that the war "was a great movement by God to end Slavery and that the man would be a fool who should stand in the way." But out of deference to the loyal border states, Lincoln still shied away from a sweeping executive decree and searched about for an alternative. On March 6, 1862, he proposed a plan to Congress he thought would make federal emancipation unnecessary—a gradual, compensated abolition program to begin along the loyal border and then be extended into the rebel states as they were conquered. According to Lincoln's plan, the border states would gradually remove slavery over the next thirty years, and the national government would compensate slaveholders for their loss. The whole program was to be voluntary; the states would adopt their own emancipation laws without federal coercion. At the same time (as he had earlier told Congress), Lincoln favored a voluntary colonization program, to be sponsored by the federal government, that would resettle liberated blacks outside the country.

On Capitol Hill Stevens derided Lincoln's scheme as "diluted milk-and-water-gruel." But other advanced Republicans, noting that Lincoln's was the first emancipation proposal ever offered by an American President, acclaimed it as an excellent step. On April 10 the Republican-controlled Congress endorsed Lincoln's emancipation plan. But the border-state representatives, for whom it was intended, rejected the scheme emphatically. "I utterly spit at it and despise it," said one Kentucky congressman. "Emancipation in the cotton States is simply an absurdity. . . . There is not enough power in the world to compel it to be done."

As Lincoln promoted his gradual, compensated scheme, advanced Republicans on Capitol Hill launched a furious anti-slavery attack of their own. They sponsored a tough new confiscation bill, championed legislation that weakened the fugitive-slave law and assailed human bondage in the national capital as well as the territories. What was more, they won over many Republican moderates to forge a new congressional majority so far as slavery was concerned. As the war ground into its second year, moderate Republicans came to agree with their advanced colleagues that it was senseless to pretend the Union could be restored without removing the cause of the rebellion.

So, over strong Democratic opposition, the Republican Congress approved a bill that forbade the return of fugitive slaves to the rebels, and on March 13, 1862, Lincoln signed it into law. Congress also adopted legislation which abolished slavery in Washington, D.C., compensated owners for their loss, and set aside funds for the voluntary colonization of blacks in Haiti and Liberia, and Lincoln signed this as well. Democrats howled. One castigated the bill as an entering wedge for wholesale abolition, another predicted that liberated Negroes

One of the many fine Mathew Brady photographs of Lincoln, taken in 1862 during the time that Lincoln was contemplating the pros and cons of issuing the Proclamation.

would crowd white ladies out of congressional galleries. Washingtonians accused the "abolitionists" in Congress of converting the capital into "a hell on earth for the white man." Republicans brushed aside all such criticism. "If there be a place upon the face of the earth," asserted a Minnesota Republican, "where human slavery should be prohibited, and where every man should be protected in the rights which God and Nature have given him, that place is the capital of this great Republic."

In June the Republican Congress lashed at slavery again: it passed a bill that outlawed human bondage in all federal territories, thus overriding the Dred Scott decision, and Lincoln signed the measure into law. Congress and the President also joined together in recognizing the black republics of Haiti and Liberia, a move that would facilitate colonization efforts in those lands. Meanwhile, a fierce debate raged over the second confiscation bill, which authorized the seizure and liberation of all slaves held by those in rebellion. Advanced Republicans not only pushed the bill with uninhibited zeal but also advocated that emancipated blacks be enlisted in the army. But even some Republicans thought full-scale confiscation too drastic, and "conservatives" like Jacob Collamer of Vermont, Orville Browning of Illinois, and Edgar Cowam of Pennsylvania sided with the Democrats in denouncing the bill as uncivilized and unconstitutional. "Pass these acts," cried one opponent, "confiscate under the bills the property of these men, emancipate their negroes, place arms in the hands of these human gorillas to murder their masters and violate their wives and daughters, and you will have a war such as was never witnessed in the worst days of the French Revolution, and horrors never exceeded in San Domingo."

On July 4, in the midst of the debate, Sumner hurried back to the White House and admonished Lincoln to attack slavery himself. Sumner was extremely disappointed in the President, for he did not seem a month or six weeks behind the senator at all. In fact, Lincoln recently had overruled another general, David Hunter, who liberated the slaves inside his lines, and again the advanced Republicans had groaned in despair. Now, on July 4, Sumner urged "the reconsecration of the day by a decree of emancipation." The senator pointed out that the Union was suffering from troop shortages on every front and that the slaves were an untapped reservoir of manpower. "You need more men," Sumner argued, "not only at the North, but at the South, in the rear of the Rebels; you need the slaves." But Lincoln insisted that an emancipation edict was still "too big a lick." And, in a White House interview, he warned border-state legislators that his gradual, state-guided plan was the only alternative to federal emancipation and that they must commend it to their people. Once again they refused.

On July 17, five days after Lincoln spoke with the border men, Congress finally passed the second confiscation bill. If the rebellion did not end in sixty days, the measure warned, the executive branch would seize the property of all those who supported, aided, or participated in the rebellion. Federal courts were to determine guilt. Those convicted would forfeit their estates and their slaves to the federal government, and their slaves would be set free. Section nine liberated other categories of slaves without court action: slaves of rebels who escaped to Union lines, who were captured by federal forces or were abandoned by their owners, "shall be deemed captives of war, and shall be forever free." On the other hand, the bill exempted loyal Unionists in the rebel South, allowing them to retain their slaves and other property. Another section empo red Lincoln to enlist Negroes in the military. Still another, aimed at easing Northern racial fears and keeping Republican unity, provided for the voluntary resettlement of confiscated blacks in "some tropical country." A few days later Congress appropriated $500,000 for colonization.

Controversial though it was, the second confiscation act still fell far short of genuine emancipation. Most slaves were to be freed only after protracted case-by-case litigation in the courts. And of course, the slaves of loyal masters were not affected. Yet the bill was about as far as Congress could go in attacking slavery, for most Republicans still acknowledged that Congress had no constitutional authority to eradicate bondage as a state institution. Only the President with his war powers—or a constitutional amendment—could do that. Nevertheless, the measure seemed a clear invitation for the President to exercise his constitutional powers and annihilate slavery in the rebellious states. And Stevens, Sumner, and Wilson repeatedly told him that most congressional Republicans now favored this. On the other hand, conservatives like Orville Browning beseeched Lincoln to veto the confiscation bill and restore the old Union as it was. "I said to him that he had reached the culminating point in his administration," Browning recorded in his diary, "and his course upon this bill was to determine whether he was to control the abolitionists and radicals, or whether they were to control him."

For several days, Lincoln gave few hints as to what he would do, and Congress awaited his response in a state of high tension. Finally, on July 17, he informed Capitol Hill that he agreed entirely with the spirit of the confiscation bill remarking that "the traitor against the general government" deserved to have his slaves and other property forfeited as just punishment for rebellion. While he thought some of the wording unfortunately vague, he nevertheless raised no objection to the sections on slave liberation. He did, however, disagree with other portions on technical grounds, especially those which permanently divested a rebel of the title to his land, and Lincoln hinted that he would veto the bill as a consequence. To avoid that, congressional Republicans attached an explanatory resolution removing most of Lincoln's complaints. Satisfied, the President signed the bill and commanded the army to start enforcing it after sixty days.

Even so, several advanced Republicans were angered by Lincoln's threatened veto and peeved by what they perceived as his legalistic quibbling when the Union was struggling for its life against a mutinous aristocracy founded on slavery. Julian, for his part, thought Lincoln's behavior "inexpressibly provoking," and when Congress adjourned, he called at the White House to find out once and for all where the President stood on emancipation and all-out war against the rebels. Julian said he was going home to Indiana and wanted to assure his constituents that the President would "co-operate with Congress in vigorously carrying out the measures we had inaugurated for the purpose of crushing the rebellion, and that now the quickest and hardest blows were to be dealt." Complaining that advanced Republicans had unfairly criticized him, Lincoln said he had no objection at all to what Julian wished to tell his constituents. In Indiana that summer, Julian announced that Lincoln had now decided on a radical change in his policy toward slavery.

In August Sumner learned that Lincoln had at last decided to issue an emancipation proclamation. Convinced that the peculiar institution could be destroyed only through executive action, Lincoln actually had drawn up a draft of the proclamation and read it to his Cabinet. But couldn't Sumner have predicted it? Lincoln had let Secretary of State William H. Seward dissuade him from issuing the edict until after a Union military victory. At the White House, Sumner demanded that the decree "be put forth—the sooner the better—without any reference to our military condition." But the President refused, and Sumner stalked out, dismayed again at what he once called Lincoln's "immense *vis inertiae.*" The senator feared that only the confiscation act would ever free any slaves.

But in September Lincoln came through. After the Confederate reversal at Antietam, he issued his preliminary emancipation proclamation, a clear warning that if the rebellion did not cease in one hundred days, the executive branch would use the military to free *all* the slaves in the rebel states—those belonging to secessionists and loyalists alike. Thus the President would go beyond the second confiscation act—he would handle emancipation himself, avoid tangled litigation over slavery in the courts, and vanquish it as an institution in the South. He believed he could do this by the war powers, and he deemed it "a fit and necessary military measure" to preserve the Union.

The advanced Republicans, of course, were delighted. "Hurrah for Old Abe and the proclamation," Wade exulted. Stevens extolled Lincoln for his patriotism and said his proclamation "contained precisely the principles which I had advocated." "Thank God that I live to enjoy this day!" Sumner exclaimed in Boston. "Freedom is practically secured to all who find shelter within our lines, and the glorious flag of the Union, wherever it floats, becomes the flag of Freedom." A few days later, Sumner announced that "the Emancipation Proclamation . . . is now the corner-stone of our national policy."

As it turned out, though, the preliminary proclamation helped lead to a Republican disaster in the fall by-elections of 1862. Northern Democrats already were angered by Lincoln's harsh war measures, especially his use of martial law and military arrests. Now, Negro emancipation was more than they could bear, and they stumped the Northern states beating the drums of Negrophobia and warning of massive influxes of Southern blacks into the North once emancipation came. Sullen, war-weary, and racially antagonistic, Northern voters dealt the Republicans a smashing blow as the North's five most populous states—all of which had gone for Lincoln in 1860—now returned Democratic majorities to Capitol Hill. Republicans narrowly retained control of Congress, but they were steeped in gloom as it convened that December.

Though most Republicans stood resolutely behind emancipation, Browning and other conservatives now begged Lincoln to abandon his "reckless" abolition policy lest he shatter his party and wreck what remained of his country. At the same time, Sumner and Wade admonished Lincoln to stand firm, and he promised that he would. On January 1, 1863, the President officially signed the final proclamation in the White House. In it Lincoln temporarily exempted all of Tennessee and certain occupied places in Louisiana and Virginia (later, in reconstructing those states, he would withdraw the exemptions and make emancipation mandatory). He also excluded the loyal slave states because they were not in rebellion and he lacked the legal authority to uproot slavery there. With these exceptions, the final proclamation declared that all slaves in the rebellious states "from henceforth shall be free." The document also asserted that black men—Southern and Northern alike—might now be enlisted in Union military forces.

All in all, the advanced Republicans were pleased. Perhaps the President should not have exempted Tennessee and southern Louisiana, Horace Greeley said, "but let us not cavil." Lincoln had now "played his grand part" in the abolition of slavery, Julian declared, and "brought relief to multitudes of anxious people." "On that day," Sumner wrote of January 1, 1863, "an angel appeared upon the earth."

In truth, Lincoln's proclamation was the most revolutionary measure ever to come from an American President up to that time, and the advanced Republicans took a lot of credit for goading him at last to act. Slavery would now die by degrees with every Union advance, every Northern victory.

Now that Lincoln had adopted emancipation, advanced Republicans watched him with a critical eye, making sure that he enforced his edict and exhorting him to place only those firmly opposed to slavery in command of Union armies. In February rumor had it that if Lincoln wavered even once in his promise of freedom to the slaves, Wade would move for a vote of "no confidence" and try to cut off appropriations. But Lincoln did not waiver. Even though a storm of anti-Negro, anti-Lincoln protest broke over the land, the President refused to retract a single word of his decree. "He is stubborn as a mule when he gets his back up," Chandler said, "*& it is up* now on the Proclamation." "His mind acts slowly," Lovejoy observed, "but when he moves, it is *forward.*"

In the last two years of the war, Lincoln and the advanced Republicans had

Abe Lincoln throws in his last card—a black ace (the Emancipation Proclamation)—against Jefferson Davis; their game is played over a barrel of gunpowder. An 1862 Punch *cartoon by the English master John Tenniel.*

their differences, but they were scarcely locked in the kind of blood feud depicted in Civil War histories and biographies of an earlier day. Several advanced Republicans did oppose Lincoln's renomination in 1864 because the war was going badly and they thought him an inept administrator. In addition, Sumner, Stevens, and Wade clashed bitterly with Lincoln over whether Congress or the President should oversee reconstruction. Sumner, Julian, Chandler, and a handful of other legislators also insisted that Southern black men be enfranchised. But Lincoln, sympathetic to Negro voting rights, hesitated to force them on the states he reconstructed. Nevertheless, in April, 1865, he publicly endorsed limited Negro suffrage and conceded that the black man deserved the right to vote.

In truth, despite their differences, Lincoln and the advanced Republicans worked together closely. And they stood together on several crucial issues: they all wanted to abolish slavery entirely in the South and to muzzle the rebellious white majority there so that it could not overwhelm Southern Unionists and return the old Southern ruling class to power. They also came to see that colonization was probably an unworkable solution to the problem of racial adjustment. All Lincoln's colonization schemes had foundered, and anyway most blacks adamantly refused to participate in the Republicans' voluntary program. In place of colonization, the Lincoln administration devised a refugee system for blacks in the South, a program that put them to work in military and civilian pursuits there and prepared them for life in a free society. And in 1864 the Republican Congress canceled all funds it had set aside for colonization efforts.

Most important of all, advanced Republicans cooperated closely with Lincoln in pushing a constitutional amendment through Congress that would guarantee the permanent freedom of all slaves, those in the loyal border as well as in the rebel South. Since he had issued the proclamation, Lincoln and his congressional associates had worried that it might be nullified in the courts or thrown out by a later Congress or a subsequent administration. As a consequence, they wanted a constitutional amendment that would safeguard the proclamation and prevent emancipation from ever being overturned. Accordingly, in December, 1863, Iowa senator James F. Wilson introduced an emancipation amendment in the Senate, and the following February Trumbull reported it from the judiciary committee, reminding his colleagues that nobody could deny that all the death and destruction of the war stemmed from slavery and that it was their duty to support this amendment. In April the Senate adopted it by a vote of thirty-eight to six, but it failed to muster the required two-thirds majority in the House.

After Lincoln's re-election in 1864, advanced Republicans joined forces with the President to get the amendment passed. In his message that December, Lincoln conceded that this was the same House that earlier had failed to approve the amendment. But since then a national election had taken place which Lincoln insisted was a mandate for permanent emancipation. If the present House refused to pass the amendment, the next one "almost certainly" would. So "at all events," the President said, "may we not agree that the sooner the better?"

As December passed, Republicans who sponsored the amendment plotted with Lincoln to pressure conservative Republicans and recalcitrant Democrats for their support. On January 6, 1865, a heated debate began over the amendments, with James Ashley quoting Lincoln himself that *"if slavery is not wrong, nothing is wrong."* A week later, Thaddeus Stevens, still tall and imposing at seventy-two, limped down the aisle of the House and closed the debate with a spare and eloquent address, declaring that he had never hesitated, even when threatened with violence, "to stand here and denounce this infamous institution." With the outcome much in doubt, Lincoln and congressional Republicans participated in secret negotiations never made public—negotiations that allegedly involved patronage, a New Jersey railroad monopoly, and the release of rebels kin to congressional Democrats—to bring wavering opponents into line. "The greatest measure of the nineteenth century," Stevens claimed, "was passed by corruption, aided and abetted by the purest man in America." When the amendment did pass, by just three votes, a storm of cheers broke over House Republicans, who danced, embraced one another, waved their hats and canes. "It seemed to me I had been born into a new life," Julian recalled, "and that the world was overflowing with beauty and joy." Lincoln, too, pronounced the amendment a "great moral victory" and "a King's cure" for the evils of slavery. When ratified by the states, the amendment would end human bondage in America.

See, Julian rejoiced, "the world *does* move." He could have added that he and his advanced Republican colleagues, in collaboration with their President, had made it move, had done all they could in the smoke and steel of civil war to right their troubled land with its own noblest ideals.

Why They Impeached Andrew Johnson

David Herbert Donald

The story of presidential reconstruction after Lincoln is told in this essay by David Herbert Donald, Charles Warren Professor of American History at Harvard University. Lincoln's approach to restoring the Union was cautious, practical, thoughtful—humane in every sense of the word. Because of his assassination, however, the evaluation of his policy has to be a study in the might-have-beens of history. The reconstruction policy of his successor, Andrew Johnson, superficially similar to Lincoln's, was reckless, impractical, emotional, and politically absurd. While historians have differed in evaluating his purposes, they have agreed unanimously that his management of the problem was inept and that his policy was a total failure.

Professor Donald's essay provides an extended character study of Johnson, and it is not an attractive portrait. Donald believes that Johnson "threw away a magnificent opportunity" to smoothly and speedily return the Confederate states to a harmonious place in the Union. But he also shows how difficult Johnson's task was and to how great an extent Southern white opinion was set against the full acceptance of black equality. Donald is the author of many books, including a Pulitzer Prize–winning biography of the Massachusetts senator, Charles Sumner.

Reconstruction after the Civil War posed some of the most discouraging problems that have ever faced American statesmen. The South was prostrate. Its defeated soldiers straggled homeward through a countryside desolated by war. Southern soil was untilled and exhausted; southern factories and railroads were worn out. The four billion dollars of southern capital invested in Negro slaves was wiped out by advancing Union armies, "the most stupendous act of sequestration in the history of Anglo-American jurisprudence." The white inhabitants of eleven states had somehow to be reclaimed from rebellion and restored to a firm loyalty to the United States. Their four million former slaves had simultaneously to be guided into a proper use of their new-found freedom.

For the victorious Union government there was no time for reflection. Immediate decisions had to be made. Thousands of destitute whites and Negroes had to be fed before long-range plans of rebuilding the southern economy could be drafted. Some kind of government had to be established in these former Confederate states, to preserve order and to direct the work of restoration.

A score of intricate questions must be answered: Should the defeated southerners be punished or pardoned? How should genuinely loyal southern Unionists
be rewarded? What was to be the social, economic, and political status of the now
free Negroes? What civil rights did they have? Ought they to have the ballot?
Should they be given a freehold of property? Was Reconstruction to be controlled by the national government, or should the southern states work out their
own salvation? If the federal government supervised the process, should the
President or the Congress be in control?

Intricate as were the problems, in early April, 1865, they did not seem insu-
perable. President Abraham Lincoln was winning the peace as he had already won
the war. He was careful to keep every detail of Reconstruction in his own hands;
unwilling to be committed to any "exclusive, and inflexible plan," he was working
out a pragmatic program of restoration not, perhaps, entirely satisfactory to any
group, but reasonably acceptable to all sections. With his enormous prestige as
commander of the victorious North and as victor in the 1864 election, he was able
to promise freedom to the Negro, charity to the southern white, security to the
North.

The blighting of these auspicious beginnings is one of the saddest stories in
American history. The reconciliation of the sections, which seemed so imminent
in 1865, was delayed for more than ten years. Northern magnanimity toward a
fallen foe curdled into bitter distrust. Southern whites rejected moderate leaders,
and inveterate racists spoke for the new South. The Negro, after serving as a
political pawn for a decade, was relegated to a second-class citizenship, from
which he is yet struggling to emerge. Rarely has democratic government so
completely failed as during the Reconstruction decade.

The responsibility for this collapse of American statesmanship is, of course,
complex. History is not a tale of deep-dyed villains or pure-as-snow heroes. Part
of the blame must fall upon ex-Confederates who refused to recognize that the
war was over: part upon freedmen who confused liberty with license and the
ballot box with the lunch pail; part upon northern antislavery extremists who
identified patriotism with loyalty to the Republican party; part upon the land
speculators, treasury grafters, and railroad promoters who were unwilling to have
a genuine peace lest it end their looting of the public till.

Yet these divisive forces were not bound to triumph. Their success was due
to the failure of constructive statesmanship that could channel the magnanimous
feelings shared by most Americans into a positive program of reconstruction.
President Andrew Johnson was called upon for positive leadership, and he did
not meet the challenge.

Andrew Johnson's greatest weakness was his insensitivity to public opinion.
In contrast to Lincoln, who said, "Public opinion in this country is everything,"
Johnson made a career of battling the popular will. A poor white, a runaway
tailor's apprentice, a self-educated Tennessee politician, Johnson was a living
defiance to the dominant southern belief that leadership belonged to the plantation aristocracy.

As senator from Tennessee, he defied the sentiment of his section in 1861
and refused to join the secessionist movement. When Lincoln later appointed him

military governor of occupied Tennessee, Johnson found Nashville "a furnace of treason," but he braved social ostracism and threats of assassination and discharged his duties with boldness and efficiency.

Such a man was temperamentally unable to understand the northern mood in 1865, much less to yield to it. For four years the northern people had been whipped into wartime frenzy by propaganda tales of Confederate atrocities. The assassination of Lincoln by a southern sympathizer confirmed their belief in southern brutality and heartlessness. Few northerners felt vindictive toward the South, but most felt that the rebellion they had crushed must never rise again. Johnson ignored this postwar psychosis gripping the North and plunged ahead with his program of rapidly restoring the southern states to the Union. In May, 1865, without any previous preparation of public opinion, he issued a proclamation of amnesty, granting forgiveness to nearly all the millions of former rebels and welcoming them back into peaceful fraternity. Some few Confederate leaders were excluded from his general amnesty, but even they could secure pardon by special petition. For weeks the White House corridors were thronged with ex-Confederate statesmen and former southern generals who daily received presidential forgiveness.

Ignoring public opinion by pardoning the former Confederates, Johnson actually entrusted the formation of new governments in the South to them. The provisional governments established by the President proceeded, with a good deal of reluctance, to rescind their secession ordinances, to abolish slavery, and to repudiate the Confederate debt. Then, with far more enthusiasm, they turned to electing governors, representatives, and senators. By December, 1865, the southern states had their delegations in Washington waiting for admission by Congress. Alexander H. Stephens, once vice president of the Confederacy, was chosen senator from Georgia; not one of the North Carolina delegation could take a loyalty oath; and all of South Carolina's congressmen had "either held office under the Confederate States, or been in the army, or countenanced in some way the Rebellion."

Johnson himself was appalled, "There seems in many of the elections something like defiance, which is all out of place at this time." Yet on December 5, he strongly urged the Congress to seat these southern representatives "and thereby complete the work of reconstruction." But the southern states were omitted from the roll call.

Such open defiance of northern opinion was dangerous under the best of circumstances, but in Johnson's case it was little more than suicidal. The President seemed not to realize the weakness of his position. He was the representative of no major interest and had no genuine political following. He had been considered for the vice presidency in 1864 because, as a southerner and a former slaveholder, he could lend plausibility to the Republican pretension that the old parties were dead and that Lincoln was the nominee of a new, nonsectional National Union party.

A political accident, the new Vice President did little to endear himself to his countrymen. At Lincoln's second inauguration Johnson appeared before the Senate in an obviously inebriated state and made a long, intemperate harangue about his plebeian origins and his hard-won success. President, Cabinet, and senators were humiliated by the shameful display, and Charles Sumner felt that "the Senate should call upon him to resign." Historians now know that Andrew Johnson was not a heavy drinker. At the time of his inaugural display, he was just recovering from a severe attack of typhoid fever. Feeling ill just before he entered the Senate chamber, he asked for some liquor to steady his nerves, and either his weakened condition or abnormal sensitivity to alcohol betrayed him.

Lincoln reassured Republicans who were worried over the affair: "I have known Andy for many years; he made a bad slip the other day, but you need not be scared. Andy ain't a drunkard." Never again was Andrew Johnson seen under the influence of alcohol, but his reformation came too late. His performance on March 4, 1865, seriously undermined his political usefulness and permitted his opponents to discredit him as a pothouse politician. Johnson was catapulted into the presidency by John Wilkes Booth's bullet. From the outset his position was weak, but it was not necessarily untenable. The President's chronic lack of discretion made it so. Where common sense dictated that a chief executive in so disadvantageous a position should act with great caution, Johnson proceeded to imitate Old Hickory, Andrew Jackson, his political idol. If Congress crossed his will, he did not hesitate to defy it. Was he not "the Tribune of the People"?

Sure of his rectitude, Johnson was indifferent to prudence. He never learned that the President of the United States cannot afford to be a quarreler. Apprenticed in the rough-and-tumble politics of frontier Tennessee, where orators exchanged violent personalities, crude humor, and bitter denunciations, Johnson continued to make stump speeches from the White House. All too often he spoke extemporaneously, and he permitted hecklers in his audience to draw from him angry charges against his critics.

On Washington's birthday in 1866, against the advice of his more sober advisers, the President made an impromptu address to justify his Reconstruction policy. "I fought traitors and treason in the South," he told the crowd; "now when I turn around, and at the other end of the line find men—I care not by what name you call them—who will stand opposed to the restoration of the Union of these States, I am free to say to you that I am still in the field."

During the "great applause" which followed, a nameless voice shouted, "Give us the names at the other end. . . . Who are they?"

"You ask me who they are," Johnson retorted. "I say Thaddeus Stevens of Pennsylvania is one; I say Mr. Sumner is another; and Wendell Phillips is another." Applause urged him to continue. "Are those who want to destroy our institutions . . . not satisfied with the blood that has been shed? . . . Does not the blood of Lincoln appease the vengeance and wrath of the opponents of this government?"

The President's remarks were as untrue as they were impolitic. Not only was it manifestly false to assert that the leading Republican in the House and the most conspicuous Republican in the Senate were opposed to "the fundamental principles of this government" or that they had been responsible for Lincoln's assassination; it was incredible political folly to impute such actions to men with whom the President had to work daily. But Andrew Johnson never learned that the President of the United States must function as a party leader.

There was a temperamental coldness about this plain-featured, grave man

A Harper's Weekly *cartoon depicts Johnson (left) and Thaddeus Stevens as engineers committed to a collision course.*

that kept him from easy, intimate relations with even his political supporters. His massive head, dark, luxuriant hair, deep-set and piercing eyes, and cleft square chin seemed to Charles Dickens to indicate "courage, watchfulness, and certainly strength of purpose," but his was a grim face, with "no genial sunlight in it." The coldness and reserve that marked Johnson's public associations doubtless stemmed from a deep-seated feeling of insecurity; this self-educated tailor whose wife had taught him how to write could never expose himself by letting down his guard and relaxing.

Johnson knew none of the arts of managing men, and he seemed unaware that face-saving is important for a politician. When he became President, Johnson was besieged by advisers of all political complexions. To each he listened gravely and non-committally, raising no questions and by his silence seeming to give consent. With Radical Senator Sumner, already intent upon giving the freedmen both homesteads and the ballot, he had repeated interviews during the first month of his presidency. "His manner has been excellent, & even sympathetic," Sumner reported triumphantly. With Chief Justice Salmon P. Chase, Sumner urged Johnson to support immediate Negro suffrage and found the President was "well-disposed, & sees the rights & necessities of the case." In the middle of May, 1865, Sumner reassured a Republican caucus that the President was a true Radical; he had listened repeatedly to the Senator and had told him "there is no difference between us." Before the end of the month the rug was pulled from under

Sumner's feet. Johnson issued his proclamation for the reconstruction of North Carolina, making no provisions for Negro suffrage. Sumner first learned about it through the newspapers.

While he was making up his mind, Johnson appeared silently receptive to all ideas; when he made a decision, his mind was immovably closed, and he defended his course with all the obstinacy of a weak man. In December, alarmed by Johnson's Reconstruction proclamations, Sumner again sought an interview with the President. "No longer sympathetic, or even kindly," Sumner found, "he was harsh, petulant, and unreasonable." The Senator was depressed by Johnson's "prejudice, ignorance, and perversity" on the Negro suffrage issue. Far from listening amiably to Sumner's argument that the South was still torn by violence and not yet ready for readmission, Johnson attacked him with cheap analogies. "Are there no murders in Massachusetts?" the President asked.

"Unhappily yes," Sumner replied, "sometimes."

"Are there no assaults in Boston? Do not men there sometimes knock each other down, so that the police is obliged to interfere?"

"Unhappily yes."

"Would you consent that Massachusetts, on this account, should be excluded from Congress?" Johnson triumphantly queried. In the excitement the President unconsciously used Sumner's hat, which the Senator had placed on the floor beside his chair, as a spittoon!

Had Johnson been as resolute in action as he was in argument, he might conceivably have carried much of his party with him on his Reconstruction program. Promptness, publicity, and persuasion could have created a presidential following. Instead Johnson boggled. Though he talked boastfully of "kicking out" officers who failed to support his plan, he was slow to act. His own Cabinet, from the very beginning, contained members who disagreed with him, and his secretary of war, Edwin M. Stanton, was openly in league with the Republican elements most hostile to the President. For more than two years he impotently hoped that Stanton would resign; then in 1867, after Congress had passed the Tenure of Office Act, he tried to oust the Secretary. This belated firmness, against the letter of the law, led directly to Johnson's impeachment trial.

Instead of working with his party leaders and building up political support among Republicans, Johnson in 1866 undertook to organize his friends into a new party. In August a convention of white southerners, northern Democrats, moderate Republicans, and presidential appointees assembled in Philadelphia to endorse Johnson's policy. Union General Darius Couch of Massachusetts marched arm in arm down the convention aisle with Governor James L. Orr of South Carolina, to symbolize the states reunited under Johnson's rule. The convention produced fervid oratory, a dignified statement of principles—but not much else. Like most third-party reformist movements it lacked local support and grass-roots organization.

Johnson himself was unable to breathe life into his stillborn third party. Deciding to take his case to the people, he accepted an invitation to speak at a great Chicago memorial honoring Stephen A. Douglas. When his special train left

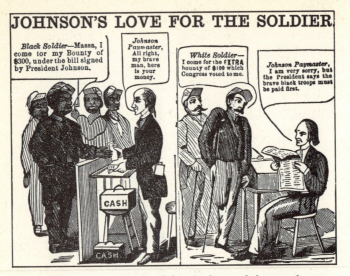

This cartoon is an example of the virulence of the attacks on Johnson by his enemies.

Washington on August 28 for a "swing around the circle," the President was accompanied by a few Cabinet members who shared his views and by the war heroes Grant and Farragut.

At first all went well. There were some calculated political snubs to the President, but he managed at Philadelphia, New York, and Albany to present his ideas soberly and cogently to the people. But Johnson's friends were worried lest his tongue again get out of control. "In all frankness," a senator wrote him, do not "allow the excitement of the moment to draw from you any *extemporaneous speeches.*"

At St. Louis, when a Radical voice shouted that Johnson was a "Judas," the President flamed up in rage. "There was a Judas and he was one of the twelve apostles," he retorted. ". . . The twelve apostles had a Christ. . . . If I have played the Judas, who has been my Christ that I have played the Judas with? Was it Thad Stevens? Was it Wendell Phillips? Was it Charles Sumner?" Over mingled hisses and applause, he shouted, "These are the men that stop and compare themselves with the Saviour; and everybody that differs with them . . . is to be denounced as a Judas."

Johnson had played into his enemies' hands. His Radical foes denounced him as a "trickster," a "culprit," a man "touched with insanity, corrupted with lust, stimulated with drink." More serious in consequence was the reaction of northern moderates, such as James Russell Lowell, who wrote, "What an anti-Johnson lecturer we have in Johnson! Sumner has been right about the *cuss* from the first. . . ." The fall elections were an overwhelming repudiation of the President and his Reconstruction policy.

Johnson's want of political sagacity strengthened the very elements in the Republican party which he most feared. In 1865 the Republicans had no clearly defined attitude toward Reconstruction. Moderates like Gideon Welles and Orville Browning wanted to see the southern states restored with a minimum of restrictions; Radicals like Sumner and Stevens demanded that the entire southern social system be revolutionized. Some Republicans were passionately concerned with the plight of the freedmen; others were more interested in maintaining the high tariff and land grant legislation enacted during the war. Many thought mostly of keeping themselves in office, and many genuinely believed, with Sumner, that "the Republican party, in its objects, is identical with country and with mankind." These diverse elements came slowly to adopt the idea of harsh Reconstruction, but Johnson's stubborn persistency in his policy left them no alternative. Every step the President took seemed to provide "a new encouragement to (1) the rebels at the South, (2) the Democrats at the North and (3) the discontented elements everywhere." Not many Republicans would agree with Sumner that Johnson's program was "a defiance to God and Truth," but there was genuine concern that the victory won by the war was being frittered away.

The provisional governments established by the President in the South seemed to be dubiously loyal. They were reluctant to rescind their secession ordinances and to repudiate the Confederate debt, and they chose high-ranking ex-Confederates to represent them in Congress. Northerners were even more alarmed when these southern governments began to legislate upon the Negro's civil rights. Some laws were necessary—in order to give former slaves the right to marry, to hold property, to sue and be sued, and the like—but the Johnson legislatures went far beyond these immediate needs. South Carolina, for example, enacted that no Negro could pursue the trade "of an artisan, mechanic, or shopkeeper, or any other trade or employment besides that of husbandry" without a special license. Alabama provided that "any stubborn or refractory servants" or "servants who loiter away their time" should be fined $50 and, if they could not pay, be hired out for six months' labor. Mississippi ordered that every Negro under eighteen years of age who was an orphan or not supported by his parents must be apprenticed to some white person, preferably the former owner of the slave. Such southern laws indicated a determination to keep the Negro in a state of peonage.

It was impossible to expect a newly emancipated race to be content with such a limping freedom. The thousands of Negroes who had served in the Union armies and had helped conquer their former Confederate masters were not willing to abandon their new-found liberty. In rural areas southern whites kept these Negroes under control through the Ku Klux Klan. But in southern cities white hegemony was less secure, and racial friction erupted in mob violence. In May, 1866, a quarrel between a Memphis Negro and a white teamster led to a riot in which the city police and the poor whites raided the Negro quarters and burned and killed promiscuously. Far more serious was the disturbance in New Orleans two months later. The Republican party in Louisiana was split into pro-Johnson conservatives and Negro suffrage advocates. The latter group determined to hold a constitutional convention, of dubious legality, in New Orleans, in order to secure the ballot for the freedmen and the offices for themselves. Through imbecility in the War Department, the Federal troops occupying the city were left without orders, and the mayor of New Orleans, strongly opposed to Negro equality, had the responsibility for preserving order. There were acts of provocation on both sides, and finally, on July 30, a procession of Negroes marching toward the convention hall was attacked.

"A shot was fired . . . by a policeman, or some colored man in the procession," General Philip Sheridan reported. "This led to other shots, and a rush after the procession. On arrival at the front of the Institute [where the convention met], there was some throwing of brick-bats by both sides. The police . . . were vigorously marched to the scene of disorder. The procession entered the Institute with the flag, about six or eight remaining outside. A row occurred between a policeman and one of these colored men, and a shot was again fired by one of the parties, which led to an indiscriminate firing on the building, through the windows, by the policemen.

"This had been going on for a short time, when a white flag was displayed from the windows of the Institute, whereupon the firing ceased and the police rushed into the building. . . . The policemen opened an indiscriminate fire upon the audience until they had emptied their revolvers, when they retired, and those inside barricaded the doors. The door was broken in, and the firing again commenced when many of the colored and white people either escaped out of the door, or were passed out by the policemen inside, but as they came out, the policemen who formed the circle nearest the building fired upon them, and they were again fired upon by the citizens that formed the outer circle."

Thirty-seven Negroes and three of their white friends were killed; 119 Negroes and seventeen of their white sympathizers were wounded. Of their assailants, ten were wounded and but one killed. President Johnson was, of course, horrified by these outbreaks, but the Memphis and New Orleans riots, together with the Black Codes, afforded a devastating illustration of how the President's policy actually operated. The southern states, it was clear, were not going to protect the Negroes' basic rights. They were only grudgingly going to accept the results of the war. Yet, with Johnson's blessing, these same states were expecting a stronger voice in Congress than ever. Before 1860, southern representation in Congress had been based upon the white population plus three fifths of the slaves; now the Negroes, though not permitted to vote, were to be counted like all other citizens, and southern states would be entitled to at least nine additional congressmen. Joining with the northern Copperheads, the southerners could easily regain at the next presidential election all that had been lost on the Civil War battlefield.

It was this political exigency, not misguided sentimentality nor vindictiveness, which united Republicans in opposition to the President.

Johnson's defenders have pictured Radical Reconstruction as the work of a fanatical minority, led by Sumner and Stevens, who drove their reluctant colleagues into adopting coercive measures against the South. In fact, every major piece of Radical legislation was adopted by the nearly unanimous vote of the entire Republican membership of Congress. Andrew Johnson had left them no other choice. Because he insisted upon rushing Confederate-dominated states back into the Union, Republicans moved to disqualify Confederate leaders under the Fourteenth Amendment. When, through Johnson's urging, the southern states rejected that amendment, the Republicans in Congress unwillingly came to see Negro suffrage as the only counterweight against Democratic majorities in the South. With the Reconstruction Acts of 1867 the way was open for a true Radical program toward the South, harsh and thorough.

Andrew Johnson became a cipher in the White House, futilely disapproving bills which were promptly passed over his veto. Through his failure to reckon with public opinion, his unwillingness to recognize his weak position, his inability to function as a party leader, he had sacrificed all influence with the party which had elected him and had turned over its control to Radicals vindictively opposed to his policies. In March, 1868, Andrew Johnson was summoned before the Senate of the United States to be tried on eleven accusations of high crimes and misdemeanors. By a narrow margin the Senate failed to convict him, and historians have dismissed the charges as flimsy and false. Yet perhaps before the bar of history itself Andrew Johnson must be impeached with an even graver charge— that through political ineptitude he threw away a magnificent opportunity.

TEXT CREDITS

ILLUSTRATION CREDITS

1   Collection of Warren Clifton Shearman
6   Culver Pictures
6   California Historical Society, San Francisco
14   Gilcrease Institute of American History and Art
21   Picture Collection, The Branch Libraries, The New York Public Library
27   Courtesy of the John Carter Brown Library at Brown University
33   Museum of the American Indian, Heye Foundation, New York
36   Museum of the American Indian, Heye Foundation, New York
41   Museum of the American Indian, Heye Foundation, New York
43   Museum of the American Indian, Heye Foundation, New York
45   Mr. and Mrs. Samuel Schwartz
66   The owners, Mr. and Mrs. William Byrd
68   The Bettman Archive
70   Library of Congress
76   The Granger Collection, New York
79   Rare Books and Manuscripts Division, The New York Public Library, Astor, Lenox and
     Tilden Foundations
81   The Granger Collection, New York
87   *Abstract of Evidence on . . . Slave Trade,* 1792
89   New Haven Colony Historical Society
96   *Harper's Weekly,* June 2, 1860
97   Courtesy of the American Antiquarian Society
102   From the Collections of the Manchester Historic Association
105   Picture Collection, The Branch Libraries, The New York Public Library
109   Library of Congress
112   Colonial Williamsburg Foundation
115   Reproduced by courtesy of the Trustees of the British Museum
117   National Maritime Museum, Greenwich
120   The Granger Collection, New York
122   Courtesy of the Society for the Preservation of New England Antiquities, Boston, Mass.
126   Courtesy of the American Antiquarian Society
130   Courtesy of the Massachusetts Historical Society
140   The Granger Collection, New York
145   The Granger Collection, New York
149   The Granger Collection, New York
150   The Granger Collection, New York
152   The Granger Collection, New York
155   Brown Brothers
163   Culver Pictures
166   Culver Pictures
171   Courtesy of the Free Library of Philadelphia, Print and Picture Department
174   Independence National Historical Park Collection
177   National Archives
185   Library of Congress
189   The Historical Society of Pennsylvania
192   National Portrait Gallery, Smithsonian Institution, Washington, D.C.
193   Library of Congress
197   Philadelphia Museum of Art: Gift of Mrs. John D. Rockefeller
199   Brown Brothers

200 Philadelphia Museum of Art: Gift of Mrs. John D. Rockefeller
201 Lauros-Giraudon/Art Resource
204 Lauros-Giruadon/Art Resource
207 Collection of Davenport West, Jr.
211 Culver Pictures
216 Picture Collection, Branch Libraries, The New York Public Library
224 Colonial Williamsburg Foundation
227 Washington and Lee University, Lexington, Virginia
235 Courtesy of the New-York Historical Society
249 Courtesy of the Museum of Fine Arts, Boston: M. and M. Karolik Collection
254 Courtesy of the New-York Historical Society
260 Courtesy of the New-York Historical Society
265 Emma Willard School
273 Shelburne Museum, Shelburne, Vermont
277 The Library Company of Philadelphia
278 The Library Company of Philadelphia
279 Culver Pictures
280 The Bettmann Archive
280 The Bettmann Archive
282 Courtesy of the American Antiquarian Society
283 Courtesy of the American Antiquarian Society
284 The Library Company of Philadelphia
286 Courtesy of the American Antiquarian Society
289 The Library Company of Philadelphia
291 Courtesy of the American Antiquarian Society
295 Courtesy of the Free Library of Philadelphia, Print and Picture Department
295 Courtesy of the Free Library of Philadelphia, Print and Picture Department
297 Culver Pictures
301 The Bettmann Archive
305 National Cyclopedia of American Biography (James T. White Co.)
309 Rhode Island Historical Society
315 The Granger Collection, New York
319 Peabody Museum, Harvard University
323 Valentine Museum, Richmond, Virginia
328 Library of Congress
331 Courtesy of the Museum of Fine Arts, Boston: M. and M. Karolik Collection
333 Library of Congress
335 Courtesy of the Cooper-Hewitt Museum, Smithsonian Institution/Art Resource
339 Culver Pictures
348 The Granger Collection, New York
355 The Granger Collection, New York
359 Culver Pictures
366 Library of Congress
368 Courtesy of the Free Library of Philadelphia, Print and Picture Department